The Food Co-op Handbook

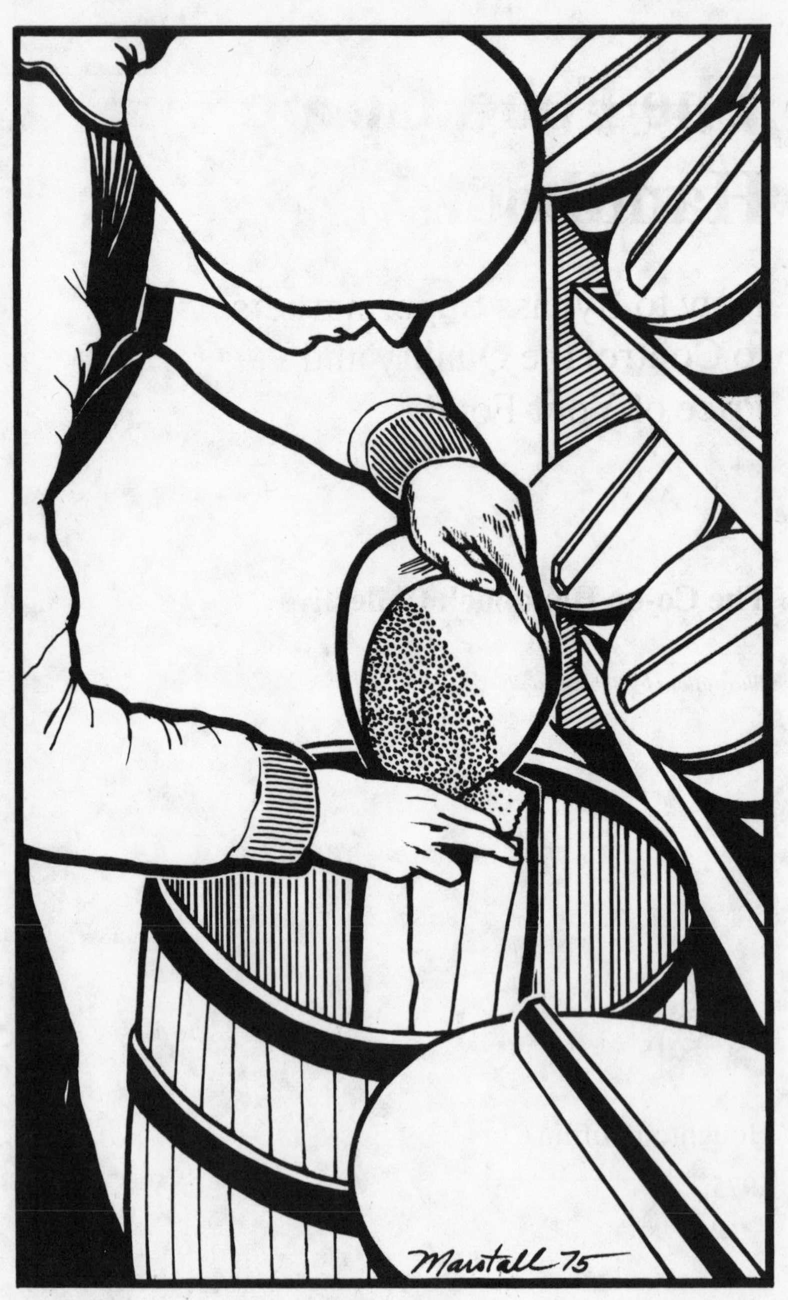
Marstall 75

The Food Co-op Handbook

How to Bypass Supermarkets to Control the Quality and Price of Your Food

The Co-op Handbook Collective

Illustrations by Bob Marstall

Houghton Mifflin Company Boston
1975

Library of Congress Cataloging in Publication Data
Co-op Handbook Collective.
The food co-op handbook.
Includes bibliographies and index.
1. Cooperative societies — United States — Management
2. Food industry and trade — United States. I. Title.
HD3284.C574 1975 658.8'707 75-22470
ISBN 0-395-21598-6

Printed in the United States of America

c10 9 8 7 6 5 4 3 2 1

To everyone who must purchase
the food he or she eats,
we dedicate this book with
cooperative trust
and affection.

Preface

IF, as is sometimes said, writing is lonely work, this book is an exception to the rule. From start to finish, it has been a collective project. The four authors were helped by more than one hundred people in the food-cooperative movement who contributed articles, advice, comments, information, and, in some cases, chapters.

The idea for a handbook about buying food cooperatively was Bill Coughlan's. Bill, a veteran of political activism at Boston University and one of the authors of *The Organizer's Manual,* had been active in the Boston Food Co-op store and the New England Federation of Co-ops (NEFCO) since 1972. David Yohalem, a friend of Bill's from university days and a founding member of the Cambridgeport Food Co-op, joined the early discussions out of which the book's structure came. They next recruited Marjorie Heins, who had moved to the Boston area after five years of free-lance writing in San Francisco; Marjorie was in the South Cambridge Food Co-op. Howie Tumlin, a member of the West Concord Food and Friendship Co-op, joined the project in the last months to tour the country visiting co-ops and help in the final writing and editing.

The four of us could not have written this book by ourselves. The people who took time from their work to help us came from food co-ops around the country. Most of the ideas and suggestions in the book reflect the orientation toward co-ops found in New England, but we were lucky to get constructive criticism and new ideas from the friends we made in other regions. We met people at food co-op conferences in Philadelphia, Ann Arbor, and Minneapolis. Howie visited co-ops from Maine to California, and we received a wealth of information from several hundred responses to a questionnaire prepared by Don Lubin of NEFCO.

We intended to produce a work useful and accessible to people with no food-cooperative experience who wished to start buying food collectively. At the same time we wanted the book to be as comprehensive as possible, to be a guide to the problems and procedures of large co-ops as well as a statement of our thoughts on growth, food politics, and the future of consumer cooperation in the United States.

The book should be read from cover to cover — not in one sitting, of course — for a sense of its structure and of the types of co-op development it charts. But this is also a reference work, and we hope it will remain on your shelf, or on the shelf of your co-op store or distribution center, its pages becoming dog-eared as you use it. The book's value will grow as you bring to it your own experiences.

At the end of most chapters you will find lists of sources. Some sources are books or articles that we have used; others are addresses of organizations that can provide information to co-ops, or leads you might follow up if you're interested in learning more about a subject.

You will encounter a number of terms that have been adopted by the co-op movement for its own uses and other words that have been so abused by the mass communications media that little remains of their original meanings. Among the co-op terms that may approach cant are collating, masterblock, work teams, work groups, blocks, branches, collectives, and direct savings. We hope that the explanations are adequate and we apologize for the persistence of the jargon.

Other terms, like participation, democracy, decentralization, and accountability, have often been misused by politicians and the media. In writing the book, we have been frustrated by the fuzziness and banality that words like these have acquired. These are crucial concepts for us. We have tried to restore meaning and integrity to them, and to use them with precision.

Some words have become so loaded and politicized that we have engaged in long debates about their use. Chief among these are gender terms; the common use of "he," "him," or "his" to denote either sex; and the acceptance of words like "middleman," "chairman," and "spokesman." Sexism is a problem in many co-ops because food gathering in our society has traditionally been women's work. In struggling against this, co-ops have used terms like "middleperson" and "chairperson," and instead of using "he" in written documents, either use "he or she" or "s/he," or, ungrammatically, substitute "they." As writers we're concerned about constantly assaulting the reader with the awkward "he or she." But as one contributor to the book pointed out, it depends on whether you value form over content. Although we value both, as feminists we think it is most important to do away with sexism in language and so have chosen to use "he or she," "middleperson," and "chairperson." If the awkwardness slows down the reading, it also provides a steady reminder of inequality's pervasiveness.

In writing this book, we've learned not only about the English language but about working collectively. The intensive input of four people and the considerable contributions of dozens more have given this book a breadth and balance that one author could never achieve. The four members of the collective and, we think, many who worked with us, experienced the kind of growth that comes from the tension of different personalities working together and the care we had to take to respect each other's needs and to offer criticism constructively.

But if we're richer personally and intellectually, we're a good deal poorer financially. Much of our royalty advance went for travel, phone, photocopying, and other expenses. When we tried to calculate the wage we'd received for our work, we found it to rival the minus thirty-six cents per hour which, according to one study, chicken farmers average when depreciation on their equipment is figured in.

We'd like all proceeds from this book to go toward building the co-op movement, but we have all gone into debt for our efforts, and therefore plan to collect royalties until we have been reimbursed for the time we put in at an average co-op movement wage of about $100 a week each. If and when this point has been reached, we intend to turn over all further royalties to a national cooperative educational fund, to be administered by the New England Federation of Co-ops.

We'd like to thank the many contributors to this book, most of whom wrote without pay. These people either wrote articles on their areas of expertise or wrote extensive comments on first drafts of some chapters. They are: Steve Amdur, Bruce Andrews, Ellen

Andrews, Roger Auerbach, Elizabeth Barker, David Barry, Nancy Burkey, Lisa Bingham, Whitney Carpenter, Albert Cassorla, Ruth Crocker, Bruce Cutworth, Bill Davis, John Davis, Jan Dubinsky, Ellen Edson, Jo Freudenheim, Felicity, Peg Gallagher, Karen Giese, Martha Gold, Joanne Green, Diane Halperin, Seth Isman, Rudy Jaeger, Jain Johnston, Ben Kellman, Barry Kissen, Carole Kouhia, Judy Liniado, Reneé Loth, Don Lubin, Bill Lundberg, Corrine Markey, Walter Matherly, Steve Matthews, Frank McGrath, Mark Miller, Jamie Mitchell, Steve Norris, Ed Padowski, Matt Perlstein, Ronnie Perlstein, Nancy Perrelli, Ed Place, Bob Pollack, Joe Reilly, Beth Reinhardt, Peg Roberts, Steve Rooney, Charlie Seitzman, Peter Simmons, Steven Stone, Richie Streitfeld, Michael Thurber, John Talvacchia, Todd Walker, Lori Weiner, Jake Williams, and Barbara Yost. For artwork, thanks to Bob Marstall and Sara Hutt.

We'd also like to thank the invaluable resource people, some of whom didn't have time to put their thoughts into writing but who contributed their ideas. Much of the information exchanged over dinners, at parties, in meetings, and on long automobile rides has found its way into these pages. Others gave us good grits and warm beds while we were traveling: Michael Bernard, Sheila Bernard, Bill Cavallini, Art Danforth, Judy Decker, Spike DeHaven, Phil Dick, John Dickerson, Joe Downing, Rick Exner, Ellery Foster, Kris Garlic, Jay Gilberg, Steven Gold, Chuck Goldberg, Bob Golden, Ron Heyford, Greg Hoke, Julian Houston, Cheryl Kennedy, Betsy Matlack, Cris McConkey, Pat McGrath, Sue Meacham, Elaine Nesterick, Karen Ohmans, Mark Ritchie, Manny Russell, Obilagi Rust, Shelly Schmalbach, Stewart Schmalbach, Bruce Singer, Dave Sterling, Ann Temple, Jacqueline Tumlin, Paul Weinberg, Peter Welsh, Sue White, Wild Turkey, Dean Zimmerman, and David Zinner.

We hope this list is complete. If anybody has been inadvertently left out, please accept our apologies.

Unfortunately, we don't have a complete list of all the people who helped with typing, but we'd like to thank particularly Susan Bigger, Peg Roberts, and Alden Waitt Tumlin.

Special thanks to our editor, Anita McClellan, who dauntlessly navigated the uncharted waters of collective authorship.

Finally, undying gratitude to our families, who endured the mountains of papers, the hogging of file cabinet space, and the ceaseless co-op talk: Harma Lee Stahl, Alden Waitt Tumlin, and Greg, Catherine, and Matthew Heins.

February, 1975

THE CO-OP HANDBOOK COLLECTIVE

BILL COUGHLAN
MARJORIE HEINS
HOWIE TUMLIN
DAVID YOHALEM

Contents

The Food Co-op Handbook

the FOO
CO~O

1. Welcome to the Food Co-op

"I USED TO DREAD going to the supermarket. I'd race through the aisles, afraid that the prices would all go up before I got to the cashier!"

A fellow member of a small food-buying cooperative was talking as we drove a van full of fruit and vegetables from the New England Produce Center to our co-op's distribution site. She had joined the co-op last year to save money on her food bills. Now she's one of the most active members.

"I don't know what I'd have done without the co-op. I guess I'd just have started one myself."

Like hundreds of thousands of other Americans, she had learned how easy it is to buy cooperatively and save 15% to 50% on food bills. Co-ops have been sprouting all across the country for a simple reason: they work. They save money for their members by buying food in bulk from wholesalers and splitting up the savings when they split up the food. Nobody makes a profit and operating costs are minimal. The result is savings like these, from a comparison between the Cambridge, Massachusetts, Food Co-op store and a supermarket down the street, in April, 1975:

	Co-op	*Supermarket*
1 lb. tomatoes	.20	.39
1 lb. carrots	.15	.29
1 bunch broccoli	.39	.59
1 lb. green beans	.23	.49
1 iceberg lettuce	.23	.49
1 lb. bananas	.15	.25
1 lemon	.07	.15

	Co-op	*Supermarket*
5 lb. white potatoes	.20	.59
2 lb. yellow onions	.18	.49
	1.80	3.73
+ 10% surcharge	.18	
	1.98	

Co-op savings: 47%

	Co-op	*Supermarket*
1 lb. mild cheddar cheese	.89	1.45
1 lb. American cheese	.87	1.26
1 dozen extra large eggs	.56	.59
1 lb. plain cottage cheese	.55	.68
½ pint Dannon yogurt	.30	.35
½ gallon whole milk	.66	.76
	3.83	5.09
+ 10% surcharge	.38	
	4.21	

Co-op savings: 17%

	Co-op	*Supermarket*
1 3-lb. chicken	1.32	1.77
1 lb. ground beef	.74	.99
1 lb. sliced ham	1.65	2.99
1 4-lb. eye round roast	6.40	7.96
	10.11	13.71
+ 10% surcharge	1.01	
	11.12	

Co-op savings: 19%

	Co-op	*Supermarket*
5 lb. unbleached white flour	.85	1.09
1 lb. kidney beans	.41	.88
1 lb. black-eyed peas	.27	.56
V-8 juice (46 oz.)	.59	.69
Log Cabin syrup (24 oz.)	1.16	1.37
Oreos (19 oz.)	.94	1.09
Cheerios (15 oz.)	.80	.89
French's mustard (24 oz.)	.49	.59
Geisha white tuna (6½ oz.)	.55	.69
Pepperidge Farm whole-wheat bread	.48	.61
	6.54	8.46
+ 10% surcharge	.65	
	7.19	

Co-op savings: 15%

As you can see, the greatest savings are on produce; the least are on groceries. Perishable items are marked up the most in supermarkets, while packaged groceries, with their high-volume turnover and long shelf-life, are marked up the least. The 10% surcharge added to the wholesale prices is all this co-op store needs to cover its operating expenses. Preorder co-ops, in which people order their food before picking it up rather than shopping in a store, usually operate with a 5% surcharge, and occasionally with none at all. Simple procedures and volunteer labor are all that's needed.

That's what we were doing, driving forty cases of produce through the streets of Boston at 8 A.M. We had volunteered to buy the food at the market that week. As we arrived at the distribution center, a second car carrying cheese and eggs drove up. We helped each other unload the food and went off to work. Other volunteers would arrive in a few hours to set out the cartons and figure out and post the prices.

After work, we returned to the distribution center. Our friends and neighbors in the co-op were picking up the food we had bought that morning. Everyone seemed happy with the quality and prices we had been able to get. We had taken the time to shop around and had even found a good deal on strawberries and purchased more than were ordered. The people who bought the extras were especially happy with this unexpected treat.

How do we do it? It's simple. Just get a group of friends or neighbors together, decide what you want to buy, shop around the various wholesale markets, and get the best quality for the lowest price. Bring the food home and split it up according to what everyone ordered. As you'll see in the coming pages, things can get more complicated as your co-op grows, but the basic principle always applies: cooperative work and no profit will beat the supermarkets any day. They just can't compete with us. They're in business to make money; food cooperatives exist to save people money.

Supermarkets are only the most visible part of the American food industry, otherwise known as agribusiness. It's the largest industry in the United States today. The giant food-marketing companies like Ralston-Purina, General Foods, and Del Monte have been joined by huge conglomerates like ITT, Boeing, Dow, and Tenneco. The attraction is profits. The growing, shipping, processing, and retailing of food are all high-profit industries.

As food prices have been rising each month, the radio and TV newscasters have been at a loss to explain who's getting rich from it all. The TV shows farmers slaughtering calves and chicks that they claim they can't afford to raise. Food processors close down operations and lay off workers. The supermarkets say the prices aren't their fault; after all, they only make 1% on sales.

Supermarkets may only make a 1% profit on sales, but their inventory turns over so fast that they make that profit fifteen or twenty times a year. Look instead at their return on investment. Most supermarkets show returns of 10% to 20%. Safeway, which in 1973 printed shopping bags advertising its 1% sales profit, made a 15% profit on investments the previous year. Supermarkets often have their own wholesaling departments, which make high profits by selling to the stores at high prices. The stores can then modestly point to their low sales profit for its public relations value.

Profit isn't the only reason for high food prices. Think of all the ingredients that go into your hamburger and French fries. The rancher sells his steer to a feedlot to be fattened on protein-rich grains and soymeal, and a healthy (though not for you) dose of fat-inducing hormones. The feedlot owner gets his cut, and ships off the fatted calf to the meatpacker. The steer is slaughtered, butchered, and shipped to a meat wholesaler, who finally sells it to a store. The potato farmer sells his entire crop to a broker who, after taking his cut, sends it to the frozen food processor. A processing company peels, cuts, fries, and freezes your potato, and probably gives it a helping of chemical food additives. Then it's off again to another wholesaler, and finally into the supermarket's freezer display case.

Along the way, workers have made wages (some decent, like the Teamsters' or Amalgamated Meatcutters', and some indecent, like the migrant farmworkers' and supermarket clerks'), everyone who owned the meat and potatoes has made a profit, and the food company executives have enjoyed very high salaries and expense accounts. We all know who foots the bill in the end. But that's only part of the cost of this simple meal.

To make sure we eat what it is producing, the food industry spends $4 billion a year on advertising. Food advertising, which dominates radio and TV, represents one sixth of all corporate advertising in the United States. Agribusiness spends $10 on advertising for every $1 spent on research. We pay for the ads in the form of high prices, and again as proportionally higher taxes, since the food industry can deduct its advertising outlay as business expenses.

Don't go away; they haven't finished with your burger and fries yet. Let's not forget about all the money spent on marketing research, packaging, the salary for the designer of the box, and the maintaining of a lobbyist in Washington to fight consumer, environmental, or labor legislation. At the supermarket, remember to pay your share of the price and taxes on the large chunk of real estate, half covered in asphalt for your car, the nice lighting and gentle Muzak to keep you in the store longer, and the latest in computerized cash registers. Now, sit down and try to enjoy your meal.

While agribusiness is concerned with squeezing the most profit out of a head of cabbage or a side of pork, food co-ops have been organizing consumers to get the best quality for the lowest price.

We were in a co-op storefront in Minneapolis one day when the mail was delivered. The mailman chatted for a while with the people behind the counter, and then walked over to a large poster on the wall and signed his name in a box reading "Thursday, 6 – 8 P.M." He had just volunteered to do his share of work in the store.

A few minutes later a young woman pulled a truck up to the side door and strode into the co-op announcing, "Warehouse delivery; let's go, folks." People stopped what they were doing — gave up their places on line, stopped weighing out grains — and hurried outside to the rear of the truck to help unload. In ten minutes the store was restocked with grains, flours, dried fruits, and whole-wheat noodles. The job would have taken a delivery person or stockclerk an hour. No one seemed put out. In fact, despite the subfreezing temperature, people seemed to be enjoying the work.

Co-op stores can keep food prices down because members do much of the work. They keep shelves stocked, weigh their own produce, record the prices, and bag the unprocessed foods bought in bulk. They clean up the spilled honey or flour.

Co-ops buy most of their food in unprocessed bulk form because it is cheaper, safer, and tastier than the packaged, processed foods that have little nutritional value and sometimes contain potentially cancer-producing additives. Members think nothing of scooping a pound of flour out of a bin, filling their own jar with oil from a 200-pound drum, or picking a few peaches out of a bushel basket.

Quality foods at low prices are not the only advantages of joining co-ops. Most members enjoy being in their co-op and feel pride and satisfaction in its success. They like working together to create a viable alternative to the supermarkets. Co-ops are real community institutions and their members' pride and affection is an important asset. We call it social capital, and it's as necessary as financial capital for the co-op's survival. A reserve of social capital will keep members in the co-op even when prices have to go up to cover a stolen cash register, or people are expected to put in some extra work in a pinch.

Co-ops are fun because the cooperative relationships that exist among members are such a welcome relief from the competitive relations that characterize most of our social contacts. The relation between members and staff hired by many larger co-ops is still very different from that of customer and worker in a capitalist market. Members don't expect the staff to wait on them, nor do they order them around and demand service. In return, the staff tries to base its policies on the needs of the co-op membership.

Paid staff members often work as a collective. There are no distinctions between managers and workers, employers and employees. Everyone gets paid on the same hourly scale, and all have equal say in the work. Paid staff exists when the complexity of the co-op reaches a point at which expertise becomes more important than voluntary participation. In many parts of the country, co-ops are alternative sources of employment for the communities they serve.

People have turned to co-ops for mutual protection and self-help for over one hundred years. A group of disgruntled weavers established the first consumer co-op in the town of Rochdale, England, in 1844. Co-ops came to the United States in the same century and many of the co-ops started around 1900 and during the 1930s are still operating today. These old co-ops have grown into large supermarkets, which sell their merchandise at prevailing prices and return any surplus to their members in the form of rebates proportionate to the amount members spend in the store. Such stores operate successfully from New England to California. The largest of them is the Consumers Cooperative of Berkeley, with 75,000 member households.

Yet what these co-ops have gained in volume they have lost in member participation. Although all members can vote, decisions in these co-ops are made by small groups of managers and directors. The new wave of co-ops, which began in the late 1960s, is, in part, a reaction to the traditional co-ops.

These new-style co-ops have replaced rebates with "direct savings" — selling at as close to wholesale as operating costs will allow. They have also chosen to stay small, while consolidating their buying power through federations. The largest contemporary co-ops have several thousand members, and most have fewer than 500.

While co-ops try to remain small and responsive to their members, agribusiness has become larger and more powerful. Many companies have been bought by international conglomerates. Tenneco, for example, owns gas pipelines, oil refineries, chemical plants, and other heavy industries, in addition to Heggebladde-Marguleas, the country's largest marketer of fresh fruits and vegetables. Tenneco produces insecticides, fertilizers, and farm machinery, controls more than 70% of the U.S. date production as well as 10% of the table grapes, and owns a chunk of California agricultural land equal to twice the size of Rhode Island.

As one student of agribusiness wrote: "The Sunday dinner table today can be laden with turkey from Greyhound, ham from ITT, vegetable salad from Tenneco, potatoes from Boeing, pork chops from Ling-Temco-Vought, applesauce from American Brands, lettuce from Dow Chemical, roast from John Hancock Insurance, strawberries from Purex, and after-dinner almonds from Getty Oil."

Among the remaining food companies, consolidation is also the rule. In most food lines, a few companies control the market. Kellogg, Quaker, General Foods, and General Mills control cereals. Campbell and Lipton dominate soups. Kraft has cheese wrapped up; Minute Maid controls 20% of frozen orange juice sales for its owner, Coca Cola; and Heinz does even better, with 38% of the ketchup sales. There are more than one thousand canning companies in the U.S., but four — Campbell, Heinz, Del Monte, and Libby — take 80% of the industry's profits. Of 32,500 food manufacturers, the largest 100 receive 71% of the profits.

All this consolidation means monopoly control of the food industry and high prices for us. According to Federal Trade Commission standards, an industry group is capable of monopoly pricing when four firms share at least 35% of the market. Although monopoly pricing is illegal, it exists informally when a few companies have a friendly understanding to charge whatever the market will allow. Just remember what happened in 1974 with the prices of sugar and flour. It all adds up to $2.1 billion in overcharges every year, according to the F.T.C.

Here's one way that monopoly pricing works. ITT's Continental Baking was charged by the Justice Department with having dropped the price of Wonder Bread in one part of the country to the point where they were taking a loss, and covering it with increases in other areas. Once the competing bread manufacturers went under, the price of Wonder Bread went back up.

Conglomerates can be very good at this trick. Oil profits in one department allow a conglomerate to cut prices in a food subsidiary until smaller competitors disappear. Food co-ops are one way for consumers to fight this price-gouging by taking control of the distribution of food. They exercise this control through democratic decision making.

In a New York City apartment building, twenty-five neighbors are having dinner together. They are members of a block in the Broadway Local Food Co-op. (A block contains from 10 to 30 households.) Sitting on the floor of a living room sharing a potluck supper of guacamole, rice and vegetables, potato salad, bean salad, green salad, fruit salad (you get a lot of salads at food co-op potluck suppers), bread, wine, and coffee, they are discussing a new food source. The federation of co-ops in New York is considering trucking to Lancaster County, Pennsylvania, to buy fresh organic produce.

In a co-op like this, meetings are often combined with potluck suppers or parties. Usually, no one chairs the meetings, and there are no votes or parliamentary procedures. A group of friends discusses an issue and comes to a consensus. When decisions affecting the entire co-op have to be made, representatives of each block discuss them at a bi-weekly meeting and return to their blocks to talk with member households before making a final decision.

In New York, the Broadway Local Co-op has become a venerable institution. The co-op is able to consolidate its members' buying power to get better deals from wholesalers, while at the same time keeping most of the co-op's operations small and personal. As agribusiness becomes more and more consolidated, food co-ops often choose to decentralize their operations to foster more personal and friendly experiences.

Co-op members control their own institutions because no one is going to do it for them. By participating in the operation of the co-op, they get the experience they need to make informed decisions. They must decide what food to carry, where to buy it, how to divide the work, do the books, and hire and fire staff, and an endless stream of operational and policy questions. For many people, co-ops are the first community institutions they've joined that are really open to their direction. Co-ops can become training grounds for community activists. Once you've taken a little power over your life, you're likely to want to take some more.

Can you imagine consumers walking into the board meeting of ITT and saying, "Now listen here, Mr. Geneen, we want protein-rich whole wheat flour in Wonder Bread, instead of that aerated rubber. And while you're at it, leave out the calcium propionate; it *should* get stale if it's been on the shelf for two weeks."

They're not likely to receive a very warm welcome. Nor should they expect much from Earl Butz, who acts as if he's still working for Ralston-Purina instead of the Department of Agriculture, or from the people at the Food and Drug Administration or the Federal Trade Commission, many of whom are also recruited from industry. If consumers want to have a say in the decisions affecting food, they'll have to organize themselves. Food co-ops are a step in that direction. They'll also have to educate themselves about food. Co-ops are trying to do something here, too.

Americans probably know more about an automobile when they buy one than they do about the food they eat every day. Everyone knows the difference between six and eight cylinders, but how many people know the difference between whole wheat and white flour, or between prime and choice meat?

Many co-ops have educational programs to inform members about nutrition, the food industry, and the history of cooperation. One of the most extensive is run by the Boston Food Co-op, a large store with about three thousand members. At the B.F.C., signs and posters cover the walls, articles and recipes appear in the newsletter, and all new members attend orientation classes. Informal education occurs whenever new and experienced members work together, or when people ask each other questions while shopping.

In Denver, the Common Market encourages attendance at its orientation classes by serving free beer afterward. They have some of the best informed members in the country.

While large co-ops have the resources to mount major educational programs, even the smallest do some educational work. Simple newsletters often include recipes and tips on getting more protein for less money. Meetings considering what foods to carry turn naturally into discussions of what kinds of food are safe and nutritious. Our food habits are deeply ingrained, and we often find it hard to change them. We are influenced by what we ate as children and by what the food industry advertisements lead us to believe we need.

Four billion dollars a year buys a lot of ads. Agribusiness isn't trying to educate us about nutrition, but to swindle us into paying high prices for sweet junk. They aim their ads at our ignorance and insecurities. Will I really be young and sexy if I drink Pepsi? Will my husband and children ridicule me if I burn the rice? Will I have the energy to start the day without my Wheaties? It matters little that Pepsi will clean the rust right off a nail, that white rice has little of the protein value of brown rice, or that most of the nutrition in a bowl of Wheaties comes from the milk and fruit you add to it. The food industry wants to make its products marketable, not nutritious.

When the companies saw a new market opening up, they started advertising "nutritional" foods. What the hell were they feeding us before? So we endured the "natural cereal" boom of 1974. Each major cereal manufacturer brought out a natural cereal in which sugar was the second largest ingredient. Each spent millions competing to see who could come up with the most wholesomely bucolic package and ad campaign. High-priced natural cereals skyrocketed into the top-selling bracket with Cheerios and Corn Flakes. Although the ingredients on the box look healthful, the high proportion of sugar significantly reduces their nutritional value. When asked why they put so much sugar in an otherwise wholesome product, industry spokesmen replied that Americans like things sweet. They didn't add that corporate advertising and marketing is largely responsible for our national sweet tooth.

Food advertising, over the years, has created a vast market for precooked, frozen, and packaged foods. These ads have convinced many consumers that cooking is a drag to be avoided with the help of fast foods. Instead of cooking inexpensive nutritious meals, they have been brainwashed into putting TV dinners in the oven, canned ravioli in the saucepan, or packaged noodles Romanoff on the table. These foods don't save that much time, taste nothing like the real thing, have little nutritional value, and often cost twice as much as the equivalent raw materials. They are a basic part of the American diet because their high price translates into high profits for the companies that make and market them.

These ads are effective because of the public's ignorance about nutrition. As we become aware of the relation between food and health, they will become useless to agribusiness. Co-ops are only part of the growing movement of people becoming conscious of the value and hazards of the food we eat.

Food co-ops represent a workable alternative to the profit-making food industry. Based on the foregoing examples, we would define food co-ops as nonprofit, democratically controlled groups of consumers that distribute high quality food, try to educate themselves, and seek to influence food production and distribution.

Where is all this energy going? Oddly enough, both the co-op movement and agribusiness are heading in the same direction. Both are trying to gain control of food from production to consumption, farm to dinner table. The corporations are doing this to gain even greater profits. Co-ops are trying to gain more control over food quality and in the process to cut out as many profit-making middlepeople as possible. Gaining this control is called vertical integration.

Agribusiness corporations buy farms or contract with independent farmers. They often prefer contracting because it guarantees them a source of supply without incurring the risks of farming. They save millions of dollars by not having to pay minimum wages, workmen's compensation, social security, or medical insurance premiums for the farmers who aren't technically their employees.

Ninety-eight percent of all chicken farmers are under contract to one of the several large poultry firms. The same contract that assures farmers a market requires them to buy their chicks, feed, chemicals, and equipment from the firm. Often one firm dominates an area, and the farmer has little choice but to sign up. If he doesn't, he faces prohibitive transportation costs to get his product to another buyer. The result is that most chicken farmers make barely enough to survive, and many are going out of business.

A company that controls food "from seedling to supermarket," as a recent Tenneco annual report so aptly put it, has a great competitive advantage over a company that has to buy its food from an independent farmer, processor or middleperson. There would be nothing wrong with vertical integration if decisions affecting the food were decentralized and democratically made. Unfortunately, this isn't the case. A few corporate executives control the quality and price of the food we eat in any given food line. Their monopolistic control results in high prices, and their concern for profits above all else results in poor quality, over-processed, preservative-laden food. The widespread use of pesticides, chemical fertilizers, growth hormones, antibiotics, and ripening sprays is the result of a system in which profit comes before health. The emphasis on processed, packaged foods full of coloring agents and flavor enhancers, the bleaching of flour, and the preponderance of sugary, nutritionless junk food has created a nation of overfed but undernourished Americans.

Food co-ops have started to move in the direction of vertical integration too, but it is for the benefit of the consumer and not a corporate executive or stockholder. Co-ops have recently developed the means of getting food directly from farmers rather than waiting until it has moved all the way to the wholesalers. Many individual co-ops do this when local crops are in season, but most farm contracting is being done by federations that co-ops have created in their regions. By contracting with farmers, setting up warehouses, mills, and bakeries, and handling their own transportation, co-op federations can get fresher food for their member co-ops at lower prices.

The following diagram shows why cooperative vertical integration can save co-op members money:

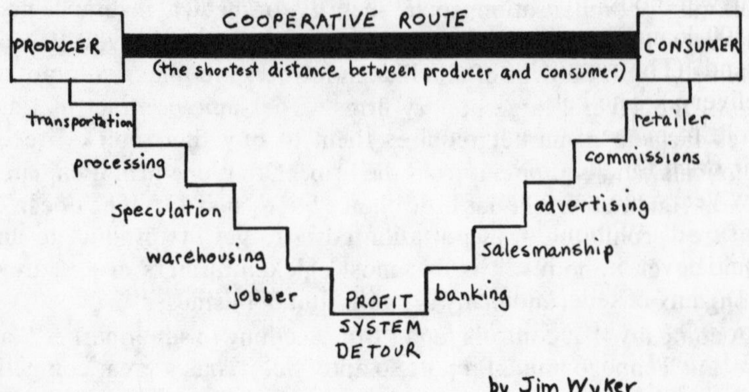

Jim explains:

> Some years ago I studied the profit plunder in detail by tracing the route of wheat from a farmer's field to his dinner table. On the profit detour the wheat had twenty-one ownerships before this farm family could eat its own bread. A farmer pays seven times more for the wheat in a loaf of bread than he sold it for . . . By contrast, the cooperatives in England buy our wheat and sell the bread for a third less than you pay in your favorite supermarket. How can they cut out so much middleperson profit? They own their own freighters; there is no speculation; storage is very limited; there are no jobbers, salespeople or advertisers; financing and retailing are kept at a minimum cost.

A good example of how direct deals can work for co-ops comes from Minneapolis. The North Country People's Warehouse recently purchased the entire honey production of a local apiary. They bought sixty-eight barrels for 52¢ a pound. Their newsletter gave the following breakdown on the deal:

Beekeeper	$23,646.44	52.00¢/lb.
Insurance Co.	70.00	.154¢/lb.
Bank (interest on loan)	406.25	.893¢/lb.
Trucking collective	330.00	.725¢/lb.
Wages	50.00	.110¢/lb.
Lunch (tequila & lemons)	7.10	.016¢/lb.
Labels and markers	3.00	.007¢/lb.
Rent on little red wagon and gas	3.00	.007¢/lb.
Warehouse brokerage	245.15	.539¢/lb.
Cost to co-op stores		55.00¢/lb.

The warehouse financed this deal with a $15,000 loan from a bank, a $3500 loan from its own building fund, and a $1500 loan from a friend. (The remaining $3,646 was to be paid a few months after delivery.) The bank and insurance company were the only ones to profit from the transaction, apart from the farmers, who received a fair price for their honey. The stores that set up the warehouse a few years ago got honey for only 3¢ a pound over what the farmer was paid. Without vertical integration through the warehouse, they could never have gotten so good a deal.

Dozens of federation buying services and warehouses have been started by co-ops in the last few years. They are the co-ops' co-ops. NEPCOOP, the federation of Vermont co-ops, buys almost the entire production of New England's Natural Organic Farmers Association. In Madison, Wisconsin, the Intra-Community Cooperative (ICC) buys cheese from local producers and transports it to its warehouse in Madison and to other warehouses throughout the Midwest. ICC members bring cheese and grain to Chicago once a week when they go there to buy from the produce market. In Austin, Texas, the Austin Community Project sends volunteers out to the cooperative farms that supply the city's co-ops with fresh vegetables. Rochester's Clear Eye Warehouse recently received a tractor-trailerload of dried fruit from organic farms in California. The fruit had been bought by the San Francisco warehouse and shipped on a truck owned and operated by Dick-Freeman, a nonprofit trucking collective based in Bloomington, Illinois.

Not bad for a movement that is still in its infancy. Wait till we grow up. We will soon grow our own food or contract for what we need, ship it and warehouse it cooperatively, and sell it through thousands of co-ops for as close to the farmers' costs as logistics allow. Nobody along the line is going to profit from our need to feed ourselves.

> There was once a foolish old man who at last decided to move a mountain that had been in his way for many years. He set out with his family to dig up the mountain with his spade and haul it away by the bucketful. Soon a wise old man happened by. "Old man," he said, "can you be so foolish as to believe you can move this great mountain?" "Why not?" the foolish old man replied. "I may not see this mountain removed, but my children will dig, and their children's children, and someday we will have moved the mountain." The wise old man laughed, but soon many people from far and near heard about the foolish old man. They joined him and together they moved the mountain in seven days.

The co-op movement is the foolish old man in this Chinese parable. The mountain is agribusiness. We've been digging steadily. Why don't you pick up a shovel and join us?

Sources

Agribusiness Accountability Project, 1000 Wisconsin Avenue, Washington, D.C. 20007. This is the best source of information on agribusiness. Write and ask for a list of their publications and reports, which are based largely on U. S. government surveys and statistics. The description of the Sunday dinner table is by James Hightower from his "Farmers — Corporate Middlemen — Consumers," an A.A.P. publication.

Appalachian Cooperative Development Exchange, Knoxville, Tennessee. *People Not Profit: Cooperative Economic Efforts in Appalachia.* This pamphlet is the source of Jim Wyker's diagram.

Cross, Jennifer. *The Supermarket Trap.* Bloomington, Indiana: Indiana University Press, 1970.

EAT IT: Agribusiness, Farming, Food, and You. Rifton, N.Y.: *WIN* Magazine, 1972.

Hightower, James. *Eat Your Heart Out: How Food Profiteers Victimize the Consumer.* New York: Crown, 1975.

Lerza, Catherine, and Michael Jacobson. *Food for People, Not for Profit.* Official Food Day Handbook. New York: Ballantine, 1975.

Lobenstein, Margaret, and John Schlommer. *Food Price Blackmail.* San Francisco: United Front Press, 1973.

Robbins, William. *The American Food Scandal.* New York: Morrow, 1974.

U.S. Senate, *Hearings Before the Subcommittee on Migratory Labor of the Committee on Labor and Public Welfare in the 92nd Congress,* headed by Senator Adlai Stevenson III, 1972.

Wellford, Harrison. *Sowing the Wind: Food Safety and the Chemical Harvest.* New York: Grossman, 1972.

Zwerdling, Daniel. "The Food Monopolies," *The Progressive,* January, 1975.

2. A Little History

A BROCHURE published by a food co-op in Wichita includes this remarkable sentence: "The concept of buying food cooperatively started in the summer of 1973." Actually, the concept of buying food cooperatively is more than a century old; human cooperation itself is older than civilization.

Even before agriculture had become the basis of human economy, cooperation was a necessity. Hunting and gathering societies shared their food. In most early agricultural societies, land was owned communally, with perhaps small plots reserved for individual households. In many places the concept of land ownership simply didn't exist. "Sell the land?" the American Indian leader Tecumseh once said. "Why not sell the air, the clouds, the great sea?"

In Europe, communal villages and cooperative economics lasted until the Industrial Revolution, when the enclosure of land and the demands of the rising bourgeoisie began to wreck the cooperative structure. Today, cooperation is still the economic norm in many villages in the Third World. Even in modern Western society, old habits of cooperation persist. Rural Americans still have barn raisings; volunteer fire departments protect thousands of small towns.

There is, then, something very old about cooperation. But it would be wrong to suggest that modern cooperativism is an outgrowth of premarket cooperation. Although both early and modern cooperativism share a common human impulse, today's co-ops are a product of the Industrial Revolution and the rise of capitalism.

Before consumer co-ops developed in the mid nineteenth century, cooperative producing and fire insurance societies had been formed. In the late 1700s, flour was being milled and baked cooperatively in England. In the United States, the first cooperative venture was

Benjamin Franklin's mutual fire-fighting society, formed in Philadelphia in 1736. Each member was required to furnish "six leather buckets and two stout linen bags."

The devastating effects of the Industrial Revolution spawned many radical social movements, among them Chartism, cooperativism and utopian socialism. In France, the Comte de Saint-Simon, Charles Fourier, and Louis Blanc, and in England, Robert Owen, developed theories based on organization of utopian communities that would own, live, consume, and produce cooperatively. Owen's New Lanark in Scotland was a model cooperative factory town. When Owen tried his principles in the United States, the experiment failed. At New Harmony, Indiana, "members shirked their duties, fought with each other, and, in some cases, made off with community funds."

Meanwhile, in England, a less utopian movement was taking shape. Dr. William King, sometimes known as the "father of distributive cooperation," began publishing a newsletter called *The Cooperator*. His idea was to start small distributive ventures with co-op members supplying the capital. By 1830 about three hundred stores had begun under King's influence. The movement died by 1840, partly because of poor management, unwise extensions of credit, and inadequate capital reserves.

One of the towns where a King co-op had begun and failed was Rochdale, England; it was here that consumers' cooperation really began.

In 1844, twenty-eight weavers registered with Parliament under the hopeful title, "Rochdale Society of Equitable Pioneers." Their effort was rooted in poverty and desperation. The previous year they had been fired and then blacklisted by employers after an unsuccessful weavers' strike. The one woman in the group, Ann Tweedale, suggested that if they couldn't organize to gain better wages, at least they might organize as consumers for lower prices.

It took them a year to accumulate the £28 necessary to start the venture. They opened on December 21, 1844, a bitterly cold night, on the ground floor of an old warehouse on Toad Lane. Their initial goods were flour, butter, sugar, and oatmeal. Anyone was welcome to join.

The Society decided to trade for cash only. This wasn't simply because the members were concerned with unpaid debts, although debts had been a problem with the earlier consumer co-ops. Many members regarded credit as a social evil. Later, people looking back over ten years of membership in the Rochdale Society felt grateful for learning to keep out of debt.

Most members actually saved money for the first time. This was possible because of a unique innovation. Profits were divided up in proportion to the amount each member spent on purchases, instead of in proportion to the capital invested. This "rebate" principle is the basis of most traditional co-op stores.

Capital was raised when members used their dividends to buy shares in the Society. New members had to promise to reinvest their dividends until they had bought four shares at one pound each. The Society decided to pay a limited interest of 3½% per year on capital invested.

The Rochdale store did not compete with other local tradesmen by underselling. They knew they could never win at price wars since larger stores could always wait them out. The result of the market price policy was significant dividends for members at the end of each quarter. It also gave the store some working capital.

Voting power, like dividends, was unrelated to the amount of capital invested. Each member had one vote at general meetings and in elections of the board of directors. All women had equal voice with men, and could receive dividends and hold shares. This was remarkable for the time, twenty-five years before married women were allowed to hold property in England.

Responsible, democratic control requires knowledge. While the store was still struggling to survive, the Pioneers decided to allot 2.5% of the surplus to education. Most of this fund went for a library and newsroom on the store's premises. A room was set aside for instruction in both store operation and cooperative philosophy. The shop on Toad Lane became a lively meeting place where many members congregated each evening after work.

In 1850, a group with evangelical views began to push for exclusiveness. They proposed to close the meeting room on Sundays and to forbid religious controversy. Such controversy had already broken up many friendly societies in England; the members decided that cooperation must be founded in toleration and rejected the evangelical view.

In ten years, the Rochdale Society's membership grew to 1800.

General meetings had to be moved to the town's public hall. The *London Daily News* observed: "Eighteen hundred workmen are brought into weekly intercourse with each other, under circumstances which have raised the tone of society among them all."

This isn't to say that the Society made no mistakes. In an anxious effort to produce for their own consumption and to begin employing members who were still blacklisted, the Pioneers rushed too quickly into buying a mill. It produced more than the members of the Society could purchase. Furthermore, the members were accustomed to the taste and color of flour bleached with alum, and were reluctant to buy the unadulterated product. The Society almost had to give up the mill at a great loss. Fortunately, enough people wanted to support the venture and learned to appreciate the more healthful flour. Meanwhile, townspeople in Lancashire and Yorkshire heard that something called consumers' cooperation was working nearby. People in Rochdale were undeniably beginning to live more comfortably. So the Pioneers were invited to speak at workmen's meetings in the area. Other co-op stores began. These new stores helped purchase all the flour that the mill could produce.

In 1855, eleven years after its beginning, the Rochdale Society helped set up a wholesale department to supply co-op stores in the area. The Pioneers also formed a manufacturing society for cotton and wool. It employed forty-two people. By then, the Rochdale store had departments of shoemaking, tailoring, drapery-making and butchering. The *London Daily News* described the scene:

> Buyer and seller meet as friends; there is no over-reaching on one side, and no suspicion on the other . . . These crowds of humble workingmen, who never knew before when they put good food in their mouths, whose every dinner was adulterated . . . now live like lords. They are weaving their own stuffs, making their own shoes . . . grinding their own corn . . . they slaughter their own cattle, and the finest beasts of the land waddle down the streets of Rochdale for the consumption of flannel weavers and cobblers.

The Rochdale store continues to this day.

One way of assessing the Pioneers' experiment is to enumerate the cooperative principles that they applied:

1. Open membership
2. Democratic control based on one member-one vote

3. Promotion of education
4. Dividends in proportion to purchases (rebate principle)
5. Limited interest on capital investment, and limit on number of shares any member can own
6. Political and religious neutrality
7. Cash trading; no credit
8. Active cooperation among cooperatives

Most of these principles had been used in cooperative ventures before Rochdale; the particular contribution of the Pioneers was to combine them successfully. All kinds of consumers', housing, health, handicraft, farming, and banking co-ops have since looked to these principles for guidance.

In Great Britain today, consumer co-ops have 9% of the retail trade. The large wholesale society and the many small retail co-ops have been aligned with the Labour Party for many years. British co-ops follow the traditional Rochdale policy of selling at market prices. Members attach great importance to the size of the dividend, or "divi." According to Jerry Voorhis, former President of the Cooperative League of the United States: "No matter how large the margins or markups on the various items sold, the British co-ops have tended to take the going market price and then to increase the 'divi' correspondingly. This clearly leads to a strong interest in the dividend on the part of co-op members. But it means that the consumer co-ops are exerting little influence on the price structure of the British economy as a whole."

In contrast, many Scandinavian co-ops like Sweden's huge wholesale, the Kööperativa Forbundet, try to control the overpricing often practiced by profit-making competitors by keeping its own prices low. Though this means lower dividends for co-op members, it also means lower prices for everyone. In this sense, the Swedish cooperative does a service to all consumers and exerts a powerful influence on the economy. Swedish consumer co-ops account for about 15% of the country's retail trade and one-third of the food business. Cooperative structures can be found in Swedish insurance companies, utilities, housing developments, and production industries, including most food lines.

Cooperativism is widespread in Scandinavia. Cooperative agriculture and banking are encouraged in Denmark, where "folk high schools" teach co-op principles along with a variety of agricultural and cultural subjects. In both Denmark and Iceland, most human needs are met by some form of cooperation.

In Belgium, co-ops are closely allied with the socialist movement. Co-op profits are not all rebated; some are used for services that a socialist government might otherwise provide: old-age pensions, life, health, and unemployment insurance, maternity benefits, medical and nursing care.

Russia before the Bolshevik Revolution had the largest cooperative movement in the world, a network of consumer and agricultural co-ops with a People's Bank at the center. After the revolution, the Bolsheviks incorporated the co-ops into the state-controlled economy. The existence of co-ops in Soviet Russia and, during the 1930s, in fascist Italy, indicates how politically malleable co-ops can be. They exist today in almost every nation on earth.

Canada has perhaps the greatest variety of cooperative organizations in the world: *caisses populaires* (credit unions), farmer co-ops that handle 80% of the grain crop, fishing co-ops, consumer co-ops, cattle co-ops, and insurance co-ops. The "direct charge" co-op stores, such as Montreal's Cooprix chain, put a strong emphasis on consumer protection and education. Cooprix, says the Cooperative League of the U.S.A., is "North America's only current effort to develop consumer goods cooperatives on significant scale in major metropolitan areas." Cooprix's weekly sales run from $75,000 to $200,000 per store. The stores, which carry a variety of foods and dry goods, are managed by a regional co-op, which is supported in turn by labor unions and individual co-op members in the province of Quebec.

During the First World War, according to Albert Sonnichsen, there were many spontaneous demonstrations of the international spirit of cooperation:

> On the French front were instances of cooperative buildings being spared by the German gunners. Chateau-Thierry, at its first bombardment, was such an instance. The cooperative store was not injured. The French troops withdrew and many of the civilian population with them. The manager of the cooperative store and his clerks remained. The German soldiers entered the town. The manager expected harsh treatment, but when the soldiers entered the store, they bought what they wanted and paid for it; some even insisted on shaking hands with him. The puzzled manager was finally able to understand what it meant when he saw that the

> Germans had written in chalk over the word "Cooperative" on the front of the store, the German equivalent, "Konsumgenossenschaft." They had also added in German, "These are cooperative comrades, boys, do them no harm."

Compared to Europe, the United States is backward in cooperative development. Much of the impetus for early American consumer co-ops came from Scandinavian immigrants. Yet there is a long American cooperative tradition.

In 1844, a consumer co-op was organized by a Boston tailor; its first purchases were soap and tea. Known as the Workingmen's Protective Union, this co-op expanded and soon other stores were opened in the area. By 1857, there were 1106 stores that had been established as far west as Illinois. They served only members and had broad social interests: temperance, the ten-hour day, and abolition of war, capital punishment, and slavery. By the end of the Civil War, most of these co-ops had failed. They had lacked stable membership and some had been poorly managed.

In the late nineteenth century, a wave of radical agitation swept the country in response to the depredations of the "robber barons" and the uncontrolled corporate exploitation of the American people. The populist movement expressed the resentment of farmers who saw themselves victimized by the big railroads and other corporate interests involved in transporting and marketing food. In the Midwest, the Grange and the Farmers Alliance organized cooperatives to market farm products from a position of collective strength. They soon began to distribute farm equipment to members, and later to distribute groceries and other goods. Many of these co-ops, unable to compete with private corporations, eventually failed. Others have survived, with the help of government programs, and have grown into huge federated organizations. The cooperative spirit remains strong in the Midwest, where members of today's new-style co-ops are beginning to communicate with representatives of the older tradition through the Minnesota People's History Project.

Farmers' co-ops represent the real beginning of cooperativism in the United States. Their example soon spread to the cities. Labor societies such as the Knights of St. Crispin and the Knights of Labor organized co-ops. In 1874, the Sovereigns of Industry became the first labor group to put its main organizing efforts into cooperatives, and the first to operate on the Rochdale principle of rebate in proportion to patronage. By 1875, the Sovereigns had 40,000 members in about twenty states. But the movement declined quickly and was apparently over by 1879. Art Danforth, Secretary-Treasurer of the Cooperative League of the U.S.A., attributes the failure to high debts and poor management.

The farm co-op movement also declined toward the end of the nineteenth century. By 1900, only about 1200 farm co-ops remained, mostly grain elevators, cheese factories, and creameries. According to Richard Margolis, "Thousands had perished for lack of capital, credit, and political influence. In many states co-ops had trouble coaxing charters out of their legislatures. There was a general feeling in state capitals that cooperatives were at once 'communistic' and 'monopolistic' and this feeling was carefully encouraged by that tireless defender of laissez-faire: the railroad lobby."

In an expanding frontier economy where the self-made man was an object of fascination, and where huge fortunes were made in a short time, co-op principles had to fight an uphill battle against transience, stubborn individualism, and profit-motive ideology. In addition, their difficulty financing themselves, their frequent bad management, and their lack of firm commitment to education and consumer democracy, contributed to their decline. This pattern would be repeated after the cooperative upsurge of the 1930s.

The early twentieth century saw a new wave of cooperativism. Immigrant groups, especially Scandinavians, formed consumer co-ops, one of them as early as 1907 in Maynard, Massachusetts. It lasted for more then sixty years. The consumers' co-op formed in 1910 by the Finnish community in Fitchburg, Massachusetts, is still operating.

Many Finns came to the mining areas of Wisconsin, Minnesota, and northern Michigan before World War I. With them came their cultural institutions: temperance halls, socialist parties, and co-ops. Consumer cooperation was the one element of economic freedom they had in a situation otherwise dominated by the mining companies.

The first Finnish co-op in Minnesota opened in 1905 in Menhaga. It was named *Sampo,* meaning "magic mill." In Finnish folklore, the *sampo* produced food from one spout and gold from the other. The 1974 Minnesota Homefires Calendar tells us:

> In 1909 the *Jukola* [housing co-op] opened its doors to the miners and sawmill workers of frontier Virginia, Minnesota. It was one of many *osuusruokalat,* cooperative boarding houses, started by Finnish immigrants . . . You bought a share of co-op stock; then a meal ticket and perhaps a room ticket. By 1912, expansion provided beds for 100 men. The kitchen served up to 450 persons a day . . . In the *Jukola* lounge, people could meet after work and hash over any topic — from the latest slur against Finns muttered by the mine boss to the dream of building a farm in the woods. The *Jukola* boarders helped put up the Socialist Opera House nearby. It soon became a haven of political meetings, union organization, gymnastic and musical groups, Shakespearean theater and original plays — all in Finnish.

In 1909, Boston department-store magnate Edward Filene financed the first credit union in the United States. Credit unions grew steadily until by 1940 there were 9000 of them, serving three million members. Today more than 28.5 million Americans belong to these financial co-ops first developed in the mid nineteenth century in Germany by the mayor of a small town.

In the 1920s, a serious political conflict began to weaken the co-op movement. Over the years, the Communist Party had supported a great number of co-ops with office space, loans, and labor. Many co-op members were Communists, having joined the new American CP when it formed, in the years following the Bolshevik Revolution in Russia. Such was the prestige of this first successful socialist revolution that many socialists in Europe as well as in the United States became supporters of the Bolsheviks. Debates over forming a Leninist-type party in the United States split the old American Socialist Party and also split the largely socialist Finnish community.

Throughout the 1920s, the cooperative movement struggled with its relation to the Communist Party. Some co-ops customarily contributed money to the party. But eventually, the Communists were expelled from most co-ops; in many areas, such as Fitchburg and Minneapolis, they started their own, alternative co-ops, some of which lasted twenty years or more.

Old-time cooperators remember the bitterness of the factional fighting. Those who sympathized with the party felt that the co-ops had "sold out" and betrayed the cause. Certainly it's true that the early co-op movement lost much of its crusading vigor after the political schism. But anticommunists felt that the party was trying to control the co-op movement. The CP's intoxication with Bolshevism in its early days committed it to a mode of operation that alienated it from most Americans. For the co-ops, the choices were limited: either alliance with a cadre-type party, or political "neutrality." There was no party that really represented their aspirations. The lack of such a party through the years has contributed to the absence of strong political direction in the co-op movement.

Co-ops and their wholesales continued to grow, but they were organized on a top-down basis with little attention to member education and little coordination among them. Some closed with heavy losses. It was partly in response to this lack of coordination that the Cooperative League of the U.S.A. was formed in 1916. In 1917, the relatively conservative American Federation of Labor endorsed consumer cooperation as a "twin remedy" with trade unionism for the hardships of workers. Miners' and railway workers' unions formed co-op stores.

Co-ops had struggled for years, first for recognition, then for help, from the government. Technically, they could have been considered violators of the Sherman Antitrust Act, which prohibited monopoly pricing and combinations in restraint of trade. By the early 1920s, a variety of cooperative-minded groups were lobbying for legislation favoring cooperatives, or at least recognizing their right to exist. In 1922, they succeeded. The Capper-Volstead Act provided that farmers could form co-ops without fear of violating antitrust laws. The act stipulated that a co-op must be operated for the mutual benefit of its members and either conform to the one member-one vote principle or keep its stock dividends under 8% a year.

The government began giving co-ops credit and technical help, and putting up money to start co-op banks. These early measures paved the way for government programs of the Depression such as the Rural Electrification Administration. Over the years, the government's cooperative programs began to favor big co-ops over small ones.

The first gas and oil co-ops were formed in the 1920s, starting in 1921 with a co-op gas station in Cottonwood Falls, Minnesota. By 1935 oil co-ops were the second largest distributors of gas and oil in Minnesota. Co-op housing on a large scale also got started in the twenties, although boarding houses had been organized by immigrant groups earlier in the century. A cooperative housing project was started by the Amalgamated Clothing Workers in New York City in 1926. Co-op City in the Bronx now houses about 65,000 people.

Co-op or mutual insurance companies, many of which have since grown enormously, also began in the 1920's, as did the first cooperative health plan, established in Elk City, Oklahoma. A cooperative hospital was built in Elk City in 1931. Throughout the thirties this small community was a model of what could be done in cooperative health care, but it was never widely imitated, partly because of opposition from the American Medical Association, long a vociferous defender of private enterprise.

The foundations laid by immigrant co-ops, the unemployment, poverty, and social idealism of the Great Depression, and the beginnings of government aid all helped create the co-op movement of the 1930s. Because of the Depression, Americans developed a sense of collective need. Not only were there a wide variety of cooperative ventures, but a great many people were interested in cooperation as one possible alternative to a profit-making system that seemed to have failed. Marquis Childs's book, *Sweden: The Middle Way,* and Upton Sinclair's *Co-op,* were both published in 1936.

Farmer and consumer co-ops had developed along parallel lines, without a great deal of contact. Partly through the efforts of the Cooperative League, the two groups began to communicate. Sounder business methods were developed. Co-op banks were growing. By the mid thirties, consumer co-ops were supplying groceries, baked goods, meat, shoes, clothing, housing, furniture, hardware, paints, farm supplies, radios, refrigerators, electricity, gasoline, motor oil, tires, and auto accessories. Co-ops supplied telephone and water service, auto insurance, lending libraries, plays, parks, orchestras, summer camps, health plans, and burial services: the ultimate in horizontal growth.

Minnesota politics was dominated by the Farmer-Labor Party, whose platform included proposals for a cooperative commonwealth. This platform helped elect Floyd Olson Minnesota governor from 1930 to 1936. The Farmer-Labor Party conducted vigorous educational campaigns to promote trade unionism and consumer cooperation.

By the 1930s most urban homes had electricity, but because of the long distances involved, utility companies had not built electric lines to most farms. The Rural Electrification Act of 1936 provided for low-interest government loans to organizations intending to build rural electric power lines. Farmers organized their own electricity cooperatives. Occasionally, in response to exorbitant wholesale rates, co-ops bought plants to generate their own power as well. The spirit of rural electrification is reflected in a song from the period (to the tune of "Solidarity Forever"):

> We have set transmission towers
> On their march across the land,
> Soon to place electric power's
> Strength at every farm's command;
> We have shown the world what happens
> When the farmer takes a hand,
> For in union we are strong!

This decade also saw the beginning of many modern consumer co-ops. In Berkeley, California, cooperation began with small preorders, or buying clubs, organized during Upton Sinclair's nearly successful 1934 gubernatorial campaign. Sinclair's slogan was "End Poverty in California," or EPIC. Most of the EPIC-inspired buying clubs didn't last long but some were progenitors of better-organized groups.

Today the Consumers Co-op of Berkeley, with about 75,000 member families, accounts for 2½% of the retail food trade in the San Francisco Bay Area. On one block in Berkeley there are a co-op supermarket, gas station and auto repair shop, hardware store, pharmacy, bookstore, taxi service, and natural foods emporium.

The Berkeley co-op is organized along traditional Rochdale lines. It has an elected board of directors and a hired staff. It sells at market prices and in good years returns sizeable rebates to its members, who must invest $100 of accumulated rebates in co-op stock before they are elegible to vote. There are committees, festivals, political information tables, and cultural groups like the co-op chorus. The co-op offers insurance, meeting rooms, a credit union, consumer information, "kiddie korrals," and a travel agency.

Political reaction after World War II contributed to cooperatives' general decline. With the onset of the Cold War, everything about the Popular Front mood of the 1930s became suspect, and people grew afraid to join organizations with even the slightest left-wing tinge. Co-ops suffered not only from bad management and lack of capital but from loss of the cooperative spirit. The co-ops that survived and grew affluent sometimes differed little from supermarkets.

These large consumer co-ops today often can't give rebates because they need so much money for capital. In recent years the whole rebate idea, and with it the concept of selling at market prices, has come into question. The Swedish co-ops have long seen their role as one of keeping all prices down, and thus of helping consumers wherever they shop. The Berkeley and Palo Alto co-ops have both attempted some discount pricing. Palo Alto sold meat at a loss several years ago in an attempt to bring down meat prices of local competitors. In 1974, the Berkeley co-op rolled back beef prices 13%, while warning members to eat less beef because of its high level of saturated fats.

If by the late 1950s and early 1960s some of the consumer co-ops were big and impersonal, many of the producers' co-ops were fat and complacent. Seven of them are now on *Fortune*'s list of the nation's 500 biggest corporations.* The merger movement that produced these giants is continuing, just as it is throughout agribusiness, and in the process the small farmer is being squeezed out. The giant co-ops are run on a top-down basis by boards of directors that often include corporate executives. Even the principle of open membership has been violated. Some co-ops admit only large growers, or discriminate against poorer members through price adjustments. Recently, producer cooperatives have entered into joint ventures with profit-making firms. They act like corporations too; the dairy co-ops made illegal contributions to Richard Nixon's re-election campaign with the understanding that milk price supports would be raised. Richard Margolis, a student of co-op history, writes:

> Several white co-ops in the South have pointedly refused to sell fertilizer to their black counterparts; and on the West Coast some of the larger co-op grower associations, like Sunkist, have been charged with creating intolerable conditions for Mexican-American farmworkers.
>
> Moreover, some co-ops have made a shambles of the Rochdale principles: they have closed their doors to new members, failed to keep old members duly informed, and, in a few flagrant instances, have even

* They are: Associated Milk Producers, Inc. (AMPI), Land O'Lakes, Farmland Industries, Agway, Gold Kist, Dairylea, and Farmers Union Central Exchange.

> scrapped the one-man one-vote rule, preferring to parcel out voting power on the basis of each member's selling performance . . .
>
> The one thousand rural electric co-ops . . . now consistently shun the thousands of black, Indian and chicano families whose shacks are still dark. Not one black man sits on the board of a single rural electric co-op.

This perversion of cooperativism may be due, in part, to the vitality of American capitalism, which sometimes seems to either destroy or absorb everything in its path. It's also due to the lack of political direction that has characterized most American cooperatives.

The old consumer co-op movement has lost much of its early vitality and purpose, but it survives and in many places continues to provide both an alternative to profit-making food distribution and a center of community activity and consumer awareness. About 50 million Americans belong to co-ops of one sort or another today (28.5 million of them to credit unions).

The most recent wave of cooperative activity has its roots in the political and social changes of the 1960s. The civil rights, student, and antiwar movements created a new political awareness among many young people. The importance of open democratic structures and the participation that gives them life in co-ops come out of the New Left's emphasis on participatory democracy. Many co-op organizers stress the need for democratic control as a way of teaching communities to take control over their own lives.

The New Left's critique of monopoly capitalism led people to look for new economic possibilities. Contemporary co-ops are nonprofit, low-cost alternatives to profit-making retailers. The emphasis on direct savings rather than rebates is based on an awareness that many people have difficulty meeting food bills. The desire to keep co-ops small and personal is a reaction against the bureaucratic extremes of big government and big business.

The contemporary co-op movement also grew out of the cultural changes of the sixties. With many young people rejecting the values of middle-class suburban affluence and "dropping out" of the world they were expected to inherit, downward mobility brought unpleasant economic realities. Dropouts faced the problem of supporting themselves on low incomes, and were forced to consider economic alternatives undreamed of by their parents.

Counterculture values also included a new awareness of food and nutrition. Unprocessed foods took their place on health-food store shelves next to more traditional items like vitamins and brewer's yeast. Macrobiotics introduced a new vocabulary and Eastern food consciousness to America. Brown rice and tamari sauce became staples of the counterculture diet.

This new food consciousness created a boom in so-called health- and organic-food stores. Many co-ops developed as alternatives to the high prices of these capitalist health-food stores; others as the first source of natural foods in an area.

For many, co-ops began as attempts to create new institutions to help turn the counterculture into a countersociety. The new cultural values of the sixties had not yet created viable alternative institutions. Co-ops were part of the same thrust as daycare centers, women's centers, and alternative producer cooperatives (people's garages, carpenters, free presses, etc.).

At the same time, the Office of Economic Opportunity's Community Action Program began to organize buying clubs among the urban poor. From Atlanta to Chicago, OEO organizers and VISTA volunteers set up small food cooperatives for poor people. Many co-op organizers of the 1970s had their first experiences with collective buying as antipoverty workers in the 1960s.

By 1968, a variety of groups were starting co-ops. The Diggers had free stores in New York and San Francisco out of which they distributed free food. The Food Conspiracy was getting underway in Berkeley. The Mifflin Street Co-op storefront was being organized in Madison. Within two years, there were food co-ops throughout the country.

The rapid expansion of co-ops in the last few years has been partly a response to inflation. People of all races and lifestyles are now in co-ops. There are probably half a million Americans today who get some if not all of their food from new-style co-ops. If the American economy continues to falter in the 1970s, co-ops will probably grow at an even greater rate. Much of the infrastructure of federations, warehouses, trucking collectives and producer collectives is being established and there are now many people with the experience needed to start new co-ops. While traditional food co-ops all too often satisfy themselves with providing rebates and consumer information, many new-style co-ops are animated by the vision of a rapidly expanding movement that can grow into a real alternative for America.

Sources

American Academy of Political and Social Science. *The Annals: Consumers' Cooperation.* Philadelphia: AAPSS, Volume 191, May, 1937.

Buber, Martin. *Paths in Utopia.* Boston: Beacon Press, 1949.

Cooperative League of the U.S.A., 1828 L St. NW, Washington, D.C. A good source of information on co-op history and traditional rebate-style co-ops.

Danforth, Art. *Why (Some) Co-ops Fail.* Washington, D.C.: Cooperative League of the U.S.A., 1973.

Danforth, Art and Emil Sekerak. *Consumer Cooperation: The Heritage and the Dream.* Palo Alto: Consumers' Cooperative Publishing Association, 4294-G Wilkie, Palo Alto, 1975.

Giese, Paula. A series of three articles on co-op history, centering on the experience of immigrant groups in the Midwest. *North Country Anvil,* May-June, 1974; October-November, 1974; July-August, 1975.

Holyoake, Jacob. *History of the Rochdale Pioneers.* New York: Scribners, 1893. Reprint of a series of articles in the *London Daily News* by the historian of nineteenth century cooperation.

———. *History of Cooperation.* New York: Dutton, 1906.

Kropotkin, Peter. *Mutual Aid: A Factor in Evolution.* 1915. Reprint. New York: Sargent, 1971.

Margolis, Richard J. "Coming Together the Cooperative Way: Its Origins, Development, and Prospects," a special issue of *The New Leader,* April 17, 1972.

Minnesota People's History Project. *Minnesota Homefires Calendar,* 123 E. 26 St., Minneapolis 55404. Write for current and back issues of the calendar.

Neptune, Robert. *California's Uncommon Markets.* Richmond, California: Associated Cooperatives, 1971.

Sonnichsen, Albert. *Consumers' Cooperation.* New York: Macmillan, 1919.

Voorhis, Horace J. (Jerry). *American Cooperatives.* New York: Harper & Row, 1961.

Warbasse, James P. *Cooperative Democracy.* New York: Macmillan, 1927.

3. Models of Contemporary Co-ops

FOOD CO-OPS today exist in an amazing diversity of forms and structures. Residents of a single city block get together once a week to buy produce and distribute it out of someone's living room. Neighbors in Vermont get together once a month to buy grains and other staples. In Minneapolis, anyone can walk into a small co-op storefront and buy items ranging from aduki beans to popcorn. In Massachusetts, the 3000 members of the Boston Food Co-op all work two hours a month to keep their store operating. In Madison, the Mifflin Street Co-op is run by a collective and is open to all, while the Eagle Heights Co-op is run by its 350 member households, and is open only to members. In the same town, another co-op, Common Market, feeds 1600 people. There are co-ops in Oxford, West Virginia, Fargo, North Dakota, Laramie, Wyoming, Wolf Creek, Oregon, and Caribou, Maine.

Some co-ops are highly participatory and others lean more toward community service. In participatory co-ops most, and often all, of the work is done by the members, who are also expected to make decisions for the co-op. Community service co-ops are run by small groups of committed activists. They are concerned with bringing inexpensive, high quality food to as many of their neighbors as possible and creating a source of alternative employment at the same time.

In practice, there are few purely participatory or purely community service co-ops. Paid coordinators or management collectives often help run participatory co-ops, and most community service co-ops expect some degree of input from their members.

Some co-ops carry only organically grown food, while others carry TV dinners and Coke, but this in itself doesn't tell us much about them. To write a handbook for co-ops, we were concerned with how they function, survive, and grow. The models we describe are a way to make sense out of the diversity of food cooperatives, and they can also tell us some important things about how structure influences the co-op experience. Keep in mind that co-ops are eclectic and not all will fit neatly into any one model.

Preorders are co-ops that buy only enough food to meet their members' orders. We use the term *preorder* because it decribes the process of ordering before picking up food. Other common terms for these co-ops are conspiracy and buying club. Stores don't buy food to cover orders; they maintain an inventory from which people can choose. Preorders are the invisible co-ops. If you visit a town you can find a co-op store, but you may never see the preorders unless you know where distribution occurs and are there on the right day.

People in the co-op movement sometimes debate whether a preorder or a store is the more desirable structure. Advocating one over the other is an injustice to the different ways in which we can cooperate. Both are useful, and they don't preclude each other. A store can help a preorder by serving as a training ground or possibly by allotting some of its storage space for warehousing. A preorder can help a store by serving as an example of full participation and preventing the store from falling into the "super duper" trap. Preorders often have stricter nutritional standards than stores do. Some people like to be in both types of co-ops at once.

Preorders are usually smaller and more intimate than stores, are generally run by volunteers, but don't yet carry everything that people need or want to eat. There's no reason, however, why preorders couldn't fill all food needs if they built up a system of cooperative warehousing. Stores are large and can be alienating. But they can and should carry a complete line of necessary foods and paper goods. They can also become centers of community activities. Stores can be more reliable sources of food because they keep inventories, but preorders can impede impulse buying by having people order only what they need.

Types of Preorders

While some preorders are small unified groups of friends and neighbors, others are large decentralized bodies with hundreds of members. The larger the co-op, the more apt it is to break down into smaller, more workable units. Because of the limitations of space and time at distribution centers, a co-op may be broken down into two or more units that distribute food to their members. Some co-ops also decentralize the work, rotating it among different groups of members. Combining these characteristics, we come up with three types of preorders:

Unified preorders have a single distribution point and allocate jobs from among the entire membership.

Branch preorders have several distribution points — one for each branch — and central committees to do the work.

Block preorders have both decentralized distribution and decentralized participation; the work of the co-op is done by the blocks on a rotation basis, rather than by central committees.

UNIFIED PREORDERS

The Cambridgeport Food Co-op in Cambridge, Massachusetts, started in the fall of 1969. It was a homogeneous group of friends and neighbors who met each week in the largest living room available. This is typical of unified co-ops; in many of them, the entire membership can fit in one room.

Some unified preorders don't have members request individual orders. In Ann Arbor, Michigan, in the late 1960s, the White Panther Party started the People's Food Co-op, whose members could order as many $3 bags of food as they wanted. Whoever went to the Detroit market that week would get a balanced selection of fruits and vegetables according to the best buys in the market. Members would preorder the number of bags they wanted.

In, 1970 a group split from the People's Food Co-op to form the Itemized People's Co-op. Individual households could request the number of apples or pounds of potatoes they wanted. As one member said, "We started the new co-op because we were sick of eating cabbage every week." Itemized ordering is much more common than collective ordering. Most preorders use order forms and let members choose what they want.

Most unified preorders discover that the energy put into organizing smooth-running systems of ordering, buying, and distributing pays off very quickly. How much structure a unified preorder needs depends on its size and the values of its members. Most unified preorders are run with very simple procedures and are characterized by friendship and high participation. In small preorders, members may have to do a job every week to help get the food.

Young co-ops tend to grow faster than their organized structures can handle. The advantages of inexpensive, high quality food attract new members at an alarming rate. The Cambridgeport Co-op doubled in less than six months. Dallas's People Buying Together quickly expanded to a membership of 600. This kind of expansion has a marked effect on a co-op's operation. Procedures established for a co-op of 20 households quickly become overtaxed when there are 100. People who spend hours getting their apples out of a barrel, their pound of onions weighed, their cheese sorted, and their order added up usually don't spend years in food co-ops.

As a preorder grows, it faces two key problems. It becomes difficult to allocate jobs equitably from among the entire membership, and the distribution set-up becomes taxed by overcrowding. Eventually, it can become necessary to divide the co-op into smaller units, branches and blocks, to facilitate both job allocation and food distribution.

When these decentralizations occur depends in part on the values of the membership and in part on the physical structure of the co-op. One co-op may remain a unified type with 200 members while another may decide it is too big and in need of change when membership hits 100. A co-op that emphasizes social relationships among members will decide to decentralize before one that doesn't care so much about personal interaction. Likewise, a preorder that distributes food out of the small basement of one member's house may decide to set up two distribution centers faster than one that has a large storefront.

A unified preorder has numerous options open to it before it is forced to decentralize. Before breaking down job allocation into blocks, it can change its *method* of job allocation (see Chapter 8). Rather than divide into two distribution points, a co-op can have its overcrowded distribution center open earlier, close later, or operate more efficiently with more helpers.

Breaking down a unified preorder into separate distribution units changes the entire structure of the co-op. Ordering and collating orders must also be separated, and the co-op develops the feel of two or more distinct organizations buying together.

BRANCH AND BLOCK PREORDERS

The major difference between branches and blocks is that in the branch preorder, volunteer central committees do the work of purchasing and distributing food for the entire co-op, while in the block preorder, this work is performed by co-op members according to a rotating schedule. Each week, one block is "masterblock," and its members collate block orders into the master order list, buy the food, and sort it into the block orders. In both systems, each individual block or branch takes care of collating its household orders into a block or branch order list, picking up the block or branch order at the central distribution point, and sometimes sorting it into the member households' orders. In the block system, both weekly in-block jobs and occasional masterblock jobs are assigned to every block member. In branch co-ops, only in-branch jobs are assigned to all members.

Broadway Local Food Co-op on the Upper West Side of Manhattan is split into two groups of five or six blocks each. A handbook for the education of co-op members describes how the block structure evolved:

> The Broadway Local Food Co-op was started by three high school students in the early spring of 1971. It operated out of a formerly abandoned city building in which we were squatting. The Co-op rapidly expanded from a few people to over 150 families. Originally, each family came to the storefront and picked up its food, but once we reached 30 or 40 families, this procedure became chaotic. To handle this problem, we reorganized into several blocs. Each bloc geographically encompasses as little as one building or as many as ten streets, and consists of 10–30 families. We have found that the bloc system enables us to distribute food efficiently as well as providing small enough working groups so that people can get to know each other.

Because blocks assign the responsibility for doing the work of the whole co-op each week to a different block, a coordinator is necessary to make sure that keys, money, and books pass from one masterblock to the next. To help with this transition, newsletters usually list the masterblocks and their coordinators for the coming month.

Most block co-ops have booklets for their members detailing all the responsibilities of the masterblock. The "booklet" for the South Cambridge preorder is a five-pound looseleaf filled with receipts, financial reports, tips on buying, and complete directions for doing masterblock work.

In Madison, Wisconsin, the Common Market is made up of 180 small branches. Each branch is responsible for making the decisions that affect its operation. Each branch assigns branch jobs such as collating orders, picking up food at the central distribution center, distributing food to the members, and keeping track of money. Co-op members are also expected to volunteer for the central committee jobs and to work at the central distribution point. Individual branches have to make sure they are represented on the central committees, which take care of work, food, finance, newsletters, nutrition, and orientation. Members sign up for work on a large chart at the distribution site. There is also a paid staff and a substantial inventory; this is not true of most branch preorders.

In branch co-ops, not all members have to be on central committees. There are usually enough activists in each branch to represent the branch on these committees. Block members, on the other hand, are almost always called upon to share the masterblock work when it's their block's turn to do it. Blocks therefore place greater responsibility on their members by decentralizing the allocation of jobs as well as the distribution of food.

Both branches and blocks are successful ways to decentralize ordering, collating, and distributing, but blocks can begin to have problems with their work systems as they get into memberships of over 100. Having a large co-op run by rotating masterblocks limits the interaction among members who aren't in the same block. In the branch system, people in the different branches get together in the central work committees. With different people doing masterblock jobs each week, the block system prevents the development of job expertise, and makes it difficult for the co-op to form the steady, trusting relations it needs with other co-ops and with wholesalers. Lack of expertise can keep the block co-op from carrying hard-to-handle foods like fresh meat and fish.

Blocks may not be so efficient as branches, but they are valuable social experiments. Decentralization is important in our overly centralized society. If blocks can learn to operate on a large scale as well as they can on a small scale, they'll make a significant contribution to the development of decentralized economic institutions.

Types of Stores

Stores are not categorized by their methods of distributing food or allocating voluntary labor, but by how they make decisions and cover their operating expenses. The three common decision-making structures are general meetings, elected boards, and collectives. The three common financial systems are rebate, direct charge, and direct savings.

Many stores delegate decision making to the entire membership or interested nonmembers through periodic general meetings. These can be held as often as once a week or as infrequently as once a year but are commonly held monthly or quarterly. Small, all-volunteer storefronts like Powderhorn in Minneapolis have weekly meetings in which all decisions are made. In larger stores with paid staff, general meetings are less frequent. A store in the Jamaica Plain section of Boston has monthly meetings and a steering committee that runs the co-op between meetings.

Elected boards are the most common decision-making structures in old-line co-op stores and are common in new co-ops too. Boards are often used by stores to fulfill the requirements of incorporation, though they aren't always necessary.

The Boston Food Co-op, a large store with 3000 active members, has an elected board of 15. The board members serve for one year and elections are held biannually, with half the members up for election each time. The board holds meetings every two weeks, and opens them to co-op members. The BFC board is a good example of how different members create different boards. When a board was elected with members who were not nearly so activist and vociferous as their predecessors, the tone of meetings changed noticeably. The year before, board members would chant together when arguments became too heated. The new board started its meetings with a moment of silence.

A collective can be viewed as a self-selected board. It's a tightly knit group of members who take it upon themselves to make decisions. These members can also be the staff of the co-op, the most active members, or the initial organizers.

Collectives are as common as boards of directors in co-op stores. They often run the store as well as make the policy decisions. Collectives that also manage stores are usually paid on an "equal pay for equal work" basis; they are nonhierarchical and practice worker control. Co-ops in which collectives do the work and make the decisions tend toward community service rather than high member participation. Glut, a Washington D.C. area storefront, is a good example. Participation from people outside the collective is minimal. (You'll find a complete discussion of decision-making structures and the problems that may arise with each in Chapter 7.)

FINANCING

A rebate is the surplus a co-op store distributes among members proportionate to their purchases. If a store finishes the year in the black, a set proportion of its earnings is given to the members. A co-op's earnings can be totally rebated or divided into rebates and capital investments.

Traditional co-op stores like the Consumers Co-op of Berkeley, with its 75,000 members and eight shopping centers, use rebates. The operating costs of such stores are high. They resemble modern supermarkets and have large staffs of unionized employees.

The opportunity for capital investment is a major advantage of the rebate system. By deferring members' savings till the end of the year, the co-op can use the surplus wealth of the store as it chooses during the course of the year. If the co-op decides to expand by renting a larger store or building another shopping center, it has the money available to do so.

This availability of funds leads to one of the disadvantages of the rebate model. Having lots of money on hand tends to centralize control. The co-op lets its directors and controllers make financial decisions. Elected boards with a million dollars at their disposal behave very differently from elected boards of stores run on a shoestring. All the traditional co-op supermarkets we know of use rebates and have centralized boards of directors.

An advantage of rebates, as the Rochdale Pioneers discovered, is that they help members save. Members of new-style co-ops with lower prices and no rebate have sometimes noticed that they spend as much money at a co-op store as at a supermarket because the lower prices encourage them to buy more and different foods, which would otherwise be out of their price range. They couldn't do this in a traditional rebate model co-op, for the shelf prices are no lower than a supermarket's.

Direct charge co-ops are a development of the Canadian cooperative movement. In Nanaimo on Vancouver Island in British Columbia, a direct charge store grew out of a fuel oil co-op, which in turn was tied to a credit union. The food store sells to its members at only 2% over wholesale price. The operating expenses of the store are covered by a direct charge of $1.75 per week per member, which is collected whether or not the member buys anything in the store (except for two vacation weeks at any time the member chooses during the year).

The 2% surcharge does not cover operating expenses but is used for loan capital and is redeemable with interest after three years. Whenever the 2% surcharge adds up to $10, the co-op issues the member a $10 "loan certificate." The loan capital is separate from the direct charge.

Advocates of direct charge feel that this system is the best way to insure that members do all their shopping at the co-op store. "Direct charge, in effect, commits the member to deliver his purchasing power because he is required to pay his share of operating costs, whether he buys anything or not," writes Nanaimo's manager. "If we have enough members under contract to pay operating costs of a store, it doesn't matter whether they buy or not." At present Nanaimo's membership isn't sufficient to have the $1.75 weekly fee cover all operating expenses; the rest is covered by a surcharge of 5% on nonfood items like razor blades.

The main advantage of direct charge is that it guarantees the money needed to run the store. Operating expenses are not tied to volume of goods sold. There's no need for a store manager to try to push more products to cover costs. Experience in Canada indicates that direct charge co-ops save their members 10 to 15% on food purchases.

One disadvantage of direct charge is that the weekly charge is regressive: everyone is taxed the same for unequal use of the store. An elderly couple pays the same per-member charge as a family of six, which may spend four times as much on food. (Some direct charge co-ops do have flexible fees for elderly and single members.) Direct charge also depends on a stable community.

Direct charge is being tried in a few co-ops in the United States. A co-op in New Salem, Massachusetts, asks members to pay $5 membership equity for five years and 60¢ to 75¢ per week in direct charges to run the store. The co-op also asks two hours of work per month from its members. The Consumers Co-op of the Monterey Peninsula and Co-opportunity in Los Angeles are other direct charge co-ops.

Most of the new American co-op movement follows the third financial model, direct savings. Here the operating costs and need for capital are met by charging a set percentage of the price of food purchases. This percentage can be added to the price of individual items, in which case it is called a markup, or to the total bill, in which case it is called a surcharge or bump. The latter method is preferable because it lets members see the wholesale price of each item and, through the bump, the operating costs of the store.

Direct savings, like direct charge, is based on selling as close to wholesale prices as possible. It shouldn't be surprising that operating costs in stores using direct charge or direct savings are lower than costs in stores using rebates. The operating costs of a rebate-type store are only revealed at the time of the annual report. The operating costs of the other two are evident to the members each week. Traditional co-op supermarkets using rebates employ paid staff and managers in a structure that differs little in appearance from the A & P. Stock is set out on shelves, prices are marked on all items, and the layout of the store is as modern as any other. Most direct charge and direct savings stores don't look like the A & P.: members commonly price their own food, open crates, or sweep the floor.

Both direct charge and direct savings stores keep operating costs low through volunteer work from members. This participation helps keep overhead down so that surcharges don't get high enough to wipe out savings. The percentage over wholesale that a store must charge is directly related to the amount of member participation it has. Stone Soup, a collectively run community store in Washington, D.C., uses little volunteer labor and therefore has a 25% markup.

The Common Market, a Denver preorder that became a store in 1973 and now has about 1500 members, uses direct savings. It adds a percentage markup on individual items to cover overhead; the markup varies with the kind of food. The Boston Food Co-op adds a 10% surcharge to the total bill at the cash register, and markups, if any, are small and reflect only spoilage or packaging costs.

An advantage of the surcharge is its flexibility. A store can decide to buy a truck and raise the money for it by increasing the surcharge for several weeks. If a store has more capital than it needs for present operations and for expansion in the foreseeable future, it can decrease the surcharge. Food Front, a store in Portland Oregon, did just this in 1974: eggs and milk were sold at cost to absorb the surplus.

Some Conclusions

Whether co-ops save their members money immediately through direct charge or direct savings, or subsequently through rebates, is very significant. In practice, this distinction results in two very different types of co-ops. Traditional co-op supermarkets like those in Berkeley, California, Fitchburg, Massachusetts, Hyde Park, Illinois, or Ithaca, New York, have high operating costs and are run by professional managers. Direct savings co-ops have created a new element in cooperative enterprises: voluntary work or member participation. Participation is not just an attempt to keep labor costs low. It is an offspring of the marriage between the political values of participatory democracy and the economic requirements of shoestring operations. Increased participation means informed membership and informed membership means more democratic control.

Voluntary labor is the social obligation that balances the rights of consumer control and democracy. Co-op members learn from the start that they don't get something for nothing. The savings on food costs and the quality control are paid for by work the members perform to keep the co-op going.

In dividing food co-ops into the various types of preorders and stores, we were struck by a factor common to all our categories: decentralization. As preorders grow from simple, unified roots, they usually break down food distribution and may also decentralize work allocation. The decision-making structures of stores range from centralized collectives and boards to decentralized general meetings. Among financial systems direct charge and direct savings decentralize money by making savings immediately available to members whenever they shop.

The financial and decision-making structures are related. Direct charge and direct savings stores, by encouraging participation to keep expenses down, result in more decentralized forms of control. This seems to be mitigated somewhat in the Canadian direct charge co-ops where top-down control is combined with decentralization of money.

It's not a coincidence that these characteristics should be related. Financial systems and decision-making structures, work systems and methods of distribution, all affect how co-ops feel and function. New-style co-ops have chosen certain systems and structures because they allow for decentralization.

4. Initial Organizing

MANY CO-OPS have started with nothing more than the desire of a few friends to buy food together. Organizing with friends is a natural way to start, but there are two disadvantages. One is that when you open your friends' refrigerators, you'll find the same familiar food. The other is that after a while you won't have any friends who aren't in food co-ops, and sometimes you can get to the point where you have to promise not to talk about the food co-op when you get together.

Still, as a place to begin, you and your friends should be able to offer each other a lot of tolerance, trust, and love, not only essential ingredients on which to base a food co-op, but essential reserves to bank on while you work out the bugs in your cooperative system.

One of the rewards of cooperative activity is meeting new people. It will be to the advantage of your co-op to include as many different people as possible in the initial organizing. Your community, be it a city neighborhood, small town, or rural area, has a wealth of skills, greater than that found in a group of friends. For these reasons, we suggest that people organize their community rather than just their friends.

You should not assume that the rest of your community will join a co-op started by you and your friends. A group of friends can appear to outsiders to be a clique. Such a group may also set up a co-op to meet its own needs, without being aware of the needs of other people in the community. Most of the information in this chapter is aimed at helping people organize their communities rather than just their friends. This effort should not be attempted by a single individual. You'll need the help of at least a few others to do the job well.

No matter what method of organizing you choose, it's essential to know the community with which you're involved. You need to have a good idea of who'd be interested in a co-op: talk with community activists, opinion leaders, and church people. One organizer in a small town knew enough about the community to guess who would object to a co-op. She went to these people first and talked to them about cooperating, thus defusing the potential opposition.

How do you find interested people? Two different approaches that work are: to organize directly for a first meeting of interested folks, or to get together a core group of people who will share the responsibility for organizing the first large meeting. The core group is probably the better approach, as one or two people can run themselves ragged trying to organize a food co-op.

Potential core group people exist in every community. Just keep your eyes and ears open for people who, with a little support, can bloom into leaders and organizers.

In reality, a core group, whether consciously organized or not, forms in most food co-ops. The main danger is cliquism or elitism. The core group has to be flexible and open to new people and new ideas.

Whether you organize a large meeting first or try to assemble a core group, there are some common ways to approach people. Go to community organizations and present your idea. You may be able to get a notice printed in a church bulletin or union newsletter. Community organizations include granges, PTAs, YMCAs, local settlement houses, church groups, welfare groups, tenants organizations, community-improvement associations, credit unions, trade unions, Kiwanis clubs, Knights of Columbus, American Legion, VFW, benefit associations, sports clubs, daycare parents, and elderly organizations — any group that meets regularly. The Broadway Food Co-op in Somerville, Massachusetts, and the Allston-Brighton Co-op in Boston were both started by local tenants unions. In Atlanta, twenty families in the Highland-Virginia-Morningside community came together in 1969 to fight a proposed highway in their neighborhood. After their success, they stayed together and organized the Stone Soup Food Co-op.

Your organizing success will depend on whether or not the community organization has a good reputation and grass roots participation. If it doesn't, you may be wasting your time. Beware of professional service agencies like OEO, Model Cities, or Head Start;

the people who work in these agencies are sometimes known in the community as the social worker or the politician. An agency's ability to move people in a community depends on the degree to which the community controls and actively participates in the agency's work. It's easier to find this out from people in a bar or hairdresser's shop than from the director of the program. If the professional agency does seem to have good community participation, it can be approached like any other group. In the Jamaica Plain section of Boston, an organizer respected by the Spanish-speaking community was able to bring about one hundred members into the co-op.

You can also approach existing co-ops. They may be overcrowded and glad to give you any waiting lists. Having sections of a co-op break away and form a new co-op is one way to deal with growth. Of course, don't try to raid a small co-op. In any case, visit the nearest co-op and learn what you can about its sources, logistics, and participation.

Canvassing door to door may be one way to find some interested people. It's helpful for a male and a female to canvass together, to have people of the same race or language group as those you'll be meeting, and to have a simple leaflet to leave behind. This should tell people where and when to reach you. While canvassing may intimidate people, it's one way to find out who's living around you and sometimes will give you leads to follow up. Don't canvass when people may be eating dinner, putting young children to bed, or watching a big sporting event on TV. Evenings after eight or weekends are good times.

With the people you've contacted from friends, community groups, or canvassing, you should be able to gather a core group. If none of this has worked, get a keg of beer and throw a party, inviting everyone you can think of, and see who's interested in a co-op before you start on the beer.

It's a good idea to have potluck dinners, Sunday brunches, socials, etc., with your core group and others interested in the co-op. Related to parties, but more sober in approach, is the kitchen meeting. Quite often in big meetings, folks need time to think about a new idea. If the co-op idea is introduced at a large union meeting, for instance, it's wise to get interested people together later around someone's kitchen table where everyone can express him or herself freely. Kitchen-sized discussions are an invaluable way to build trust and realistic expectations of what jobs may need to be done by a core group. Kitchen meeting size can also be achieved in large meetings by breaking them down into small groups. This enables everybody to participate and is a very effective organizing tool.

The core group should research food sources. Have some idea of likely sources before your first big membership meeting, and draw up a probable co-op price list based on your research into wholesale prices or the prices of neighboring co-ops. It's a good idea to write up a price list comparing projected co-op prices with current supermarket prices.

The food distribution system in this country works pretty much like this:

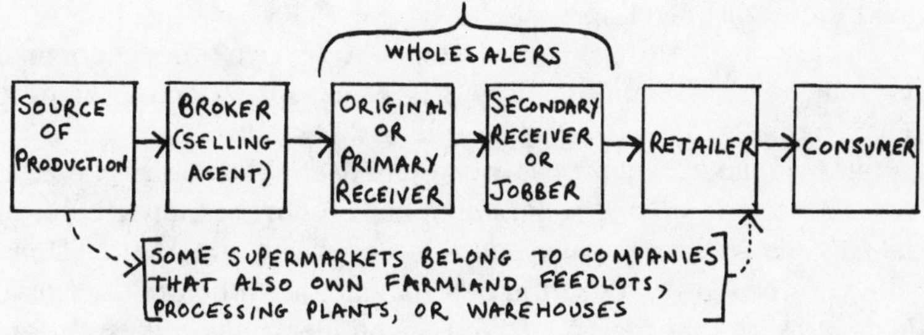

The flow chart shows the many people who handle your food before it reaches you. The rule is to try to buy at or close to the source of production.

In Boston, a large co-op wanted to buy Wisconsin cheese. They checked with three or four cheese wholesalers in the city. Prices for the same or similar cheese differed as much as 10¢ a pound. The difference is explained by the flow chart. The wholesaler with the cheapest price, a primary receiver, bought directly from the source of production, without even dealing with a shipper-broker. The higher-priced wholesalers, secondary receivers, didn't buy from the source of production but from a primary receiver. Remember: the more people who handle your food, the more expensive it will be. A small co-op may not be able to meet the volume required to buy from primary receivers, but it's still worth checking.

If you are unsuccessful in assembling a core group, you may still want to go ahead with a co-op by calling a large community meeting. Many co-ops have been started by one dedicated, persistent person. Once the co-op is underway, a group usually takes over.

The First Meeting

PUBLICIZING

You might want to write an article describing what you're doing, where you can be contacted, and where the first meeting will be. Write it in dispassionate news style, with a headline like "Food Co-op Being Formed in West Concord." Make it about 200 to 400 words and submit it to your local paper. The smaller the paper is, the happier the editor will be to see you. Small papers thrive on local stories and always need filler. Submit your article a couple of weeks before the meeting.

You may be able to get some free public service time on community radio or TV stations. Radio is especially effective in rural areas. Keep the messages short — 15 to 20 seconds.

Your own media will probably be more useful than other people's. Put up posters in grange halls, union halls, churches, civic centers, business places like laundromats, and even supermarkets. Don't make your posters so beautiful that they get lifted before the event. But make sure that they're attractive and clear, and give sufficient information about whom to contact and where to go for the meeting.

In urban situations and some suburban ones, leafletting can be another means of reaching people. Here it may be important to include written support from known community members. Food Conspiracies of Philadelphia suggests the following simple leaflet:

> We are starting a neighborhood food co-op. A food co-op is a good way to meet people, eat good food, and save lots of money. Come to our first meeting and help us get started.

If you think people need more of an introduction to co-ops, provide additional information in the handout. You can have a few well-researched facts about food prices and profits. Or include a comparison of prices in profit-making stores and in nearby co-ops. The leaflet should be neat, uncluttered, light and personal in tone, and short.

A leaflet is always more useful when used in conjunction with another means of communication. If you've been invited to talk to a church group, you can leave your leaflet with them afterward. No matter what kind of medium you use, it never takes the place of person-to-person contact. Talking at a bar or over a kitchen table is the most effective type of organizing.

Now for the place to meet. It shouldn't be too large because if too few people show up, a large place can be depressing. Don't set up too many chairs and risk ending up with empty ones.

Choose a neutral territory — that is, a place where people will be comfortable and that doesn't have partisan associations. If there's recently been a strike on which people took sides, the hall of the union involved wouldn't be neutral territory. The location should be accessible by public transportation, if possible. Quite often a large living room will do.

In scheduling your meeting, don't try to compete with the night of the bowling league or other popular activities. You might decide on a meeting at night or on a weekend to encourage working people to attend. Plan for children and pets if you think any of either will show up. Have some coffee or other refreshments since the meeting may take a while. If the meeting is long, be sure to plan for a break so folks may stretch their legs and socialize.

CONDUCTING THE MEETING

You'll need a chairperson, preferably someone who knows how to run a meeting flexibly but who can keep it from straying off the track and who knows when people are ready to move on to the next topic. A posted agenda might be helpful. Sample:

What is a food co-op?
The work-price exchange: the reason co-ops save money is that members work.
What should we carry?
How shall we divide up the work?
Are we ready to begin?

To help set the tone, have people introduce themselves and say why they came and what their expectations for a food co-op are. This may be impossible in a very large meeting, but people should still introduce themselves when they speak. You may be surprised at how many people give reasons for joining a co-op other than cheap eats. It's an eye-opener for people only interested in prices to hear that they can make friends through a co-op too. That's how the word friendship got into the name of the West Concord Food and Friendship Co-op. Be sure core group members introduce themselves too, and say where they work and why they want to start a co-op.

Most people are aware that they're being hammered on food prices and quality, but that awareness must be focused. A short discussion of how agribusiness makes its profits will help people understand how co-ops can begin to eliminate some of these profits. This awareness will also influence your co-op's decisions about what to carry. Members save a lot buying apples co-operatively, but not much buying frozen, processed apple strudel.

Establishing the fact that food co-ops mean working together should help to clarify the work-price exchange on which most co-ops, and all preorders, depend. If people aren't clear in the beginning about the need for participation, then your co-op may last only as long as a core group can carry it. One means of reinforcing this notion without being heavy-handed is to solicit volunteers for any concrete work that the group needs to get done: researching sources, recruiting more people, finding a distribution site.

A discussion of what to carry may flow naturally from talk about co-op expectations and work requirements. If it doesn't, you should initiate this discussion before the meeting goes on too long. It's an exciting nuts and bolts discussion in which everyone can participate. Organizers shouldn't let their preconceived notions of what to carry get in the way of members' making their own decisions. But they should stress the importance of nutritional and unprocessed foods, and should provide people with the information needed to make informed decisions. (See Chapter 6 for some ramifications of what-to-carry decisions.)

People may have some unrealistic ideas about how much food, or what kinds of food, to start with. In general, it's best to start with one kind of food that is easy to get, requires no immediate refrigeration, special handling, or capital equipment, and offers substantial savings. In Boston, this food is produce, and this may be true of other cities with large produce markets. Co-ops in the Midwest often start with grains because of the proximity of grain farmers, grain elevators, mills, and warehouses.

Some considerations in deciding what to carry first are:

Do you have enough members to order a particular food on a wholesale basis? Core group people should know how food comes — by case lot, bushel, etc., and how many items are in each wholesale unit. Your co-op probably doesn't want to get stuck with big surpluses at the start. Except in remote rural areas, 15 to 25 households should form enough of a buying pool to begin ordering some produce, grain, or cheese. Depending on your group's size, you may be able to get some foods wholesale but not others. Oranges, for instance, usually come 80 or 100 to a crate. If an average order is five oranges, you'll need 15 to 20 households ordering them.

How easy is it to get the item? Your premeeting research on sources will tell you where wholesalers are and which ones will sell to you. Don't forget the Yellow Pages as an invaluable source finder. People can't decide what to carry without good information on sources. Produce market wholesalers are usually more accessible to co-ops than are canned goods wholesalers. Talk about buying food produced nearby, both to eliminate middlepeople and to strengthen the local economy. You'll probably want to talk about any nearby co-op warehouse or federation buying service.

Related to access is the question of *people's time and energy levels*. How many separate sources can you go to? Will people pick up food from a source or would they rather have it delivered? If you buy food in bulk, are people ready to participate in cutting or bagging it?

Discuss perishability. If you carry something that goes bad quickly, then a small error in timing will result in a loss to your co-op. This is one reason why many rural co-ops start with grains rather than produce. Transportation over long distances makes produce difficult to distribute before it spoils.

How much money will you save, and how much money do you need up front? Highest savings will be on foods that are marked up the most in supermarkets: produce, some grains, and packaged foods that you can get in bulk. Savings are generally lowest on canned goods and meat, unless you do the butchering yourself.

Will you have the space and equipment needed to distribute this particular food?

You might want to summarize this discussion on a "what to carry" chart that you can fill in on a blackboard or poster:

Item	Minimum Order?	Access-ibility	Time/ Energy	Perish-ability	Cost	Space/ Equipment
Produce						
Gains and Staples						
Cheese						
Meat						
Fish						
Groceries						
Other Dairy						

If you've gone this far, you'll have to discuss how money is to be raised to buy these items. If members pay when they order, you don't necessarily need a membership fee, although you may want one anyway to give yourselves a cushion and initial capital to pay for any equipment or expenses. If members don't prepay, you'll need either a fee (nonrefundable) big enough to cover their first order, or a deposit (refundable) based on the estimated size of the first order. If a fee or deposit is decided on, collect it from those ready to join. Also talk about what percentage to mark up, or bump, the food, to cover the co-op for errors and overhead. Five to 10% is ample for most preorders. (For more details on all this, see "Preorder Logistics" in Chapter 11.)

The next question is how to divide up the work. Some co-ops don't have clear work requirements; those who want to volunteer do so, and often it seems to work out. We feel that in the long run this is debilitating for a co-op, especially a preorder. It also denies some members the cooperative experience and the chance to control their own institution. Members should hash out this question and decide for themselves. Remember that the more people participate, the closer and stronger you will become as a community.

If you are going to require participation, do you do it by individual member or by household? Since you need as full a participation as possible, a certain number of work hours per individual may seem more equitable. But you may find that in some communities this means that the woman ends up doing the work hours for all the co-op members in her family. A requirement that each individual do his or her *own* hours may exclude from the co-op families in which the husband or teenage children will not participate. In such situations, it may be better to get these families into the co-op and then try to encourage husbands and teenagers to work. If this is discussed, men will be aware from the start that the co-op expects their help. To facilitate this, try to arrange work schedules to allow people with 9-to-5 jobs to do co-op work on weekends, evenings, or early mornings. The produce run is a perfect early morning job and is usually done by 8 or 9 A.M. If your work requirement is by household, single people and members of small households may resent having to put in as many total hours as households with six or eight members. Some co-ops solve this by dividing work requirements and membership fees into units. A household of 2 adults and 2 small children might be 3 units.

After considering these policy questions, your meeting should discuss what jobs need to be done and who will do them. Here are the essential preorder jobs:

1. Writing the first order form
2. Collating the order forms, verifying the money
3. Ordering or buying
4. Picking up the food
5. Opening the distribution center; setting up the necessary equipment
6. Breaking down or bagging the food
7. Adding up orders, taking people's money. This can be combined with bookkeeping, or they can be two separate jobs
8. Cleaning up
9. Making the weekly newsletter and a new order form
10. Coordinating — keeping a log of co-op operations, knowing who has the keys and money, being available in emergencies
11. Membership and new-member orientation

Most of these jobs can and should be done by more than one person. Other, nonessential, jobs can be added later as you need them. Don't overstructure your co-op at the start.

If by this point your meeting has been going for some time, you may want to adjourn. Try to end the first meeting on an upbeat note. A good ending can be brainstorming for a co-op name. Some of our favorites are Food for Thought in Montgomery, Vermont, Safer Way in Los Angeles, and Hungry Chuck's Inevitable Food Co-op in Waterville, Maine.

Have a second meeting to discuss what work allocation system you want to use. The three most common systems are random, rotation, and job specific. (These job allocation systems are described in Chapter 8.) You may also want to discuss decision-making structure, distribution, equipment, and finances.

It's a great high to get the co-op rolling, but it can be a liability if jobs aren't coordinated or if you aren't clear about sources. Ask yourself:

Do we have sufficient numbers to begin? If not, more recruitment is necessary.

Do we have sufficient numbers but insufficient commitment? If not, more discussion and preliminary activity are necessary. If after two meetings some people still lack commitment, the rest can begin the co-op, without recriminations. Others may want to join later.

If you have sufficient numbers and sufficient commitment, then you're probably ready to go. Be sure you meet again after distribution to discuss how it went. People will want to share their first co-op experiences.

In general, it's not advisable to do a full-scale order after the first meeting, but you may want to get a few crates of nonperishables to split up: carrots, potatoes, and such.

Before any meeting breaks up, make sure everyone knows when and where the next meeting will be. Someone in the core group should have everyone's name and phone number. Leave a free time for discussion about what people feel was accomplished.

Before the First Order

First you should write an order form. Only include foods that you can afford to split up based on your knowledge of crate size. The first rule in setting up an order form is clarity. Don't crowd. Make the columns even. Use a good typewriter — an electric if you're typing on a stencil. Make sure the typewriter ribbon is dark. Leave space for people to figure total prices and possibly note reorders and substitutions.

A simple order form for a preorder with postpayment system might look like this:

quantity	*price*
_____apples	_______
_____artichokes	_______
_____avocados	_______

In listing items of produce, it's wise to leave easily squashable things like tomatoes and strawberries for the end. If produce is prebagged, the baggers usually follow the order form and if tomatoes are at the end of the form, they have a better chance of being on top of the bag and making it to a member's refrigerator in one piece. With these exceptions, an alphabetical list is probaby the most practical. Baggers should use common sense and sort hard items first.

After the orders are in, some people have to be responsible for collating them into a master order. You need to decide where to take the order forms by a certain time, and it's advisable to be strict about the time. If people know they can get the forms in at all hours and still have their orders accepted, some of them will do it. Of course, exceptions can be made, but a too-flexible policy can lead to frustrated collators.

The next job may be ordering, if you have an arrangement with a wholesaler that you'll call in an order and he or she will either deliver it or have it ready for you to pick up. If no ordering is done, the next job is buying. You need to get your collated master order and your money to the buyers, and to make sure you have enough truck or car space to carry all the food you will buy to the distribution center.

Breakdown or bagging is the next step. In the beginning of the Minneapolis co-op movement a neighborhood back porch, or "people's pantry," was used, but you may want a more sheltered spot. Try to find the largest possible free space for your distribution center. Members' houses, garages, barns, or sheds, or donated space in churches, schools, or community buildings may be available. You can even check out big companies and government agencies.

If you decide on a member's house for distribution, plan to rotate the location fairly often. The closer the distribution point is to the life center of the household the more unavoidable the human friction will be on distribution day. One co-op member suggests six weeks as the upper limit for distributing out of someone's basement, eight weeks for garages, and ten weeks for detached structures like barns or sheds. The West Concord Food and Friendship Co-op moved five times in its first twelve months, thriving in garages, barns, and basements alike. Those who distribute in this way often view all that human friction as the most attractive part. In fact, there are many exceptions to the six-eight-ten week rule. One co-op in Newton, Massachusetts, has distributed out of the same member's basement for over a year with no noticeable adverse effects.

There are many ways to deal with bagging. Your co-op may either prebag orders or have members bag their own. You should decide how you'll deal with overs and unders (surpluses and shortages), and substitutions. Bag-your-own co-ops generally have more lively distribution centers, while prebagging is more efficient and equitable. On the over-under question, it's probably better to get extra food to meet crate sizes and try to sell it at a surplus table than to have a lot of shortages and disappointed members. Buyers need good intuition about how much of a particular item the co-op can sell from a surplus table. Surpluses can also be given away or sold to nonmembers. See Chapter 11 for details on overs, unders, and bagging.

At the end of distribution, the coordinator or people responsible for the books should make out a financial report. Chapter 12 describes bookkeeping in detail, but here's a simple system you can start off with:

Amount Collected
- Produce _________
- Cheese _________
- Bread _________
- Etc.
- Bump _________
- Total _________

Amount Spent
- Produce _________
- Cheese _________
- Bread _________
- Etc.
- Operating Costs _________ (should be itemized)
- Total _________

Left Over
(Sometimes known as
"Bump passed on") _________
Discrepancy? _________

A cleanup crew is very important. If you're using a member's house as distribution space, don't leave cleanup to the member family. In a church or other institution it's important to clean up both to avoid attracting insects and rodents and to keep the landlord happy.

You might keep some written record of how your system evolves and what sort of values you think are important. This can become a guide for new members who didn't go through the co-op's initial stages.

Store Organizing

A co-op store may evolve in several ways. It may grow naturally out of a preorder that begins to expand its space and selection, to carry inventory, and to be open more than one day a week. It may be a regular small grocery that goes cooperative, or that goes out of business and gets bought by a co-op. It may be organized by members of another co-op store. Or it may be started from scratch.

Stores that grow out of preorders have one great advantage: a base of active members who know what participation means and who guarantee a certain volume right from the start. Many co-op stores that start from scratch, or as transformations of profit-making groceries, lack a participatory base. Although they may have adequate volume, they often find it hard to build a cooperative institution when expectations of member participation aren't set from the start.

Organizing is much the same as for a preorder: know your community, approach local groups, ask all your friends, have kitchen meetings, and possibly do leafletting and canvassing. In Harlem, New York City, a large co-op store was organized through door to door canvassing and sound trucks in the street.

In seeking a membership base, look for support from existing preorders and stores and from established community groups. If few or no established organizations exist in the community, this may be a sign that your co-op will be hard to start. A lack of community organizations may indicate that the anomie level is so high that other groups with far more resources than yours haven't been able to organize.

As in preorder organizing, it's important to get the right people in the community on your side. Don't neglect anyone in your organizing campaign. Go to local businessmen for loans of money, advice, and equipment. Even your prospective landlord may help out. Some people can help just by lending their names. Mentioning that you have the support of a respected person can open many doors for you. But if you hook up with a group of people regarded by the rest of the community as opportunists, your co-op may never get off the ground.

Whether your store is evolving from a preorder or being built from scratch, you'll need a dedicated group of people to make sure it all happens. These people shouldn't do everything themselves or form an unapproachable clique. They should concentrate on organizing and coordinating all the activities that need to go on. They should seek out people with knowledge of community organizing, publicity, bookkeeping, business management, legal matters, food sources, and nutrition.

Hold open meetings to attract these people. Then break down into small talk-idea groups. Come together again to pool ideas. Then break up into ongoing committees.

Some communities may want to consider hiring one or two full-time organizers. Be careful, though. This could lead to undue centralization, top-down organizing, and expenditure of precious funds.

Making the first decisions for a store can be difficult. Everyone is afraid to make the first commitment. Decisions can be made by the entire group, by the community or, de facto, by a few people doing the work. When the decision-making structure is unclear, people from outside don't know how to relate to the new store that is forming. Spend some time initially with the entire community group that comes to open meetings to outline a process for making decisions that is not overly cumbersome or frighteningly centralized. Logically, it should fit into your committee structure.

The test of this structure is how well it handles disagreements. If at all possible, avoid factional fights. There may be power struggles of all kinds going on under your nose. Try to steer the problem people into activities they will enjoy without aggravating the rest of the group.

No matter how participatory your co-op is, there will always be some people who are more active than others. These regular volunteers should be encouraged; they are usually dedicated and unselfish. They know a lot about the co-op and take a tremendous burden off the paid staff. Frequently new staff is recruited from among them.

A co-op store can get by on much less participation from its members than a preorder can. Some co-op stores don't require member participation or else the participation is so haphazard and unplanned that both members and store get little out of it. You may be able to overcome this problem by developing work teams. They give people a chance to get to know and work with a small familiar group. Work teams can do all sorts of jobs, from managing a section of the store to preparing newsletters and orientation programs.

Before the store opens, the entire community group should agree on a work scheme to staff the store. If the store is to be run by volunteers, a schedule needs to be established. If a paid staff or collective is to coordinate the volunteer labor, expectations, requirements, and duties must be delineated.

Establish committees for building and equipment, membership and publicity, fundraising, finances, legal matters, education, food sources, and hiring staff. These groups should continue once the store is open.

The membership and publicity committee should spread the word and gather members. Guide the new recruits into other committees. Start everyone out participating. When the store opens, everyone will feel that a part of him- or herself is invested in the store.

How many members does a co-op store need to start? This depends on the size of the planned store and the amount of sales it will need to meet expenses. We'd say a minimum of 200 committed people for a medium-sized store. Don't try to start without this number and expect people to join once the store opens, although they may.

The education committee should be active before the store opens. It can create leaflets and give presentations at meetings to make sure that members understand what a co-op is and what participation is expected of them. It can also educate about nutrition and recycling.

Hiring staff can be a painful task. The employment or personnel committee must seek out and select people capable of encouraging and organizing people in a friendly way, keeping track of inventory, buying astutely, and handling financial matters. Personalities make all the difference. Don't be afraid to say no to a prospective worker if this person might alienate members or stimulate factional fighting. Equally important, of course, is competence. Before you start interviewing, set up a list of criteria and stick to it. Almost certainly the entire community group will want to have the final say about who is hired.

The building committee must find an appropriate location for the store. Important things to look for include structural soundness, parking, delivery access, loading docks, lighting, security, plumbing, electrical system, storage areas, office space, and room to grow.

It's important to have a building before you do a lot of community organizing. It gives you credibility. You may be able to have the space held for you on deposit while you gather the members and raise the money necessary to start your operation.

The equipment committee has a tricky job. You must know how much space you have and what you're going to carry before you can start rounding up store fixtures. Make a list that includes shapes, sizes, tolerances, etc. Now the scrounging begins. (See Chapter 6 for more on equipment.)

Plan for installation and moving costs. Moving equipment is a difficult job and you can break something if you don't know how to dismantle and move it. Find people who can use dollies and jacks. Seriously consider getting insurance in case somebody is injured by heavy equipment.

The first step for the fundraisers, financial wizards, and bookkeepers is to draw up a preliminary budget. Second is to scheme and plot to get the initial capital you need. At the same time set up books to handle all the money clearly and sanely.

Ideally all your money should be raised from membership in the form of fees, but this may be impossible. Grants and interest-free loans may be gotten from other co-ops, government agencies, student activities funds, churches, or community groups. Banks are a last resort. You may also get presents: somebody walked into the Jamaica Plain Co-op in Boston one day with a $5000 loan. But remember that you'll have to start repaying these loans in the first struggling months.

It may take $5000 to $7000 to start even a small storefront. Estimate your needs realistically; undercapitalization has been the ruin of many an otherwise viable co-op. If you don't have enough money to build at least a moderately varied inventory, or if you don't have reserves to buy more when things run out, you'll have dissatisfied members right from the start. Of course, this doesn't mean you have to look like a supermarket. Overordering can be as disastrous as undercapitalizing. Many co-op stores do very well without meat or canned goods, and quite a few deal almost exclusively in grains, nuts, oils, and seeds. Make sure there's a lot of member input into the inventory planning committee. Know the staples of the community diet.

Your preliminary budget should include initial capital investment into site and equipment, initial inventory, and operating loss for the first few months. Calculate when you can reasonably expect to reach break-even volume. Include a budget for monthly operating expenses.

The following is a revised version of a start-up budget for the Jamaica Plain Co-op store in a low-income area of Boston:

Original Start-up Budget:	
1. Equipment	
Walk-in and display coolers — gifts from other co-ops	
Cash registers — lease or buy	$ 400.00
Carts, baskets	200.00
Shelving — wood, metal, etc.	200.00
Produce scales	40.00
Meat scales (calibrated)	200.00
Miscellaneous — knives, markers, etc.	200.00
Office equipment — desk, calculator, etc.	300.00
2. Security, alarm system	500.00
3. Licenses — dairy, meat, etc., incorporation fee	100.00
4. Security deposits — phone, building, gas	1300.00
5. Initial inventory (may not be able to get credit)	2000.00
6. Pre-opening salaries: 1 to 3 full-time organizers	250.00
7. Estimated operating loss over first three months (Jamaica Plain forgot to estimate this important one)	
	$5690.00
Estimated Income from membership fees	
$2 per individual adult (18 or over)	
$1 per individual aged 65 or over	
$5 per blood-related family of three adults or more	$1000.00
Left to raise	$4690.00

See Chapter 12 for a sample operating budget.

A final note: watch your finances! The number of co-op stores that fail due to sloppy accounting is enough to make your hair curl. A co-op with a modest overhead charge can make it. But remember that you're a business and can't spend money you don't have. The financial committee should report to everybody on a regular basis.

5. More on Organizing

PART of an organizer's job is to make opportunities for people and encourage them to assume responsibility. Whenever someone comes into your co-op and shows even a flicker of interest in how it's organized, grab her or him and rack your imagination to find things that she or he can do. There isn't a co-op that doesn't have lots of jobs that need doing, or lots of committees that need organizing. You may have to think a bit to get some people started. If your volunteer doesn't have much leadership experience, your patience may wear thin before he or she becomes competent. You may find you could have done the job quicker and more efficiently yourself, but you wouldn't have helped anyone along the road to self-reliance.

In the following discussion of the needs and problems of various groups some of our categories, like students, welfare recipients, and the elderly, are self-defining. Others, like working class and working poor, are delineations of some controversy. People differ about what these terms mean and how useful they are for analyzing American society, but from the point of view of food co-ops, there are recognizable differences among groups of people. These differences influence the style and content of successful organizing. Class distinctions are subtle amalgams of differences in income, educational level, cultural attitude, type of neighborhood, ethnic identity, and many other factors. The characteristics we've isolated for each group are what define the group for us.

The Elderly

No matter how badly inflation hits, it hits some groups harder than others. Rising prices take their greatest toll on those with fixed incomes. Most elderly citizens fall in this category. So it's important to think about the elderly as a potential source of food co-op membership.

The initial problem is to get them to join. Based on the experience of co-ops that have successfully recruited the elderly, you can probably approach them best through the groups they themselves have formed. The elderly are more accessible to strangers at drop-in centers, social gatherings, or recreation nights than they are in their apartments. If possible, the elderly should be recruited for co-ops in the groups in which they were initially contacted. As a transitional step, they might be given a specific job to do together so they can work with their friends and not feel lost in a new organization.

If your co-op is a preorder that has occasional surpluses, you might want to sell them at an old people's housing project or drop-in center. The savings are a good enticement for people who have learned to shop intelligently. It's a good idea to have the same person sell the food each week so that a policy of how these surpluses are sold is established and so that the old people can get to know and trust someone in the co-op. It helps to reinforce co-op goals if the elderly see that things are done the same way each week and that people are treated fairly. The Common Market in Denver recently agreed to sell food at membership prices to the Senior Mobile Market, a state government-sponsored bus that travels to ten different locations around the city (eight of them public housing projects for the elderly). If you can bring the food to old people at housing projects or community centers, you can easily recruit them for a co-op. If this isn't possible, a transportation system can be organized to get them to and from the store or pickup point. Responsibility for such transportation could count toward the work hours of younger members.

If you're starting a co-op, decide if you'll recruit the old right away or wait until the co-op is functioning smoothly. If elderly people are recruited from the start, they can help the co-op set up an operation acceptable to their peers. Unfortunately, the problems they might have in dealing with the flexible and often chaotic first month of a co-op's life may be too much for them. (It's too much for some younger members.) Old people are often less flexible and accepting of change than young people are, and the early days of a co-op might not be the best time to get them into the swing of things.

Elderly people, because of illness or habit, frequently require fairly rigid diets or have strong food preferences. Although many older people may have grown up on unprocessed food, they have since become accustomed to the convenience of prepackaged items. They may find it hard to adapt to a store that doesn't stock different flavors of instant Jell-O but does carry whole-wheat macaroni and carob powder. Many old people, however, are delighted to find the unprocessed foods they ate in their youth. In Minneapolis, elderly people form a significant part of the co-op membership and are valuable resources for younger people who want to learn how to cook bulgur and millet.

Older people aren't so physically mobile as younger ones are. They may have problems getting to the store or distribution center. The Boston Food Co-op, for example, is located on a narrow, rutted street, and walking there can be difficult for some old people. The co-op itself is quite different from a modern supermarket. Since there are no shopping carts, members provide their own cartons or bags; they also weigh their own produce and occasionally have to wait in long lines. All this can be difficult for an older person in poor health, with poor eyesight, or without a taste for rugged surroundings. It may help to have younger members assist the elderly with weighing food and carrying cartons. This is easily done if members are attuned to the needs of old people. But don't get patronizing about it. Many old people are in excellent health and enjoy the novelty of shopping at the food co-op.

As young and old attempt to adjust to each other, some tension may be inevitable. Elderly people have been obliged to accept services without being asked to contribute to a society which has more or less discarded them. If this is perpetuated by the co-op, it could be genuinely disspiriting for the elderly and in the end would not benefit the co-op. The co-op should ask its elderly members to participate but should also take into account their particular limitations and skills. Obviously you're not going to ask an eighty-year-old man to help load crates, but elderly members can do almost all other co-op jobs. One retired plumber in Minneapolis now plies his trade at the Mill City Co-op. Skills acquired over a lifetime do not disappear upon retirement. Probably the best way to resolve the work requirement is to ask older members what they would like to do.

Many old people will prefer to do the same job every time. They can become experts and feel secure about the quality of their contribution to the co-op. An elderly woman in the Cambridgeport preorder food co-op volunteered to do the same job each week even though the co-op requires work only once a month. Furthermore, she developed the job herself when she discovered that there were often no eggs left for the people who came late on distribution day. She decided to sit beside the eggs and check everyone's order form to make sure people weren't buying more than they ordered.

Old people's special needs warrant the attention of an organizer, at least while they are being recruited and during their first months in the co-op. The organizer should be around to work with the elderly as they shop — to answer questions, smooth over problems, and listen to gripes. Many elderly people have been isolated from the language and lifestyles of the young, and the organizer can help them get adjusted by giving them a chance to air their frustrations at having to work and communicate with young people whose ways may upset them. In the Cambridgeport co-op, elderly women members were distressed to see a young cashier breastfeeding her baby. They complained to the organizer and he asked the young woman if she didn't want to take a break and let him cashier for a while. She took the hint and retired temporarily. The elderly women were still hot under the collar, so the organizer explained that the young woman didn't think anyone would be offended and was sorry she had upset them. The older women took the apology with cooperative spirit.

The elderly, generally living alone or with a spouse, buy smaller quantities than families with children or households of young people do. If a co-op carries only large sizes, it may be unsuited to elderly members. If you're in a preorder, be aware that many elderly people prefer not to have substitutions, since their likes and dislikes are often rigidly established and they no longer have others at the table on whom they can pass off the zucchini that came instead of carrots. Elderly members may also prefer to pick and choose their food from open crates rather than having their orders prebagged. To make shopping more convenient, you might want to set aside specified hours when only they can use the co-op store. This shouldn't preclude them from coming in at other times too.

If the co-op wants the full participation of elderly members, meetings shouldn't run too late at night. Transportation to meetings and social functions will encourage more of them to attend. Small committees might meet at the home of an elderly member to avoid that person's transportation problem and permit participation.

Shopping can make up an important part of the social world of an older person. The food co-op can offer a more pleasant and personal way of shopping than a supermarket can. The initial reaction among a group of thirty elderly men and women from a Jewish Community Housing Project who joined the Boston Food Co-op was one of thorough enjoyment and great fun. A sense of experimenting and reaching out into new experiences was unmistakable.

Students

The community surrounding a university, particularly a university with a large off-campus population, is one of the richest areas for co-op development. A student community contains lots of idealistic people who have spare time, energy, and willingness to work for nonmonetary rewards. Many students are concerned about food quality (although a perhaps larger number subsist on pizza and coke). Married students in particular are often in dire straits financially; food co-ops, like babysitting pools, spring up naturally in married students' housing projects.

In an academic community you should be able to find students and faculty members to help you out: business professors and students for your finances, law professors and students for legal help, engineers for structural and mechanical problems. Some colleges have well-established student cooperative organizations that can offer a new food co-op a pool of experienced helpers. Co-ops in student communities may be able to get space from the university or from campus-based religious groups. Remind school officials that you'll be providing a significant service. But keep in mind that, as one member of the Freedom Foods Co-op in Stony Brook, New York, said, if you get big enough to infringe on the "quasi-monopoly of campus food service," the university may try to shut you down. What the university gives it can just as quickly take away.

The Boston Food Co-op store started with a $10,000 grant from the student activities fund at Boston University. Common Market in Denver started with a $2,000 loan from the student senate. Some university towns have housing co-ops, and you might try getting in touch with them about loans or ideas for financial sources.

One warning about "free" money. Be sure that any funds you get from the school don't have strings attached. The administration may try to control your political activities or membership policies. Make sure you're explicit in your insistence on autonomy.

You may be able to get used equipment from the school. Check the cafeterias, the dorms, the fraternities, and the office supply department for used items.

A major problem with primarily student-membered co-ops is transience. Most students aren't around for more than four years, and although this is usually long enough to provide continuity in voluntary work teams, it becomes a problem as the co-op grows and may need a permanent, stable, full-time staff. In addition, students often leave town for intersession, winter and spring holidays, and summer vacations. Your co-op's volume and efficiency may fall precipitously during these periods.

You can mitigate the negative effects of transience through planning. Plan to keep your store inventory low before vacations, and to increase your orders as vacations end. Expect enormous volume in September. Anticipate running in the red for about four months of the year and plan to build up a good surplus in the fatter months to carry you over the lean.

Block-style preorders can merge their blocks during the summer, and can skip ordering during vacations if most members want to. Both stores and preorders can try to mix membership. If your co-op consists solely of students, try to expand it to include townspeople. If you're just beginning to mix membership, be sure that students respect the different schedules and habits of nonstudents. Members of one Cambridge preorder got quite miffed when students brought in their block orders at midnight. An educational program and some social functions can help ease these natural tensions.

Don't think that because you've got a primarily student co-op the members will know anything about cooperation. Most will be attracted to the co-op solely for its good, cheap eats. In addition, students sometimes lack work experience. For both these reasons, it's important to establish a good education program. Some members may even become intrigued by cooperative history and decide to write a paper on it in fulfillment of that long-overdue social-science requirement.

Middle Class and Working Class

The distinction between middle class and working class is a hard one to draw; most people probably like to think of themselves as middle class. Yet for co-op organizers, especially if they're not from the community they're working in, subtle differences in neighborhood attitudes and lifestyle necessitate different approaches to organizing.

In a solidly middle-class community there should be no lack of managerial talent; there may be lawyers, accountants, and business people in the group. What middle-class co-ops may lack is a sense of collectivity. Middle-class families, especially in suburban areas, are isolated in their own private houses with their own private yards, and may not feel as much identification with a community as do working-class people who have lived in the same neighborhood all their lives.

The reason middle-class people join co-ops, in fact, has as much to do with feelings of isolation as with the urgent need to save money. Many join co-ops partly to regain control over a small portion of their lives, to try a little *ad hoc* social management, or to find a sense of commitment. Because of this need for community, co-ops of middle-class people can easily form spinoff activities like cooperative babysitting or volunteer political work.

Middle-class people are often more successful in homogeneous co-ops than in co-ops with members from a variety of social groups. Co-op organizers have sometimes found that working-class people are better at cooperating with students, "hippies," and the elderly. They associate with different types of people on the job and may live on a street with a commune two houses away.

In all kinds of co-ops, it's best if people from the community are involved in the initial organizing, so that they'll have a voice in policy and structure, and create a co-op amenable to the people who will be using it. But often outside organizers play important roles as catalysts. These organizers may have more radical political views and more knowledge of nutrition, than do most people in middle-class or working-class communities. The result is differences over what food should be carried and how work should be allocated. Such differences may occur even without outside organizers. In any case, compromises have to be made. Outside organizers and core groups should be prepared to compromise, but not at the expense of their own values. There are two principal points that we feel should not be compromised, and must be worked on from the start. These are fighting racism and sexism. Members must accept, as a condition for joining the co-op, that the group is open to all and that it must actively recruit others as it has recruited them. In the Jamaica Plain section of Boston, working-class members accepted the need for having meetings in both English and Spanish so that both the Puerto Rican and English-speaking communities could be part of the initial organizing of the store.

Both working-class and middle-class co-ops often suffer from lack of male participation. In any community in which nuclear families predominate, wives are usually responsible for food-buying, even if they also have jobs. Although middle-class men may be more subtle about it, they can be just as sexist as Archie Bunker, refusing to do any but the "executive" jobs. In one middle-class co-op near Boston, a wife is coordinator while her husband, otherwise inactive in the co-op, retains the post of president and chairs meetings once a year.

While many men *consider* themselves "liberated" in their attitudes toward women, it's not unusual to find one who proudly proclaims his blissful ignorance of menu-planning or food-budgeting. His forays into the supermarket are generally confined to buying snacks or occasional TV dinners when the "little woman" is indisposed. Similarly, many middle-class and working-class women insist that they like their subordinate roles. The result of such attitudes is often an all-women co-op. The situation isn't healthy for the co-op or its members, although it can build skills and self-confidence among previously house-bound women.

Men can be integrated into co-op work if the co-op actively sets a nonsexist example for them. In the early stages of organizing, you'll probably have to reach a balance, recognizing that co-ops need to be nonsexist but that attitudes change slowly, through experience.

Both working-class and middle-class men will participate more readily if their skills are tapped. Many are homeowners and know how to take care of day-to-day problems in a distribution center or store. Others have valuable job skills or connections. A mechanic may be able to keep the truck in order; an accountant to set up books; a plumber to explain how the new cooler works. A member may know somebody in the meat business, or at city hall.

Working-class people can be appealed to on the basis of their pride, of the spirit of voluntarism in their community, and of their experiences in buying food with their neighbors. Friends often get together to drive out of a neighborhood to a discount supermarket or even to buy meat and produce from wholesalers. Recounting these experiences at open meetings helps get the idea of cooperative buying across.

Working-class communities often have histories of voluntary group action that may have centered around churches, workplaces, schools, community agencies, or labor unions. The pride that people have for their community and for their personal accomplishments or victories can be tapped when starting a co-op. A knowledge of the neighborhood's history may turn up some interesting facts.

The political and social values of members, if different from those of organizers, must be respected. One woman stopped going to the initial meetings for a co-op store in a working-class section of Boston because, as she told one organizer, "I still believe in America." The best advice for organizers is to be straight with people, but not inflammatory.

The structure of a co-op depends on its class base. Most working-class members, and many middle-class ones, don't feel comfortable in anarchic structures. If things are too loose and open, they may see only disorganization, and want no part of it. One organizer of the Holyoke Food Co-op remembers men muttering after the first meeting, "This is some way to run a business!" Some co-ops may thrive on little or no structure, but it's not recommended for people who are used to and more comfortable with clearly defined responsibilities. The elusiveness of authority becomes exclusionary to those who don't want to play the game by the new rules. Organizers have found that people in working-class co-ops often want centralized authority; middle-class co-ops can usually tolerate more decentralization, as long as the operation is efficient.

If you're opening a storefront in a working-class neighborhood, its appearance will be important in attracting members. The Roxbury-Dorchester Food Co-op in a working-class section of Boston found that it was able to recruit new members when it put up shelves and stocked them with canned goods. Passers-by recognized it as a store and came in to find out what the sign Food Co-op meant. A quick look at the quality and low prices of the food, a conversation with the person behind the cash register, and the co-op had some new members. Most working-class people prefer modern-looking, well-lit stores.

Working Poor and Welfare

Poor people need food co-ops most. Malnutrition and often starvation are still facts of life to many Americans. But poor people need more than just cheap food. They need to control institutions in their own lives.

If it weren't for this second need, it would be easy to recommend community service co-ops for poor communities. They're easier to run, more efficient, and more direct in meeting poor people's needs for inexpensive nutritious food. But in serving this need they perpetuate the powerlessness of the poor. Participatory co-ops offer poor people cheap food for a price — their labor and commitment. They may be harder to organize and keep going in a poor community but their rewards warrant the risk and extra work.

The terms participatory and community service refer to tendencies in the co-op movement and not specific types of co-ops. For a participatory type co-op to work in a poor community it has to borrow many of the structures of a community service type co-op. Someone, or some group, has to be in charge to a much greater extent than in other participatory co-ops. It's best if the coordinators or store managers are from the community. A group of white middle-class co-op organizers isn't going to be successful in a poor black or Chicano community. In San Francisco, a community service co-op named Seeds of Life opened in the largely Latino Mission District, but none of the organizers knew Spanish. The store has had serious theft problems.

It's important to bring poor people into the initial organizing for a number of reasons. The co-op must be structured to meet their needs and these needs must be voiced from the start. Too, the organizers' reasons for doing things must be clear at the beginning. If nutritious food is an important value to the organizers, they must let people know why. It's a good idea to have a newsletter that can double as a recipe book and nutritional advice column.

Poor people can also benefit enormously from being part of the initial organizing. The political experience of organizing a food co-op can be put to use in any number of self-help projects. Finally, poor people are used to relating to public services: survival means knowing how to get around the social worker or government bureaucrat. If they're active in the co-op from its inception, they'll know that the co-op organizers and managers aren't just another brand of social service worker.

Procedures should be as clear as possible. Poor people's co-ops usually avoid elaborate ordering forms and complex systems of paying that require debiting and crediting. You may want to allocate jobs according to a "job-specific" system in which people master one job before taking on another. Job specific work teams also allow for on-the-job training, with experienced members teaching new ones.

Co-op members must be aware that the co-op has collective rights that take precedence over the desires of individual members. The co-op cannot let itself be used as a daycare center, hangout, credit or loan institution, or easy source of free food. Security may sound like an uncooperative word, but for a co-op to survive in a poor neighborhood it has to be together. Members will respect the co-op more if it's tough and surviving than if it's an easy mark and going under because of constant losses.

The co-op may decide on a closed membership policy so that only co-op members can even be inside the store. It may be advisable to have members serve each other rather than having them pick out their own food. Pricing and adding up the final order should also be the responsibility of the co-op, not the individual member. Large sums of money shouldn't be left to accumulate in the co-op, and a safe way of getting them to the bank should be set up. (This is true for all co-ops.)

A strong co-op in a poor community can be its own best security. In *How to Start Your Own Food Co-op,* Gloria Stern points out that at the Harlem Consumers Co-op in New York, ripoffs aren't a major problem. "The lower pilferage rate is because of people's involvement. Every customer is a set of eyes," says Cora Walker, one of the co-op's organizers. "I've been in Harlem for twenty-six years . . . and I have never seen anything that has brought the people together like this."

The co-op must be able to accept food stamps or welfare vouchers. Food stamp authorization differs from state to state and is usually easy to get. (See pp. 256–57.) Welfare vouchers require payment by the welfare department, which is notorious for being several months behind on its debts. Don't accept welfare vouchers unless people have no other way to pay for food. Credit should also be discouraged and, better still, denied. It just creates too many problems. If these decisions are made at the start, people will understand and respect them.

It's not difficult to attract poor people to food co-ops. A comparison price list may be all you need. It takes a little more to get them involved in setting up their own co-op. Someone from the community who has been working as an organizer may have the trust and respect that are necessary for people to come together and make an economic commitment to each other. People have to put money up front, either as dues or as prepayments, and to do this they must trust the organizers. Public meetings should be run by experienced community people with any outside co-op organizers speaking as guests.

The Rich

In Lexington, Massachusetts, one of the local food co-op's hardest-working members is a woman who bags tomatoes every week, except during the summer when she's off vacationing on the island she owns in Maine. Rich people do join co-ops because co-ops offer many things aside from lower prices. The spirit of community, the good feeling that comes from working together, the practical democracy, and the sense of productive activity are co-op advantages that cut across economic lines.

So, if you're organizing in a suburb or an urban neighborhood that includes high-income areas, you may well have rich people in your co-op. Here it's extra important to have a good education program, especially in cooperative philosophy and egalitarian manners.

Equally important, if your co-op has rich members, is to guard against the trend toward expensive gourmet foods. The savings on luxury foods bought wholesale can be substantial. But if you start carrying lobster, lox, and truffles to the exclusion of more proletarian fare, you'll discourage poorer members and may end up with a "Park Avenue Co-op." Even in a debate over short- versus long-grain rice, members may line up by income.

If you guard against these hazards, the rich can prove an asset to your co-op. They often have business expertise, access to equipment and transportation (a Mercedes is very reliable), political connections, and knowledge of available space and money in the community.

Locations: Urban — Suburban — Rural

Depending on where you live, you'll have different considerations in organizing a co-op. The most obvious of these are physical: how far do people live from each other, where is distribution space available, how far away are your sources? There are also social considerations: how do people relate to each other, and what are the community patterns, in big cities, small cities, suburbs, and rural areas? What media in each area will be most accessible to you, and most likely to reach your potential members? The following observations are generalizations from our experience; your best guide will be *your* experience.

BIG CITIES

The best way to organize co-ops in big cities is by neighborhood. Cities are too confusing and diverse for most people to feel common bonds with people across town, and the logistical hassles will multiply in a geographically spread-out urban co-op. Neighborhoods, especially those dominated by one ethnic, religious, or social group, often already have strong community bonds that facilitate co-op organizing. Co-ops within one block or even one apartment building can work very well. In a large apartment house, a co-op can be a tremendous humanizing tool. In Cambridge, the Peabody Terrace Harvard married-students housing complex has blocks in the South Cambridge preorder. A massive building in Boston's South End, which consists of artists' studios and living spaces, has its own co-op that buys through NEFCO.

Cheap or free storefronts are hard to come by in wealthy or downtown areas, but may be readily available in poorer areas or those slated for urban renewal. Many co-ops, such as New York City's Broadway Local, use properties slated for redevelopment and pay nominal rents like $1 per year. Of course, these cheap ample spaces may be snatched from under you if and when urban renewal gets underway. (It sometimes never does.) Don't be discouraged by the temporary nature of this arrangement unless you think renewal is really imminent. A co-op store, however, should try to find a more stable site. In poverty areas, you may be able to coax cheap or free space out of city, state, or federal service agencies.

If you can't find a large cheap or free distribution space or if you want to distribute out of members' homes, a decentralized structure is in order. Branches and blocks are common in cities for this reason. Decentralization also works well because it provides small group cohesion in an otherwise fragmented social environment. Try keeping your distribution groups under ten families, a number whose orders will easily fit in a small apartment.

Big city co-ops are at an advantage because they're close to large markets and wholesaling centers. Transportation is less of a hassle than in small city, rural, or suburban co-ops, although a co-op of any size may still want a truck of its own. Coastal cities are usually importers of foreign foods as well.

If you're centering your organizing around a city neighborhood, using the big city newspapers or radio and TV stations won't do a lot of good. You need more local media. Many neighborhoods have community newspapers. If the neighborhood contains a group such as Spanish-speaking people, you may be able to reach them through local Spanish language radio stations. Otherwise, your best bets are attractive, clear, not too arty, posters on telephone poles and in laundromats and other gathering places. Leaflets may be of value in some communities (student, perhaps), but most people treat them like junk mail. House-to-house canvassing may work in some neighborhoods. In many city apartment buildings, however, you can't even get through the front door unless you're visiting a specific person.

Security can be a problem for urban co-op stores. You can't always depend on the watchful eyes of your members or neighbors. In fact, since the only available cheap space may be in commercial areas, there may be no one around to keep an eye on the store at night.

SMALL CITIES

The main problem in small cities is access to markets. You may be near a regional market but the prices will be higher, and the food less fresh and varied, than at a terminal market. (For a discussion of these differences, see Chapter 10.) Eventually, you'll face the choice of trucking to a terminal market yourself or continuing to let wholesalers do the trucking and reap the profits.

You may be closer to some sources, though. Your city may be near a regional center for cheese, meat, fish, or grains. You're probably closer to farmers than big-city folks are, and may be able to deal with them directly. Industrial cities may have factories where you can get some products directly. In any case, a small- to medium-sized city probably has enough wholesale resources to make a food co-op viable with a minimum of transportation hassles. In this respect you're ahead of suburbs and rural areas.

Neighborhood or block-by-block organizing may not work in small cities. At first there may not be enough people in any given neighborhood interested in starting a co-op. Depending on the city's size, neighborhood boundaries may not be so rigid as they are in big cities, though as the co-op grows, it may be able to decentralize on a neighborhood basis.

You may find cheap or free space more readily than you can in the more desirable parts of big cities. The city newspaper and TV and radio stations will be useful media, and most will take public service ads without charge. But use your own media — posters and leaflets — as well.

SUBURBIA

The biggest physical problem for a suburban co-op is finding a distribution center. Land exploitation is so intense in most suburban areas that it's almost impossible to locate an affordable storefront. What decaying commercial areas there are quickly become parking lots and shopping centers. Nearly all suburban co-ops are therefore preorders and distribute either out of neighborhood churches or members' houses.

Many of the suburban co-ops near Boston operate out of churches. Most churches offer large, well-lit, linoleum-floored meeting rooms, occasionally with adjoining kitchens, which they are willing to rent on a day-by-day basis to nonprofit community organizations. Frequently, arrangements can be made to use the refrigerator in the church kitchen for short-term storage of meat, fish, or dairy products between the time they are delivered and the time of distribution. Make sure your church has parking facilities; this will spare the co-op neighborhood complaints of blocked driveways and hit-and-run flower beds.

But none of this comes cheap, either in terms of finances or of human community. You may have to pay $10 a day and up for use of the meeting room. Although the Lexington, Massachusetts, Food Co-op uses the room they rent for only a couple of hours each Friday afternoon, they are currently paying $40 a month without the use of the kitchen.

At greater cost to the co-op, however, is the fact that it's trying to work from inside an institution that exists to serve its own needs. Besides the physical limitations of the rooms themselves, which for some reason are almost universally designed to resemble high school cafeterias, you must deal with church boards as landlords. Lease provisions often insist that nothing be displayed on the walls and everything be returned to its original location at the end of the day. An outside institution dictates its needs to the co-op and insists on institutionally oriented solutions. Floor space suddenly begins to get unusual consideration in co-op discussions of optimal membership size; church availability determines the nature and length of work schedules and contact among members; and all equipment, signs, and materials are limited to what is portable and either storable on the premises or easily carted around.

Church availability and rental costs can push suburban co-ops to short midafternoon distribution hours. Having thus nicely excluded that portion of the population that works from 9 to 5, the church-renting co-op then often evolves into the most prevalent suburban type: the "housewife" co-op. This isn't to say that suburban churches cause the nonparticipation of suburban husbands; many city co-ops have the same problem. But rigid church hours don't facilitate any attempts you might want to make to get more men involved. The suburban co-ops that are most committed to community and sexual equality often stay out of institutions and provide their own distribution place: garages, sheds, barns, basements, and, in good weather, back porches and driveways.

Getting the word out is relatively easy in the suburbs. Probably most effective are brightly colored handmade posters placed in local stores; in the suburbs, this is the medium of Girl-Scout outings, church suppers, and garage sales. Local businessmen are usually willing to put the posters in their windows if the cause is nonprofit and community-oriented. Be prepared to explain what a co-op is.

In Acton, Massachusetts, the food co-op even persuaded a supermarket manager to put their notice in his window.

RURAL

In the country, transportation will be your number one problem. Not only will most of your sources be far away, but your members may be miles from each other. Organizing trucking in and out of the nearest city with a sizeable market and getting the food to your remotest members will demand a lot of time, energy, advance planning, and centralization of resources.

The main thing to remember, as you centralize what must be centralized in rural co-ops, is to keep everything else decentralized. In rural areas people relate on a small-town level and it's important to preserve the integrity of the town. Don't make each town just a drop-off point for a regional co-op; decision making and participation should begin at the town level. In Vermont, the seven co-ops in the New England People's Cooperatives (NEPCOOP) do trucking and some buying centrally but every operation that can be decentralized is.

There may be a major trucking route that cuts through your area and has a truckers' stop; if so, you might be able to arrange with commercial truckers to carry goods as far as the truck stop for you. Investigate commercial routes and stops so you can figure out your best method of transportation. This includes knowing where diesel fuel is available if you're planning to rent a diesel truck. People in Vermont assumed that it would be best to be self-reliant in trucking from the start. They believed that if the energy crisis got worse, hilly up-country areas would be among the first trucking routes to be cut. (See Chapter 11 for more on trucking.)

The Vermonters base their distribution system on using the least gas for the most good. For NEPCOOP this has meant that areas that develop into 100-household co-ops have their own distribution centers whenever possible. Instead of having each household travel a long distance to get its food, a small truck brings all the orders for one group to some local common point. As more orders come in from areas around a distribution center, secondary centers can be set up. This decentralized system has helped build the self-reliance of the ordering groups, which are actually extended preorder branches.

The necessity of traveling long distances for food has its positive side. People who must travel far often plan better; if it's a 75-mile drive back home to get your list, you don't often forget what you need. People are used to buying enough food to last a fair amount of time. Both these facts make rural people very amenable to preorder buying.

Getting space for a distribution center may be difficult. However, we've heard of using, renting, or buying grange halls, churches, community centers, and American Legion posts. It's probably best to have distribution centers in town, so that people can go to the co-op and do other errands on the same day. Rural co-op stores, such as Growing Tree in Spencer, West Virginia, have found that with folks living miles apart, their in-town location makes them energy and communication centers.

Rural co-ops have begun to develop regional autonomy by contracting with local farmers. The Natural Organic Farmers Association sells its entire output of root crops and grains to NEPCOOP. We discuss this sort of relation in more detail in Chapter 10.

Since transportation is a central focus of time and energy, many rural co-ops start with grains, nuts, oils, nut butters, and dry goods that are nonperishable. With produce, unless it's available locally, spoilage is a serious problem. With canned goods, it may be difficult to realize any savings. So while grains and dry goods may not draw so wide an initial group, they minimize problems and give you a chance to work out any bugs in your distribution system before you tackle perishables.

You may also want to consider carrying nonfood items. Many rural co-ops stock books on organic farming and alternative energy systems, wood-burning stoves, chain saws, tools, and even cross-country skis. These items have sometimes been discontinued because of pressure on the manufacturers from local retailers. But equipment and tools are major needs for country people.

Communication will be a problem in the country only if you're not tuned into the media people use. In most rural areas there are one or two radio stations that people listen to all day. Get co-op announcements on their calendars. Local newspapers are good media for public service notices. Most important, as in any organizing situation, is person-to-person contact. Talk with established groups: churches, organic farmers, 4H, and Future Farmers of America clubs. (The members' parents may be interested.) County employees, teachers, and the elderly are other possible contacts. NEPCOOP participates in "home demo" groups sponsored by the local agricultural extension service. Demonstrations include various crafts and home canning techniques. By doing some demonstrating, NEPCOOP organizers have been able to bring new people into co-ops.

Be aware of the pace and flow of your community. If you've lived there a while, you know how people get things done. If you're new, take a substantial amount of time to get attuned. A speedy urban pace and aggressive organizing campaign may be out of place in the country.

Sources

Several co-ops or individuals have published pamphlets or books with useful organizing information:

All the People at Food Conspiracies. *Food Cooperatives: How to Start One and Make it Prosper*. Philadelphia: Food Conspiracies, 165 West Harvey St., Philadelphia, Pa. 19144. Mimeographed.

Angelides, James. *The Organization and Structure of the Greenwich Neighbors Food Club*. Washington, D.C.: V Line Action Publishers, undated.

Community Crisis Intervention Project. *Organizing a Consumer Food Co-op*. St. Louis, Mo.: Social Science Institute, Box 1202, Washington University, St. Louis. Self-published pamphlet, undated.

Mack, John, *How to Run a Food Co-op*. Self-published manual. C/o John Mack, 615 W. 164 St., Apt. 51-D, New York, N.Y., undated.

Prejean, Frederick, Sr. *The Buying Club*. Atlanta, Ga.: Federation of Southern Cooperatives, 20 Marrietta St. NW, Room 1200, Atlanta. Self-published, undated.

Ronco, William. *Food Co-ops*. Boston: Beacon Press, 1974. A journalistic survey based mainly on New England co-ops.

Stapleton Community Buying Club. *Preparation and Organization of a Community Buying Club*. Self-published. C/o Pennie Monroe, 5168 Sherman, Denver, Colorado, undated.

Stern, Gloria. *How to Start Your Own Food Co-op*. New York: Walker & Company, 1974. Based on correspondence with co-ops around the country and visits to New York area co-ops. Contains an excellent chapter on buying meat.

Vellela, Tony. *Food Co-ops For Small Groups*. New York: Workman Publishing Company, 231 E. 51 St., New York, N.Y. 10022, 1975. Includes flow charts illustrating several possible systems of operation.

On community organizing:

Alinsky, Saul. *Rules for Radicals*. New York: Vintage, 1971. Of the many books on community organizing, this is perhaps the most famous.

anti-mass pamphlet, *methods of organization for collectives*. P.O. Box 7411, New Haven, Connecticut.

Brown, Samuel, Jr. *Storefront Organizing*. New York: Pyramid Communications, 1972.

O.M. Collective. *The Organizer's Manual*. New York: Bantam, 1971. We recommend this for detailed information on canvassing, small groups, and the problems of different constituencies.

Project One Community Handbook. Millerton, N.Y.: Glide Publications, 1972. Good on community organizing and alternative economic projects.

NASCO, the North American Student Cooperative Organization, publishes a monthly magazine, *The Journal of the New Harbinger,* as well as a variety of pamphlets on co-ops. Write them at: Box 1301, Ann Arbor, Michigan 48106. The Cooperative League of the U.S.A., 1828 L St. NW, Washington, D.C. 20036, also publishes pamphlets with organizing information. You might also try the Office of Economic Opportunity, Washington, D.C. 20506, the Superintendent of Documents, Government Printing Office, Washington, D.C. 20402, and local university extension services.

6. Food

THERE are many factors you'll have to consider in order to decide what to carry. The first is availability. Are there local sources? If not, how far will you have to go? How close to the source of production can the item be purchased? Can it be delivered, or will you have to pick it up? This leads to the next factor, transportation. If the food is being delivered, how much are the freight charges? Is the co-op's location suitable for large deliveries? Will you need a loading dock? If you're going to pick up the food, is your vehicle large enough, or will you need another?

Next you'll have to consider the space and equipment you'll need to distribute or inventory the food. Does your store or distribution center have enough room? Do you have the necessary equipment or can you afford to buy it? If the product is perishable, can you move it fast or store it safely?

Along with space and equipment you'll have to analyze your logistics and work system. If you're a preorder distributing on Monday afternoons, can you get the food that morning? How much time and energy will it take to handle the food? Will it require expert volunteers, as in the cases of butchering meat or filleting fish? Is your work allocation system suitable for the required jobs?

Finally, you'll have to study your financial situation. Can you buy on credit or will you have to come up with the money when you order? Do you have, or can you raise, the necessary capital for a large order? If you're inventorying a staple, how long can you tie up your capital in inventory? How fast can you turn it over?

This list isn't comprehensive but just contains some clues about where to focus your attention before you can meet any and every food demand of your members. Specific requirements for specific foods will be discussed later in this chapter. But first, we ought to discuss a few basic questions about food policy.

Nutrition and Food Quality

Nutrition is a crucial and difficult question for the co-op movement. It's often raised in extensive debates over what to carry. In Minneapolis, people in the storefronts and warehouse argued for months over whether to carry white as well as whole-wheat flour. In the end, they decided to carry only whole-wheat and to educate their members about its nutritional advantages.

Co-ops should accept their responsibility to safeguard their members' health by not carrying junk foods, and to educate them about nutrition by carrying whole unprocessed foods and by posting recipes, articles, and nutrient charts on co-op walls and in newsletters. The buying policy of the co-op can be an effective educational tool in itself. If the majority of the members decide they want air-filled white bread, TV dinners, and tortilla chips, it's the responsibility of the minority to try to educate them and try to change the policy. In stores, staff should remain responsive to the desires of the members, but use their ordering responsibility wisely. If members want cookies, the staff can buy, or ask a work team to bake, healthful ones. In Madison, Wisconsin, a co-op bakery makes "beeple bar" candies out of seeds, nuts, and honey. If some co-op members or staff take the time to learn about nutrition and food quality, they'll be in a position to move the rest of the membership a step at a time.

Our food habits have developed over years and we can't expect to change them overnight. A balance has to be reached between having no awareness of what we eat and therefore carrying anything the membership desires, and being so purist as to restrict the co-op to only those people with totally whole-grain, unprocessed food diets. If a good food consciousness is to grow, we must bring people into co-ops so they can be exposed to better food. This may mean offering people some of what they're used to at the start, and continually adding better foods as people learn about them.

Some co-ops have become restrictive by limiting the variety of food they carry. A manager of Food Front in Portland, Oregon said, "Unless more people turn on to meatless diets, the co-op won't have growth problems." This may be to Food Front's advantage, but what of all the meat-eaters in Portland? The other extreme may be equally unfair to people wanting to join co-ops. If a co-op carries anything and everything, is it really operating in the best interests of its members?

We feel that a bottom line has to be drawn at the start and continually raised as members become more aware of food quality. Junk food with almost no nutritional value should not be carried. If people want Hostess Twinkies and Fruit Loops they can go elsewhere for them. The Roxbury-Dorchester Co-op needed the extra revenue that cigarettes, potato chips, and candy would have brought in but maintained its food values and continued to struggle along. Once a co-op starts carrying junk food it may find it hard to stop. Nutritionally conscious members of the Boston Food Co-op have been battling for years to get bottled soda off the shelves, so far to no avail. The majority of members want soda.

Additives

Processed foods like packaged dinners and frozen vegetable combinations are costlier and less nutritious than the raw foods that comprise them, and also contain a wide range of food additives. Some additives, like monosodium glutamate, USDA red #2, or saccharin, enhance flavor, color, texture, or aroma. Some, like BHA or calcium propionate, increase a product's shelf life. This in turn increases shipment size and therefore cuts down on the cost of shipping.

Other additives are used to prevent growth of pathological organisms in food. This is one purpose of the nitrites and nitrates used in processed meats. Nitrites and nitrates combine with amines to form potentially carcinogenic (cancer-producing) nitrosamines. Amines are found in coffee, tea, cigarette smoke, beer, wine, some medicines, paprika, pepper, and other spices. Many foods also contain residues of pesticides, herbicides, growth hormones fed to livestock and tranquilizers fed to chickens.

There's no general rule about the safety of food additives. Some are safe at low concentrations, but toxic at high concentrations. Some are themselves harmless but make possible the industrial fabrication of nonnutritious junk foods. Some have been found to be carcinogenic in combination with other substances. Probably of most concern is the synergistic effect of having so many additives in so many different foods. Many times the Food and Drug Administration has been reluctant to ban potential carcinogens because of pressure from food manufacturers. We think it's best not to wait for problems to be discovered or additives to be banned. Co-ops should avoid high-additive foods whenever possible.

You can do this by checking out sources of food and by reading labels. Buy simple forms of food: fresh chicken rather than chicken roll, plain turkey instead of "butterball." Make soups and desserts yourself and supply co-op members with recipes.

In its search for new profitable commodities, agribusiness manipulates basic foods into endless varieties — potato chips, curls, flakes, crackers. Half the potatoes grown in the United States are now processed into frozen French fries or instant mashed flakes. Thanks to corporate-inspired "food science," an innocent wheatberry may be shaped like wagon wheels, taste like bananas, have little of its original nutritive value, and contain possibly harmful additives that make it last forever. The process of making banana-flavored wagon wheels out of wheat is a not-so-funny example of how a wholesome food can be made into a low-nutrition, high-profit commodity. The result of all this manipulation is the approximately 18,000 items that confound the supermarket shopper.

There are enough economic and nutritional reasons to prefer relatively unprocessed foods to highly processed ones that the decision doesn't have to rest only on the question of potential health hazards of additives. Fresh produce is cheaper than either canned or frozen, and hasn't lost any of its vitamins and minerals in processing. White bread, even if made of "enriched" flour, lacks wheat germ, which is high in protein, minerals, and vitamins. Enriched bread contains only a few of the minerals and vitamins, and none of the protein, of whole-wheat. But whole-wheat bread is usually more expensive than white, and the co-op must try to deal with the problems of a member who has to make sandwiches for five lunchboxes each day and may feel he or she can't afford the extra expense. The New Haven Food Co-op, with a basically low-income membership, carries several brands of white bread in addition to whole-wheat.

Further arguments over food quality begin with discussions of "organic" versus "nonorganic" foods. Organically grown food is grown without chemical fertilizers or pesticides. Organic farming also preserves the health of the soil. But organically grown food may be more expensive and less readily available than nonorganically grown food, and most people won't recognize its advantages.

Many co-ops carry organically grown foods at prices that compete with nonorganic. They do this by contracting directly with local farmers, usually through co-op federations. The Food Conspiracy in Tucson relates the following example: "The top market price (wholesale) with the exception of the Food Conspiracy is 9¢/pound, for zucchini, which retails at around 27¢/pound, organic or not. The Food Conspiracy buys organic at 18¢/pound and sells it for 18-20¢."

If the quality and price are competitive, co-ops can sell organically grown food as easily as nonorganic. When prices differ greatly, you might consider carrying both, as Food Front does; they carry both organic and nonorganic whole-wheat flour.

As co-ops create alternatives to the present distribution of organic food, the price difference will diminish. The higher expense of organically grown food today is at least partly a result of the dominance of chemical-, efficiency-oriented agribusiness in setting research goals. As co-ops increase buying power, and as the land reform movement gathers strength, the number of organic farms will increase, their methods will become more sophisticated, and their prices will be able to compete with nonorganically grown food.

A word of caution: many foods labeled "organic" or "natural" have been treated with chemicals. All food is technically "organic." "Natural" may mean grown without chemical sprays, or it may not mean anything except that the manufacturer is trying to fool you. Even food labeled "organically grown" is sometimes mislabeled, if rumor has any validity. So know your sources. Some co-op federations have labs test organicity of the food they buy.

Another major food controversy is over meat versus alternative sources of protein. Much of the grain in this country is used to feed cattle. It takes 21 pounds of grain to produce a pound of beef, 8.3 pounds of grain for a pound of pork, and 5.5 pounds of grain for a pound of chicken. In the U.S., beef consumption has more than doubled in the past thirty years. This excessive consumption of meat uses up grains that could otherwise feed hungry people.

Whether people want to switch from animal to vegetable protein for humanitarian reasons, religious principles, or just economics is their own business. Co-ops should offer members alternative protein sources and the information with which to balance their diets to get the same nutritional value as meat.

Nutrition Information in the Co-Op

Here are some points to keep in mind when distributing or displaying information in the co-op:

Remember that people's eating habits are the result of a lifetime of acculturation. It takes time to internalize changes. Be firm, direct, and insistent, but also sensitive and understanding.

Check the sources of information for accuracy and have reference materials on hand. (See bibliography, page 124–26.)

Keep information simple, understandable, and graphically attractive.

Respect members' cultural and ethnic food patterns.

Offer recipes for foods that require a lot of preparation or that people are just learning to include in their diets.

Here are samples of nutritional information that co-ops have given:

"What *are* green leafy vegetables and legumes anyway?"

green leafy vegetables	*legumes*
dark leaf lettuces	soybeans
kale	lentils
mustard greens	dried peas
beet greens	(green, black-eyed, etc.)
collard greens	pinto beans
turnip greens	kidney beans
swiss chard	lima beans
spinach	black beans
	navy beans

How to Be a Vegetarian

Eating a vegetarian diet means getting protein from vegetables instead of meat. Some vegetarians eat fish, milk, eggs, cheese, grains, beans, seeds, and nuts. Others eat only grains and legumes for protein.

The Problem: The proteins our bodies use are made up of 22 amino acids in various combinations. Eight of these amino acids cannot be synthesized by the body and must be obtained from outside sources. All eight must be present at the same time. If one essential amino acid is missing, protein synthesis will fall to a lower level. By themselves, grains, beans, seeds, and nuts are deficient in one or more essential amino acid.

The Solution: Fish, milk, yogurt, cheese, buttermilk, and eggs all have plenty of essential amino acids. If a small amount of one of these is eaten with a nut, seed, bean, or grain dish, the amount of total essential amino acids will increase substantially. Or legumes and grains can be combined to complement each other's amino acids. The key is to find out which foods complement each other. Frances Moore Lappé explains the process simply in *Diet for a Small Planet*.

A Minor Problem: Some vegetarians find it difficult to get enough Vitamin B_{12} when no meat is eaten. There are no good vegetable sources of this nutrient. People who get all their protein from vegetable sources may need a Vitamin B_{12} supplement.

A Quick Protein-Balancing Chart

Foods can be combined to make complete proteins by balancing the amino acids, the building blocks of protein. The hardest amino acids to find in plants are tryptophan, lysine, isoleucine, and sulphur-containing amino acids. The following are some good food combinations:

Seafood with grains or nuts and seeds
Milk with grains, legumes, nuts and seeds, or potatoes
Legumes with grains, milk, or nuts and seeds
Nuts and seeds with legumes, milk, or grains
Fresh vegetables with sesame seeds, brazil nuts, mushrooms, millet, or rice
Meat: small amounts suffice to complement plant foods, especially grains

Produce

Fresh fruits and vegetables are best, cheapest, and most plentiful in season. Plums, nectarines, peaches, strawberries, and blueberries are all summertime fruits. Apples are abundant in the fall and winter but their quality goes down over the summer. Pears, tangerines, tangelos, oranges, and grapefruit are all winter fruit. In California, where about one-third of the country's produce is grown, fresh fruits and vegetables of great variety are usually available year round. Elsewhere, try to buy in season. Prices on summer produce may triple from summer to midwinter. Avoid buying at the very beginning or end of any fruit's or vegetable's season, as prices will be higher because of scarcity. Try to get members used to the idea of buying in season.

How do you judge good produce? This takes time to learn. The main things to look for are firmness, size, color, taste, and season — and when the shipment came in. Oversized, waxed appearance doesn't necessarily mean high quality. Taste everything you buy at the market, or if it's a vegetable that has to be cooked, like squash, cut it open and look inside. Compare prices at different vendors. You can get good quality at a high price and good quality at a low price. When you're new to produce buying, you might want to go through cases from top to bottom before loading. You may find beautiful quality on top but rotten produce buried underneath. And no matter how much you trust your supplier, it's always wise to spot check crates.

The U.S. Department of Agriculture (USDA) has grades for produce but most states don't require grade labels. Produce grades are used mostly by growers, shippers, and wholesalers. They're not too important since you can judge produce best by appearance. However, you may see "USDA Inspected" on some packaged vegetables. This means that the product was inspected during packaging. Washington state requires its fruits to be grade-labeled: Number 1, Fancy, and Extra Fancy. Number 1 is usually the best buy. Fancy may just mean bigger, prettier, or more evenly colored. Sometimes a receiver will grade fruits Number 2s. Number 2 oranges and grapefruits may have scabs on the outside but are O.K. inside; some even taste better. Try to make members realize that uniform appearance is not equivalent to high quality.

If you buy small sizes, you'll probably save money. Small peppers are cheaper per pound than large ones are, and are a good buy if your members accept them. Certainly non-brand-label bananas can save you money over the known brands, with their high advertising budgets.

You may be able to save money if you buy ripe fruit. But be sure you can sell it immediately. Preorders shouldn't buy all ripe fruit as it has to last members a week (or in some preorders, two). Produce is also cheaper unbagged than bagged.

Remember, in your search for bargains, that co-ops aim to become reliable sources of high-quality food. Most people will forget a bad price sooner than they'll forget a bad peach. See Sources, pp. 124–26, for more help in buying produce.

HOW MUCH PRODUCE TO GET

Most produce comes in crates; the wholesaler may sometimes sell you half crates, or partials. The number of items in a crate varies with the size of the individual items. Florida oranges generally come in 60s, 80s, 100s, and 125s. Eighties and 100s are the moderate sizes. Learn what your members want and stick to one size. You'll pay more per pound for bigger fruits although they're not necessarily better.

Don't overbuy on produce, as it's highly perishable. For preorders, a good system of substitutions may work better than heavy surpluses if these can't be sold at distribution time. See section on preorder logistics in Chapter 11 for details on surpluses and substitutions.

Deciding how much produce to get for stores is tricky. Consider the amount sold the previous day, and also the amount sold the previous week on the day you're buying for. That is, for Wednesday's order, consult the produce sales for Tuesday, and also for the previous Wednesday. Wednesday may be a particularly heavy day at the co-op. Also take into consideration holidays, seasonal variations, and weather. (Melons don't sell well in cold weather.) Food for Saturday should be included on Friday's order. Try not to have excessive inventory — especially greens — left on Saturday night to sit over the weekend.

WHERE TO GET PRODUCE

There are two types of produce markets: terminal and regional. The terminal markets are larger, and receive railroad carloads or tractor-trailerloads directly from the point of production. Regional markets get much of their stuff from the nearest terminal market.

Longwharf Market in New Haven is merely an outpost of Hunt's Point in New York. Washington, D.C.'s wholesale market is supplied by the terminal market in Baltimore. In smaller cities, there may be only one jobber who trucks produce in over some distance. This wholesaler probably walks the nearest terminal market, fills a tractor-trailer, and charges everyone back home exorbitant prices. If you can organize the trucking, you can walk the same terminal market for 50¢ to $2 a crate less than if you bought from the local jobber. Consider how much you'd save and weigh it against the cost of trucking; then decide if you're ready to go to a terminal market. (See Chapter 10 for more on this.)

At a terminal market, some wholesalers are original receivers of shipments direct from growers or brokers in California, Florida, etc. They may deal in only a few items, or as many as 15 or 20. Other wholesalers, or jobbers, are secondary receivers. They buy small lots from the original receivers and resell them to you. Jobbers and original receivers may be next door to each other, so don't be fooled. Ask where the commodity came from and when it arrived. If you buy from an original receiver, you'll eliminate one more middleperson in the food-buying chain. You may not have the volume an original receiver requires, but it can't hurt to ask. Often they have to get rid of partials, ripes, or Number 2s and they'll be happy to have your business.

It's important to get along with wholesalers, and to gain their respect. They're one step ahead of you. They know what's available and what's good quality. They also know how old their produce is. The more you get to know them, the more honest they'll be with you, and the more willing to give you deals. At the New England Produce Center in Boston, some wholesalers know that New England Federation of Co-ops (NEFCO) buyers usually take ripe fruit and will give them excellent buys on it.

Whether you shop around the market for the best buys or buy consistently from one wholesaler depends on your time, energy, and work system. Shopping around is time-consuming, especially for small or new co-ops that should be concentrating their main energy on organizing a smooth, reliable operation. When your system is functioning well, you might begin to shop around. Co-ops that have different people buying every week also might not gain much from shopping around. Buying produce requires some experience and expertise, and it also helps immeasurably to know the wholesalers personally. Consider combining with other co-ops to share a paid produce buyer, joining a federation buying service if one exists in your area, or trying to organize one. (See Chapter 15.)

Part of establishing trust and friendship with a wholesaler is telling him or her when you've received an inferior product. Complain in a firm but nice way. If you find moldy or rotten produce when you're spot checking, the vendor should replace it. If you come across it back at the store or distribution center, let the vendor know and expect a price reduction on the next crate proportional to the amount you lost through spoilage. But be judicious. You can't blame the wholesaler for poor handling on your part.

It goes without saying that you should try to check out local farm sources. Buying from local farmers is a difficult art, but one that's entirely worth learning. Co-ops in Los Angeles' Southern California Cooperating Community buy about two-thirds of their produce from local organic farmers. The New York People's Warehouse trucks in organic produce from Pennsylvania. NEFCO gets much of its produce from farms during the summer, but returns to the wholesale market come the frost. Farmers' markets are another possibility. (See Chapter 10 for more on farms and farmers' markets.)

Co-op members may have individual gardens or you may be able to find some land and set up a community garden. Farm members of the Austin Community Project supply produce to the co-ops, which in turn supply labor and compostible waste to the farms.

A possible problem is that members will have such big gardens that they won't need the co-op for produce during the growing season. You can then use the co-op as a bartering center; few gardeners grow everything they like to eat, and anyone who's grown zucchini knows how large the surpluses can get. Try to organize canning and pickling operations. Finally, to keep gardening members active in the co-op over the summer, carry other foods: grains, dairy, bread, meat, fish, groceries.

PRICING PRODUCE

You'll have to get your prices from the produce buyers and break them down into individual items, bunches, or pounds. Divide the total price of a crate by the number of items, bunches, or pounds in it, round off to the next highest whole number, and add a penny or two for loss due to mold or spoilage. This doesn't include the bump for overhead that's usually added on at the cash register or at the end of the order form.

TRANSPORTATION, HANDLING, AND STORAGE OF PRODUCE

Produce has to be packed properly for transporting. Some fruits can be crushed by their own weight. Don't pack tomatoes more than two deep, three deep as a maximum for green ones. And don't stack tomato crates more than two high. Stack crates carefully, too. If a heavy box falls onto the strawberries or mushrooms, you're sunk. You'll learn how to pack a truck through trial and error, but caution and common sense can help a lot at the beginning.

When the crates arrive at your store or distribution center, check to make sure you got what you ordered. Unpack produce from damaged crates immediately and repack it in sturdy boxes. Remove any moldy or bruised produce; mold and rot spread rapidly. A bruise will grow into a brown spot or rot.

If you have a cooler, try to pack it quickly so that the produce doesn't freeze in the winter or wilt in the summer. Quickly, yes, but carefully and neatly. Lettuce should be stacked on lettuce, apples on apples, and so forth. Flimsy or soggy crates will not stand up very long without support. We almost lost a very dear friend to a stack of eight cases of lettuce. Boxes in poor condition should be replaced or at least put in corners so they'll have two walls to lean against.

When packing a cooler, it's tempting to toss the cases in, but every time you do so, you're bashing or bruising something inside.

Once a fruit or vegetable is picked, it's cut off from its life source. Most produce is picked green. It's shipped in refrigerated cars or trucks and sometimes packed in ice. Commercial produce is bred to withstand bruising and deterioration during shipping and display. But you still have to be careful. Different foods have different needs. Berries are superperishable. Greens will wilt and need refrigeration. But don't refrigerate tomatoes unless they're in a cooler all the time; they shrivel if moved from cold to warm. The same is true of eggplant. Bananas have to be kept at about 58° F. Take their plastic wrapping off to prevent them from getting too hot. They generate heat as they ripen. Root vegetables (potatoes, onions, carrots, turnips) don't need refrigeration, but they do need air to circulate and can't stand much moisture — unlike greens. You may want to spray greens with a plant mister to help keep them from wilting.

When you open a crate of lettuce, you may find that a quarter of the box is loose leaves. Pull them out and trim the heads. The leaves are good for soup stock. Other produce items need constant sorting or cleaning up: tomatoes, strawberries, melons, citrus fruits, peppers, onions, and potatoes. If an orange has been banged or crunched, it's going to be the first to mold and rot. You can lose a whole case of oranges in two days, or a case of strawberries overnight, if moldy or rotten fruit isn't removed.

Produce is very sensitive to cold and heat. Set up your display away from cold drafts near doors or open windows. An ideal spot is out of direct sun but with a little sunlight. Check your local supermarket for inspiration.

It's logical to keep fruit with fruit and vegetables with vegetables. Try to make a beautiful display; both stores and preorders that have members bag their own must make the food look attractive. Cutting off loose flaps of cardboard, cutting wires, and removing wooden slats, makes the produce department look great and also prevents scraped arms, punctured hands, and torn clothing.

Dairy Products

Organizing and maintaining a good co-op dairy operation is a matter of coordinating a variety of factors and of weighing resources against needs. What storage equipment do you have? What products do you want to carry? How much of each can you store? How can you be sure your're getting a quality product?

With adequate refrigeration and cheese-cutting equipment you can carry a full range of dairy products. Many preorders carry only cheese because it doesn't require refrigeration immediately. A scale, a good knife or cheese wire, wrapping material, and a cutting surface are the only necessities. (Check licensing requirements in your area.)

Think about each dairy product carefully: how good it is nutritionally, what particular problems it presents, and what you need to know about production, storage, and distribution. Judging quality may take a different form with each product, but there are some standard questions you should ask:

What kind of processing has the product had? What additives, if any, does it have and what do they do? Is it made with whole or skim milk? Most imported cheese is made from whole milk; most domestic cheese from skim.

What kinds of transportation and delivery are dependable?

Why and how quickly does the product spoil? How is it packaged? How do you interpret its date codes?

What does it taste like?

What does it cost?

If you have problems finding these things out — particularly coding systems and standards — don't hesitate to consult consumer protection agencies and state or federal food and drug departments.

CHEESE

Cheese is an excellent source of protein. There's an incredible variety available, each produced in its own way. You can learn a lot about different cheeses by reading "Cheese Varieties," USDA handbook #54. Pass your information on to the people in the co-op.

Availability and price depend on your location. Feta cheese is widely available around Boston because of the large Greek population. Monterey jack cheese is found more easily on the West Coast. Imported cheeses are cheaper if you're near a large importing city. Domestic cheese is cheaper if you're near the source of production. Remember that there's a difference between domestic cheese and American cheese. American cheese is a type of processed cheese.

Probably the best test of cheese quality is taste. Get different kinds of a particular cheese and compare them. You may find quite a difference among similarly priced brands. You don't have to be a connoisseur to know if a cheese tastes mostly like the plastic it comes in and has the consistency of rubber. Stay in touch with members' comments.

While quality depends on different factors with each cheese, there are some standard quality indicators. The older and more carefully cured the cheese is, the better it will be, so find out as much as you can about the curing and ripening processes for the cheeses you want. Cheddar, if it meets certain standards, is packed in cases stamped with the outline of the state in which it is produced. Domestic Swiss cheese doesn't hold a candle to imported Swiss. In Swiss cheese, the bigger the holes, the better the cheese. (No kidding.)

Avoid cheese dips and spreads; they're full of preservatives and flavor enhancers and they usually cost as much, if not more, per pound than unadulterated cheese. Don't buy prepackaged cheeses from general grocery wholesalers; they are almost always inferior. Processed (American) cheese, though sometimes cheaper by the pound, has more moisture than unprocessed cheese. Most yellow cheeses are dyed and some co-ops may prefer to get undyed cheese. It's not clear if the dye is a health hazard. The Intra-Community Cooperative in Madison has enough buying power to order undyed colby.

Cutting big blocks or wheels of cheese is usually done with a two-handled knife or piano wire. The Noe Valley Store in San Francisco has made its entire back room into a beautiful cheese-cutting space, complete with blown-up photographs showing each step of the cutting process.

YOGURT

Yogurt is a nutritional house of wonders, with protein, B vitamins, and benign bacteria for your digestive system. It's a staple in many parts of the world and can be included in countless sauces, casseroles, and marinades, eaten straight, or drunk mixed with fruit juices. It's also a terrific baby food.

You can get yogurt from big commercial or small independent producers. It can stand unrefrigerated for several hours — the yogurt culture grows at 100–113° F. — but if you let it go unrefrigerated too long, it will get too sour.

Yogurt can be bought in countless different brands, flavors, sizes and qualities. Let people know the nutritional and caloric differences between plain and flavored yogurt, and give them ideas about how to dress up plain yogurt. Some commercial yogurts have no additives; others have a great many. Try to find an independent yogurt producer or work toward setting one up. Also consider teaching people to make their own yogurt; it's quite simple.

Check local and state regulations concerning yogurt production for nonprivate use. Common Market of Madison must buy yogurt from Continental in Ohio, even though Wisconsin is a major dairy state, because state regulations are so stringent that local dairies have shut down their once active yogurt production.

MILK

Milk is a primary protein source and a staple of the American diet. It is pasteurized and homogenized by the processor from the original whole raw milk. Every carton should clearly indicate ingredients and processing information, as well as a stamped date on the carton or cap. This is an open code that indicates the limit of the milk's shelf-life. Check this date when your milk is delivered and make sure, considering your co-op's delivery schedule and volume, that you're getting a reasonable amount of time to sell it. If there's a distributor in your area who sells milk in returnable bottles, you might consider buying from this company for ecological reasons. The bottles should be dark, as milk can lose Vitamin D if it's in the light too long. Also look for local sources of certified raw milk and goat's milk; both have nutritional advantages over pasteurized cow's milk. Milk should be kept at 37–38° F. Forty-five degrees is the "shock temperature" at which bacteria growth accelerates drastically, and the milk usually can't be saved even if it's cooled again. Remind people to keep the cooler doors closed, as the equipment will be working hard to keep the temperature down.

Many states have milk price supports to help the farmers in their region. This means that the wholesale price of milk is regulated, and is usually so high that small stores and co-ops often carry milk as a convenience to their customers or members, with no markup, or as a "loss-leader," meaning selling below wholesale and at a loss. Large supermarket chains, on the other hand, receive a "fluid discount" on milk because of their high volume and get illegal but government-condoned kickbacks from wholesalers. One Western co-op has gotten large enough to be eligible for these kickbacks. California co-ops, in frustration over this problem, recently organized a statewide boycott on milk that even the large Berkeley Consumers Co-op supported. Atlanta's Stone Soup Co-op doesn't carry any dairy products because they can't compete with the supermarkets' low prices.

You'll need to decide what quantities of milk to buy and whether to carry skim, butter, or fat-free milk. And you'll need to educate people about the whole process, telling them, for instance, to get dairy products last when they're shopping, particularly in the summer, and posting articles about the nutritional differences in different types of milk.

You might also look into powdered milk, which is very nutritious, useful in baking, low in cholesterol, and increasingly popular as the price of whole milk rises. Some families drink only powdered and once they get used to the flavor, find whole milk too rich. Grocery or bakery supply wholesalers are possible sources. Noninstant is cheaper and more nutritious than instant.

BUTTER AND MARGARINE

Butter is a fairly stable product, both in production and price. It's often labeled with a closed code. For example, a three-digit number which indicates the day of the year; 359 would be Christmas. Butter is also unique in that it is frequently coded with the day of production, not the shelf-life limit.

Margarine is a widely used substitute; it's cheaper than butter, though the gap seems to be closing. There's a great difference in margarines both in quality and price. You'll probably want something in between the expensive, whipped, fancy-packaged stuff and the quarters of lard-based margarines that are dirt cheap and terrible for your health. Safflower, peanut, soy, and corn oil margarines are highest in healthful unsaturated fats. Try to avoid margarines with linseed or cottonseed oil; they may contain high pesticide levels.

CREAM

Cream can be a problem, not only because of high price, but because its production and processing have been complicated to insure long shelf-life. A lot of cream is "ultrapasteurized," which simply means boiled, and countless additives are used to keep cream from turning. Different additives do different things, however, and you ought to investigate them as you need to. Some, like sodium phosphate, are preservatives; others, like sodium alginate, prevent the cream from coagulating but don't affect its longevity.

Your co-op might consider carrying cottage cheese, cream cheese, ricotta, farmer cheese, sour cream, and ice cream. There are innumerable sources for all of these, and you should shop around for the best quality for the lowest price. Dairy wholesalers aren't congregated in central markets as produce and meat wholesalers often are.

Finally, consider carrying tofu — soybean curd packed in water and cubed. It's an excellent inexpensive source of protein. If there's a Chinatown near your co-op, a wholesaler of tofu should be easy to find; if Oriental foods are scarce in your region, try a distributor of "natural" foods. *Diet for a Small Planet* is only one book listed in Sources, pp. 124–26, that gives recipes for tofu.

WHERE TO GET DAIRY PRODUCTS

Each distributor has its specialties and its ties to producers and other distributors. They all trade with each other. Find out who is the major importer in your area for foreign cheeses. A primary receiver may require a minimum order, which you can meet by buying with other co-ops. Through the USDA's *Dairy Market News,* keep tabs on the Wisconsin cheese market, which is the basic trading center in the United States. Changes in that market, based on the current value of cheddar and Swiss, are the standard for pricing among all domestic cheese distributors.

Cheese is usually priced at assembling points in Wisconsin and shipped by brokers in mixed lots to local wholesalers. A big wholesaler may contract directly with a plant or creamery.

Whole milk is distributed mostly by industrial processors and packagers. The closer you can get to the dairy farmers, the better off you'll be, but this isn't always possible. Most milk companies maintain a price schedule; the more you buy, the lower the unit price. You should ask for prices at different companies. If you don't like the answer Dairy A gives you, tell them you've been quoted X dollars by a competitor.

EGGS

Both preorders and stores can get eggs from local wholesalers who are sometimes located at produce markets. Of course, the closer you can get to the chicken, the lower your prices will be. Rural co-ops are at an advantage here. Some farmers will sell fertile eggs ("blood spots") cheap or even give them away, because they're not commercially acceptable. Actually they're more nutritious than infertile eggs. Many producers or graders and packagers will sell malformed or cracked eggs for a large discount. Be sure to buy only cracked eggs that have their membranes intact.

If you're in the country, try to get eggs from farmers who don't feed their hens a lot of growth hormones. This is hard for urban and suburban co-ops, but a federation or a good food sources committee can help.

We think it's worth it to get eggs packaged rather than in flats. Although they'll be a few pennies cheaper in flats, it's usually more of a mess than it's worth. Some eggs invariably break. Your distributor may even give you free extras to cover anticipated breakage. Styrofoam egg cartons aren't biodegradable; cardboard ones are.

Egg grading is voluntary and most producers don't want to pay for it. On size, a good rule is: the larger size is more economical if it's less than 7¢ more expensive than the next smaller size.

Grains and Other Staples

Most supermarket cash registers don't even have a key for grains and staples, but these basic unprocessed or minimally processed foods are extremely important in co-ops. When combined, many of them yield the same complete proteins as meat, fish, or dairy. (See *Diet for a Small Planet.*) When bought in bulk, they're quite inexpensive. Ecologically and nutritionally, they form the basis for a sound diet.

Staples include beans, flours, legumes, nuts, oils, nut butters, pasta, dried fruit, seeds, and honey. It's a real challenge to find good prices and locate sources for these foods.

The supply system right now is undergoing some fundamental changes. Co-ops are working together to buy grains and staples directly from farmers at prices far below wholesale. NEFCO recently bought rice and wheat at 30% below wholesale, and kidney beans at half the wholesale price. Small farmers, stimulated by co-op demand, are beginning to grow grains specifically for the co-op market. Some grain companies, even though they're high-price capitalist operations, are sympathetic to cooperative principles. They want our business and we can learn a lot from them.

If you're interested in organically grown grains, deal with a reputable grain business that tests the items it advertises as organically grown but be prepared, in some instances, to pay substantially more for this. With rice, the yield per acre on organically grown is about half that on nonorganically grown, and the price reflects this difference. With soybeans there isn't a substantial difference in price.

What grains and staples should a co-op provide? If you're a small operation, you probably want to start out with only a few commodities for which there is high demand. A good starting list might be brown rice, whole-wheat flour, granola, rolled oats, raisins, honey, peanut butter, and a few kinds of beans and vegetable oils. A more complete list would include:

Unbleached white flour	Sunflower seeds
Oat flour	Sesame seeds
Soy flour	Wheatberries
Rye flour	Dried apples
Corn meal	Dried apricots
Millet	Tamari (aged soy sauce)
Barley	Whole-wheat noodles
Wheat germ, toasted and raw	Chick peas (garbanzos)
Bulgur	Split peas
Sprouts	Black-eyed peas
Maple syrup	Cashews
Lentils	Peanuts
Soybeans	Walnuts

Popular beans include kidney beans, mung beans, white beans, black beans, pinto beans, and aduki beans. Among oils, safflower, sunflower, peanut, sesame, corn, and soy are high in polyunsaturates. For a comprehensive list, get a catalogue from a grain supply house.

Many preorders purchase and distribute grains every month or every two months. It's important if you do this to tell your members just how long it will be before the next order. You can do the grain order the same way you do the weekly produce order, with an order form, collating team, and, preferably, prepayment.

If you don't have enough orders of one item to buy a full bag — *e.g.,* sesame seeds come in 100-pound bags but you only have orders for 40 pounds — arrange to share the order with another co-op in your area, or see if you can buy from a nearby co-op store. If you have orders for 70 pounds, you'll have to decide if you can sell or store the 30-pound surplus safely.

To distribute grain, a preorder needs a more accurate scale than it would for produce, plus bags or containers, which should be provided by members.

Grain operations in stores involve ordering, stocking, pricing, and packaging. It's important not to run out of items between deliveries. The best way to ensure this is to have a good inventory system, and to keep accurate records of sales. (See section on inventory pp. 203–7.)

When you order for a store, take into account seasonal fluctuations in demand. People's eating habits differ with the seasons; you'll sell twice as much oatmeal and rice in the winter as in the summer, when people eat fewer hot meals. When fresh fruits are in ample supply, cut back on dried fruits. Avoid overstocking grains whose oils get rancid in warm weather: wheat germ, sunflower seeds, cornmeal. Summer eating habits and vacations make August a month of low volume in staples. Buy extra for September as people and appetites return.

WHERE TO GET GRAINS AND STAPLES

Most co-ops buy their grains from a single wholesaler who serves their area. To locate a wholesaler, contact co-ops, health food stores, and other retail stores, and look in the Yellow Pages. The Boston Food Co-op once let its fingers do the walking to a wholesaler in beans whose prices were 25% below other wholesalers. The others bought from this large bean dealer themselves, then marked up the prices. A NEFCO buyer once found out about a grain company by accident in the backroom of The Good Life, a small store in Brattleboro, Vermont.

In some parts of the country co-op warehouses supply many of the grains previously available only from capitalist wholesalers. These warehouses are probably the best sources in the areas where they exist. The Natural Alternatives Co-op in Jacksonville, Florida, and The Food Co-op in Tampa regularly place orders with the Washington, D.C., Community Warehouse because it offers them many items at prices lower than they could get from local wholesalers. Co-op warehouses will share any information they have about sources. The Minneapolis People's Warehouse and San Francisco Cooperating Warehouse have source lists that are available to any co-op that writes for them. See Appendix I for a list of co-op warehouses and their addresses.

Even without a warehouse, federations of co-ops can order large quantities of grains and staples from brokers or farmers. Wholesalers must have gotten their food from somewhere, since it is not growing in their warehouses. Research can turn up fine results and lower prices. It was this kind of research that led NEFCO from the wholesaler to the broker level of buying and in turn made it advisable for co-ops in New England to combine their orders.

The point of buying is to get as close to the source of supply as is economically feasible for your co-op or federation. If the minimum order required ties up too much time or is too large to handle, then the extra price you'll pay for the privilege of a smaller order may be more reasonable for you, but remember the direction in which you want to be heading: that of paying the people who have grown the food, not those who have touched it along the way, unless their handling is essential, such as the miller who turns grain into flour.

A good way of going directly to the source is to read labels. Some grain companies print the name and address of the farmer on their bags. You can also write to organic farmers' associations (see Appendix II) and put ads in their newsletters.

Many co-ops get stuck in the rut of buying grains exclusively from one wholesaler who also sells to health-food stores, organic restaurants, etc. Although these wholesalers often have high-quality food, it may be best economically to look around for other suppliers. The large grain companies that supply restaurants, cafeterias, and supermarkets often have low prices and will deliver to your door. Commodities like raisins, beans, oats, flour, and vanilla can be purchased from standard wholesalers at prices far below those of businesses that specialize in whole or organically grown grains.

Always look around for local sources of honey, sprouts, granola, and other items. Granola and sprouts can easily be produced by a work team of co-op members.

If all else fails, try to get a discount of about 10% from local retailers.

STORAGE OF GRAINS AND STAPLES

Where health regulations allow, many co-op stores sell their grains directly out of homemade wooden bins, twenty-gallon garbage pails, or five-gallon plastic buckets. The Good Harvest Co-op in Middletown, Connecticut, persuaded the local Dunkin' Donuts to donate about forty used buckets on the condition that the Dunkin' Donuts labels not be removed.

Visit other co-op stores to get some ideas about how to display and move grains. Bigger bins are needed for fast-moving items like rice, flour, and oats. One-gallon glass jars may suffice for slower movers like dried fruit. Check local bakeries for five-gallon containers and institutional kitchens for one-gallon jars. The Good Harvest called the cafeteria of the biggest corporation in town and asked for some one-gallon jars. The man in charge of the cafeteria hemmed and hawed but a few days later showed up with three dozen of them.

Some stores that have space and lots of volunteer labor prepackage their grains. This saves members a lot of hassle, probably results in the loss of less food through spillage, reduces congestion around the grain bins and scales, and may be necessary in any case to meet local health codes. Arizona health codes require that everyone handling foods for nonprivate consumption must have a TB test and display a picture ID health clearance while working with the food. Tucson's Food Conspiracy store has a special room that only health card-carrying volunteers may work in to package grains and staples. Hats and aprons hang next to self-service bins in San Francisco stores to be worn while weighing out your grains, as required by local ordinance.

If you allow members to bag their own grains, be sure to urge them to bring bags. Soon you'll find people coming in with thirty-five years' worth of A & P bags for you, and huge grins on their faces to boot.

Sacks of grain should be stored on pallets, and grain storage rooms should be kept clean to prevent infestation. Stack grain sacks in layers of equal number to facilitate inventory, leaving room between pallets to allow ventilation.

A final word on storage. Fresh ground whole-wheat flour, raw wheat germ, and a few other staples require refrigeration. In summer, oils should be refrigerated also. Remember this when you plan a store. You may want to buy commercial flour instead of fresh ground if you can't afford the cooler space.

With the rise in sugar prices, honey has become a staple in most co-op members' diets. It comes in sixty-pound tins with 2½- or 3-inch screw-on caps. If you try to pour it directly from the tins, you'll end up with many a hellish mess. Ask your honey supplier about spouts or gates that screw onto the tin in place of the cap.

Honey pours easily when warmed. Minneapolis' Mill City Co-op wraps its six-gallon tins and fifty-five-gallon drums with a heating tape normally used to wrap exposed cold water pipes in northern basements. The tape has a filament like a heating pad or blanket, and when plugged in keeps the honey pourable but well below the 160° F. at which some of its nutrients are destroyed.

Bread and Baked Goods

A grain of wheat has three main parts: the kernel, the outer husk, and the germ. White flour is made in steel mills that take out the husk and the germ, leaving only the kernel. Most of the protein, vitamins, and minerals are removed along with the germ. White bread is then "enriched" with a few of these nutrients in chemical form. The outer husk is usually sold as animal feed, while the germ is sold as a food supplement. Some manufacturers add a little caramel coloring to their enriched white bread and pass off the darker product as "natural."

As bread buyer for your co-op, you should know what ingredients and preservatives are in each bread you buy, and should see that your members are informed of the comparative nutritional values. This doesn't mean you should buy only whole-grain breads; most of us are too fond of bagels, English muffins, and sourdough to settle for that. But you can cut down considerably on additives, and you can search for good oat, rye, corn, and seven-grain breads, as well as nutritious whole-grain sweets if members want them. Many preorders get day-old bread from manufacturers at considerable discounts. Washington, D.C., co-op stores carry the entire selection of nutritious breads baked by the Columbia Union College, a Seventh Day Adventist School in Takoma Park, Maryland.

If a bread can be squeezed down to a small bundle, it's full of air and not a good buy. However, much as we dislike air-filled white sandwich bread, we know some co-ops that carry it because it's cheaper. They often serve low-income communities, and are trying to meet all their members' needs, so they don't have to spend any of their earnings at profit-making chain stores. This is where the co-op's educational function comes in. Many people have never heard about the advantage of whole grains from someone they respect and work with.

You can put recipes in your newsletter or post them near your grains and flour. A great source is the *Tassajara Bread Book*. Along with baking at home, try doing what the people at Famine Foods in Winona, Minnesota, do. Every Thursday night they rent the local YMCA kitchen and bake breads for their small co-op.

WHERE TO GET BREAD

There are several nationally known bread manufacturers that provide nutritious products, among them Thomas, Arnold, and Pepperidge Farm. These companies will usually fill even small orders at wholesale prices, usually 10–20% below retail, and they often deliver.

In addition, try to support local bakeries. Their bread can be incredibly fresh and delicious, without any preservatives, and you can observe their operation. You may even be able to convince a local baker to make bread to your specifications. Be careful with very small bakeries, though; they can be unreliable and will often substitute one bread for another. Better still, see if there's a co-op bakery in your area, or work toward setting one up. (See Chapter 15.)

Try to keep your bread fresh. In a store, rotate stock, check dates, and pull out old stuff. In a preorder, get a wholesale price list, start with a few varieties on your order form, rotate them, and see what members like. Or make arrangements with a good local bakery for pickups on certain days. Stores should set up a system with dealers so they'll accept returns on items that don't sell.

Fish

Fish is high in protein, vitamins, and minerals, and as a co-op fish buyer, you can introduce members to many new varieties. Fish, like meat, may not give you a significant price break unless you order large quantities or find a direct supplier. Preorders with small volume may have to buy from retailers rather than wholesalers. But buying fish is still worthwhile in terms of quality and convenience for members.

You can get either fresh or frozen fish, or both. Either way, you'll need freezer space, because fresh fish has to be frozen if it is not sold within one or two days.

Two popular frozen fishes are turbot and shrimp, and they're at almost opposite ends of the price scale. Turbot fillets, which often come in unsealed cellophane bags, are one of the most reasonably priced of all fish. They're also delicious. Shrimp is sold by size; the more shrimp to the pound, the smaller they'll be, and the lower the price. Look also for crayfish, which are much cheaper and resemble shrimp in taste and appearance.

Fish cakes and fish sticks consist of ground-up odds and ends that are precooked, breaded, and sold frozen. Cheap cost and easy preparation make them popular. Get cakes rather than sticks as they're cheaper and have a higher fish to bread ratio.

What fresh fish you'll get depends on your location. If you're on either coast, you'll have access to a wide variety of saltwater fish and seafood: cod, flounder, swordfish, pollock, bass, mackerel, whitefish, bluefish, squid, hake, porgy, whiting, butterfish, lobster, crab, clams, mussels, scallops, and shrimp. Inland you may be able to find good sources of freshwater fish like trout, bass, perch, and catfish. There are many more types; try different ones when they're plentiful, and see what members like. Provide recipes and fish stories.

WHERE TO GET FISH

If you're near either coast or any large city you can get plenty of saltwater fish from wholesalers, fishing co-ops, or individual fishing ventures. Most wholesalers will sell you whole fish or fillets (without the bone). Ask around for names of good wholesalers, and try the Yellow Pages.

In Boston there is a message recorded daily that indicates what fish were brought into the harbor and what price was paid for them. Most coastal states compile statistics on types and quantities of fish landed each month. A look at these will give you an indication of seasonal volume patterns and help you decide what might be a good buy that month. Just as you sample and shop at the produce market, sample and shop at the fish pier or other wholesaling areas. Your price will go down as your steadiness as a customer goes up.

Both on the coast and inland, do what you can to encourage small fishing ventures. Check out fishing towns as well as big city piers. Several Massachusetts co-ops are supplied with fresh fish caught by a fisherman in Gloucester, twenty miles northeast of Boston. The fisherman cleans the fish and removes the heads; co-op volunteers scale the fish and sometimes fillet them. Fish is delivered to the collectively run Stone Soup store in Washington, D.C., cleaned but not scaled. A sign over the fish counter explains, "We don't wish to do anything we feel you can do yourself. Therefore all fish is sold unscaled. We will teach you how to scale it for 5¢ a fish."

Some large wholesalers specialize in frozen fish. Use them, as they'll probably have the most variety and the best prices. Elsewhere, you'll be getting your frozen fish from regular wholesalers.

In addition to the normal wholesale outlets for fish, there are a number of fishing co-ops around the country. These co-ops unload the fishing boats and pack the fish in boxes of ice for shipment. The boxes hold about 100 pounds of fish and 25 to 30 pounds of ice. The fish stays fresh for three or four days, plenty of time for distribution to either preorders or stores nearby. All you need is a reliable truck.

Another, more seasonal source of fresh fish are the many sport fishing boats that are chartered daily by amateurs. You can arrange to buy surpluses from boat owners. This can be a comparatively cheap source of very desirable fish like bluefish and striped bass. When these fish are running, the catch is high, providing a good chance to stock up freezers for a winter's supply. You'll have to provide ice or refrigeration, and clean the fish yourself.

FILLETING AND STORAGE OF FISH

When you've got your fresh fish, make sure it's clean. Then you can either sell it whole or fillet it. If you sell it whole, weigh it, bag it, price it, and chill it. If you're going to fillet it, find someone to teach you. If there's no one in the co-op with experience, go to a friendly fish store and learn how. Essentially, you'll be making two cuts lengthwise across the ribs and peeling off two boneless fillets, one on each side of the fish. Save the remains and either sell them or give them away to members for bouillabaisse, cat food, etc. If you fillet the fish, make sure to adjust your per pound price upward to account for the bones that have been removed.

Stores must have adequate refrigeration and freezing space for the quantities they buy. Preorders can circumvent the refrigeration problem if they buy fish iced (keeping it at a temperature of 33–36° F.) and distribute it the same day. Sinks are almost a necessity.

Fish keeps best in shaved ice, which preserves the moisture balance. Solid ice, ice water, and dry refrigeration are workable alternatives. Freezing, of course, is the ultimate preservative. Freeze as fast as possible; freeze only cleaned fish; and try to use frozen fish within one to three months.

Remember, fish smells. It must be handled separately so that your lettuce, cottage cheese, and meat don't begin to smell and taste like fish.

Meat

There are many ways for a co-op to handle meat. Some co-ops get only cold cuts; others buy hamburger, chicken, and stew meat. Still others make arrangements with butchers or small wholesalers to cut a variety of fresh meats, and some co-ops even cut their own. But butchering requires cutting room, tables, knives, lots of cooler space, and even more expertise, not to mention health inspection and licensing. For many co-ops, and almost all preorders, meatcutting is not yet feasible.

Because of its high perishability, meat, like fish, is probably not a good item for a beginning co-op to carry. The problems meat poses will make it harder for you to get off to a good start. Meat does not offer the same kind of savings as produce or grains do.

A good way to start is with ground beef or chickens, neither of which require cutting. All you need is refrigeration. Co-ops that plan to do butchering usually start with beef, and may later get pork and veal. Liver is also a good buy; lamb liver is cheaper than beef liver which in turn is cheaper than calves' or chicken liver. Other meats you might try are hearts, kidneys, and brains. They're all relatively cheap and highly nutritious, and can be delicious if properly prepared. Be sure to supply recipes for your members. One co-op we know got kidneys free from the wholesaler because he couldn't sell them. (Organ meats, though, do retain harmful chemicals more than other parts of the animal.)

Cold cuts like bologna, salami, liverwurst, ham, chicken and turkey loaf, corned beef, smoked tongue, and "mystery" meats present a nutritional dilemma because most of them contain the potentially carcinogenic sodium nitrite and sodium nitrate. Hot dogs and bacon do too, of course. If your co-op decides to carry cold cuts you may want to search for brands that have fewer or none of these chemicals, and that have lower fat content. Check the labels to be sure. The Common Market in Madison has sausages made to order without these preservatives. The Laramie People's Market in Wyoming carries buffalo salami with no chemicals or preservatives.

Wholesale beef and veal can be bought in sides, hindquarters, forequarters, square chucks, arm chucks, rounds, rumps, loins, short loins, and loin ends. Wholesale pork comes in loins, shoulders, butts, back ribs, spare ribs, and hams; wholesale lamb comes in legs, rounds, shoulders, and loins. These are just the names of different size portions of half an animal. It's useful to know where these parts are and what cuts of meat they contain. Hindquarters are usually preferred to forequarters because they yield more steaks and roasts. But they're more expensive and have less usable meat. Forequarters yield rib roasts and a variety of other cuts that require moist cooking. You can easily learn what cuts are produced by other pieces of meat.

Meat must be federally inspected and graded if it crosses state lines. If it doesn't cross state lines, it must be state or locally inspected and graded. Prime grade is the most tender and marbled (fatty); then comes choice, still tender, with less marbling. Prime grade is too expensive for most folks, and the best buy all around is probably Choice Yield 1 or Choice Yield 2.

Yield refers to how much meat the animal's carcass yields. Yield 1 is usually steers; Yield 2, heifers, and there are also Yields 3, 4, and 5. Other grades are *standard* and *commercial*. Standard has little fat and must be cooked moist; commercial is fatty but tough.

Poultry is graded A or B, and comes in various brands. Chickens come in three sizes: roasters (four pounds); broilers (three pounds); and fryers (under three pounds). You can also get fowl, which are older chickens — cheap but tough as hell and mainly good for stewing or soups.

Don't buy more meat than you can realistically sell in a few days, or, if you're butchering, more than your meat collective can realistically cut. Meat goes bad quickly. If you've overordered and don't have adequate freezer space, you'll suffer a considerable financial loss. Stone Soup in Washington, D.C., had a freezer full of meat after demand for meat fell in their poor neighborhood as a result of increasing unemployment.

Co-op stores should try to sell meat as fresh as possible so people can let it sit in their refrigerators for a few days without having to freeze it. Get fresh meat on Wednesday or Thursday and try to sell it all by Saturday.

WHERE TO GET MEAT

In big cities, meat wholesalers are often located at a central meat market. Friends in other co-ops or in the restaurant business may be able to tell you which wholesalers have good reputations. A major packing house that doesn't have to go through a broker to get its meat but raises or slaughters its own will have better prices. When acquainting yourself with wholesalers, ask about grades, methods for cutting meat, and procedures for ordering and picking up.

Large wholesalers may not be interested in you unless you can guarantee them a certain volume of business every week, sometimes as much as $1000. But most preorders can establish good relations with smaller wholesalers who will butcher for them. The Lynn, Massachusetts, co-op has been dealing with the same wholesaler for many years; he and the co-op grew together. He will split cases of cold cuts or bacon for them, which large houses won't do. The co-op usually plans its orders so that the wholesaler won't have to buy a great many different cuts. For example, one week they may order center cut pork chops, pork loin, and end cuts of pork; other weeks they may not order pork at all. If London broil is on the order form, they'll usually include shoulder roasts as well, since both come from the beef shoulder. They save 10–20% over supermarket prices.

If your preorder can't find a good local wholesaler, you might start with a regular butcher and ask him or her for a discount. The quality will exceed the supermarket's, and you'll be able to order to your specifications.

Always order a specific grade. Never let wholesalers sell you ungraded beef. They will try. When you're there, watch to see how well it is trimmed before it is weighed. When it's delivered to the co-op, check that it is stamped with the grade you ordered, and that the weight given on the bill is the weight you received.

You need to keep the wholesalers honest. They have to move bad pieces as well as good, and if they discover they can move the bad ones on you, they'll do so. Any time a piece of meat has excess fat on it, is getting old, or was poorly graded, make a note to tell the vendor; if it's bad, don't hesitate to send it back. Watch the meat for freshness; ask to make sure the wholesaler hasn't already frozen it once.

As with many other foods, it helps to alternate buying from two or more meat wholesalers. That way you can compare products and prices.

Sometimes you can bypass meat middlepeople. The Ecology Food Club in Philadelphia gets beef directly from a local rancher, who also happens to be president of the Pennsylvania Organic Farmers and Consumers Organization. The beef is free from hormone injections. The Common Market in Madison gets its meat from Herbert Hoover Organic Beef, Lambs, and Rabbits.

Some meat distributors now cut up hindquarters and ship the pieces in *cry-vac* (tight plastic seals). This saves wholesalers and retailers the trouble of cutting up a hindquarter; they can buy individual rumps, rounds, and sirloins instead, without additional cost. This can save your co-op money, but if you've got a meatcutting collective, they may view butchering as more than a chore; at the Boston Food Co-op, the meatcutters didn't want to give up the fun of cutting the hindquarter.

MEATCUTTING

For meatcutting, you'll need an extremely responsible work team or collective. Find at least one member with butchering experience; meat is too expensive to experiment with. If you don't have such a member, try to borrow one from another co-op or go to a friendly butcher or your wholesaler to see how it's done.

You'll need a coordinator to schedule meatcutting sessions. It's important for meatcutters to understand the seriousness of their commitment; once a piece of meat has been delivered, it has to be cut immediately. A meatcutting session usually lasts 2 to 2½ hours. If a member of the meatcutters' collective can't make it, he or she should call the coordinator at once.

A good meatcutters' collective may take a while to organize. Be patient and meanwhile learn all you can from the wholesalers you deal with. The New Haven Co-op started out buying from a local butcher and has since learned to cut whole steers.

A separate committee may come in regularly to cut whole chickens into legs, thighs, breasts, wings, and backs, if members like to buy it that way. Cutting chicken yourself is somewhat cheaper than buying breasts or other pieces from the wholesaler. But if members only want breasts and aren't buying the other parts, it may not be worth your while to cut them up yourself.

If you grind your own hamburger or have bones left over after butchering, you might give them to co-op members for soup stock.

PRICING MEAT

If you're doing your own butchering, you'll be cutting the meat into smaller pieces of varying quality, so you'll have to vary the prices accordingly. It's a tricky business to make the different prices for steak, roast, stew, and hamburger average out to the wholesale price.

Let's say you bought a square chuck for $34 — 50 pounds at 68¢ a pound. You figure you'll get 15 pounds of chuck steak out of it, 20 pounds of chuck roast, 5 pounds of hamburger, and 10 pounds of bone and fat. If you charge 85¢ a pound for the 15 pounds of steak, you'll get $12.75. If you charge 80¢ a pound for the 20 pounds of roasts, you'll get $16.00. And if you charge 70¢ a pound for the 5 pounds of hamburger, you'll get $3.50. So your total return will be $32.25, and you'll be losing $1.75. You can't come out exactly right on every piece of meat, but, with experience, you'll be able to come up with approximate prices that average out to wholesale cost.

Mistakes and spoilage are not figured into the above price analysis, but you should allow for these as well. Always set prices a little higher than exact return to allow for mistakes in cutting, markdowns of old meat, and spoilage.

For packaged meats — canned hams, bacon, knockwurst, cold cuts — mark the wholesaler's price per crate divided by the number of items in a crate. Be careful, though; you may get 20 pounds of bacon packed in 12-ounce packages. If the wholesaler charges by the pound, make sure you don't charge that per-pound price for only 12 ounces of bacon.

Groceries

Groceries — canned, bottled, and packaged goods — are not a high priority with most co-ops. Not only do they have less nutritional value than fresh foods, but they go through so many hands before they reach the retailer that the wholesale price is relatively high.

Supermarkets make their money on volume, not markup. Co-ops, which have lower volume, may be able to save only a few pennies on most grocery items.

Nevertheless, groceries are worth carrying. Most co-op members consume some canned goods (tomato paste, tuna fish, pet foods, etc.), and almost all use toilet paper. If members don't get these things from the co-op, they'll have to get them from the supermarket. This isn't just inconvenient; it weakens the co-op movement. From the members' point of view, one-stop shopping is a real advantage. From the co-op's point of view, there's no reason why the co-op shouldn't get the extra surcharge on these items to help defray its own operating costs, rather than letting the supermarkets get the profit by default (provided, of course, that the food isn't objectionable from a nutritional or health-safety viewpoint).

Although the amount of money to be saved is minimal, groceries are easier to carry than many other foods. Preorders can get them every three or six months, depending on how much money members can invest and on the amount of storage space they have. Stores with any sizeable turnover usually have to order groceries every week; if they ordered too much in advance, they'd be tying up capital in merchandise that's sitting in the storage room. There's little spillage or spoilage with groceries, and there are no big equipment needs. The main requirements are shelf and storage space, and good inventory control. And the rewards are great: the appreciation of the members, the convenience of one-stop shopping, and the knowledge that you're coming close to providing a complete alternative to the supermarket.

Supermarkets carry thousands of different grocery items. For a co-op, 200 to 250 are more than sufficient. The difference is that co-ops carry basic foods and unless their members demand them, generally avoid frivolous or junk foods, frozen processed foods, and canned fruits and vegetables. Co-ops also avoid duplication of brands and sizes. The largest size of most groceries is usually the best buy. When an item is considered necessary, try to carry one size and one brand only. Try not to carry groceries that duplicate your fresh foods.

The basic groceries include soups, juices, condiments such as mustard and ketchup, spreads, cleaning supplies, paper goods, minimal toiletries and housewares. A priority for a beginning grocery section might be canned tuna; find out which brand and size offers the best value. (Some co-ops avoid chunk light tuna because many dolphins are killed when these fish are caught.) Powdered milk is another good choice. Be open to member suggestions and stimulate discussion of comparative nutritional advantages.

Groceries need considerable stocking and display space. Many co-ops use one quarter to one third of their space for groceries. Because of this you'll need especially good inventory control.

Inventory control is the delicate art of balancing projected needs against amount of money and space available. If you're ordering groceries weekly, base your inventory system on weekly turnover. Don't use a figure for daily sales and multiply by the number of days you're open during the week. Most people's shopping habits are pretty regular, and you may have twice as many people shopping on Monday as on Thursday. Be sure to take seasonal fluctuations into account.

WHERE TO GET GROCERIES

National Cooperatives, Inc., distributes a wide variety of groceries under the twin-pines Co-op label, which is registered to the Cooperative League of the U.S.A. If you're near a warehouse that distributes Co-op label groceries, this may be your best source. (See page 126 for addresses.) Quality is usually high and costs are lower than for nationally advertised brands or even supermarket brands. One reason for this is the lack of advertising. Many co-op products have explanations of government grades on their labels. Some commercial labels don't even have grades, much less explanations of them. The Common Market in Denver makes a monthly order with the Associated Cooperatives warehouse in California. Community Warehouse in Washington, D. C., is organizing a periodic run to Mid-Eastern Cooperatives in New Jersey.

But not all food co-ops are near these distributors, nor is it a good idea to order exclusively from one source, You should always look around for the best deal; with a little research you may be able to bypass the wholesaler altogether. Several Boston area co-ops get Tampax straight from the factory. In addition, if one wholesaler is out of an item — a frequent occurrence — you can order it from another wholesaler with whom you've already established business relations. And you can take advantage of specials and promotions offered by different suppliers.

Wholesalers provide ordering sheets or books that you fill in before you call or mail your order. If you call, you can determine which items are out of stock, and can decide what substitutions you want to make. Unfortunately, when the shipment arrives, some items will be missing anyway. To minimize inventory problems, note which ordered items were not delivered, so you won't forget to reorder them.

You may occasionally come across a bulging or otherwise suspicious-looking can. Put it aside to return for credit. Even dented cans should not be sold due to the danger of botulism.

A word to preorders: don't let one person get stuck with preparing the entire grocery order. It may look simple, but it's a hell of a job. A small committee can handle it nicely.

PRICING GROCERIES

Divide the crate price by the number of items in the crate. If you pick it up yourself, add transportation costs to the markup. The West Concord Food and Friendship Co-op exempts groceries from the bump because bumping them would wipe out the savings. The co-op considers grocery buying purely a service to members, and relies on the bump on other items to meet its operating expenses.

STORAGE OF GROCERIES

Groceries should be placed on the shelves and in storage in a systematic manner. This makes it easier to take inventory and to place orders. Since most wholesalers maintain their ordering system according to like items or code numbers corresponding to those items, it's a good idea to set up your inventory based on their systems as much as possible. If the wholesaler's book starts with cereals, stock cereals in the first section. This enables a member doing inventory to go down the line and check things off in sequence.

Once you place items in particular locations, don't shift them around if you can help it. People get used to looking for the same items in the same place. If something is moved, place signs announcing the change on the old spot.

Plan for adequate storage for a week's (or two weeks') supply of groceries, depending on how often you order. Make sure they can be stacked and reached easily. Rotate your stock; that is, sell your old groceries first. This is especially important when prices fluctuate. Sell the item with the old price before you put those with the new price on the shelves.

Teas, Herbs, Spices

To spice up your co-op, add teas, herbs, and spices. The savings in bulk buying are amazing — often from 50–300%. Bulk buying is relatively simple; all you need is an idea of what to carry, where to buy it, and how to store, sell, and package it.

Deciding what to carry is the first step. Draw up an extensive list, including everything from the most common items like garlic powder, cinnamon, and tea, to more obscure things like saffron, hibiscus, and yarrow flowers. Ask members to check off items they want and to add others.

Sources are more of a problem. Ask for suggestions from friends who work in restaurants, check the ever valuable Yellow Pages under Herbs and Spices, and send letters to other co-ops that might be distributing herbs in bulk. The best co-op source of herbs is the Red Star Apothecary at the People's Warehouse, 123 East 26th Street, Minneapolis 55404. They supply a full range of items to co-ops in the North Country, and are glad to give any co-op information about their sources.

Compare price lists from your sources. The suppliers of organically grown food are considerably more expensive, and don't always sell in bulk. Many teas and spices are imported, which makes it difficult if not impossible to guarantee that they're organically grown.

Local dealers may not carry all the items you want, particularly things like peppermint, camomile, and sassafras. The Boston Food Co-op gets some of these items from a small herb dealer in New Hampshire. This dealer has an interesting shipping arrangement. The order arrives anywhere from one day to one week after it is placed, depending on the class schedule of the dealer's neighbor, who teaches at one of the colleges in Boston and drops off the order when she comes into the city.

In storing and packaging herbs, teas, and spices, it's essential to keep out air, moisture, and, in some cases, light, to protect their color and potency. Seeds and branchy herbs or roots such as rosemary, fennel seeds, whole rose hips, and sassafras, store best. The green leafy herbs are most affected by light. Tarragon, for example, starts off bright green, but deteriorates to a dull brown and loses a lot of its flavor. You can store and display spices in large glass jars, which you may be able to round up for free or very cheaply by tapping large local institutions with cafeterias. Paint some jars to keep light out if the herb requires it.

Label all lids and jars with the name of the item and the per ounce price, the price on masking tape so it can be changed and the name in paint so it can't. Be sure to label both lids and jars in case they become separated. When the cinnamon lid ends up on the oregano, it will be noticed immediately, but the red pepper lid might stay on the saffron indefinitely, a misleading and expensive proposition since red pepper is about one-fourth the price of saffron, and their uses are miles apart. Price herbs, teas, and spices as you would any other bulk commodity, remembering to protect the co-op for loss due to spillage or deterioration. Your display can be set up so that members weigh, price, and package everything themselves. Ask members to bring their own containers. An accurate scale that can weigh ½-, 1-, and 2-ounce quantities is essential. Postage scales costing only a few dollars may suffice, but a more accurate scale is probably worth the investment. You may be able to get a triple beam scale for less than $50.

Ask the most knowledgeable people in the co-op to post information about the medicinal use of various herbs. The North Country Co-op in Minneapolis and the Food Conspiracy in Tucson devote entire rooms to the display of medicinal herbs and homeopathic cures.

Finally, encourage members to grow their own.

Equipment

Equipment for most preorders may be little more than a hanging scale or two, an adding machine, a large kitchen knife, a blackboard for prices, and a second-hand refrigerator. Hanging scales turn up at auctions for around $15. Scales with hanging pans shaped like a scoop are preferable to the older deep-dish produce scales because they allow grains to be poured out after weighing without being spilled. Newer scales usually have adjustment screws at the base of the dial to correct readings.

An adding machine with a tape will reduce addition errors and provide the co-op with a record of the day's purchases. Self-duplicating tapes are available for about $1 a roll and will allow the cashier to give each member a receipt while retaining a record of sales. Adding machines run about $20 to $40 used.

A refrigerator is a necessity if your co-op is going to carry dairy, meat, or fish; it's also valuable for storing produce and some staples. Have someone put perishables in upon delivery and allow members to serve themselves. Fresh fish shouldn't be refrigerated with other foods unless you like fishy-tasting cottage cheese. Used refrigerators are readily available for under $50. Often, refrigerators are simply donated.

An outgrown children's blackboard is nice for posting prices. A sharp kitchen knife, a good cutting surface, and waxed paper or plastic wrap are about all small preorders need to cut cheese. You shouldn't have to buy paper bags; tell people to bring their old ones and start the recycling habit.

Refrigeration is the largest equipment expense that a store faces. A fleet of refrigerators may do for a while, but to handle perishables properly in store volumes, nothing can replace the efficiency of a walk-in cooler. With the exception of tropical fruits and root crops, all produce not on display should be refrigerated. Cheese, fish, meat, and grains with natural oils must also be refrigerated. During the summer, unfumigated dried fruits must be squeezed into a walk-in cooler already crowded with members socializing out of the heat.

Unassembled, a walk-in cooler is comprised of six insulated panels that easily bolt together to form the box, and accompanying compressor, blower, heat exchanger, tubing, and other hardware. Prices range from about $300 for a small 4′ x 8′ cooler to several thousand dollars for larger room-sized lockers. Newer models are air-cooled, lighter, and more efficient than older models, which may be quite bulky and awkward to move. The newer coolers only require 110 volts while older ones may need 220-volt sources. You may even find an occasional model that is water-cooled; avoid it if your municipality requires you to supply your own closed water-cooling system.

Your cooler will need constant attention. You should learn as much as you can about how to use and maintain it, although in some situations professional help will be required. Share the labor and education rather than letting a poorly understood machine drain one person's energy. A work team should be responsible for maintaining the coolers, and training groups are a good way to spread knowledge about the machines. Good advice is available in *The Co-op Cooler Book*. (See page 126.) Check out local libraries for manuals and guides, but don't expect to learn all you need to know about coolers from books; try to find somebody who's knowledgeable to teach a group of interested co-op members. And find out about any repair collectives in your area.

Most stores have refrigerated display cases that allow members self-service access to milk, cut cheeses, frozen juices, etc. Display cases are essentially large commercial refrigerators operating on the same principle as home refrigerators. Cases may be either upright or chest high, and either open or close-faced. Open-faced display cases use a buffer of chilled air instead of a glass sliding door to keep the contents well-cooled, and they should never be filled beyond the line marked inside. Wholesalers of dairy products may be persuaded to furnish a display case to a co-op with a high potential volume.

Health regulations and good sense require that each cooler unit have a clearly visible thermometer inside.

Most people consider a cash register a kind of musical cashbox. In fact, a cash register is primarily a bookkeeping tool. Properly used, it provides a record of sales with an instant breakdown of volume into as many different categories as the keys allow. Most stores have organized their registers to give them an end-of-the-day sales reading for meat, dairy, grocery, produce, bread, nonfood items, and bump if the co-op bumps the entire sale.

A used cash register should only be bought from a dealer who's willing to guarantee the machine for six months and to service it in case of breakdown. Registers are very intricate instruments that will need repairs with greater frequency as they get older. It's best to establish a good working relationship with an office-machine repair service near the store. Check the Yellow Pages and shop around. Used cash registers sell for several hundred dollars; the least expensive new register will be nearly $1000. Registers may also be leased.

Accurate hanging scales are as necessary for stores as for preorders. Many stores also need more precise measurements, and there are an endless number of scales to fit the bill. For spices and teas, you'll need a scale that measures in ounces or grams. Calibrated scales that show the price as well as the weight are best for meats and cheeses. (They're also expensive.) San Francisco stores have chosen to use digital readout pricing scales to reduce losses caused by misweighing. Usually co-op stores use whatever scales they can find cheaply at auctions. Whatever you use, it will probably have to be certified for accuracy by the local weights-and-measures inspector at least once a year.

There are a multitude of small items that may not be missed at first, but once acquired will become instant necessities. Dollies, two-wheelers, and carts to move stuff onto the floor, case knives with disposable razor-blade inserts for opening cardboard cases, price stampers, taps or gates for oil and honey tins, and so on, make tasks easier. A supermarket auction can be quite an education in solutions to the most trivial problems.

Perhaps the most important equipment in your co-op will be a well-stocked and well-organized tool box. Having the right tool for the right job at the right time will remove endless irritations.

If your co-op is considering taking advantage of the considerable savings it can achieve by cutting meat, you should examine the idea carefully to ensure that savings are not outweighed by the expense of equipping a butchering room. You may have to redesign an entire room to meet local health regulations. In many areas of the country, cutting rooms must be refrigerated to 45° or lower, and be equipped with a floor drain for proper cleaning. You may also be required to install stainless steel sinks, large tables with legal cutting surfaces, and a hot water system that will keep water temperature at 180° or more.

Cutting blocks are usually polyethylene or wood. Some butchers think wood is preferable, but it's also more expensive. In Boston, plastic is the only legal cutting surface because wooden boards were found to harbor bacteria in the gashes. Make sure you know the local regulations. Plastic boards must be cleaned with disinfectant and scrubbed with a wire brush.

Depending on what kind of cutting you're going to do, you'll need knives to fit your needs. A meat knife has a curved edge, rather than a straight edge like a cheese knife. The simplest and smallest meat room will need at least one big knife with a blade 1½–2 inches wide. If you're doing some serious cutting, like a hindquarter, you'll need a boning knife and a handsaw.

You must keep your knives sharp. This means you either send

them out every week to be sharpened or learn to do it yourself. In either case you'll need a sharpening steel. Take care of your knives; put a good edge on them with the sharpening steel before you cut, and don't ever misuse them by, for instance, using them as screwdrivers.

Knives should probably be bought new to avoid inheriting saw-toothed edges and abused blades. A good wholesale supply house should not only sell you the knives, but grind and hone them and be a source of information for their care. With properly sharpened knives, you won't need a meat cleaver. Not only are cleavers unnecessary, but they'll quickly destroy a planed cutting surface. Stainless steel knives require less care than the older carbon steel blades, but need sharpening more often.

You may think you need a meat grinder. Before you get one, compare the cost and time of grinding your own hamburger with the economics of buying bulk hamburger. Some co-ops have found that wholesalers, because of their larger volume, can sell hamburger cheaper than the co-op could grind it.

Meat must be wrapped. A heat-sealing wrapper has a spool of wrapping film, a hot wire, and a hot pad of metal. The wire melts and cuts the film and the pad seals it together under the meat. If you work with sealing plastic, make sure it's in a well-ventilated area, as the plastic is usually polyvinyl chloride, whose fumes can be dangerous if inhaled over a long period of time. An alternative wrapping material is the safer polyethylene.

Cheese-cutting wire, or piano wire, is made of stainless steel and never has to be sharpened, although it may break or knot. Mounted, with wood on each end, it's excellent for cutting large blocks of cheese. A two-handled knife will also do.

When buying equipment, be very careful. Prices may vary as much as 1000% depending on condition, age, and circumstances under which you're buying. Shop around and you may save a lot of money. There are several sources you should explore before going into the retail market. Call the main offices of the supermarket chains in your area. They may be able to sell you used tools, shelves, coolers, office equipment, etc. Used equipment places are also worth trying, including those that specialize, like butcher's supply houses.

Ask potential suppliers if they can help you, either by donating or loaning equipment or giving you leads on where to get it. Tell them you'll be able to maximize the sale of their products if you have the right equipment to store and display them. And let the word out in the community that you're accepting donations.

Auctions can be excellent sources, but beware of the persuasive wiles of auctioneers (and "plants" who are there to up the bids) or you may end up with stuff you don't need. Bring somebody who knows about equipment.

Many co-op stores have been messed up by members' sloppy attitudes toward equipment. You should feel neither scared by equipment, nor cavalier about its care. Staff or volunteer work teams that take responsibility for the maintenance of equipment are a necessity. If your scales are not accurate or your coolers are faulty, you'll suffer a loss not only in money but in social capital as well.

Sources

Many nutrition education groups, vegetarians, and people who just want to cut down on meat consumption, find the single most useful guide to be Frances Moore Lappé's *Diet for a Small Planet*. (New York, Ballantine, 1971). We strongly recommend that you stock this book in your co-op. Among the many other books and pamphlets on health, cooking, and nutrition:

Berkeley Women's Health Collective. *Feeding Ourselves*. Berkeley, California, 1972. Available from New England Free Press, 60 Union Square, Somerville, Mass.

Bethel, May. *The Healing Power of Herbs*. Hollywood, California: Wilshire Publishers.

Boston Women's Health Book Collective, *Our Bodies, Ourselves*. New York: Simon and Schuster, 1971.

Brown, Edward. *Tassajara Bread Book,* 1970, and *Tassajara Cooking,* 1973. Berkeley, California: Shambala Press.

Davis, Adelle. *Let's Eat Right to Keep Fit*. New York: Signet. This, like two of Davis's other books, *Let's Get Well* and *Let's Have Healthy Children*, offers a wealth of information on what different nutrients do and what foods they are found in. But Davis's style is occasionally hysterical; she favors large expenditures for nutrient supplements.

Ewald, Ellen. *Recipes for a Small Planet*. New York: Ballantine, 1973. The sequel to *Diet;* more recipes for combining vegetable proteins.

Gregory, Dick. *Dick Gregory's Natural Diet for Folks Who Eat*. New York: Harper & Row, 1973.

Guthrie, Helen A. *Introductory Nutrition*. St. Louis: Mosby, 1971.

Hall, Ross H. *Food for Naught: the Decline in Nutrition*. New York: Harper & Row, 1974.

Hunter, Beatrice. *Consumer Beware — Your Food and What's Been Done to It*. New York: Simon and Schuster, 1970. Has information on additives and on inadequacies of FDA regulation.

Jacobson, Michael. *Eater's Digest: The Consumer's Factbook of Food Additives*. New York: Anchor, 1972.

———. *Nutrition Scoreboard*. Washington, D.C.: Center for Science in the Public Interest, 1973.

Kotz, Nick. *Let them Eat Promises: the Politics of Hunger in America*. New York: Doubleday, 1971.

Margolis, Sidney. *The Great American Food Hoax*. New York: Pocket Books, 1972.

National Academy of Sciences. *Recommended Daily Allowances*. 8th edition. Washington, D. C., 1974.

Rodale, Jerome I. *The Complete Book of Food and Nutrition*. Emmaus, Pa.: Rodale Books, 1966.

Science Teaching Group. *Feed, Need, Greed: Where Will it Lead? A Classroom Approach to World Hunger and Population Growth*. Science for the People, 9 Walden St., Jamaica Plain, Massachusetts 02130.

Turner, James S. *The Chemical Feast*. New York: Grossman, 1970.

Union of Radical Political Economists. *Food Packet*. URPE, P. O. Box 331, Cathedral Station, New York, N. Y. 10025.

U. S. Department of Agriculture. *Composition of Foods, Raw, Processed, Prepared*. Handbook #8. Washington, D. C., 1963.

Wickstrom, Lois. *The Food Conspiracy Cookbook*. San Francisco: 101 Productions, 1974.

Williams, Sue R. *Nutrition and Diet Therapy*. Second edition. St. Louis: Mosby, 1973.

Some of the magazines dealing with nutrition are *Prevention*, *Food Technology*, *Organic Gardening and Farming, Today's Health*, *Nutrition Today*, and *Science for the People*.

The U. S. Government Printing Office publishes pamphlets about food. Some of the most useful are:

"How to Buy Fresh Vegetables." Home & Garden Bulletin #143.

"How to Buy Fresh Fruits." Home & Garden Bulletin #141.

"How to Buy Beans, Peas, and Lentils." Home & Garden Bulletin #177.

"USDA Grades." Bulletin #196.

"Cheese Varieties." Handbook #54. Has complete information on almost all cheeses: their methods of preparation, quality variations, and analysis (moisture, fat, protein, salt, etc., in percentages).

There are many more on fish, meat, and home canning, freezing, and storing.

Full-color charts from the Government Printing Office ($1.50 each) show the different edible marine fishes of the North Atlantic and North Pacific. Write to the Superintendent of Documents, Washington, D. C. 20402, or check out the nearest government bookstore. Subscribe to the USDA's *Dairy Market News* (Federal Office Building, 970 Broad St., Room 930, Newark N. J. 07102) and *The Packer* (1 Gatewy Center, Kansas City, Kansas 66101) to keep tabs on the food industry.

You can find repair manuals and books on equipment in the library; in addition, we highly recommend *The Co-op Cooler Book*, published and distributed by the Red Star Repair Company, 123 E. 26 St., Minneapolis 55404. See also: *Public Works*, edited by Walter Szykitka. New York: Lynx Press. Distributed by Quick Fox, Inc.

Warehouses of Co-op label groceries are:

Associated Cooperatives, Inc.
4801 Central Ave.
Richmond, CA 94804

Mid-Eastern Cooperatives, Inc.
75 Amor Ave.
Carlstadt, NJ 07072

Midland Co-ops
2021 East Hennepin Ave.
Minneapolis, MN 55413

7. Decision Making

MOST CO-OPS make decisions democratically according to the Rochdale principle of one member one vote. But voting, either in meetings or in elections, can often be a means of ratifying decisions rather than making them. How are decisions really made in general meetings, elected boards and collectives? And what are the less visible informal ways in which decisions are made? A little discussion about this process in the beginning can save your co-op a lot of problems later on.

General Meetings

General meetings can work as decision-making bodies if they are not too large. The larger the general meeting becomes, the more likely it is to be a ratifying body — approving or vetoing decisions that have already been made by formal committees or informal caucuses.

Way back in 1969 when the Cambridgeport Food Co-op was just getting started, every Monday night members packed into Eddie's big living room to discuss what had gone wrong the previous week and how they could solve it this week. There was no problem with absenteeism since each meeting ended with food ordering. The co-op's membership of thirty people was small enough to ensure workable meetings.

A different person chaired the meeting each week. Fresh out of the political activism that had shaken universities in the late 1960s, co-op members were determined to avoid having leaders. It wasn't until many months later that they realized that a natural leadership had developed, without which the co-op could not have operated smoothly.

The weekly meetings of the early Cambridgeport Co-op made all decisions because there was no other formal structure and no informal groups had yet developed to make decisions between meetings. Usually, a sense of the meeting would be reached before an actual vote had to be taken. When the question before the group split it into opposing factions to such a degree that compromise and consensus were impossible, it would resort to votes. Many small co-ops still make decisions this way.

The ease with which this co-op made decisions at its inception did not last long. The co-op eventually grew to over two hundred members — a heterogeneous group of students, college graduates, working-class families and elderly residents of Cambridgeport. General meetings are still the formal means of making decisions, but they are held once a month at the permanent distribution center. Attendance by thirty or forty people is considered a big success. A group of active members makes most of the decisions, with the others at the meetings ratifying them. The informal decision makers often discuss problems among themselves, reach tentative solutions, and place topics on the agenda for the next meeting, where the recommended solutions are usually accepted.

This situation is common in co-ops. Informal decision making is often as important as, or more important than, formal decision making. It is the cement that holds the formal, structural bricks together and keeps the building standing. As most Americans realized, the decision to impeach former President Nixon was not made during the televised Judiciary Committee debate but in the corridors of Congress and in the houses of individual representatives.

Americans are not accustomed to exercising control over their own institutions. Occasionally we do vote for our elected representatives and then we defer to them the right to make decisions that affect our lives. All that we retain is the right to bitch about the lousy decisions they make. This lack of control over our own institutions influences how we behave in co-ops.

Most co-op members are more willing to participate in the tasks required to run the co-op than they are to participate in decision making. Co-ops for their part are often willing to deprive members of the right to order food or buy at the store if they are lax about doing their work, but hardly ever use this sanction to get people to come to meetings. Instead, most co-ops prefer to rely on positive inducements such as having meetings double with potluck suppers, boogies, or other social functions. The Avenues Co-op in Austin, Texas, regularly serves beer at the end of meetings. Publicizing the meetings and discussing the issues on the agenda in newsletters, leaflets and posters are also effective means of increasing attendance; word of mouth communication is even better. But the best means of assuring good attendance is to have good meetings. Boring, drawn-out meetings at which issues do not get resolved are the surest way to stifle interest and create attendance problems. "Meetings that produce nothing but further meetings are perhaps the main organizational disease of the movement" (*The Organizer's Manual*).

How to Have Good Meetings

Try to keep meetings informal. Don't use parliamentary procedure unless the meeting is so large that you have to. *Robert's Rules of Order* can be self-defeating. At a meeting in Chicago, it took three quarters of an hour to go through one page of minutes because of various points of order.

As a first step establish an agenda in advance and post it at the store or distribution point with plenty of blank space for members to write in their own subjects for discussion. This not only increases attendance but it allows people to prepare their own ideas on the issues. During the meetings, the agenda can act like a road map, keeping everyone on course and letting people know how much time they can spend before moving on to other questions.

Time control is essential. A delicate balance must be established between cutting off a good discussion and letting things run too long. Here's where a sensitive chairperson helps, although collectives often run their meetings without a chairperson. Chairing a meeting consists of more than wielding a heavy gavel and calling on people to speak. The chairperson should be sensitive to the relative importance of the issue and to the feelings of the participants. Some decisions warrant more discussion than others. To limit debate or call for a vote too early can result in feelings of resentment and in a poor, hastily made decision. Letting debate run too long can be equally damaging. The chairperson must also be sensitive to when a meeting is getting blocked by a tough issue. If a decision is not pressing, it may be best to table the discussion and let people think and talk about the problem in the interim before the next meeting.

A distinction that is sometimes missed by meetings using rules of procedure is the difference between "tabling" and "returning to committee." Tabling means postponing the decision. It presumes that all the necessary information has been presented. "Returning to committee" means that more research must be done.

The tone, quality, and direction of a meeting depend largely on the chairperson. The chairperson should see that everyone gets a chance to talk and that a few aggressive people don't dominate. The chairperson should look on his or her role as arbiter, not powerbroker. Rotate the job to develop different people's abilities.

One of the hardest things to deal with in a meeting is the behavior of obstructionists. The best-run meetings can be disrupted by one dogmatic loudmouth. Friendship and cooperative respect often mitigate this problem in food co-ops, but try to keep alert to what's going on, and find out what's really bugging the obstructionist. Someone other than the chairperson may be able to take him or her aside and discover what the real problem is.

A calm tone is important. If things get antagonistic, someone might request a moment of silence. This gives people a chance to think, and allows quieter members to voice their views after the silence has ended. At the Boston Food Co-op's board meetings, a requested moment of silence takes precedence over all other business. Simply not making noise together helps members to keep perspective. Other hints:

Divide into small groups whenever issues are complicated or when there is uncertainty about people's feelings. Sometimes you can break into smaller groups just to get more participation and feedback. Be sure there's enough space in the meeting room for small groups to work without disturbing each other.

Know the members' level of interest in the topic. Watch carefully for signs of people nodding out.

Keep your members' schedules in mind when planning meetings. Many preorders have meetings just after order forms are brought in or food is picked up. Early evening may be best for most members.

Too many meetings or meetings that are too long make for frustration. Discussing nuts and bolts that could be taken care of by a good work system can drain people's energies. Items that small groups can deal with might be given in summary reports to the whole meeting.

If specific decisions are made, make sure you know how they'll be implemented. Too many people debate and O.K. work that goes by default to others. Gentle reminders of our interdependence are essential.

Consensus and Voting

Consensus means reaching a unanimous decision through discussion and compromise. The spirit of a cooperative allows for consensus, as well as majority rule. Consensus may require full discussion, but it assumes that members are prepared to cooperate. People are more likely to make an idea workable if they haven't been forced to accept it without full discussion. Those with criticisms are less likely to sabotage an idea if their opinions are heard and considered.

People are sometimes scared away from the idea of consensus decision making without even trying it. Getting everyone to agree may seem impossible. In practice, reaching consensus need take no longer than bringing a question to a vote. Discussions work around an issue and in a short time zero in on a consensus. Someone may say that it seems that the group feels this way or that way, or the discussion may just peter out and someone may volunteer to see that the decision is implemented.

In the fall of 1974 the South Cambridge Food Co-op, a block-style preorder, was considering changing its weekly ordering and buying schedule from Friday-Monday to Tuesday-Thursday so that members would have plenty of food for the weekend. All blocks favored this except one, which had many members with 9 to 5 jobs from which they could not easily take time off. They were able to participate in co-op work by filling weekend job slots, but on the proposed new schedule they wouldn't have been able to participate at all. After some discussion the coordinators' meeting decided not to change the schedule after all. One person complained that this was "minority rule," but actually it was consensus decision making in which the overwhelming feeling of the group was that full participation was more important than strict majority rule.

Voting based on majority rule sets up conflicting sides of an issue and creates a dissatisfied minority. Decisions based on consensus do not create losses in the same way, but tend to foster cooperation and compromise. A decision reached by compromise more accurately reflects the feelings of the membership. And without voting, meetings are looser.

Decisions can be made well or poorly with either consensus or voting. When decisions are made well, they are made with maximum input from those in attendance and without undue conflict and labor. Poorly made decisions create dissension, are unequitably made, and result in bad solutions. Neither voting nor consensus has a monopoly on any of these tendencies. Yet they both influence how decisions are made and how the co-op will operate. As Eugene V. Debs once noted, voting is the menu, not the meal. The trouble with voting is that people can too easily become involved in taking sides and winning, rather than in examining issues and finding ways to use their differences creatively.

Co-ops do not need to use one method at the total expense of the other. Sometimes the nature of a decision determines the best way to make it. Nonpartisan issues and specific problems are more conducive to consensus decision making than "either-or" questions are. The decision to spend money on refrigeration to handle meat is not really open to a great deal of compromise. You either carry meat or you don't. This decision would probably be made by voting rather than consensus if everyone is not in agreement.

Don't masquerade majority rule under the guise of consensus. Unanimity means everyone. A consensus is not reached by ignoring the objections of a few dissidents just because their number is small. Vocal activists should not speak for the group, or claim knowledge of the sense of the meeting, before it is evident to all participants. The People's Warehouse in Minneapolis has some useful guidelines for consensus decision making:

> To make decisions by consensus implies that: a) those on the majority side have a special responsibility to question those in the minority so as to understand fully their position, to answer all their fears and misgivings, and to assure the minority that the majority will continue to reevaluate the question; b) the minority has a special responsibility to point out to the majority the shortcomings of the majority position and to suggest an alternative that can accommodate all sides. The minority, however, must be willing, in the interest of unity, to set aside their demands for the time being.

Making decisions by consensus is a skill that takes time and practice to develop.

Weekly meetings may be necessary at the start of your co-op, and may be enjoyable in small groups, but they are usually asking too much of the membership. Biweekly or monthly meetings are more common. Meetings held less frequently usually require the formation of a body to make decisions between meetings. These steering or coordinating committees often develop into the real decision-making bodies. A strong steering committee, made up of members elected at the general meeting, is similar to the next type of decision-making structure, the elected board.

Boards of Directors

Elected boards are the most common decision-making bodies in large food co-ops. They are a compromise between the ideals of mass participatory democracy and the efficiency and centralized control necessary in an economic organization that may have annual sales in the millions of dollars. Mistakes become too costly to be tolerated as easily as they can be in a small preorder. It helps to have some specific people accountable, rather than having responsibility reside in the whole membership.

Participatory democracy need not be totally lost with an elected board. The Boston Food Co-op has twenty committees with open membership, giving members a chance to make decisions about numerous issues and influence board decisions. Board meetings are open to everyone in the co-op.

Co-op members can also contribute to decision making through debate on policy questions during quarterly general meetings, referenda on key issues, and election campaigns of board members. If elections are based on issues rather than personalities, they can effectively influence co-op policy. It helps to have candidates form opposing slates to clarify the issues.

In stores with paid staff, boards are often a necessary check on the day-to-day power of the store collective. They usually have the responsibility to hire and fire staff. Staff members, for their part, usually find it easier to deal with a limited number of elected representatives than with the entire membership at a general meeting.

Limiting staff membership on the board protects the board from the more specific interests of the staff. These interests are harder to counteract in general meetings, where the staff is often deferred to because of its expertise.

The terms of board members and the frequency of elections are important. Board members should be on the job long enough to insure that they learn the task well and to provide stable leadership. Terms should be short enough to insure that board members remain accountable to the membership and that they neither become entrenched nor burn themselves out. A one-year term seems to meet this balance. Elections need not be this infrequent. If half the board is elected every six months, the co-op has a biannual opportunity to discuss issues. This system also allows for continuity within the board, with newly elected members learning from those already on the job.

Boards usually number between five and twenty members, and meet anywhere from weekly to monthly. They develop a specific style of working together based of their members' personalities. Their small size and the frequency of their deliberations are usually advantages. If a board is split by political factions or personality conflicts, these advantages become liabilities.

When factionalism is a problem, boards should discuss it openly and try to discover the real issues behind the conflict. Is it policy differences or just personalities? If board members have strong disagreements, it's better if they're over matters of policy than if they've degenerated into personal feuds. You might try to combat personal clashes by centering attention on issues. Or, to take a rather different approach, try planning a weekend together in the woods to help people iron out their personal differences.

People who run for boards may sometimes be ambitious and egocentric. Even unassuming people may get defensive and competitive in a board situation. To guard against board members who are basically interested in their careers and not in the co-op, you might make sure that a board position is not just a prestige post but is a job requiring real work and concern. Board members should be involved in the day-to-day work of the co-op. At Kokua Country Foods in Honolulu, board members work in the co-op three hours per week. But you can overdo it. Common Market in Denver, in an attempt to get a board of directors that knew something about the operation of the store, required that candidates work at least sixty hours in the store during the three-month period before the election. This idea ran aground when it was discovered that in the next election, none of the candidates who weren't part of the store's permanent staff were eligible. The by-law has since been changed.

Boards are in some sense naturally antagonistic. Each member is elected to represent certain people or interests. (Collectives, by contrast, often represent a collective interest; people who don't get along don't usually form collectives.) A board may by accident wind up with ten completely uncongenial tender egos. To combat this natural antagonism and individualism, it may help to form caucuses within the board. Women's caucuses, black caucuses, and caucuses organized around political or policy issues can at least break up individualism by getting people together around common concerns.

Boards may have other problems. Decisions can only be made with the information available. Most board members are generalists, not experts in food sources or store management. Without expert, or at least well-informed, advice, their decisions will lack clarity and depth.

One way to bring expert information into decision making is to have subcommittees of the board, made up of board members and volunteers from the general membership. These committees can supply the board with needed expertise and give nonboard members a chance to participate more actively in decision making.

Problems can develop around the relation of the board to the store staff. A worker can have an inflated ego as easily as a board member, and may think that his or her views are the only ones the board needs to make its decisions. This can be worsened by the fact that most workers are hired and fired by boards. Experienced workers and perceptive board members can help prevent natural and healthy differences of opinion from becoming disruptive.

If enough information is flowing into the board, and if the members have ample time to digest it, they should be able to make intelligent decisions. Like general meetings, boards can work better if decisions are made by consensus instead of voting. If the board has all the information it needs, the discussion can move ahead and the decision may almost make itself. Questions of politics and long-range co-op policy should be deferred to general meetings, referenda, or other means of polling the membership.

It helps to have the relevant people present when deliberations about a certain issue are taking place. If you're thinking about eliminating the bump on canned goods, people working with groceries and finances should be present so that they can give their opinions, be informed of the decision immediately, and know that they've taken part in the decision-making process.

Once a decision is made, it has to be administered. Just informing people of a decision is not enough. Here again, boards can get into trouble if they don't have good communications, or if they are having problems with paid staff. Any decision must be communicated to those responsible for administering it, and to the membership at large.

If subcommittees of the board exist, it's worthwhile to have one responsible for administering decisions. The board should also be aware of the problems of administering a decision while they are drafting it. Too many decisions are made because they sound great, but they may be unenforceable. This can be a problem when political ideals get the better of operational realities. A board may decide to carry only honey from China, but this may be unrealistic because of transportation costs. This isn't to say that you should avoid decisions that make demands on the membership.

Collectives

Collective decision making is often found in community service co-ops that don't require or encourage member participation or that have an open membership policy. It also exists in most warehouses, restaurants, bakeries, and mills that require full-time, committed staff. In Glut and Stone Soup, two storefronts in the Washington, D. C., area, collectives do the work and make the decisions. Both have open community meetings, but usually only workers show up. This is because collective work and collective decision making generally go hand in hand.

Collectives work best in small community stores where the collective is in close face-to-face contact with the rest of the membership. The collective keeps informed of the needs of the membership, and the members of the decisions of the collective. Collectives may be a formalization of a situation that exists in many co-ops. The informal leaders, who develop as the more concerned and active members bubble up through the ranks, are here given a formal role.

The fact that they're self-selected doesn't mean that collectives are antidemocratic. A collective, like an elected board, is accountable to the membership. Its legitimacy resides in its performance. If the collective is out of touch with the desires of most co-op members, its decisions will not be accepted and will have no force or value. In a small store, face-to-face contact between members of the collective and the rest of the co-op can result in a more democratic situation than that achieved by an elected board accountable only at elections.

If collectives discourage other willing co-op members from joining in decision making, they may become cliques, groups that, often unintentionally, exclude outsiders. This cliquism is a symptom of a larger organizational disease. It indicates poor member access to decision making and lack of shared responsibility. If cliquism is a problem, you should try to stimulate discussion of the process of decision making and access to it in your co-op. Please don't ignore this issue if you know it's there. The health of your organization is at stake. If a co-op depends on a small group of people to run it, it will be helpless if the collective burns out or leaves. No members will have been actively learning the skills necessary to take over.

In Minneapolis, all but one of the North Country Store's original collective left the city after less than a year to start Winding Road Farm. The one remaining collective member struggled to get new people into the management of the store and give them the needed skills. In contrast, Mill City Co-op, also in Minneapolis, was able to keep its collective open to new members and had a new collective running the store eight months after its opening.

Decision making in collectives is different from that in elected boards. The closeness of the collective means that members can deal with interpersonal problems and conflicts. Personal ties are much stronger and people can be more open with each other. Consensus decision making is also easier to handle because people are more willing to compromise, having worked together all day.

If internal conflicts are troubling a collective, members can set time aside at the end of meetings to express their feelings about each other and about what has been said. Having time set aside at the end will keep people from bringing feelings up during substantive discussions.

Since collectives are commonly found in co-ops that are just getting underway or are in a state of transition, it's worth discussing how they can pass on their decision-making powers to other bodies. In the case of a collective that becomes an elected board, the situation is self-explanatory. All they have to do is hold elections. If the original members of the collective have been doing a good job, they'll probably be elected. If other people are elected to the board, the change will be one of personalities or policies, but the basic relationship of delegated decision making remains the same.

If a collective chooses to turn power over to the membership at large and have the co-op make decisions through general meetings, more preparation is needed. The co-op members must be educated and informed of the problems they are going to confront. It's advisable for the collective to continue its active role during this period. But it must also be sensitive to when the co-op can take care of itself.

Activists whose co-ops have weaned themselves have important roles helping new co-ops get started. Depending on the backgrounds and experience of the people being organized, many co-ops start as *de jure* or *de facto* collectives. If the activist organizers see themselves as catalysts who come into a community, help it get itself together into a food co-op, and then leave to establish other co-ops, they will have to know how to turn power over to the people they organize. Organizers must be open so that the new co-op will know all the steps it took to get it running; members must have as much information at their disposal as the experienced organizers had. Organizers must also be patient and willing to allow people to make the mistakes by which they learn, rather than jumping in and doing everything for the new co-op.

General meetings, elected boards, and collectives are the three most common formal decision-making structures in co-ops today. But the formal structures don't tell the whole story. Informal decision making is equally important.

Informal Decision Making

Imagine that you are doing the produce buying at the local wholesale market for a preorder co-op. Members have ordered five dozen quarts of strawberries, but at the market you learn that the price has skyrocketed because a wholesaler in California has bought up the last of the harvest. Rather than pay 50% above the usual price, you look around and find a great deal on plums. Your co-op does not have a system of substitutions, but you buy a couple of bushels of plums instead of the strawberries anyway. The plums are sold from the surplus-table without any leftovers, and the people who ordered the strawberries thank you for saving them the money and congratulate you for being a smart buyer. All except one person who spent the previous night making shortcakes and whipping cream.

This is one kind of informal decision making that occurs all the time in food co-ops. Many operating procedures are established this way. Impromptu solutions often become co-op policy without ever being formally ratified. The Central Cambridge Co-op, a large block preorder, has a handbook that details the job of being master-block. The last pages of the booklet are left empty, but are rapidly being filled with suggestions that come out of members' experiences. Rather than being a rigid set of rules, the handbook is a constantly self-amending guide to the co-op's operation.

Impromptu problem-solving is only one form of informal decision making. Decisions can be planned in advance and still be informal, if they are made outside formal structures. A group of members may decide that they want the co-op to carry yogurt. They contact a company that makes good yogurt locally and find out the wholesale price and conditions for delivery. They arrange to get a used refrigerator and come to the next meeting with all their information and a proposal to start buying yogurt. The meeting accepts the idea after five minutes of discussion. The meeting may have formally made the decision, but in fact it was made by the small group of yogurt-hungry cooperators.

Decisions are made before meetings by all sorts of co-op members. They may be a small specific interest group (as in the preceding example), or they may be the "heavies" in the co-op — those who are concerned about the co-op and determined to make it a viable alternative to the capitalist food system. Active members are needed in any co-op to spark the rest of the membership and keep the co-op moving.

Leadership: Organizers and Managers

Some co-op leaders tend to be managers; others tend to be organizers. Managers usually hold elected positions or salaried jobs, or are recognized spokespeople for the co-op. Organizers work at keeping the co-op in motion and at articulating problems, and may shun positions of formal responsibility.

Organizers are concerned with increasing member participation. Their work is getting other people to work, spreading the wealth of participation and expertise. They light fires under people and try to make the co-op more responsive to the members.

Managers take care of problems when they come up, or get others to take care of them. They are mainly concerned with how well the co-op is running. They are often putting out the fires that the organizers are setting. They tend to do the work themselves rather than spreading it around and organizing others to do it. But their egos should not be tied to the exercise of authority. All leaders in fact should be committed to undermining their own authority by educating other people to assume responsibility.

Leadership may be formal or informal. The president of the board is a formal leader. But an active co-op member may be considered a leader by others because of his or her participation, knowledge, past position, or charisma.

Managers are more likely to be formal leaders than organizers are. Positions of authority make it easier for them to do their jobs. Organizers, on the other hand, may be able to work better if they avoid formal leadership positions. Many a valuable organizer has been lost to a co-op through the "reward" of being elected to office. Once elected, the organizer may find it hard to create as much turmoil as is necessary for change. People in positions of authority are less likely to want to attack the *status quo* of which they have become a part.

There are many other types of leaders in co-ops. Opinion leaders are people who have lots of friends and are generally trusted; they may or may not be co-op "heavies." A friend of ours is convinced that opinion leaders always live in the corner house on the block, and figuratively, if not literally, this is so.

Real leadership in a co-op may be informal because people in democratic participatory institutions may try to avoid explicit leadership. But no organization can function without leadership. By ignoring the informal leadership that does exist, co-op members may be giving tacit approval to something they formally oppose. The sudden recognition that a co-op, or any committee within it, does have a group or an individual leading it may cause discontent and

alienation among members who thought that no such leadership existed. This doesn't mean that informal leadership should necessarily be formalized with a title or job description, but that co-op members should try to recognize where informal leadership exists.

Sometimes informal leadership should become formalized. Someone may have been holding the newsletter together without anyone realizing that the newsletter committee even had a coordinator. When this person moves, everyone starts asking, "Where's the box of stencils?" and "Whom do we call now that Carol's not here?" In this case, informal leadership had become essential for the operation of a particular committee without anyone realizing it. Perhaps a formal job should be established.

Informal processes are vital. If things become so overstructured that people don't feel free to be innovative and contribute more than is expected of them, the co-op can become cold, formal, and lacking in the flexibility needed for both survival and growth.

Strong leadership is not antithetical to democracy in co-ops or in any other organizations, provided that the leaders remain accountable to the membership and that democracy is built into the formal decision-making structure. But the most democratic formal structure can be hollow if it is not animated by member participation. People who work in and for the co-op will naturally have more informed and committed contributions to make to decision making.

8. Participation

IF there's one thing that distinguishes the new co-op movement from its predecessors, it's participation. Participation means members actively running the co-op. A co-op may not be run by all members on a voluntary basis, but even with paid staff responsible for day-to-day operations, there are many ways in which members can participate. The larger the number of members who run the co-op and the more kinds of jobs they do, the more participatory the co-op is. Many co-ops *require* participation as a condition of membership. The requirement generally ranges from two to four hours per month, but more active members often spend twice or three times that amount of time working for the co-op.

Voluntary participation in running the co-op saves money for everybody. Jobs done by paid workers in supermarkets are often done for free in co-ops. This cuts operating expenses, keeping the prices close to wholesale.

Participation makes the co-op more democratic. If a co-op is run by a handful of hard-working, dedicated members, there is a tendency to centralize knowledge about co-op operations. Without decentralized knowledge, the members can't make informed decisions and any kind of general meeting or member-elected decision-making body usually becomes a rubber stamp for decisions already made by staff or dedicated volunteers. Knowledge is power in co-ops, and participation yields knowledge.

Furthermore, co-ops run by a few "heavies" tend to fall apart if and when they leave. Burn-out is frequent if the hard workers aren't helped and supported by the rest of the members. Although there are always some people who work harder than the rest — this in itself is not unhealthy — co-ops should try to prevent burn-out, both to avoid making activists bitter and to build up a strong group of people who are comfortable enough with their roles to stay in the co-op movement indefinitely.

There are many advantages to participation for the general membership. As people participate, they learn about the food-distribution process. Going to the produce market, dealing with wholesalers or farmers, and running a small business are educational experiences in the world of food buying and selling. These experiences lead to a deeper understanding of the politics and economics of the whole food process. Running our own community institutions is especially valuable: it's a way of assuming control over a portion of our economic and social lives. The importance of this experience can't be overstated — especially in a country where political passivity is a major obstacle to change. Food co-ops can help teach people the skills they'll need to change the American corporate economy.

Historically, cooperatives have grown in bursts of enthusiasm, then declined when beset with financial and managerial woes. Often overlooked is the fact that a decline of cooperative spirit usually accompanies the other problems. Managerial and money troubles can be remedied, but the spirit, once lost, is hard to regain. Participation can help keep that spirit alive. Without it, today's new-style co-ops may face the situation of the huge Berkeley Consumers Co-op, as described in a recent newsletter:

> The most critical problem facing us is the almost complete uninvolvement of our members . . . Our co-op, one of the largest and most successful in the country, is directed by a clique of no more than 100 members. The inner circle who really participate in decision-making is made up of no more than twenty-five. This from a membership of more than 75,000!

Participation creates social capital. That is, working cooperatively creates positive feelings toward the co-op, which are as necessary to its operations as financial capital is. These good feelings motivate co-op members to relate better to each other and to support the co-op in bad times as well as good.

When a retired man on a fixed income gives $50 of his savings to the Boston Food Co-op after it has just been robbed, we can see social capital converting itself into financial capital. When people shopping at the different co-op stores in Minneapolis drop what they're doing to stand in the cold to help unload the delivery truck from the People's Warehouse, social capital is again at work.

A co-op can earn social capital by being successful. Efficient procedures, quality food at low prices, and cooperative spirit all help generate the positive feelings that create social capital. But the best-run co-op, in itself, may not produce much social capital. It's necessary for the members to feel responsible for that success. Participation is the best way to foster that feeling.

The cooperative experience is at the heart of social capital. It's based on people working together to achieve something unattainable to them as individuals. Whether people are raising a barn or pushing a car out of the snow, they feel exhilaration from working together.

The first day of operations for a preorder co-op is amazing. After weeks of preparation, everyone gets together at distribution and usually just stands around grinning at the cases of food. "Look at all that food!" "And those prices!" "Far out, we really did it." It's quite a high. Maintaining that high and making it work for the co-op takes both planning and effort.

Interdependence — Accountability — Sharing Expertise

Interdependence describes the nature of the cooperative relationship. Co-ops work best when members are neither completely dependent on, nor completely independent from, each other. When we need other people, and at the same time are needed by them, we create an interdependent relationship. I depend on you to buy the food this week, and in turn you depend on me to cut up and wrap the cheese.

The more co-op work can be structured so that people work together, the more interdependence grows. One person may be able to cut the cheese, but the experience is more rewarding if two do it. They can then do the work faster, get to know each other, share their cheese-cutting skills, and have a better time.

In the competitive capitalist society, interdependence is ignored and people find themselves in roles that are usually dependent and occasionally independent. Generally, we work for a boss or an institution. We know what is expected of us; someone else sets the goals. Dependency is an agreement to relinquish control over our lives to someone or something else. Independence is the narrowly defined "freedom" we have to compete with each other. People in co-ops can learn that they need be neither dependent nor independent, but can become interdependent.

Accountability is the co-op members' responsibility to each other. It's a two-way street. Members are accountable to the co-op for their work requirements, dues or fees, and participation. The co-op is accountable to its members for its operations, policies, and service. Staff is accountable for its work and its day-to-day decisions.

Accountability means that one member can feel comfortable telling another member that she or he is not doing her or his job well. It means that the member at the door can tell you without feeling guilty that you can't shop in the store this week because you haven't fulfilled your work hours. It also means that you can go up to last week's buyer and complain about the overripe tomatoes or too expensive pears.

Accountability works best when people know each other, and can give and take advice and criticism without offense. When co-ops become very large, impersonal rules may replace personal accountability. In a large co-op, accountability is most effective within small work teams.

Sharing expertise is essential in a participatory co-op. Some members always have more knowledge about a specific operation than does the average member. If we want people to participate, we have to share the "expert's" know-how with the rest of the co-op. Co-op heavies are often so busy working that they don't realize that they are monopolizing knowledge. This problem cuts two ways. The heavies must make the time to share their experience. They can do this formally through orientation or training programs, newsletter articles, or job-description leaflets or posters; or informally through conversations with members. At the same time, members should be aware of, and try to overcome, their socially conditioned passivity and to ask questions and demand instruction.

Nonmember Policy

Most co-ops have members; in fact, co-ops are traditionally defined as member-owned organizations. But in the contemporary co-op movement, some nonprofit service stores that subscribe to co-op goals do not have strict definitions of membership. They feel that a membership policy prevents the store from serving the whole community; some people are simply not joiners, but all people are entitled to fresh, wholesome foods at nonexploitative prices.

Many other co-op stores, and even some preorders, have rather loosely defined membership policies. A member may be anyone who pays a fee, fills out an application, does voluntary work, comes to meetings, or buys shares. Some co-ops distinguish between working members and nonworking members, and charge a higher markup to nonworking members.

In addition to these variations in membership policy, some co-ops allow nonmembers to shop. They generally either charge nonmembers higher prices for food or add a higher surcharge onto their total purchases. The Puget Sound Co-op in Seattle charges members a 16% markup and nonmembers a 32% markup. The Ecology Food Co-op in Philadelphia charges nonmembers a 40% markup, nonworking members a 25% markup, and working, or participating, members a 12½% markup. Many other stores have variations on these policies. Although such policies make the co-op tradeoff of participation in exchange for lower prices very clear, they also create a stratification that may conflict with cooperative values, and they perpetuate the notion that the rich are privileged to have others work for them.

Allowing nonmembers to use the co-op permits it to increase its volume. Small preorders may do this to meet crate sizes; that is, they buy full crates, then sell the unused fractions to anyone. Such a policy can be a good organizing tool for a co-op wishing to grow, or one that is about to expand by starting another distribution center or storefront. A co-op in Waterville, Maine, allows nonmembers to order twice before deciding whether or not to join.

An open nonmember policy is also a good intermediate step for a capitalist store evolving into a co-op. The patrons of such a store may not be quite ready to pitch in and join the work. While the store is considering becoming cooperative in terms of finances and staff, some informal education can be going on as customers come in. This is how the St. Anthony Park grocery in Minneapolis became a co-op. The Growing Tree Co-op in Spencer, West Virginia, was also originally a profit-making store. Gradually, some of the customers may become participating members.

In Minneapolis-St. Paul, most of the fifteen co-op stores are open to nonmembers who pay a higher surcharge than members do. These small storefronts are generally well-integrated into their neighborhoods. Their nonmember policy has increased volume, resulting in a greater variety of food and a lower surcharge all around.

The cohesion of the community has helped mitigate problems of ripoffs by nonmembers. This might not hold true in a neighborhood lacking such cohesion. In fact, ripoffs have been a serious problem in several co-op stores and they sometimes can be traced to an open nonmember policy or to a nonparticipating, uninvolved membership. The Roxbury-Dorchester storefront in Boston doesn't let anyone in the store without a membership card. Their security needs are dictated by the desires of their membership and their location in a poor, urban neighborhood.

There are numerous problems with opening a co-op to nonmembers. The members must see some advantage to the rights and obligations of membership. Although price differentials are the most common way of favoring members, many people would gladly pay a little more to be freed from work obligations.

The Freedom Foods Co-op in Stony Brook, New York, used to sell at 30% markup to nonmembers and 10% to members. "We ended this policy," writes one co-op worker, "because it was in violation of the cooperative spirit. To enjoy the benefits of the co-op people should have to contribute labor and themselves. To be able to buy co-op buying privileges for a higher price is a contradiction of what cooperatives are all about."

Co-ops with a high proportion of nonmembers or with a very loosely defined membership sometimes take a paternalistic attitude toward their community. That is, the organizers in the name of efficiency behave as though people are incapable of taking care of themselves and must therefore be *helped*. This condescending attitude enforces dependency among the people who use the co-op, and perpetuates their powerlessness. A co-op that assumes it can't serve all the people if it insists on a membership policy may be writing its community off before really trying to organize it. The assumption that people won't buy in a store if they have to work there denies them power and keeps them dependent.

Systems of Job Allocation

At the Freedom Foods Co-op, one member relates, volunteers crowd behind the counter, bumping into each other, until there are sometimes more volunteers "working" than members shopping in the store. The problem seems to be lack of a job allocation system.

Every participatory co-op needs some way of deciding who does what. This is important not only so that all necessary jobs get done, but so that people learn new skills and feel that they've contributed to the co-op.

The three most common systems of allocating voluntary labor are random, rotation, and job specific. In the random system, people volunteer for whatever jobs they feel like doing that week or month. They can express their preferences at meetings or on a sign-up sheet at the store or distribution center. Or they can communicate with a job coordinator by phone.

The least structured of the three systems, random job allocation, sometimes gives the appearance of being no system at all. In fact, there is a system and when things are flowing as they should, people are exercising their free choice to participate in whatever way they want. As we pointed out in Chapter 3, organization is important to create the necessary structures that allow the co-op to operate efficiently. Beyond this, unnecessary structures can block the natural flow of people's energies and thwart their free participation. A balance must be reached between the organization necessary for an efficient operation and the freedom necessary for spontaneous participation. Where random job allocation works, it maintains that balance.

The smaller the co-op, the easier it is to use the random system effectively. Breaking down a large co-op into smaller work groups or blocks is helpful in this respect. Each work group or block is responsible for operations for a certain week or month, and within this smaller group, people may know each other well enough and communicate easily enough to use random job allocation.

Rotation is a more structured system. A cycle of all the necessary jobs is established, and every time a member works, he or she does the next job in the cycle. The rotation system can provide the order that may be lacking in the random system. It guarantees that most members learn to do most jobs. Its disadvantages arise from its rigidity. Rotation prevents people who like one job from doing it all the time. As a result, people trade jobs with their friends, who may then forget to show up. The price of order and equal distribution of work and knowledge may be the discontent of members who are inclined to participate but who feel that the rotation system is too structured. In addition, certain skills like truck maintenance or buying food require more expertise than others and may demand more continuity than the rotation system provides.

The job-specific system is probably the most efficient because people get to be expert at their tasks. Everyone in the co-op has a specific job or joins a job-specific work team for a fairly long period of time (three months, six months, etc.). Members of work teams can get to know each other well and enjoy working together.

In a store with a permanent staff, job-specific work teams can take care of many special operations. Food Front, a co-op store in Portland, Oregon, has an extremely well-organized spice and tea section. All items are prepackaged by a crew of volunteers who bag each Wednesday evening at a member's house. There are typed-up explanations of the medicinal values of the various teas. This is the only area of the store not run by the paid staff and it's a good example of how volunteers can take full responsibility for a particular part of the co-op.

A job-specific system encourages a proliferation of jobs. The Free Venice Food Co-op in Los Angeles has twenty-one separate job-specific teams. In addition to the usual preorder jobs of collating, buying, trucking, sorting, bookkeeping, setting up, and cleaning up, there are work teams for individual foods like fish and bread, the container team keeps the distribution center well-stocked with bags, cartons and jars, and there are even teams for babysitting and beekeeping.

As the membership grows, more and more jobs can be established. Newsletter committees, study groups, and free stores can develop. These "nonessential" jobs can grow into important co-op activities and help build a community out of a band of consumers.

If you use a job-specific system, you will need a good education program to inform members of the overall operation of the co-op so that they can be as effective making decisions as they will be doing their jobs.

These three job allocation systems — random, rotation and job-specific — exist in many combinations. You might want to experiment with each to see which suits your co-op. If your co-op has problems getting the necessary work done, examine your job allocation system and see if another might be better. Of course, not all work problems are traceable to unsuitable job allocation. It may just be a matter of inconvenient times and places. Or there may be real problems of participation that have to be dealt with on an educational level.

Problems of Participation

American society is not the best breeding ground for cooperative participation. People join co-ops with preconceived notions and values that can impede full participation. Some of the common problems include noncooperation, supermarket manners, the mystique of certain jobs, sexism, and ageism.

Noncooperation happens when people just won't do their share. Many co-ops have a requirement that says no work, no food. Or, in more positive terms, equal work for equal savings. You can be flexible about such a policy, but you can apply it firmly when you have to. There may be many reasons to overlook a member's temporary lapse, but a chronic noncooperator should probably be asked to leave the co-op. Very often the mere endorsement of such a policy by the membership can raise people's awareness of the need to participate to the point where the policy never has to be enforced.

Here are some other suggestions for dealing with people who aren't doing their share:

Remind them that part of the reason they save money is that people put in the work themselves. Add that a commitment of two to four hours per month really isn't much, considering all the advantages of membership.

Ask them if anyone else in their household can work. Find out the schedules of all household members and provide options that fit in.

Ask them what they like to do. If you have a big co-op, you should be able to find something. At the Boston Food Co-op some members fulfill their work hours by playing music in the store, and one member does it by donating his services as a dentist.

Drop hints about how well their neighbors, who have equally busy schedules, are doing their work.

Remind them that if something is important enough, people make time. Food is certainly important.

If all else fails and they remain uncooperative, ask them to leave. People who won't contribute shouldn't expect to benefit.

*

"Supermarket manners" refers to the ways people relate to each other in capitalist retail stores. When people join co-ops they often bring this old behavior with them. For example, Bill had just stepped out of the walk-in cooler when somebody approached him and asked, "Are you working here?" When he said yes, the person's attitude changed immediately and commands began to flow. "I want some pears and there are none left in the crates. Will you get me some? And while you're at it, I didn't see any lettuce." Bill explained that they were both co-op members and not employee and customer in a supermarket. After a short discussion they both went into the cooler and together carried out the pears and lettuce.

In supermarkets, the customer expects service as the minimal return for high prices. Stock clerks are ordered to check for items not on the shelves. Butchers are expected to cut it the way the customer wants it. No one attempts to clean up the broken jar of applesauce — someone is paid to do that. Customers wait on check-out lines reading *TV Guide*s or the backs of cereal boxes rather than talking with those around them. People rarely help each other, or ask about the quality or economy of food.

In co-ops, member participation and education create cooperative manners to replace the old supermarket manners. Though this is a natural development of cooperative experiences, it has to be encouraged in some people more than others.

The mystique of certain jobs is a two-sided notion: the fear people have of doing something new, and the expectation that others will do it for them. "I can't do the books" or "I've never driven a truck before" are common excuses to avoid certain jobs. Some people mystify a job to make it seem overly complicated or important. The best way to destroy the myth is to help them do the job.

In a small co-op, all the jobs are easy enough to do. In more complex co-ops, certain jobs may be done by full-time staff but even these can be simplified so that all members can understand what's happening. Often, proper instruction and little time are all that's needed to help a member learn to do a job. If certain jobs require some skill, a training program can be set up.

The Eagle Heights Co-op in Madison, Wisconsin, has a good system of teaching store operations to new members. The jobs are broken down into job-specific work teams. There are eight "affinity groups" in each team; each affinity group does its job in the store for half a week at a time. Within each affinity group a volunteer coordinator assigns experienced and inexperienced members to work together as a form of job training. Once new members have learned the job they can do it themselves. As the more experienced members get into the subtleties of the job they can become coordinators. This system has been very successful and Eagle Heights is run entirely by participating members.

Food co-ops can teach their members how to run a small business. This experience can prepare people for taking greater control over their lives and the lives of their communities. Co-ops would be doing their members a disservice if they reinforced the attitude that experts are needed to do for us what we can do for ourselves. Job descriptions, education programs, and on-the-job training are all it takes. The first step is refusing to allow people to avoid work just because they don't think they can do it.

Sexism refers to our society's deeply held attitudes toward women's and men's roles. To assure participation by all co-op members, we have to be aware of the many ways sexism influences the roles people play in co-ops. The major problem is the avoidance of cooperative responsibilities by husbands who assume that gathering food is women's work. This problem exists in rich, middle-class, working-class, and poor households; in suburbs, cities, and country towns. It robs the co-op of the energies of many of its members and it denies those members the rewards of cooperative experience.

The other side of the sexist coin is that women often think they're incapable of handling "men's work" in the co-op. For some people "men's work" includes driving the truck or carrying heavy crates and bags; for others it can be coordinating, chairing meetings, or filling other positions of responsibility. Here too the co-op is denied the resources of its female members, and women cut themselves off from rewarding experiences.

Although a fuller analysis of sexual roles is given in Chapter 16, we want to mention several ways in which you can combat these twin results of sexism. Men can be encouraged to participate if this situation is discussed during the initial organizing of the co-op. Men should know that participation is expected of them and the co-op does not share their view that co-op work is women's work. Work times must be adjusted so that working people can participate. Ask men to contribute the skills they have learned on the job or around their homes. These can range from accounting to plumbing — anything that will get them involved.

Men can also learn from the example of other men. Young and elderly male members, who usually have the time and inclination to work, can set an example of male participation. If, after public discussion and private cajoling, there are still some men who won't participate, you might consider a policy of requiring each member to do his or her own work hours.

Encouraging full participation by women is easier. Examples within the co-op or from other co-ops can help. Co-op women run warehouses throughout the country. Their jobs range from supervising the finances to unloading fifty-pound bags of grain. A women's trucking collective was active in Washington, D.C., for several years.

A bigger problem may be women's participation in decision making. Invisible husbands often appear at meetings when the "big decisions have to be made" and immediately dominate their wives. Active women at meetings should set an example by asking the silent women for their views. If the co-op has a policy of equal participation by men and women in decision making, members can be brought to task for sexism.

Discrimination against people because of age may also prevent full participation. Both the old and the young can make important contributions to the co-op, yet too often they are ignored or taken for granted. People assume that teenagers are irresponsible and that old people are weak or incompetent. Both assumptions are false.

The young and old are major resources for co-ops. They have time, energy, skills, and the desire to contribute. Retired members have a lot of time to devote to co-op work, if the co-op is receptive and set up to make use of it.

Fighting ageism also means being aware of the cultural differences among age groups and having respect for the needs of those who may be a minority of the membership. Elderly people may be put off by the language, dress, and behavior of the young, and vice versa. For the young, being considerate doesn't mean cutting your hair or wearing a bra, but it may mean tying your hair back while you're cutting cheese, or watching your language while shopping. Cooperative contact may help both old and young reevaluate some prejudices.

Informal Participation

So far we've been talking about formal participation, but informal participation is important too. Co-op members who know and like each other, who eat, drink, dance, and do other social things together will look forward to working together on co-op jobs. It's a good idea to have a social committee to organize boogies, potluck suppers, picnics, and even weekend retreats. Getting the ingredients together for these bashes is often a fair amount of work, but it's rewarding for co-op members to have social events to look forward to, and to have some way to relate to each other aside from food. In some parts of rural New England, co-op square dances are regular events. Whether you're planning city or country dances, try to find the necessary musical talent within the co-op.

A potluck supper is one of the best means of combining business with pleasure. A small co-op in Allston, Massachusetts, which was converting to a block structure, held a series of block potluck suppers to help ease the transition. Long after the immediate need for them had ended, these block potlucks continued.

You may be able to borrow films from your library or buy tickets to events in wholesale quantities. You might try co-ed baseball, basketball, or touch football — or have one co-op challenge another.

Spinoff Activities

Organizing spinoff activities related to membership needs is an excellent way to build social capital. Volunteers may put in their work hours by organizing these groups. One typical spinoff activity is child care. The child care committee can organize a drop-in center for parents shopping, doing co-op work, or attending meetings; it can organize cooperative playgroups among parents, or co-op babysitting services in which parents swap sitting time. Eventually it can look into setting up a permanent daycare center in the community.

For a group at the other end of the age spectrum, it's often wise to form a committee concerned with the special needs of the elderly. This group might provide transportation to the co-op, assistance in getting food orders together, and help in carrying heavy loads. It can bring older people into co-op activities. One committee of this sort organized co-op parties for elderly members who lived in nursing homes.

A skill-swapping bank can easily grow from random notices posted on a co-op bulletin board. It can operate as many babysitting co-ops do, with "chits" or index cards representing hours of work. People pay each other in chits for work done, be it painting, roofing, hauling, plumbing, wiring, etc. The Food Conspiracy in Tucson has a "Work Conspiracy," which lists 132 different skills, from goat husbandry to foot massage.

A good project is a free store that can exist in a spare corner of the co-op. People bring in what they no longer need and trade or get what they now need. It's surprising how much stuff will come and go, and a small group is needed to keep it all in order. A friend of ours once collected a whole wardrobe for a two-year old from such an operation.

You can establish any number of small producers' collectives for granola making, juicing, milling, etc. You can have an organizer's committee for people who like to problem-solve, for those starting new co-ops, and for those in other co-ops who want to swap organizing information. Finally, men's and women's consciousness-raising groups can be formed through notices on the co-op bulletin board. See Chapter 9 for more ideas on spinoff activities.

Staffs and Collective Experiences

Many co-op stores and some preorders have permanent staffs that, since they participate more intensively in the co-op, have their own unique set of problems and experiences.

Most, but not all, co-op staffs are collectives. They think of themselves as a unit. They are collectively, not individually, responsible to the co-op, and they make decisions and structure their work democratically, not hierarchically. Co-op members may work together several hours a month; collective members usually work together twenty to sixty hours a week. Responsibility is shared by a much smaller group.

Along with the extra responsibility and work come extra rewards. These are not only monetary, though co-ops try to pay their workers living wages. Collectives break down the worker-boss dichotomy; no one makes a profit from others' labor. The collective does the work and the collective makes the decisions. The job is also satisfying because you're serving the people of your community. Collectives not only run co-ops but supply grains and other staples to entire regions and bake all the bread sold to the cooperative community in some cities. The Seattle Workers Brigade, an organization of producers' collectives, supplies food to co-ops, mills flour, runs a restaurant, provides accounting help to alternative businesses, and fixes automobiles.

The collective relationship lies somewhere between the accountability of a co-op and the intimacy of a family. In co-ops, accountability controls public cooperative behavior. People do not hold each other accountable for personal or political behavior. In collectives, people are held responsible for a much broader range of views and actions. The collective requires intensive constructive criticism to work effectively. Not only does the job have to get done, but the example of the collective to the rest of the cooperative community must be positive. Political criticism and self-criticism is an active part of many collective relationships. Here is where the balance between friendship and intimacy is hardest to draw. Collectives are still made up of individuals who have different needs for privacy and communication.

Collectives must develop comfortable situations in which criticism is not a threat. Constructive criticism is hard to give and even harder to take. A base of friendship, trust, and mutual respect is needed. We all have to learn that we are not perfect and need criticism to develop as fuller and more cooperative individuals. Compliments, though, are as important as criticism. We can learn from each other's strong points and a little ego support is not going to hurt. In writing this book, our collective has found that constantly and routinely reading, criticizing, and rewriting each other's work has made us used to and more willing to take criticism from each other.

If you enter a collectively managed co-op, you may see people who seem casual about the work they are doing. But behind this exterior lies an entrepreneurial spirit unmatched by the leading corporations. Just the values are different. People aren't working for a profit, but for a decent wage. Costs aren't cut to increase profits, but to decrease prices. People move from ordering food to doing the books to unloading a truck. There are no executives, no professionals, and no differences in pay scale, except those based on need. No job is demeaned for being either manual or "intellectual." All are necessary for the total effort, hence all are respected.

A collective embodies the idea of worker control. The means of production (the tools and machines used to produce a product) may be owned by the co-op, but the collective controls the process on a day-to-day basis. This is radically different from working in a capitalist enterprise, even a hip or a benign one.

The work experience in a collective is also influenced by the collective's politics. In San Francisco, half the members of the warehouse collective must be women. With an equal ratio of men and women set up by rule, the struggle against sexism can proceed on an equal footing. Women are not second-class citizens in collectives. They are not relegated to typewriters or telephones. They drive trucks, unload sacks, and take an equal share in decision making. Working collectively offers an alternative to the isolation of working for oneself, or the exploitation of working for "the Man."

Collectives sometimes have trouble relating to the rest of the co-op, especially if the co-op is participatory. A balance has to be established between the responsibilities of the collective and those of the other co-op members. If the collective keeps in mind the concepts of interdependence, accountability, and sharing expertise, it should be able to create a relationship acceptable to both groups. There are no tight definitions of this balance. Each co-op must study its own operations and values to find the answer that meets its needs.

In defining these needs, co-op and collective members must weigh two often conflicting values — the need for member participation and the need for permanent staff. Either need in the extreme can rule out the other, but a balance can be reached. The nature of the job will often decide whether it should be done by a paid collective or a volunteer work team. Jobs that require a great deal of expertise, responsibility, or personal contact with wholesalers may lend themselves more to paid staff positions than to rotating groups of volunteers. But if food co-ops are to remain participatory, the members who have the final control must have the information and experience on which to base decisions. Collectives must share that experience and knowledge with them.

9. Communication and Education

In a purely economic relationship, two people can go into a room, each with a dollar. They can exchange dollars. In a cooperative situation, two people can go into a room, each with an idea. Each can come away with two ideas. This is the essence of cooperative education.

Communication and education in your co-op can start with orientation and continue with training programs, study groups, newsletters, posters, committees of correspondence, and innumerable other formal and informal means. In Denver, the Common Market has monthly orientation meetings with guest speakers and free beer afterward. In San Francisco, people from the four co-op stores and the warehouse get together to produce one newsletter. *The Scoop* in Minneapolis provides detailed news of activity in co-op stores, restaurants, farms, and other production units. The Austin Community Project has one member who concentrates on maintaining a photographic file of co-op activity.

Orientation

Education starts with a good orientation program. Orientation may take the form either of formal classes or informal gatherings at people's houses. Hopefully orientation will give new members an understanding of the interdependence of theory and practice. Those interested in pursuing co-op history and philosophy can set up study groups.

To start a formal orientation program, organize a small group of volunteers, with or without teaching experience, and write a curriculum. People should probably team-teach, and classes should be small enough for people to get acquainted in one meeting. If you have the resources, get a committee together to provide audiovisuals: slide shows, photographs, video tape, film, etc. Although far from necessary, these can be useful in orienting new members, and in helping to start new co-ops.

It may take a while to organize an orientation program. The Boston Food Co-op decided to have one a year and a half before it actually got started. A class situation was decided on, although it's not a formally structured class in the sense of a teacher dispensing wisdom and students passively absorbing it. Of course, you may convey information to new members in nonclass situations as well. At the Cambridge Food Co-op store, orientation doubles with sign-up and payment of membership fee.

It's good to begin with a little history and philosophy. It's important for people to know that co-ops were around in the1930s, and that most of them disappeared, and why. You should also discuss the history of your own operation, to give new members a sense of its trials, tribulations, and successes.

You should cover the varieties of co-op evolution and structure. Even if your co-op is a store, provide a brief description of preorders. Some members may eventually decide they would rather organize a preorder than remain in a store. Preorders should describe store structures to give people a sense of one possible direction for growth.

Discuss the extended co-op community. The Boston Food Co-op's orientation leaders emphasize that their co-op has friends throughout New England and in other parts of the country. Co-op people get together frequently to combine buying power and share experiences. Talk about the economic and political importance of building federations.

All your members should understand how the co-op operates, so that if they see something wrong, they can correct it, even if it isn't their "job." Show how the different departments operate, and have people knowledgeable in those areas available to answer questions. Point out that members can help the co-op even while they're shopping, by cleaning up, straightening out displays, closing cooler doors if they're left open, cutting cheese, or bagging grain if supplies are running low. As the folks in Austin say, "When a member comes in and says, 'Do you have butter today?' something's wrong. When a member comes in and says, 'Do we have butter today?' we've come a long way."

Ask new members how they want to relate to the co-op. This gives less active people a chance to talk with more active ones. It's also an excellent way to find out who the potentially more active members are. Once you know their interests, you can direct them to people who are working on a project they'd like to join. You might ask people to sign up for committees or work teams after orientation.

Preorders may want to provide new members with a booklet or notes about the co-op. Even better, if you have periodic potluck suppers, these provide a personal opportunity to acquaint new members with your philosophy and operation. Some co-ops ask new members to attend one coordinators' meeting. The West Newton, Massachusetts, co-op decentralizes orientation by assigning each new member to an old member for an informal introduction.

Training Programs

Education shouldn't stop with orientation. Training programs are one means of continuing co-op education. They become necessary when procedures for a particular job demand more than common sense and experience. The goal of any training program should be to demystify the skill and to build a pool of people familiar with a variety of tasks who can take the place of paid members or highly experienced volunteers. The New England Federation of Co-ops' buyers' collective periodically gives guided tours of the New England Produce Center to people in participating co-ops, explaining what wholesalers are used and how buying decisions are made.

You can encourage any member with a particular skill to offer a training program; we've seen successful programs in anything from carpentry to economics. At training sessions, somebody should keep a written record so that the information will be available to others. The Boston Food Co-op writes down all procedures in a looseleaf folder, which is kept in the store. The constantly changing manual is available to interested members and is very useful in emergencies.

Resources for training programs may range from conferences and materials of the Cooperative League of the U.S.A. to regional and interregional conferences of the new co-op movement. In the summer of 1974 the Minneapolis co-ops offered a month-long living and working experience in their stores and warehouse to co-op people outside the North Country region. Participants in this program evaluated its usefulness afterward and made recommendations for future training.

Going outside the co-op movement takes discretion. You need to know exactly what expertise and advice you're looking for. Your co-op may decide to train people in store management, but our feeling is that on-the-job co-op training is far more useful. You may not want chain-store ethics to be applied to your co-op. Occasionally, though, a person trained in store management will come to work for the co-op. This is how the Roxbury-Dorchester store got its manager. He was willing to take a cut in pay to be able to work in and for his community.

Study Groups

Study groups can investigate anything from nutrition to consumer law to cooperative history. A simple way to start is for one member to take the initiative of posting a topic and having people sign up. You might include interested nonmembers as a way of introducing them to the co-op.

A cooperative study group shouldn't be restricted to an academic concern for a problem. If members of an ecology study group find a new recycling possibility, they should try it out within the co-op. Nutrition study groups commonly function as lobbyists for carrying better foods and eliminating foods of dubious quality from the shelves.

Study groups interested in doing research on agribusiness can start at the library with *Moody's Industrial Manual,* for company histories and financial data, *Standard and Poor's Register of Corporations, Directors, and Executives,* for tracing interlocking directorates, or the *Fortune Plant and Product Directory,* for locating the plant of a major corporation. For specific information on a company, you can write a letter saying you're interested in buying stock; they'll send you plenty of material on what they're doing and the profits they make.

You might consider forming a people's history study group. Co-op folks in Minneapolis did this to discover and preserve some of their state's rich history of labor, immigrant, and women's movements; much of this history is still in oral form and is ignored by academic historians. The Minnesota People's History Project now produces a "Homefires" calendar containing pictures, speeches, anecdotes, recipes and important historical events. Six thousand copies of the calendar were printed for 1975. (If you'd like one, write to Minnesota People's History Project and send $2.00 plus 25¢ for postage. See page 174 for address.)

Small co-ops may not have the need or human resources for a great many study groups. Please don't feel overwhelmed by all the suggestions we're making. Simply make a list of priorities and decide what educational functions would benefit your co-op most. In our estimation, one of the most important is a long-range planning group, known in the capitalist world as a think tank. In co-ops, this group often exists relatively informally, but there should always be some people thinking about the future.

Get together some people in the co-op who have interest in or knowledge of a particular area that deserves consideration. Then brainstorm. Have one person write down all the ideas, good and not so good, that the discussion generates. Encourage hitchhiking on each other's ideas. Go on until you get to a blank wall, then begin to evaluate and develop what you've discussed. A little wine may be useful on such occasions. Remember that co-ops should sanction the exploration of all human cooperative possibilities.

Newsletters

As a booklet put out by the Food Conspiracy in Philadelphia says, "The newsletter is the neighborhood co-op's back fence." Newsletters are an excellent way to get the word out and activate the grapevine. Chock them full of notes on nutrition, recipes, community events, gardening hints, facts about agribusiness, organizational problems, philosophical meanderings, work schedules, distribution hours, social news, phone numbers, political controversies, lists of foods that are being boycotted, birthday greetings, business of active work teams, co-op finances, letters, and lists of bounced checks. Try to get a wide range of co-op members to write articles — and sign them.

A newsletter can't be a substitute for educational happenings or face-to-face encounters about what's going on. Exhortations in print must be part of a nexus of activities. But not having a newsletter will mean a lot less communication in your co-op.

While it's possible for one or two people to put out a newsletter, most of us aren't I.F. Stone. We have to share editorial, technical, and business tasks, and have a regular group of volunteers put the newsletter together. One-person operations tend to disappear with that one person.

For preorders, the order form can double as a newsletter. For stores, you may need to make arrangements with a collective print shop. Or you can shop around for a mimeo machine. Your method of printing should depend on the size of your co-op. For a small co-op, photocopied newsletters may be the least expensive. For a group of up to 200, dittos will do. A mimeo stencil is good for up to 2000 copies, and after that you need a printer.

If your co-op has its own mimeo or ditto machine, we suggest that you limit its use to a few competent operators. It will greatly increase the life of the machine. If your co-op is part of a university or has members connected with universities or businesses, you may find someone who has access to a mimeo or ditto. A friend who works near a copying machine is a good friend indeed.

Your newsletter should be attractive and readable. Try to include graphics and headlines. Short articles in columns and reasonable space between articles also help. Most of all, have good editors. The more concise your articles are, the better chance they have of being read to the end. For a sample of a first-rate co-op newsletter, write to the Food Conspiracy in Tucson, Arizona (address on page 175), and have them send you one of theirs.

When debate over an issue like growth or new capital equipment comes along, encourage full explanation of the various positions in your newsletter, with a tear-off sheet for responses. This is a useful way to draw out people's satisfaction or dissatisfaction about almost any co-op matter. If you have such a tear-off sheet, your newsletter staff should include a response and complaint processor who gets this feedback to the people who can do something about it.

If you want a picture of national co-op happenings, subscribe to the national *Food Co-op Nooz* (address on page 175). You can get a six-month subscription to the *Nooz* plus two copies of the most up-to-date food co-op directory for $3. Bulk copies of the national food co-op directory are available for 10¢ apiece plus postage (minimum order 20 copies). Regional newsletters exist in Austin, San Francisco, Minneapolis, and New England. See if you can get nearby co-ops to exchange newsletters with you.

If you're considering doing a regional newsletter, apply for a bulk mailing permit. It doesn't cost much and it significantly reduces the postage per item. Rather than hand-addressing or retyping labels, consider getting labels that can be Xeroxed. If you have a stable mailing list and access to an addressograph machine, investigate addressograph plates.

Posters, Signs, and Leaflets

Posters, signs, and leaflets are the basic communications media for co-ops. Walk into any distribution center and if you see impromptu graffiti, announcements, drawings, notices, leaflets, and hand-written notes, you can feel the health of that co-op. Necessity and enthusiasm make the walls of newly formed co-ops blossom with signs. People stop writing notes when they feel that nobody is listening. After the signs go, newsletters and meetings may follow. Many co-ops that distribute from churches and other institutions where signs cannot be left on the walls find that communication begins to dwindle; newsletters fizzle out and meetings are held either once a year or "as we need them," which may turn out to be as often as the visit of distant relatives.

The graphic advice offered for newsletters goes for signs and leaflets too. Keep them neat and well-organized. Avoid a jumble of signs, or crowded lettering on individual signs; few people will bother to decipher them. Keep signs current. If there are graphic artists in your co-op, try to get them involved in making signs, both for announcements and for informational purposes (names of food items, prices, directions).

Back-to-the-Farm Committee

A group that researches food sources, sometimes called a back-to-the-farm committee, gathers information crucial to your co-op. Whenever the co-op considers buying a new item or getting into a new area of business, good investigation will help make up for lack of experience.

The back-to-the-farm committee can establish contacts with local growers or other producers. Such arrangements mean saving what you'd otherwise pay middlepeople, strengthening beleaguered small producers, and guaranteeing co-op members fresh food. Careful development in this area can bring you organically grown food at prices comparable to nonorganically grown.

For example, somebody you know has a friend whose mother is a duck farmer. It may seem simple enough to call her and arrange for duck eggs. But you really ought to find out first whether there's sufficient demand for duck eggs, whether the farmer has sufficient supply for your demand, wheather her prices are good, what the laws are concerning duck eggs, and whether there are various grades of duck eggs. Research might include a trip to the duck farm to check out both the ducks and the farmer. Another consideration might be how much extra work this project will add. Does the duck-egg deal mean you have to have a duck-egg person in your co-op?

In another situation, you may be carrying brand X, but you hear that brand Y is a better deal. This committee can find out whether the better deal really exists, and if it's temporary or permanent. It can develop reliable contacts in the industry.

It can also develop new sources by tracing the various commodities as far back as the original producers. Sometimes you can do this just by reading labels. The Boston Food Co-op didn't carry Tampax because preliminary investigation indicated that they couldn't do better than the local discount store. But someone found a more direct source — the factory — and now BFC and a few other Boston co-ops carry Tampax.

Recycling Committee

Many co-ops have recycling programs for containers. Members bring in glass jars, tins, and paper bags. This not only saves the co-ops the cost of new containers, but it makes sense: whole-container recycling is much more sensible than breaking materials down to be reprocessed.

Members may be able to trade their old bottles, bags, and containers for other recyclable materials. We know somebody who made a shirt from a grain bag, and another inventive cooperator made pillows from one. A free store is an excellent form of recycling.

Co-ops can also organize recycling projects on a regional scale. At present, recycling often helps wasteful enterprises: glass is ground up and used for landfill in highway construction rather than being remade into bottles. Newsprint is shipped abroad or used in making construction materials like sheetrock. It's questionable how many trees this really saves. But as co-ops organize their own recycling projects they'll be able to have some say in how materials are recycled.

In Austin, the cooperating community gets much of its produce from several co-op farms where members can work in lieu of store participation. Organic waste is brought to the co-ops, where farm workers pick it up and take it to the farm for composting. This could conceivably be done on a larger scale. Trucks commonly come to the East Coast with food and leave only half full of commodities going West. The other half of the truck could be filled with one of the major products of the densely populated East: compostible (or composted) wastes. This compost could be delivered to farmers in the Midwest, who could then avoid the damage and expense of chemical fertilizers. In addition, Eastern cities would reduce their garbage disposal problem.

Any recycling program that your co-op can develop using compost will increase members' awareness of the nature of the soil and the miracle of plants that take our dead cells and organic wastes and build them into new life.

Speakers

Whether your co-op is mainly concerned with the continuing education of its own members or with spreading the co-op idea among wider circles of people, you'll need to *organize* the process of bringing speakers and audiences together. In the early stages when the immediate task is member education, you may want to supplement the talents of your own best-informed members with the expertise and experience of people from longer established groups. A small committee can get speakers for meetings and leaders for seminars or workshops. Later on, when your co-op is prepared to help new groups, you may want to set up a speaker's bureau.

A speaker's bureau needs only three or four members. The work consists of making arrangements by phone or mail, keeping an up-to-date file, and attending to a multitude of small but important details. Members of the speaker's committee should be able to communicate clearly and keep systematic records. They should have tact and social presence since, as a rule, they'll be asking someone to volunteer his or her time.

To compile a speaker's list, begin with your own active members and expand to include leaders of other co-ops, community organizers and educators, farmers, nutritionists, students of agriculture and economics, people involved in various self-help projects, and perhaps even members of city and state legislatures. (The Common Market in Denver had the current governor of Colorado as a speaker.) Develop a card file of potential speakers and include all you can find out about each person's background, experience, area of special knowledge, and views on the co-op movement. Note on the cards requests to speak, dates of actual engagements, and pertinent comments.

Even before its roster of speakers is complete, the bureau may advertise its services by mail or phone. The strong appeal of food co-ops in time of rising prices, shortages, and deteriorating food quality will produce a response from labor unions, consumer, welfare, and tenant councils, daycare centers, women's groups, churches and synagogues, community centers, organizations of the elderly, and various groups of people organized around particular beliefs or seeking alternative lifestyles.

Whether you concentrate on getting speakers to educate your own members or on sending emissaries to speak to others, success depends on following a few commonsense procedures:

1. Know your audience: its interests, economic level, ethnic composition, age, stage of organization, and degree of familiarity with the co-op movement.

2. Try to fit your speaker to your audience. To a group hearing about food co-ops for the first time, send someone broadly versed in their history, achievements, and various ways of functioning. To a newly organized co-op, send a speaker who can talk about work systems, decision-making processes, bookkeeping, logistics, crate sizes, and sources of supply.

3. Make sure your speaker's name, background, and topic are known in advance to the chairperson or program director so that

publicity can be done. It's a good idea to have your speaker arrive at least fifteen minutes ahead of time to talk over the purpose of the meeting with the chairperson or other members.

4. Make sure all technical arrangements are clear. When possible, get written confirmation. Be sure your speaker knows what he or she is expected to talk about, where he or she is going, how to get there, what time to arrive, and whom to ask for. Supply transportation if possible. Often groups inviting speakers will pay for transportation and expenses. Some may even pay a fee.

5. Confirm the date by telephone with both the group and the speaker about forty-eight hours in advance. If there's any slip-up, you can arrange for a substitute. Nothing so discourages a group eager to organize as to wait for a speaker who never arrives.

6. Supply speakers with literature. If the meeting is large or if the literature must be sold, an assistant should go along. If you plan to set up a literature table, get the consent of the sponsors and ask their help in arranging it.

7. Your speaker's bureau should acquaint itself not only with the literature of the co-op movement but with the available audio-visual materials: film-strips, tapes, charts, etc. If your speaker plans to use any of these, notify the sponsors so they may arrange for equipment.

8. Panel discussions, debates, and question-answer formats are usually more productive of organizational activity than straight lectures are. People ready to learn about food co-ops or taking steps to form one normally have many questions to ask and quite a few ideas of their own. The speaker who introduces a subject briefly and then opens the floor to audience participation will often accomplish more than the one who makes a full-length presentation before asking for questions. The point is to achieve maximum rank-and-file involvement. When a meeting is too large for general participation, your committee might propose that it be divided into workshops and should be ready to supply discussion leaders for them.

9. Since the main purpose of sending out speakers is to educate people to take practical steps to organize co-ops, your speaker's bureau might expand its function to arranging visits — of your members to some well-established store or preorder, or of a newly forming group to your own operation. In either case, knowledgeable guides will be needed.

10. Be sure to thank a speaker who comes to your own meeting or who goes at your request to educate some other group. Unless your organization or theirs is large and well-financed, you'll have to depend on speakers willing to volunteer their time because of their commitment to co-ops. Let them know that you value their contribution.

Media — Your Own and Other People's

You'll probably have to deal with the communications media at some point. It's useful to know how to use the media to spread your message. But remember that other people's media will reflect their points of view. Don't be surprised if you're quoted inaccurately; there are limits to the usefulness of corporate-owned media in spreading the co-op message.

Be resourceful about using the media. Since you're nonprofit, you can get free TV and radio time. Make sure you send in public service announcements a week or two in advance of desired broadcast. The same goes for press releases to newspapers and magazines. The Boston Food Co-op got 1000 new members in a matter of days by putting spots on several local radio stations.

If you have something important to tell the media, call a press conference and prepare press releases of a few hundred words. Quote people — even yourself. You'll be surprised how many papers print all or part of your press release verbatim or else quote from it as if from a live person. Write press releases in a style congenial to the mass media; avoid rhetoric, slogans, slang terms, or clearly subjective writing. Written statements are important at press conferences; if you don't have one, the media will inevitably leave out the one fact you consider crucial.

Make sure you have adequate facilities for a press conference: a big enough room, nearby telephones, electrical outlets. Have one person clearly delegated to read a prepared statement and answer questions. Even if you wish to have a collective represent your co-op, the press will focus on one person. But have others available to answer questions in case the delegate of the day is stymied or doesn't have the specific facts asked for.

Don't call too many press conferences or the press will stop coming. Try to give them a good reason to come. Boycotts, picket lines, rising prices, or atrocious food quality are good reasons for press conferences. In Washington, D.C., Fields of Plenty, a community service store, called a press conference to protest a local food sales tax.

If a newspaper or TV station wants to do a story on your co-op, assign at least one knowledgeable person to deal with the reporter. Make sure you explain fully and clearly what you do, and why and how you do it. Don't take any knowledge on the reporter's part for granted. Give the reporter as much written material as possible to refer to when he or she sits down to write. Misconceptions and misinformation frequently creep into articles by reporters not familiar with cooperative philosophy. Be prepared for a long background talk. Remember to expect the health inspector the day after you've been on TV.

When publicity is in the offing, be prepared to deal with waves of people interested in joining your co-op or others nearby, or trying to organize their own. If the groundwork is not prepared, then you may not want a lot of media exposure, since this will lead to frustration for interested people.

More productive than relying on outside media is to encourage co-op members who are writers to contribute articles to local newspapers and magazines. Study groups can circulate and publish results of their research. For "in house" communication, you may want to commission videotape shows, slide tape shows, or movies. Or you can put together your own radio show if a listener-sponsored station, FM music station, or local university station will let you.

Here's a discussion of four major forms of audio-visual presentation, in order of increasing cost:

1. Lecture with photographs or slides. Although this can be the least expensive method, it requires plenty of time and thought. If several different people will be presenting the program, you should prepare a detailed script. A piece of paper divided in half with text on one side and corresponding picture cues on the other is very efficient:

Soybeans supply most protein requirements	Picture #13: chart of nutrient percentage in soybeans

If you're using photographs, they should be at least 16″ x 20″ and mounted. The cost will depend on whether or not you have facilities to process, print, and mount them yourself. Minimal cost would be about $100 for film, paper, board, and photographic chemicals. If you have to pay for processing, printing, and mounting, triple the budget figure.

Because of the cost of 16″ × 20″ prints, you may find a simple slide show is cheaper. You'll need color film, processing, and a projector with rotary tray. Figure on shooting ten slides for every one you use in the show.

The nice thing about a lecture with photographs or slides is that it doesn't require sophisticated equipment or vast experience to produce a pleasing result. Lectures can be more specific and detailed than any of the more expensive media techniques because they're easily updated and altered.

Try to avoid excessive length; people start nodding out after about 25 minutes.

2. Slide tape show: These are basically slide shows with a synchronized tape-recorded lecture, and they avoid the necessity of having a knowledgeable speaker on hand. They require 1) a slide projector with rotary tray, 2) a tape recorder with two tracks, and 3) a synchronizer. Cost of this equipment varies with your sources. Gifts are best; loans are second best. If you have to buy the equipment new, expect to pay several hundred dollars for it. Materials will probably cost another few hundred, mostly for film and processing. If you have a friend who develops color film, you may cut your film costs in half.

Slide tapes require some skill in production; they must be carefully timed and edited, and usually require two hours of production time for every minute of show. Expect to spend 90% of your production time in editing.

Since you'll spend a lot of time producing a slide tape, you'll want it to last, so don't make it too topical. Try to stress things that you don't foresee changing. Slide tapes are excellent for general concepts and information that may be boring in a lecture situation. Keep them light; use as much humor as possible. The show should be a maximum of 25 minutes long or you won't be able to fit all the slides into one tray. Use music to break up long stretches of gab; keep it moving and interesting, and make sure that everything on the tape is clear, audible, and correctly synchronized. A bad slide tape is worse than none at all.

3. Videotape: Equipment for videotape costs several thousand

dollars. So unless you get a grant or have a member who can raid the local college's media department, this probably won't be feasible for most co-ops. The Broadway Local Co-op in New York got a New York State grant to videotape their buying procedures to train other people interested in preorder logistics. Video is much less versatile than a slide tape because unless you have access to a videotape studio, you can't edit.

Videotape is excellent for lectures and talks when it is impossible for a speaker to be there. If you have to reach a lot of people with specific information, videotape is great. It has short production time and so can be very topical. Programs can be produced cheaply and quickly once you have the rather expensive hardware.

4. Film: Unless you have professional filmmakers in your co-op, you probably shouldn't attempt a film. For an hour-long film in Super 8 with sound, expect to pay several hundred dollars for projector and screen and close to a thousand for production, assuming that you don't have to buy hardware such as cameras and editors. Film is the most versatile and least boring medium. Like a slide tape, it requires hours in the editing lab and is impractical for most co-ops. But as co-ops grow, grants will become more widely available, and you shouldn't discount the possibility of doing a film in 16 mm. at some point.

Committees of Correspondence

Committees of correspondence, as we learned in our history classes, were both essential and fruitful means of communication during the American Revolution. They can serve a similar purpose in food co-ops today. The British may be gone, but agribusiness is looming on the horizon. Ideas, news, and information about new food sources sometimes take weeks to cross relatively short distances. We are just starting to build contacts, networks, and methods of information-sharing.

Have your co-op answer all mail in as personal and complete a way as possible. If your co-op gets only bills, you are not listed with the national *Food Co-op Nooz* (address on page 175). If you want folks you can write to, get a copy of the National Directory from the same address.

Your committee of correspondence should have a number of responsibilities besides answering letters. It can maintain a phone tree so that people can get in touch with each other quickly, either about food co-op problems or about other needs such as fighting tenant evictions or coordinating babysitting. Your correspondence committee can communicate with other co-ops in the area concerning their resources and needs. It can take care of inquiries for speakers and organizers if a speaker's bureau doesn't handle this. It may decide to set up a ham radio group. While the FCC prohibits discussion of actual business, people may keep in touch through ham radio, and exchange other forms of information.

Your committee of correspondence should keep its roots deep in the community. It ought to create a communications network within the co-op and with other co-ops and community organizations. Then perhaps it will be worthy of its namesake.

Informal Processes

Remember while setting up formal structures that much of the real communication happens informally. One member taking personal responsibility to talk to new people and explain how jobs are done may be a more effective orientation program than any formal class.

As in decision making, informal processes in communication and education go on all the time. They may reinforce formal processes and constitute their human element, or they may counteract, replace, or fill in missing structures. Being aware of your co-op's informal processes is necessary to understand how it functions in fact as well as on paper.

How do people communicate informally in a co-op? Usually there's a grapevine; this should be developed rather than ignored. Identify those people who are pivotal in the chain of communication, and keep in touch with them.

It's often useful for organizers to keep a list of items to bring up personally with particular people or with members in general. If you're working steadily, you may easily forget what you intended to discuss. Leave yourself a few minutes at the end of the day to review the people you talked with and to decide what you might want to share with them in the future. Keep track of follow-through if someone expresses interest in a particular activity. Write a note so you'll remember to put this person in touch with whoever else might be interested.

In a large co-op, a suggestion box or log helps to find out what

members are thinking. The Boston Food Co-op got little input into its suggestion box until the name was changed to "karma box." At Kokua Country Foods in Honolulu, members who suggest new products are encouraged to research the sources themselves.

In both small and large co-ops, people ought to set aside time for heart-to-heart talks with other members. The spirit of a co-op is nurtured by love as well as by business. When you enjoy working with others, let them know. The strength of face-to-face discussion is that it satisfies our social needs. Discussions clear up misunderstandings and yield a lot more air time for each participant than meetings, newsletters, or study groups do. We need to be aware of our social capital; it's one strength with which exclusively economic institutions can't compete.

Sources

For pamphlets, films, and other materials useful in orientation, study groups, and training programs, write to:

Agribusiness Accountability Project, 1000 Wisconsin Ave., Washington, D.C. 20007.
Center for Science in the Public Interest, 1779 Church St. NW, Washington, D.C. 20036.
Cooperative League of the U.S.A., 1828 L St. NW, Washington, D.C. 20036.
Minnesota People's History Project, c/o People's Warehouse, 123 E. 26th, Minneapolis, Minnesota 55404.
North American Student Cooperative Organization, Box 1301, Ann Arbor, Michigan 48106.
Office of Economic Opportunity, Washington, D.C. 20506.
Rodale Press, Emmaus, Pennsylvania 18049.

See also:
Buber, Martin. *Paths in Utopia*. Boston: Beacon Press, 1949.
Freire, Paulo. *Pedagogy of the Oppressed*. New York: Herder & Herder, 1970.
Groves, Frank, and Dick Vilstrup. *Cooperative Communications*. Madison, Wisconsin: University Center for Cooperatives, 4 volumes.
NACLA *Research Methodology Guide,* available for $1 at some bookstores or from the North American Congress on Latin America, P.O. Box 57, Cathedral Station, New York, N.Y. 10025.

For newsletters:
Food Co-op Nooz, 64 E. Lake St., Chicago, Illinois 60601.
Tucson Food Conspiracy, 412 N. 4 Ave., Tucson, Arizona 85705.

For recycling committees or ecology study groups:
Clark, Wilson. *Energy for Survival*. New York: Doubleday, 1974.
Commoner, Barry. *The Closing Circle*. New York: Bantam, 1975.
Kelly, Katie. *Garbage: The History and Future of Garbage in America*. New York: Saturday Review Press, 1973.
Schumacher, E. F., *Small is Beautiful*. New York: Harper & Row, 1973.

For information on press conferences, leaflets, and newsletters:
O. M. Collective, *The Organizer's Manual*. New York: Bantam, 1971.

10. Sources

FOOD SOURCES vary from item to item. You can get fresh produce at large terminal markets, at smaller regional markets, at farmers' markets, or directly from farmers. Meat, like produce, is usually available at large central markets, but for other foods you'll have to go to individual wholesalers scattered around town. Although there is a central cheese exchange in Wisconsin, we know of no regional cheese markets. Grains come from big wholesaling companies, although some co-op federations have arranged for trucking of grains directly from farmers. Finally, co-op warehouses exist in some areas of the country; Chapter 15 describes how they work and how to set one up.

Terminal Markets

If your co-op is near one of the country's twenty-one major terminal markets, you'll have lots of choice of fresh produce and will probably be able to get low prices. Terminal markets are the central receiving points for produce shipped from the big growing areas. They're usually located in or near major cities.

Wholesalers who are primary receivers at these terminal markets deal in a few items for which they're known among the secondary receivers as reliable sources. A primary receiver might specialize in Florida oranges and grapefruits generally supplied by the same Florida broker. If he or she runs out of oranges, he or she may even buy from somebody else and sell at a loss rather than disappoint regular customers. A primary receiver in the morning may become a secondary receiver by afternoon.

Wholesalers who are secondary receivers, or jobbers, buy from a variety of primary receivers and generally have a large selection. Co-ops and small capitalist stores usually buy from these jobbers because it's more convenient and less time-consuming than going around to various primary receivers to find the best buys. Also, primary receivers may require a minimum order that individual co-ops can't meet. If your co-op has the energy, however, it's worth checking out primary receivers. Some will sell to you because they need the business of a few small groups to sell their extra few cases. At the New England Produce Center, one primary receiver refers all inquiries from co-ops to NEFCO. NEFCO operates a produce buying service for about forty co-ops. With this volume, NEFCO can get good prices from primary receivers. Even with NEFCO's 10¢ per crate brokerage fee (which supports two full-time produce buyers), the participating co-ops pay less for produce than they would if they went to jobbers.

Food supplied by jobbers is more expensive and usually older than food from primary receivers. Standard jobber markup is about 50¢ a case. Co-ops with access to terminal markets should decide whether they want to shop around or buy from one jobber. The decision should be based on how much time members have, balanced against how much they want to save money or seek the best quality. Even with an efficient federated buying service, co-ops are likely to spend more time at the market if they pick up from various receivers than if they buy from one. Some co-ops don't use the NEFCO service because of the extra couple of hours it takes to pick up produce from the different receivers.

The most important consideration in weighing one-stop buying against shopping around is the strength of your organization. A new co-op should devote its major energies to organizing a smooth operation. You might want to stay with one wholesaler until your co-op is running smoothly and you've become a reliable source for your members.

There's another consideration: you have to be on the market frequently to know what wholesalers are charging, to follow trends, and to compare quality and price. A co-op that's buying once a week, and that may have different people buying each time, might not accomplish very much by shopping around. It may be better to establish a good trusting relationship with one jobber, but be aware that if you're too dependent on one distributor, he or she will be tempted to charge you more or pass inferior produce on to you. Personalities play a big role in determining which wholesaler will sell to which buyer at what price-quality combination.

Primary receivers buy from brokers in various ways, and since produce is perishable and therefore chancy to deal with, business practices are often complicated. A receiver can either buy by paying a price set at the shipping point or buy "on the arm," which means that the broker at the shipping point agrees to accept the price for which the food is later sold at the receiving point, minus the receiver's markup. Local farmers who truck their produce to a terminal market usually deal with wholesalers on the arm. This is an undesirable method from the broker's or farmer's point of view, but one they often have to accept, especially when there is an oversupply of their commodity.

The receiver takes chances too: the market may go way down between the time he or she orders and the time the produce is received; the produce may be bad or may not sell fast enough, which means spoilage and cash flow problems. If the shipment is bad, the wholesaler may either reject it, send it into auction, or sell it to a jobber who has customers that can use it (restaurants, hospitals, etc.). In any case, the receiver calls the broker, explains the situation, and tries to change the buying agreement. If the shipment is rejected, the receiver may have to send it back, though this is rare.

Receivers also sometimes sell on commission. The broker or farmer may call and say he or she has some beautiful avocados on hand and the receiver may agree to try to sell them on a commission basis. When receivers get shipments from big farming companies or from individual farmers, the business procedures are much the same as they are with brokers. The receiver, since he or she has to buy sight unseen, must trust the source.

For long distances, the receiver usually arranges and pays for transportation by train or truck. Transportation is expensive; in 1974, shipping produce from New Jersey to Boston cost 75¢ to $1 per crate. Small farmers generally have to pay for their own transportation to the terminal market. Whoever pays, loss of a truckload of produce can be an expensive proposition. A tractor-trailerload of 40,000 pounds of produce may be worth $15,000 to $20,000, which is still not so devastating as a tractor-trailerload of cheese, which is usually worth about $40,000. Everywhere along the line, the price goes up. A $1.75- or $2-crate of California produce may cost $4 by the time it's sold by a jobber at an East Coast terminal market.

A terminal market is a good example of the classical free market.

Laws of supply and demand work just as the classical economists described them. The perishability of produce adds pressure to the wholesalers to sell. Prices respond to seasonal demand. The week before Thanskgiving all prices automatically rise, even for non-festive foods. When the first truckload of the season arrives, the price is high. There is a limited supply and a high demand. But generally the first shipment was picked prematurely to get that extra price. It may taste terrible. Wait several weeks until lots of shipments are coming in; the supply is ample so the price will go down. Such price fluctuations occur daily too. No wholesaler wants to store vegetables over the weekend. On Friday, prices will either be very high, because no one has anything to sell, or very low because the market is overloaded.

Regional or City Markets

Wholesalers at regional or city markets get some direct shipments but they also often truck to the nearest terminal market to buy food to sell back home. Prices, therefore, are usually higher at regional markets than at terminal markets, and the variety available is not as great. Nevertheless, you can work out arrangements with wholesalers at regional markets and get produce for your members at as much as 50% under supermarket price.

An advantage for co-ops buying at regional markets is that since the markets are smaller, a group of co-ops has greater comparative buying power. They may be able to influence what foods the wholesalers bring in or to demand a good price break on their volume if they're buying together.

Co-ops that reach a certain volume may consider hiring a truck and going to the nearest terminal market rather than continuing to buy at the regional market. Here, you have to balance the amount of money you'd save at the terminal market against the amount it would cost for transportation, multiplied by the energy factor — the level of energy and commitment of co-op members. Washington, D.C., co-op stores organized a trucking collective to go to the Baltimore terminal market; co-ops in the Austin Community Project make regular runs to the terminal market in San Antonio. Maine and Vermont co-ops truck into Boston to buy with NEFCO.

Because of the mechanics of food marketing, produce may actually be cheaper at a terminal market than at a regional market in the area where it was originally grown. Often the food is sent to the terminal market first and then shipped back to the regional market. Co-ops in Maine discovered that it was cheaper to buy Maine potatoes through NEFCO in Boston than from their regional wholesalers.

Similarly, Vermont cheese is often cheaper in the Midwest than it is in Vermont. The cheese is sent to Wisconsin, aged, and priced at assembling points there. Cabot Creamery, the largest in Vermont, does not age its own cheese. When the New England People's Co-ops, a federation of seven co-ops in Vermont, approached Cabot for a cheese purchase, they learned that they'd need their own ageing rooms. Ageing is a difficult art and one that the federation did not feel ready to attempt.

Farmers' Markets

There are three types of farmers' markets: those set up by state, city, or county agencies, those set up by farmers, and those set up by co-ops in conjunction with farmers. The first two are usually large enough to be considered regional markets, although they are open only during the growing season. In Atlanta, where the growing season is year round, co-ops regularly go the farmers' market because there they can buy produce in smaller than case sizes. Prices may be higher at farmers' markets but the money goes straight to the farmers instead of the middlepeople. You may also be able to make some friends among the farmers. The Minnesota Organic Growers and Buyers Association has a stall at the Minneapolis farmers' market.

The third type of farmers' market has been successful in Vermont. Usually the sponsoring co-ops get in touch with farmers they know to see if they'd be interested in making their products directly available to the public. If your co-op doesn't know enough farmers and you're interested in this idea, you can visit county agents, agricultural extension services, and farm organizations.

A co-op-sponsored farmers' market makes people aware of the existence of the co-op and may increase membership and lead to the formation of new co-ops. For the small organic farmer, it's an excellent way to supplement income, to educate the public about organic methods, and to make contacts that can later be used in direct deals.

It's helpful to have your farmers' market near adequate parking. You may be able to get permission to use curb space and close off part of a street. Or you can use space near your co-op: a parking lot, a town square, a local athletic field, or fairgrounds. One co-op in Vermont had its farmers' market partially protected under an overhanging roof in case of rain. You may want to set up stalls outdoors between eight and twelve feet wide. A farmer can back a truck into the stall or sell directly from the truck. Some farmers use tables and benches. These co-op-sponsored markets are generally open one or two days a week.

Co-ops and farmers should agree on some ground rules. These might include:

1. Allocation of market space. The co-op should try to assign space without favoritism except where produce will go bad because of heat and some shade is essential.
2. Rental fees should be low and equal for all participants. Anything from 50¢ to $2 a day should be adequate to cover advertising and incidental expenses. One Vermont co-op donates the fees to the town recreation fund.
3. Opening and closing times should be agreed on.
4. The co-ops and the farmers respectively should clean up whatever areas they use.
5. If any special vending licenses or permits are needed for packing, labeling, or weighing, they should probably be secured in advance by the co-op.

We think that only vendors who have actually grown or made their products should be encouraged to sell at these farmers' markets, although the co-op may want to sell items that are not generally available in the region. Having as direct a contact as possible with the producer is part of the idea of farmers' markets.

Finally, a key to successful farmers' markets is good publicity through newspaper ads and feature stories, posters, and radio spots.

Buying Directly from Farmers

It's a good idea for co-ops to support farmers by buying directly from them, but it should be clear that they may not save a lot of money on a small volume. At a produce market you can take advantage of gluts, which make food prices fall. With a farmer, you may decide on a price in advance and stick to it, with little variation, throughout the season. At the beginning of the season, for example, you may contract, either verbally or in writing, to buy a farmer's tomatoes at 20¢ a pound. There aren't too many tomatoes coming into market yet, so the price, even from original receivers, may be 30¢. As the season wears on, the market price will go down, first to 20¢, then perhaps to 15¢ or even 10¢ a pound. Meanwhile, you're committed to paying your farmer 20¢.

You may be able to work out an arrangement whereby you agree to help the farmer by keeping the price reasonably steady, with the understanding that you won't pay more than 5¢ per pound above the market price. This variation will change with different foods. It should be clear to the farmer that you know you're overpaying, but that you're doing it to support the farm. You'd rather see your co-op's money going into small-scale farming and ecological land use than into wholesalers' profits, trucking costs, and large-scale monocropping. It follows that you should choose the farmers you deal with carefully. A farmer who uses organic fertilizers and biological pest control may be the one you want to support.

A good way to arrive at a fair price with a farmer is to have him or her tell you what profit he or she needs to make to live comfortably and to reinvest the necessary amount of money in the farm. Figure a good price by adding that profit to his or her production costs. Check the commodity prices every so often on the financial pages and in USDA market reports. Co-op farms dealing with the North Country People's Warehouse in Minneapolis commonly submit balance sheets for the cost of their crops; these are printed in the regional co-op newsletter, *The Scoop*.

When dealing with farmers, make sure it's clear who's responsible for transportation. Relations between farmers and co-ops can be torn apart by transportation misunderstandings, and resultant spoiled food. Also make sure you have an out if the food is not up to standard.

How much you deal with farmers depends on your location. Co-ops in and around Los Angeles buy about two-thirds of their produce from local farmers. The produce is organically grown and sold at prices comparable to terminal-market prices for nonorganically grown food. The North Country People's Warehouse buys some of its grains from local organic farmers. In some areas of the country, like New England where, as the saying goes, the main crops are rocks and graduate students, it's probably not feasible to fill all food needs through direct deals with local farmers. New England co-ops, especially in the winter, buy chiefly at the terminal market. Although their money goes back into the capitalist food system instead of creating a self-sufficient cooperative distribution system, the New England co-ops are gaining valuable experience and making important friends by buying in this manner.

Co-ops in California sometimes provide labor to pick their own fruit. We the People, a co-op store in Lake Tahoe, picks apples, beans, and pears at local farms. San Francisco co-ops pick oranges through FarmCo (Farmer-Consumer), a producer-consumer cooperative that has a model project of fifty acres.

You can get in touch with farmers through regional organic farmers' associations, university extension services, county agents, farm magazines, farmers' markets, and farmers' meetings. If there are rural co-ops in your federation, they should attempt to make the contacts. *Organic Gardening and Farming* magazine has a certification service for organic farmers, as do some state and local associations. You can find a list of organic farmers' associations in Appendix II. Write to these organizations. Eventually they'll learn that you exist and will start writing to you. Put ads in local rural papers to let farmers know you're interested in buying from them. The Michigan Federation of Food Co-ops recently sent a member hitchhiking through Michigan bean country to meet farmers, and the Washington, D. C., federation has sent a representative to Florida.

Establishing direct links with small farmers may be difficult. This is partly because large farmers are easier to deal with logistically; one big shipment is easier than many small ones. In addition, as the Ann Arbor folks explain:

> A large portion of our food has to be processed before we can sell it. All our grains — the most "natural" thing we get — must be cleaned to standards far higher than even those for seeds you plant. Sunflower seeds, buckwheat groats, and oat groats must be hulled. Rolled oats, wheat flakes, and flour must be processed by expensive equipment. Naturally this equipment is beyond the reach of most small farmers. In most cases, the small farmer has only a small cleaning mill which is far from adequate for food. It requires fairly large capital accumulation to set up flaking or rolling equipment.

For co-ops dealing in produce, there's the pressure to distribute as quickly as possible. And there are the questions of quality control and storage, which become more complicated if you're buying from many different sources. Nevertheless, as federations get more experience, ordering directly from small farms will become increasingly likely.

The Michigan federation's bean scout made the following observations after his trip:

"Many farmers contract to sell their beans or other crops long before harvest. They are paid an agreed price regardless of the market price at the time of harvest. Many farmers lose speculative profits as a result, especially in this time of inflating food costs. Prices are posted in elevators prior to harvest based on speculative markets in New York and Chicago. For this reason prices of beans drop in the fall. The farmer must sell to the elevator since he or she probably has no facilities for storage and cleaning.

"The beans are bought by the elevator and then bought again by speculators although they are not physically removed from the elevator. The investment speculator holds the beans on paper for several months to wait for the price to rise. This is what happened in the 1973–74 season when bean prices went so high. The prices went up allegedly because of the rise in oil and chemicals. But this wasn't based on actual expenditure [to grow the beans]. During the summer of 1974 the prices dropped again because the last of the crop held for speculation was dumped in preparation for buying at a low price from the farmer with the new season.

"The beans are eventually sold to large wholesaling firms such as Michigan Bean, a division of a multinational conglomerate. They transport and package the beans and sell them to distributors and wholesalers, who sell to retailers. The largest profit goes to speculators and large wholesalers, and the next to distributors, elevators, and smaller wholesaling operations. The smallest margin goes to the farmer and the small retailer. (Large retail operations are generally part of the corporate chain.)

"Thus far the co-ops have done little to alter this basic pattern. We attempt to lower prices at the retail level by operating with low overhead and little or no wages. We take a first step in changing things by operating a small, low margin warehouse. These efforts are good to the extent that they maintain energy and bring us together. They are limited, however, in their ability to alter the energy flow. The prices remain controlled by speculators in Chicago. There is a need for cooperative relations between producers and consumers based on regional organization and a minimum of energy drain through unnecessary transportation and speculation . . . Some possible actions leading to this object include:

— Developing relations with existing or new cooperative elevators. The elevator is an important part of the flow since certain crops require hulling, cleaning, milling, rolling, or flaking — using machinery which is large, expensive, and not generally available. There are elevators which started as co-ops and some remain democratic in form.
— Establishing a yearly cooperative buying and selling price based on the whole yield and not allowing for speculation.
— Cooperative use of farm equipment.
— Increasing knowledge of organic and diversified farming systems. A decline in the energy-wasteful production of corn and soybeans for overproduction of beef and pork."

Since farming is not a very predictable business, it's wise to form flexible agreements with farmers. A purely verbal agreement is fine as long as good communication exists. For example, the farmer from whom the Michigan federation usually buys soft wheat, corn, and soybeans, calls them from time to time to be sure their usage isn't going up or down dramatically, and she calls before making a large sale to someone else to be sure she's reserving enough wheat for the co-op. The federation constantly re-evaluates its needs and keeps the farmer apprised. But another farmer promised the federation his whole crop of 100 bushels of rye. They picked up half of it and arranged for him to store the rest for a number of weeks. But the day before the co-op was going to pick up the rest, the farmer planted it! The federation got rye from another farmer but it wasn't clean and came in fiber-pack barrels which he wanted back.

One way to avoid these problems is to use a contract between peers, in which each side can renege in undue circumstances and neither would think of going to court. It should be a positive statement of the needs, requirements, and assumptions of each side. Some of the guidelines you may want to establish with grain farmers include:

— moisture content; this affects storage capability
— protein content

— cleanliness
— organicity; you can have crops tested for organicity at university extension services or private labs.

The University of Connecticut extension service tests food for NEFCO for chemical content and protein.

In contracting for produce, you might want to specify grades, quality, packing, and transportation.

Here's a sample contract:

July 13, 1974
Michigan Federation of Food Co-ops
&
Lone Pine Rice and Bean Farm, Carl Garrich
Re: Brown Rice Contract

Carl Garrich, of the Lone Pine Rice and Bean Farm, agrees to sell to Michigan Federation of Food Co-ops two hundred and eighty thousand pounds (280,000 pounds) of organically-grown short grain Nortai brown rice and Star Bonnett long grain brown rice @ $.30 per pound. F. O. B. point of milling is Arkansas. Michigan Federation of Food Co-ops agrees to take this rice not later than the thirtieth (30th) day of June, 1975. Any delivered because of Michigan's fault after the 30th of June will have a two cent per pound cost added, or $.32 per pound.

The terms will be fifty percent on invoice, balance thirty days. The final payment may be changed with both parties agreeing. All payments must be made by August 30, 1975.

Signed: ___________
Carl Garrich, Owner
Lone Pine Rice and Bean Farm 7–13–74

Signed: ___________
Michigan Federation of Food Co-ops 7—19–74

Perhaps the most important aspect of dealing with farmers is the frequent face-to-face contact. Farmers will often give credit if they trust the co-ops. It's worth putting a lot of time into these contacts. As food supplies tighten up, you may need them.

Dealing with Wholesalers and Distributors

There are several ways to find wholesalers. If you're looking for meat, fish, or produce, you can walk around the central market and introduce yourself. You can ask other co-ops who their suppliers are. Be sure to check out the co-op warehouse in your region, if one exists. You can also ask retailers and restaurants, although remember that restaurants usually pay higher prices than retailers do, and often get lower quality food. Don't forget to read labels. Last but not least is the trusty Yellow Pages. You'll find people who can tell you where other wholesalers are. NEFCO was looking for a source of good honey; the buyer looked in the Yellow Pages for a bee supply outfit. He called and asked who they sold supplies to. This led NEFCO straight to a honey wholesaler.

Be open and honest when you approach wholesalers. Tell them you're from a co-op, and if they don't know what a co-op is, briefly describe your distribution procedure and your nonprofit principles.

Find out the wholesaler's policies on brands, grades, prices, credit, C.O.D., delivery schedules, returns, and discount scales. If they have a published discount scale based on volume, get a copy. Find out whether or not you lose a percentage point on your discount if they deliver; weigh this information against your ability to do the trucking yourself. A new co-op may want to have as many things delivered as possible until it gets its organization running smoothly and feels that it can tackle trucking.

Talk about your volume and — very important — your potential volume. Co-ops have a proven growing power at rates far greater than supermarkets'. In 1974, the Safeway chain in Washington, D.C., had closed one store and was considering closing seven more at the same time that the three community service co-ops doubled their volume. NEFCO got a 2% discount off the regular price from one wholesaler because of potential volume.

Many wholesalers like C.O.D. arrangements because they have cash flow problems just as the rest of us do. Some prefer charge because they don't like their delivery people to have to bother making change. Some won't want to bill you because your volume isn't large enough or it takes too much paperwork; others will prefer a billing system. Find out wholesaler preferences and try to oblige. If you're getting billed, pay bills on time, especially if the wholesaler seems dubious about doing business with you. There's nothing like reliable payment to warm a wholesaler's heart. You may agree to go on C.O.D. for a while but explain that eventually you expect credit, that is, you want to be billed.

Have some knowledge of wholesale prices (via phone calls and business grapevine) before going to see wholesalers. Don't decide to deal with one company without visiting others. Weigh wholesalers' respective food qualities against their prices and the work it will take you to deal with them. One may be farther away, have less frequent deliveries, refuse to give you credit, or require that you pick up.

If you're dealing with more than one source for a particular food line, let the wholesalers know. They won't always let you know what they're doing, but your best policy is openness. If one wholesaler's price sounds too high, mention another price that you've been quoted.

If you make it clear at the start what quality you're interested in, you'll save yourself and the wholesaler trouble later on. Don't be afraid to reject shipments if they're not up to your standard and you've previously made that standard clear. You don't necessarily have to send back inferior food; you may want to sell it at reduced prices or just throw it out and let the wholesaler know how much you lost. You should get credit on your next bill. Always let wholesalers know about bad stuff as soon as possible. Otherwise they can assume that your handling is at fault.

Good personal relations based on trust and respect are the key to dealing with wholesalers. Co-op buyers should be able to establish rapport. This means that you have to understand where they're coming from. Some lasting friendships have been made between wholesalers and co-op buyers; and this is a potent way of educating people outside the co-op movement about cooperatives.

NEFCO buyers have built up excellent relations with several primary receivers at the New England Produce Center. One wholesaler lets NEFCO use part of his space at no charge to distribute eggs and cheese; another once reminded a NEFCO buyer that co-ops try not to buy brand label bananas because of the higher price. Once when two buyers got into a wrangle, a friendly wholesaler gave them a lecture on cooperation.

When dealing with large wholesalers, you may never get near the boss, but you can still make friends with the sales and delivery workers. They can give you important information about where the food is coming from and how long it's been sitting around. Their tips may even lead you to some direct sources.

If you're not satisfied with a wholesaling company, you shouldn't deal with it. This doesn't preclude coming back later if they offer you a better deal.

11. Logistics

Preorder Logistics

PREORDER CO-OPS have evolved various systems for ordering, distributing, and paying for their food. In deciding which of the methods described below you want to use, consider the size of your co-op and the preference of your members. If you're not sure, you can try out different methods and see which one works best for you. Each preorder operates a little differently, and after some experience, you'll probably have much to add.

ORDERING

There are two basic ways of ordering, collective and itemized. Collective ordering is simpler; the buyers make the choice for the entire co-op when they're at the market. This may be necessary if the co-op is very small (under 20 households) and unable to meet crate size if many items are ordered each week. The buyers have the money, either from prepayment or from the previous week's sales, and they use their good sense to make it go as far as possible while at the same time getting a balanced selection. People might not be very happy if you came back with avocados, mushrooms, pomegranates, tangerines, and eggplants, but no lettuce, tomatoes, or cucumbers.

Itemized preordering is by far the more common approach. Itemized orders can be handled informally at meetings when people call out how much of a specific item they want, or can be done in writing on a blackboard or order form. Most preorders print up order forms which can double as newsletters.

Having order forms creates two jobs. Someone has to print the forms and someone has to collate them and come up with a master order. If the food is paid for after distribution, there's no need for current prices on the form, and forms can be run off in quantity every few months. If you have a small co-op and are having trouble meeting crate sizes, you can rotate items weekly on your order form. If carrots are only on the form every two weeks, it's more likely that enough people will order them to provide the wholesale volume. And carrots can easily keep two weeks.

Collating can be speeded up if order forms are printed so that the quantity ordered borders the side of the page. The collators can then line the sheets up on a table with all the numbers showing on the sides of the sheets and just add across in a straight line.

In block preorders, each block figures its block order and then turns it in to the masterblock for that week. The masterblock collates the individual block orders into the co-op's master order. After compiling the master order, you may want to put the order for each item on an index card. Some block co-ops write each block's order for that item on the index card to make it easier for those doing distribution for the entire co-op to split up the items into each block's order. After a block's order for an item has been filled, it is checked off on the index cards. This can also work if you prebag orders in a unified preorder.

ITEM Strawberries
NO. IN CRATE 12 pts.
NO. OF CRATES TO BUY 7

LIST PRICE .45/pt.
TOTAL ORDERS 77 pts.
SHORT/EXTRA +7
SUBSTITUTION? sell extras

BLOCK ORDERS

Block	Order	Block	Order
1	7	7	12
2	2	8	8
3	9	9	0
4	0	10	5
5	6	11	12
6	7	12	9

WHEN TO PAY

Some preorders have their members pay when they pick up their food; others pay with the order. If you pay at distribution, you'll need a cashier and a system for figuring prices. This adds to the time spent at the distribution center, but it does away with the problem of debiting and crediting people's orders. If you pay when you pick up, you'll have to get money for the initial purchase from dues or deposits. Deposits in this method are based on the expected order. The amount will depend on the size of the household and the quantity of food carried by the co-op; $5 or $10 per household is common. Deposits can be refunded when members leave the co-op; dues, or fees, technically, go into the co-op's capital fund. Some co-ops have small fees to provide them with a little capital, and larger refundable deposits to cover the first week of buying. Hungry Chuck's Inevitable Food Co-op in Maine charges a $10 membership fee to everyone except disabled or elderly members.

If food is paid for at distribution, prices have to be computed right away. To get the unit price, divide up the total price of the crate by the number of items or pounds in it. Raise any fractions to the nearest penny to cover the co-op for losses and keep problems of arithmetic to a minimum. (Some co-ops compute prices to ½¢.) If members are bagging their own food, post the unit prices, on a clearly visible blackboard or bulletin board. Some preorders add up total bills for the members; others let members add up their own. In either case it's a good idea to have people use their order forms to make sure they get what they ordered, and to have someone with an adding machine check addition. It's one thing to trust the honesty of your members, and another to trust their arithmetic.

The operating cost of direct savings co-ops is met by a surcharge or bump that is added either to the unit price of the product, or to the total. (If it's added to the unit price, it's usually called a markup.) We suggest adding your bump to the total. It lets the members see the actual wholesale price of foods and the exact percentage that is added to cover operating costs. Adding the surcharge individually to low-priced items like apples or oranges means fractions, greater chance of error, and often inflated prices. If apples are 4¢ apiece and the bump is 10%, each apple then costs 4.4¢, or, rounded off to the next highest penny, 5¢. Twelve apples would then cost 60¢. If the bump is added at the end, the 12 apples would cost 48¢ plus 10% (4.8¢), or 53¢, a more reasonable price.

If members pay when they order, prices have to be included on the order form. Forms must be rewritten each week with current prices. The prices can either be the same as the previous week's market prices (not order form prices), or an estimate of that week's market prices. A good buyer can make educated guesses. In any case, a system of debiting and crediting the order for the week's *actual* market prices will probably be necessary, as it is only when the buyer gets to the market that prices can be known exactly. Some co-ops do away with debits and credits by guessing high and absorbing any losses if the market price is even higher than the high guess.

If orders are debited and credited, the current prices have to be posted and computed as in the pay-at-pick-up system, and the money worked out at distribution or on the following week's order. Crediting is also necessary if something ordered is not purchased because it wasn't available at the market or the price was too high. Even when co-ops have a system of substitutions to replace unpurchased food with a suitable alternative, the price difference has to be accounted for.

SUBSTITUTIONS

Co-op orders are not always filled exactly. Many co-ops substitute another food if what's been ordered is unavailable, too expensive, or poor quality. Some co-ops use substitutes to do away with shortages and surpluses caused by the difference between crate sizes and amounts ordered. For example, if peaches and pears both come in crates of 100, and 120 peaches and 80 pears were ordered, whoever is compiling the master order might substitute 20 pears for 20 peaches to avoid a surplus of 20 pears and a shortage of 20 peaches, and to make the orders approximate the crate sizes. When ordering, don't forget to allow for the few rotten apples or squashed tomatoes in most crates.

Back to pears and peaches. If pears are more expensive than peaches, you'll have to account for this too. When peaches are 8¢ and pears are 6¢, you'll be able to substitute four pears for three peaches. The arithmetic won't always come out this neatly, but try to make it as close as possible.

If your co-op has members bagging their own orders, substitutions don't have to be so carefully calculated. Members are free to buy substitutions from a surplus table if they wish. The buyer, or person ordering over the phone, may discover that the wholesaler has no cantaloupes this week, and decide to substitute honeydews. A large sign can advise people at distribution of the change, and those who choose can buy the honeydews. Order less of the substituted item than the total ordered so that the co-op isn't left with a lot of unpurchased food, especially perishables.

If the co-op prebags food for members, you'll have to be more careful about this kind of substitution. Honeydews may be more expensive than cantaloupes, so you may not be able to substitute one for one, and it gets pretty messy if you try to cut them up.

If you are substitute buying at the market, be sensible. Cucumbers aren't the best substitute for zucchini, even though both are long and green. Yellow squash is more appropriate. Or, as one co-op member put it, "A cabbage for three pears? Not again!" If you have too many substitutions, your order form may be too long.

Some co-ops dislike substitutions because they may be forced on members. Your co-op can make a democratic decision to have them or not. The main argument for them is that if members don't get something they ordered and nothing is substituted for it, they may be forced to go to the supermarket to get enough food for the week.

OVERS AND UNDERS

Preorders are at their most inventive when dealing with the problem of selling surpluses (overs) and equitably spreading out shortages (unders). These occur because the amount of food ordered is rarely the same as the crate size for that commodity. To return to peaches and pears, if no substitutions are made, the co-op would have 20 peaches fewer than the number ordered and 20 pears too many. If the orders are prebagged, this can be taken care of arbitrarily by giving a pear apiece to the orders of 20 people who have ordered peaches.

This becomes a problem if we're dealing with broccoli, cauliflower, or dozens of eggs. It's harder to make do with an extra, or without one that is ordered. Try to subtract or add to large orders rather than to orders that include only one of an item. This discriminates against people in large households, but it's much less of an inconvenience for them than for people with small orders. Even with prebagging, some choice can be put into this system by only distributing the shortages and allowing people to pick up whatever surpluses they want.

Having an overs table at a preorder is like having a small store. People can come in and purchase things they haven't ordered. If the quality and price are right you should have no problem clearing food off the overs table. Nonperishables can always be sold the following week, and perishables can be sold at the end of the day at bargain prices. Overs can also be sold to people you are trying to recruit into the co-op, or sold or given away to needy groups in the neighborhood. The Broadway Local Food Co-op has a regular clientele of elderly people who come to buy the surpluses each week. Another Day Co-op in Florence, Massachusetts, sells extras at half price to an alcoholics' halfway house.

It's a good idea to set a policy regarding surplus. If you're willing to give it or sell it to nonmembers, make this a policy that all members understand, and set a time for the giveaway or sale. Co-ops without such policies can run into difficulties. One co-op in Cambridge discovered that some members were giving free food to the distribution center janitor who then sold it to community residents. If some co-op members give away extras and others don't, it can lead to extremely tangled co-op-community relations.

Some co-ops don't sort their members' orders at distribution time but supervise members filling their own orders. If this system is used, members pick out their food from opened cases and bags set up around the room. If there's a shortage of a certain item, they must learn to take less than they have ordered. As members help themselves, they can write the new number of items or pounds missing on a sign posted above the shorted items.

In the voluntary bagging system, the last person to arrive at distribution usually gets left holding the bag — that is, there may not be enough left to fill this person's order. If some people, because of their schedules, are always late in arriving, it may be a good idea to bag their orders for them.

The best solution to the overs and unders problem is found at the market and not at the distribution site. You may want to buy from wholesalers who will split case lots. You can also coordinate your buying with other small preorders and split up cases among yourselves. Large co-op stores may also sell partial cases to small co-ops as a service. If you have to buy full case lots, know your membership and act accordingly. Overs are easier to handle than unders, so it's usually better to buy more than you need. Good judgment at the market is half the battle.

TO BAG OR NOT TO BAG

Prebagging is the system by which someone else in the co-op bags members' orders. It can be done by a work team before distribution starts or by people filling orders at distribution. The alternative is to have members bag their own. Co-ops that do not use itemized ordering usually prebag to insure their members' getting a balanced selection.

There are arguments for and against either system. It's obvious that prebagging provides more control at distribution. In a bag-your-own system, people may buy more or less than they ordered, weigh items incorrectly, or eat food that looks tempting. Prebagging makes it easier for the co-op to distribute overs, unders, and substitutions. But what is gained in control and efficiency is lost in the freedom to choose the head of lettuce or the size broccoli you want. Members also lose the fun of picking out and weighing their own food. For more than 100 orders, prebagging may take longer than members' bagging their own from well-laid out tables.

People spend more time at distribution if they have to do it all themselves. Sometimes people like to have this time to socialize. To bag or not to bag is a typical efficiency versus social values question. Your answer will depend on the size of your co-op, the attitudes of the members, and the specific conditions of your operation.

If a co-op is overcrowded at distribution and has more than enough people to work, it may choose to prebag orders. If a co-op is small and doesn't have enough people to do the extra work of bagging, it may choose to let members do it themselves. It's not an either-or question. There are many possible combinations. Some co-ops prebag specific foods like cheese or meat. Some bag items that are sold by the pound into one, two, and five pound bags, to prevent long lines at the scales.

OTHER LOGISTICAL CONSIDERATIONS

Preorders usually pick up most of their food in members' vehicles. With good packing, 10 to 20 crates should fit into a compact or foreign car, 20 to 30 into a large sedan or station wagon, and 30 to 75 in a van or microbus. More than 75 crates requires a truck or two vehicles.

If you receive deliveries at the distribution site, someone must be there with the master order list and money if you are not billed. Deliveries should be made on day of distribution if at all possible. This is a must for refrigerated items like dairy, sprouts, meat, or fish.

If your members bag their own food, you may want to arrange for a babysitting area at the distribution site. Otherwise, nibbling by preschoolers can cause unexpected shortages by the end of the day, and young children can also hurt themselves playing with the crates.

All but the smallest, most efficient preorders will need a coordinator. This need not be a full-time or paid position, though it often is in large co-ops. Coordinators can hold their jobs for several weeks or months at a time, or they can rotate each week. Some co-ops with work teams have a coordinator for each team. However you work it, it's a good idea for coordinators to keep in mind the following questions:

Are all the jobs getting done?

Are the people who signed up to work actually there?

Do the necessary people have the keys to the distribution site, truck, etc.?

Are the cash box, scales, adding machines, order forms, etc., on hand?

The coordinator often takes care of the books, or sees to it that someone else does.

MONEY

Despite the complications that can arise with substitutions and with arithmetical calculations in the fractions of pennies, the financial operations for most preorders are simple. Bump money and money not spent but held for reorders can be kept in a cash box or bank account. If you don't have a bank account and there's a large amount of money floating around from week to week, it's a good idea to alternate the houses at which this money is kept. Bank accounts mitigate this problem, but some co-ops feel they centralize financial control too much in the hands of the check-signers. The positive side of this centralization is that check-signers are specially accountable to the co-op for all their financial dealings. With a looser operation, and more people handling large amounts of money, there's more chance of error and loss. (See Chapter 12 for more on bank accounts.)

DISTRIBUTION CENTERS

Preorders should look for the largest available free space. Those that work out of churches, union halls, social clubs, or members' houses, have to be more flexible than those that rent or find their own space. Here are a few important things to look for when choosing a center:

Is the space accessible to public transportation and reasonably close to members' homes?

Is there parking? If on-street parking only, how crowded is the street usually?

Is there room for your co-op to grow? Crowded distribution centers mean inevitable mixups and frustration when block 3 takes block 2's eggs by mistake.

Scale and refrigerator if needed?

Bathroom and sink? Highly recommended, if not required by the local sanitation code.

Space to cut and wrap cheese?

Place to keep receipts and deal with delivery people? Out of the way of the avocados, if possible.

Phone? Very useful, especially if it's a long walk to the nearest pay phone, but it's expensive and may be abused.

Burglar-proof?

Lots of shelf space, or room to put up shelves?

Store Logistics

We now come to the rather more complex question of store logistics. Although we're not going to attempt to give you a complete manual on store operations, the following suggestions may be of help to new co-op stores or stores that are in difficulty.

LAYOUT

The trick is to find a building that meets as many requirements as possible and still fits your budget. Chances are you won't be able to find a building that has everything you want. You can work around many things and substitute for others.

Size is your first consideration. The building should be large enough to support your present membership and accommodate some expansion, in terms both of membership and of goods carried. Figure for storage space as well as floor space. You'll want an office or meeting room and some space for business records. You can always work with too much space but you can't work with too little. Co-op stores we know range in size from the 10′ × 10′ Tao Food Conspiracy in Mt. Lemmon, Arizona, to the proposed 17,000-square-foot direct charge "supermarket" of Atlanta Cooperatives.

Plan to do all your distributing on one floor. It's difficult to manage, and shop in, a co-op on two floors. The stairs will run you right down. If the building you're considering has two floors, plan to do your distributing on one floor and use the second floor, or basement, for storage, meeting and office space, or other types of co-ops (clothes, books, records, pharmaceuticals). If you're going to store things on another floor, try to make it the light stuff that you'll be carrying up and down. Mifflin Street Co-op in Madison uses its second floor for a community health clinic.

You don't need aesthetic quality but you do need structural quality. A co-op takes a lot of wear and tear and bears considerable weight. Take someone with you who knows about these things — a carpenter, an architect, or a structural engineer. There are professional inspection services that you can engage if you can't find a knowledgeable friend to do it for nothing. These services aren't too expensive and can save you a lot of money in the long run.

Check heating costs and condition of the furnace. Consult your library for books having a good checklist of what to look for.

Many a cooperative spirit can be dulled by a half-mile walk with groceries in heavy snow. It's best to have parking space adjacent to your co-op, but nearby is good enough. Plan on at least 15 parking spaces (more for a large store). It's sometimes essential, and always nice, to be near a bus line or subway.

You're going to need space for trucks to maneuver. Most truck drivers are contortionists, but loading and unloading is still less trouble with ample space. A loading dock will save you a lot of energy. It should be away from the co-op entrance to prevent confusion and crowding. The larger your co-op is, the more important an isolated loading dock is. Several exits are advisable, if not legally required for fire safety; check local regulations.

Design your co-op layout to insure a smooth flow of goods and members. Consider the space you'll need for delivery, storage, stocking, refrigeration, shelving, cash out, and paths. Your layout will influence both the viability of the business and the social relations among members.

Space should be allotted for goods coming off the truck. You may not have the ready labor or space to move things right from the truck to the shelves. This receiving space shouldn't be used for storage; clear it as soon as possible. When you receive merchandise, you'll probably need several people to unload it. You'll save time and energy if you're not cramped.

Plan storage space close to the receiving dock to save members the hassle of moving stock unnecessary distances. Consider your storage setup in terms of labor. Avoid storing an item in one spot, then storing it in another, and then putting it on the shelves. Try to unload and store in one step.

Shelving and lofts are two forms of storage space. Shelving must be strong: two-by-fours and ½″ or ¾″ plywood or one-by-twelves will suffice. Build shelving against the wall with a depth and height of 3 or 4 feet. You should be able to fit about six medium-sized boxes of goods in one slot on a shelf. Vary the height of some shelves to accommodate different size items.

If you can't satisfy your storage needs with shelving, you might plan a loft. Make it very sturdy. The combined weight of food and people has done in more than one loft. Lofts are especially useful if you do projective stocking, that is, if you try to plan way ahead not to run out of stock. When you store something for a long time, a loft does the job well. If the stock is a quick mover, best keep it in shelf storage.

Lofts can have other uses. The Food Conspiracy, Tucson's biggest co-op store, has its business office in a loft atop the walk-in cooler.

When planning layout, consider traffic flow, variety of goods to be carried, and placement of refrigeration for labor convenience. Cut a piece of paper to represent the size and shape of your building. Make a list of items you wish to carry. Group appropriate items together. Cut scale-sized pieces of paper to represent the display shelves for these groups of items. Make scale representations for everything in the store: checkout counters, display cases, coolers, lofts, etc. Shuffle these parts around until you find a workable layout. Do this before you move in. It's much easier to change your layout on paper than in the co-op.

If you're planning a large co-op, it's helpful to have a separate entrance and exit. If you can't have two doors, place your checkout to one side and direct incoming members away from it. You can do without an isolated loading dock in a small co-op, but it's still wise to do your loading away from the front entrance.

It's best to keep like items in the same area. People find it infuriating to look for bread, crackers, and rolls in three different parts of the store. And it makes more work for staff and volunteers.

Since refrigerated items are often heavy and have high turnover, it's best to have the refrigerated storage close to your receiving dock. This will save you the energy of hauling stuff through the co-op, which is a hassle when it's crowded. Your walk-in cooler or refrigeration storage unit is necessary for meats, fish, dairy goods, and some vegetables. Plan your displays for these goods adjacent to your walk-in cooler or close by.

Because canned goods are heavy, they deserve an aisle close to the receiving dock and storage area as well. Lighter goods can go anywhere; it's no sweat to carry 400 sponges across the co-op, but 40 cases of canned juice is another story.

After you've considered entry, exit, receiving dock, and refrigeration, you're ready to plan aisle layout. In your aisles you'll display most of your stock. To do this displaying effectively, you need easy access. Aisles should be wide enough to accommodate at least two, preferably three, people abreast. Your stock should be easily visible from the aisles, and easily reached.

There are many workable aisle designs. Co-ops needn't imitate the row aisles of food chains. A little variety can make shopping less monotonous.

In your aisle design, consider stock exposure, smooth traffic flow, and low labor expenditure. All parts of the store should be accessible. Paths shouldn't tend to cut off traffic from any areas, or converge on a single area except at cash out. Set your aisles so they direct traffic smoothly from one aisle to another. Consider leaving space for socializing. Tucson's Food Conspiracy has a separate herb room that doubles as a library and gathering place.

Checkout requires space for registers and lines. Checkout counters should be away from incoming traffic and deliveries. Since you may not have shopping carts, you'll need a place where members can put their purchases while waiting in that swift checkout line. The Boston Food Co-op has done well with a centrally located bench. Co-op members place their boxes on the bench and fill them with food. At the front half of the bench is a line. People move up to the front of the bench until it's their turn at the register. This system works smoothly for the most part. Delays are the most frequent complaint, but this is a register problem, not a bench problem. The lines are a good place for people to meet and talk, and to have co-op news posted for member perusal.

STOCKING AND PRICE-MARKING

Sensible stocking procedures can make the difference between an overworked membership and a satisfied one. A co-op has plenty of labor time to work with. If your store is well laid out and well managed, you should have a surplus of volunteer labor to channel into growth, education, communication, and spinoff activities like daycare. One crucial factor here is design. Shelves and storage designed to enable a volunteer to do a job quickly and efficiently can lessen co-op work tremendously.

Consider a volunteer working on canned goods. Tuna fish requires stocking. If the display shelf isn't marked, the volunteer has to deduce what item is out of stock. This can take as much as half an hour. The next step is to find the tuna in storage. If your storage isn't marked, this can take another twenty minutes. Once the tuna is found, if the case isn't price-marked, the volunteer must look up the price or have someone else look it up. If the price is found, the volunteer takes two cases of tuna fish, price marks the cans, and stocks them. This whole process can take over an hour if the cans have to be stacked three high and nine deep to fit them on the shelf. The time and effort problem is aggravated by the depletion of the tuna fish two hours later. The process must be repeated by a new volunteer.

You can avoid this sequence of events by planning. Well-marked shelving will tell volunteers what stock is out and where it should be placed. Storage can be arranged alphabetically. Tuna fish can be located under T for tuna or F for fish. If it's too much trouble to alphabetize, color code your storage. Divide the alphabet into four or five groups and give each group a color, for example, A–E, red; F–J, yellow, and so on. Mark your shelving with the stock item's name and a block of color suggesting where the item can be found in storage.

Mark the unit price of an item on the outside of the box as it comes off the truck on its way to storage. To have members unceasingly requesting price searches from the staff or from knowledgeable volunteers interrupts smooth co-op operation and makes for personal friction.

You might also write the current price of an item next to its marker on the display shelf. Find someone who can do attractive lettering; it doesn't cost any more than sloppy lettering. Make good-sized markers (12″ x 3″), include the item name, a blank space for its price, and your color block if you do color coding. Cover the sign with clear plastic. Over the price space write with a marker pen the current price. Since the price is written on plastic, you can easily change it.

Conventional horizontal shelving requires a good deal of time to stock. It's a frustrating job to balance one row of cans on top of another. An easier method of display stocking is to cut the top and front (or half the front) off a carton and place it on the shelf. Several cartons can safely be stacked on top of each other.

Or you may construct sliding shelves that are slanted and load from the rear. With gravity's help, the stock rolls to the front. The shelf space should correspond to the items you wish to stock. A #303 can, for instance, requires about 5″ clearance.

This type of shelving should be built with storage space behind it. Mark your storage space so the boxes on it correspond to the items on the display shelf in front. Sliding shelves can make a volunteer's work much more productive.

You can dump bar soap, sponges, toothpaste, and packages of all sorts into self-service bins. Most of this small stuff is hard to stack on shelves and is perpetually falling. With bins, you can stock larger quantities and save labor time. Where health regulations allow, many co-ops also use bins for grains, flours, and legumes such as beans and dried peas.

You can display bulk spices in gallon jars on a rack. The rack can rise over a work table about four feet high, and members can pour and weigh their spices on this table. Extra spices can be stored underneath.

You can get most of the materials for construction and shelving at little or no cost. There's always a building being torn down. Practice recycling. Keep an eye open for free wood; you'll always have a use for it.

LIGHT, COLOR, AND SPACE

Lighting need not be the same everywhere in the store. In fact, uniform lighting is pretty dull. If you alternate the intensity and placement of your lights you will create more personal and comfortable space. But your stock should be clearly visible; people are rightfully reluctant to buy what they can't see.

Shelving in a supermarket is of uniform height. It's built so high that you can't see anything but merchandise. This regularity of shelving and unending exposure to merchandise becomes oppressive, and accounts, in combination with uniform lighting and Muzak, for the hypnotic effect of supermarkets. As a co-op is a service institution, it needn't copy these tactics, and in fact should create a non-hypnotic environment. Shelving height can vary; there can be nooks and crannies. Messages, recipes, and nutritional and consumer information should be included near the food.

Coordination of colors will make the co-op more inviting. Darker colors create a settling environment; pastels and lighter colors suggest brightness and activity. Don't just go with any color. Find someone who understands color and design and their effects. Coolers and refrigerators don't have to be black and white. We've seen dancing asparagus, singing pork chops, and big smiling eggplants. Put your co-op Picassos to work.

INVENTORY

Food is constantly moving through your store. Deliveries are coming in and members are buying. Any food in the store that has not been sold is inventory.

All stores and some large preorders will have to keep inventory records. Although inventory control systems can get quite complex, the basic principles are simple:

You don't want to run out of anything. Your co-op exists, among other things, to provide a reliable source of food.

You don't want to order too much. You're working with limited capital and can't afford to tie it up in slow-moving inventory, no matter how unperishable the product or how tempting the deal. As an example of what not to do, a co-op we know had one steady customer for cornmeal, so they ordered a fifty-pound sack, and every other week this single member came in for his one pound. The secret of successful inventory control is to have stuff turn over fast. In a food store, the bulk of the merchandise should probably turn over every week.

A good inventory system will help you achieve the balance between underordering and overordering. But there are so many unknowns in ordering that inventory control itself can only be of limited use without the experience and intuition of members and staff to back it up.

Suppose you have 10 fifty-pound sacks of flour on Monday, December 1. An order of 12 more sacks comes in, so your inventory is now 22. A week later, on December 8, you want to know how much you've sold, so you'll know how much to order for the coming week. To find out the amount sold, you must take inventory. Suppose you count 14 sacks. To find out how much you sold, add the inventory of December 1 to the order that came in and subtract the current inventory (December 8):

$\text{Sold}_{\text{Dec 1-8}} = \text{Inventory}_{\text{Dec 1}} + \text{Order}_{\text{Dec 1}} - \text{Inventory}_{\text{Dec 8}}$
$\text{Sold} = 10 + 12 - 14$
$\text{Sold} = 22 - 14$
$\text{Sold} = 8$

Once you know what you've sold in a week, you have an idea of what to order for the current week, but it's only an idea. The formula for what to order is:

$\text{Order}_{\text{Dec 8}} = \text{Sold}_{\text{Dec 1-8}} - \text{Inventory}_{\text{Dec 8}} + \text{F}$

F is the all-important fudge factor. In this case you probably don't have to use it because you've sold only eight sacks and you still have 14 on hand; you obviously overordered for Thanksgiving, thinking everyone would be making pumpkin pies. You can skip ordering flour completely this week.

Let's say, though, that your inventory was down to 4 sacks, and having sold 8 the previous week, you plug the numbers into your formula:

$\text{Order}_{\text{Dec. 8}} = \text{Sold}_{\text{Dec. 1-8}} - \text{Inventory}_{\text{Dec. 8}} + \text{F}$
$\text{Order}_{\text{Dec. 8}} = 8 - 4 + \text{F}$
$\text{Order}_{\text{Dec. 8}} = 4 + \text{F}$

Your order will be four sacks, plus or minus the fudge factor.

The fudge factor includes many things. First, there's shrinkage. This covers a multitude of sins, including spoilage, spillage, theft, and what was nibbled for lunch. Your figure for sales includes shrinkage, which may vary from week to week. If you suspect that spillage accounted for the loss of a full sack last week and are planning this week to prebag flour instead of having members bag (and spill) their own, you might reduce this week's order by one sack. On the other hand, you may anticipate a big return of members who've gone away for Thanksgiving, accounting for the previous slow week and the relative lack of pumpkin pies baked locally. Based on your knowledge of previous weekly sales and of the size of the post-Thanksgiving rush, you may want to boost that fudge factor and order another sack. Or you may know from experience that people eat and bake more bread as the winter wears on, and will up your fudge factor for that reason.

Another element in the fudge factor is membership buying patterns. People don't usually buy staples like flour every week; your store may have a pattern in which sales are cyclical: 20 sacks one week, 15 the next, 10 the next, and up to 20 again the next.

The fudge factor also includes delays between ordering and delivery. Unless there's a warehouse close by and you pick up the order yourself, you probably won't get delivery the same day you order grains and other bulk staples or groceries. Produce, on the other hand, is usually a same-day or every-other-day item; many co-op stores take inventory the night before produce is to be bought and make up the order for the following morning's market run.

A last big part of the fudge factor is intuition and knowledge of the membership. Some things will sell well occasionally but not regularly. When strawberries come into season, a smart co-op buyer might order extra sour cream or whipping cream, even though these might not be regular high-volume items. The pre-Thanksgiving buyer will stock up on cranberries, pumpkins, cider, etc.

It's important to take inventory regularly, not only to help you with week to week ordering, but to enable you to see overall trends. Your finance committee will need those sales-volume figures to calculate your assets and see whether your weekly income covers the amount you are ordering. In other words, are you increasing your debt, decreasing your debt, or keeping it constant? Most co-ops keep the value of their inventory below a certain figure to avoid getting into debt by ordering more than they can sell in the time between orders.

Decisions on total value of inventory are important because

they're a way of setting policy on external growth. If the decision-making body in your co-op, given certain information from the treasurer or finance committee, decides to increase the value of the store's total inventory, it should then be prepared to deal with growth. The Boston Food Co-op keeps the value of its inventory at $12,000 to $15,000, which is adequate for a full-service co-op with a membership of 3000 to 3500 and weekly sales volume of $22,000 to $24,000.

You can keep track of your daily or weekly inventory for different sections of the store with a record like this, with appropriate datings:

	Week 1			*Week 2*		
	Inv.	Sold	New Order	Inv.	Sold	New Order
Cream cheese						
Rye bread						
Jam						
Peanut butter						

This forms a permanent record which you can use for checking bills, judging volume, gleaning buying patterns, and getting a feel for what's "moved."

Many stores take a total inventory once a month for bookkeeping purposes. To do it, get a lot of volunteers in the store, either in the evening or on a day you're closed. Make up sheets for each section of shelving, cooler space, and storage space, with a complete list of all that is contained in that space, and its price. A typical sheet would look like this:

Spices Section 1

Item	Price	Number	Total Value
Mustard seed	.23		
Ground pepper	.79		
Oregano	.63		

The order of the items on the sheet should follow their physical placement so that no item is missed in counting. Grains should be counted by pounds. Whole sacks in storage may be counted by sacks, then converted to pounds. Just make sure that no more grains are bagged or put on the shelves after you've counted them in storage.

Give each person a sheet for a section and set him or her to counting. If someone brings a radio or record player, the music will be much appreciated. People who work in profit-making stores often dread inventory, but if it's done in a congenial manner, with refreshments afterward, it can be fun. Have people count each item, fill in each column, and then multiply by unit price across to determine total value. Add up the value columns to get the total value of your inventory. Arrange completed sheets by departments. Make a totals sheet.

ORDERING

Always keep a copy of your order. Many wholesalers provide order forms and catalogues; if you use their order forms, make a carbon for your records. If you order by phone, write down the order and file it by wholesaler. You can also buy purchase order forms from paper goods or office supply wholesalers. These usually come in triplicate.

Make sure you're clear about terms, delivery, and returns with any wholesaler you order from. Some common terms are:

Prepayment — payment must be made before order is shipped.

C.O.D. — cash on delivery, or when you pick it up.

C.O.R.I. — cash on receipt of invoice; this usually gives you a few days' credit.

Net — Pay the whole thing by the time indicated. Net 10 days means payment within 10 days of invoice. Discounts are usually shown by percentage, for example, 2% 10 days or 2-10 means subtract 2% from the bill if you pay within 10 days of the date of invoice. Take advantage of this if you can. Invoices are usually due in 30 days and interest charges may be added after that.

If you haven't made the 10-day discount, don't rush to pay the bill; you probably have others that are older. Stagger your bill-paying so that nothing goes over 30 days.

When your order arrives:

Check the packing slip against the items delivered. Make sure you got what you ordered and if not, advise the delivery person of all discrepancies. Make sure the packing slip reflects any items that are missing, and note on your copy of the purchase order which items are missing.

Check to see if merchandise is damaged. If so, tell the trucker, note it on the packing slip and on your copy of the purchase order, and call the supplier as soon as possible. Either have the trucker sign his or her manifest (schedule) to indicate damage or have him or her give you a damaged-goods statement, which truckers often carry. If your agreement with the wholesaler provides that you return damaged goods immediately, do so.

Put the verified or corrected packing slip and copy of purchase order back in the file.

Mark the unit price on the box and put in storage. Unit price may include transportation cost and markup for store overhead if you don't add these on later at the cash register.

The invoice may come with the shipment, or may arrive a few days later.

When it comes:

Check it against your purchase order. Is the price the same as that quoted to you?

Note any damaged or undelivered goods if the invoice doesn't reflect this. Is the quantity that you received the same? Are all credits for previous payments or for damaged goods accounted for?

Check the terms. Are they what you agreed on?

Is the supplier's arithmetic correct?

Check off and initial any invoice that is ready for payment.

Paying bills weekly is efficient for most co-op stores, especially if credit extends for 10 days or more. You can enter disbursements (payments) in your journal of expenses at the same time that you pay the bills. (See Chapter 12 on finances.) Many items, like bread, are delivered daily and it would be a tremendous hassle to pay for them every day, not to mention the cost of checks, envelopes, pens, stamps, and the sheer boredom of writing check after check and licking envelope after envelope. Paying the delivery person at the time of delivery is equally time-consuming and unnecessary. Weekly payment preserves the sanity and tastebuds of the billpayer.

To pay invoices, it's best to identify the invoice on your check by the seller's invoice number, if any, and by date. Often you'll get monthly statements from suppliers detailing several invoices you've received since the last statement, and payments you've made or credits you're entitled to. Your check might then look like this:

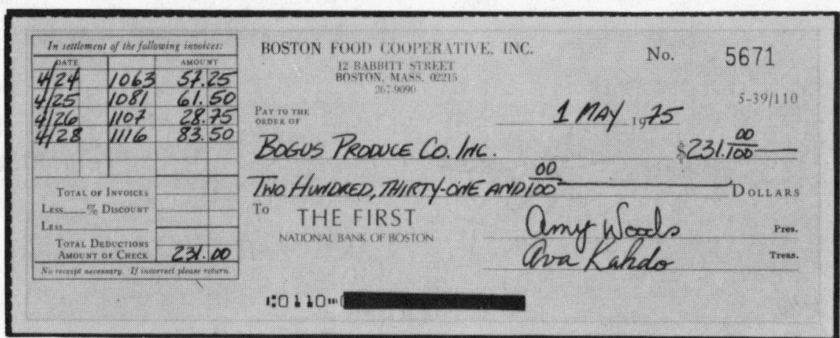

In settlement of the following invoices:

DATE		AMOUNT
4/24	1063	57.25
4/25	1081	61.50
4/26	1107	28.75
4/28	1116	83.50
TOTAL OF INVOICES		
LESS ___% DISCOUNT		
LESS		
TOTAL DEDUCTIONS		
AMOUNT OF CHECK		231.00

No receipt necessary. If incorrect please return.

BOSTON FOOD COOPERATIVE, INC.
12 BABBITT STREET
BOSTON, MASS. 02215
267-9090

No. 5671

5-39/110

PAY TO THE ORDER OF Bogus Produce Co. Inc.

1 May 1975

$231.00/100

Two Hundred, Thirty-One and 00/100 DOLLARS

To THE FIRST
NATIONAL BANK OF BOSTON

Amy Woods Pres.

Ava Kahdo Treas.

⑆0110⑈

Mark the invoice paid, with the date of payment and the check number. Then file the invoice under the name of the seller. This may sound tedious, but it causes immense satisfaction if the seller should call asking, "When are you going to pay me for the $31.05 worth of broccoli you bought on January 9?" To tell the person that the payment went out on January 12 on your check number 253, together with payments for your purchases of the 5th and the 7th, may prevent hard feelings as well as potential double payment.

If you fall behind, try to pay the oldest bills first. Know which creditors will or can wait. Credit is an important part of business; if it's available then you don't have to raise cash before sale. This is especially important for large deals in which a cash up front requirement might prohibit purchase. A good credit rating and prudent use of it allow a co-op to provide more types of food with greater economies of scale.

RETURNS

Be sure you have a returns policy established with each vendor. Small vendors who deliver will generally pick up spoiled or outdated stuff and credit you immediately. Larger wholesalers may require credit memos, which they approve before they credit your account. This may take several weeks. A canned goods wholesaler probably won't require you to send back dented or bulging cans, but many other suppliers will want you to save and return spoiled stuff. At the Boston Food Co-op, a milk distributor wanted the staff to save sour milk until the next delivery. The staff protested that the milk was smelling up the store, and a compromise was finally reached; they poured out the milk and saved the containers.

SPECIAL PROBLEMS

Special problems come up if the time between ordering and delivery is exceptionally long, if your timing is off, if you're contemplating ordering a new item, or if you're ordering the same item from two distributors. By ordering from two wholesalers you can take advantage of specials, keep yourself informed on prices, and cover yourself if one supplier is out. But you have to check records carefully to prevent duplication.

In the case of long-term ordering, if you and several other co-ops are splitting a truckload of, say, rice, or if you're dealing with a farmer and have to estimate your summer produce needs in advance, yearly inventory records are very helpful. Look at last year's inventory for the time of year that you anticipate your order will arrive, adjust it for changes in membership, and figure your new order.

On big orders of grains and staples or groceries, you can ask members to preorder and prepay, thus supplying the co-op both with necessary capital and with an idea of how much to order. If some members find it impossible to prepay in full, they may be able to give partial prepayment. You can raise the money you still may need up front from interest-free loans or fundraising events. Some co-ops sell coupons worth five pounds of rice, which members are free to buy in advance of the order if they wish to give the store this extra support. In any case, tell your supplier you expect credit next time around.

If you're thinking of ordering a new item, there are many ways to gauge member interest. Talk to people. Where face-to-face communication doesn't seem to suffice, posters and newsletter announcements may bring member feedback. Suggestion boxes will probably yield a fair number of good ideas along with a few outlandish ones. A more efficient method may be a log arranged alphabetically in which members can add their names to a request for an item. This way, whoever is ordering can see at a glance how many members are interested. As a general rule, start small with a new item. One co-op store was stuck with three cases of cocoa-orange soap for over a year.

Good member feedback will produce questions about food policy. At Tucson's Food Conspiracy, one member asked what frozen meat tamales were doing in the store, and whether there was a policy on meat. "Well, we don't have a formal one," the staff wrote in the newsletter, "but we don't carry meat and the tamales were a mistake and it won't happen again."

Salespeople will frequently try to sell you perfectly useless things, so you've got to be clear and firm about what your members want. If your volume gets big enough, you may also be offered bribes from commission salespeople trying to induce you into carrying a food that offends your sense of nutrition or good value.

Co-op Trucking

Whether you're moving six crates of produce from the regional market to the distribution center or a full tractor-trailerload of grain across the country, you have to truck. Small co-ops often get by with members' cars, station wagons, or vans, but at some point this becomes cumbersome, inconvenient, and inefficient. You may want to investigate the possibility of renting or even buying a truck, or of sharing truck rental with neighboring co-ops.

As co-ops get further along toward buying food directly from the sources of production, they'll need to develop their own trucking. Like food marketing, trucking is an important, often mystified, aspect of the economy, and one that co-ops must learn about if they are to build an alternative to profit-making food marketing. It only makes sense that sooner or later co-ops will want to eliminate the large profits of commercial truckers.

The reasons for co-op trucking are not only financial savings. In some instances, it may be necessary for co-ops to transport food themselves. The co-ops in northern Vermont found that commercial truckers simply would not go there; truckers don't like to go off major routes or into hilly areas.

When your co-op first considers renting a truck:

Check with several rental agencies to determine both per-diem rental rates and per-mile charges. These will vary, and depending on how far you're planning to drive, you may find one price arrangement better than another.

Find out what deposit is required and make sure you have it in cash.

Learn what insurance coverage each rental company offers. Most don't cover for overhead damage, but some do. Of course *your* co-op will not bang its rented truck into an overhead bridge, but we know of several that have.

Find out what the truck is made for. Find a company that rents trucks for commercial use and not for the you-do-it mover.

Decide what size truck you want. Econoline-type vans hold about 75 to 150 crates; stepvans, with 8 to 10 feet of cargo space, hold about 130 to 200 crates; and van bodies, with 12 to 24 feet, hold more than 300 crates. Pickups aren't too practical for hauling food, especially in the rain.

Find out how the truck is geared. Some trucks are geared for city driving, some for highway driving.

Learn about the capacities and ratings of trucks. Probably you'll be starting out with a truck that is rated under 18,000 pounds gross weight, its legal load, including the weight of the truck. Don't try to load a truck above its rating. It's against the law and brings a heavy fine. If you think you'll be exceeding 18,000 pounds, either rent two trucks or one higher-rated truck. In most states a higher-rated truck requires a driver with a trucking license.

If you'll be unloading at a loading dock, make sure that the truck is of loading-dock height. Most small trucks and some large ones have floors lower than standard loading docks. A metal plate can make up for about eight inches but more than that and your loading dock may be of little use.

Plan for loading and unloading. You may want to round up a handtruck or dolly, rollers for crates, cardboard to slide bags out, rope to tie boxes to the inside of the truck, or blankets to protect refrigerators and other delicate equipment.

Plan for the full time that you'll have the truck. You may be able to do a grocery or grain run during the twenty-four hours for which you've rented the truck for produce. You may have a member who needs to move furniture and can arrange to do it during the same twenty-four hours. Or you may want to share rental with another co-op.

INTERCO-OP TRUCKING

In the Boston area, three co-ops experimented successfully with interco-op trucking. The large Boston College preorder was already renting a 12-foot truck once a week. An 18-foot truck packs a good deal more food in proportion to its cost than a 12-footer does. One Boston College co-op member telephoned around and found two other co-ops to join the project: the Allston-Brighton preorder and BoJahn, a communal ashram group.

In any interco-op trucking set-up there are many details to work out. Labor and cost must be divided up; the most equitable way is on the basis of how much of the truck each co-op uses. Some logistical arrangements must be made at the market; if co-ops truck together but don't buy together, the food must be bought separately and kept separate in the truck.

Usually, three or four people are needed for trucking, purchasing, loading, and delivery. It's a good idea to have two trucking teams. One can get the truck, go to market, and return the truck to the first co-op. Team 2 can drop off goods at the remaining co-ops and return the truck to the rental company.

Try to find experienced drivers. Drivers not used to trucks must learn to be constantly aware of the size of the vehicle. Drivers should know local regulations about where trucks can and cannot go, and should have their routes planned in advance.

To divide up the work, the three Boston preorders developed a rotating system in which a different co-op was in charge of the expedition each week. The other co-ops supplied one or two members for each team.

To divide up the cost, the co-ops first computed the basic expenses of using the truck. Then they divided the cost by the number of crates bought to come up with the cost per crate. Finally, they split the cost based on the number of crates bought by each participating co-op.

Coordination is absolutely crucial in trucking. When two or more co-ops want to form a trucking cooperative, specific people from each group should meet with each other regularly. Once, Boston College and Allston-Brighton both rented trucks, a $30 error.

READY TO BUY

If your co-op is renting a truck more than once a week, you might consider buying. Add up your rental expenses over a period of time and compare them with projected expenses of ownership: maintenance, repair, insurance, registration, depreciation, parking tickets, and the rental fees you'll have to pay when your truck is being repaired. Capital outlay can vary tremendously, so if you're thinking of buying do a lot of looking around with co-op members who know something about trucks.

Another major consideration is the stability of your co-op and the energy level of its members. Truck ownership is not only a big expense but a major hassle, and only co-ops that are relatively together in their basic operations should undertake it. For big stores and rural co-ops truck ownership may *be* a basic operation.

In addition to a stable membership, you'll need a small group responsible for the truck. This should include people who can do maintenance and repair or who have good relations with a competent local repair collective. Someone in the group should keep track of registration, insurance, and inspection, and the co-op should maintain a trucking fund for emergencies.

When shopping for a truck, consider your co-op's present volume and leave room for growth. You may find an 18-foot truck not much more expensive than a 12-footer, and it would be a mistake to limit growth unintentionally by buying too small a truck. Once you have the vehicle, you'll discover additional uses for it, and perhaps get more types of food. But of course don't saddle yourself with a dinosaur that will eat up gas and drive around half-empty most of the time. Plan for the biggest normal load you anticipate; as for the once in a while big move (equipment), it will be cheaper to rent a truck than to pay operating expenses on a truck that is bigger than your usual need.

Most co-ops will probably buy used trucks, so it's important to learn all you can about the different makes and models of bygone years. Consider where the truck will be used and how it's rated. (Similar-looking trucks can vary tremendously in their hauling capacity.)

It's a good idea to have a limited number of people driving the truck, and any new drivers should be thoroughly coached in the vehicle's idiosyncrasies. Drivers should communicate in person whenever possible, otherwise through a log left with the truck's keys. Regular meetings are advisable. If you let too many people drive the truck, accelerate your depreciation schedule.

Whether you buy or rent, your trucking collective is a good place to put sexual equality into practice. Make sure that women get equal time at the wheel. All-women trucking collectives have operated in several parts of the country, and women are equal members of most others. A women's trucking crew regularly does the Tucson-L.A. run and a large grain deal was recently completed entirely by women, including driving a tractor-trailer. Both men and women should be aware of the fears and inhibitions they may have about driving big trucks.

Most co-ops that have their own trucks do some minor repairs and maintenance. How much you do depends on your members' skills and their interest in learning mechanics. Co-ops should practice preventive maintenance, which, like preventive medicine, means regular check-ups, tune-ups, and lube jobs. Don't forget such necessities as snow tires, antifreeze, and a working heater in cold climates. Some cities have co-op garages where for a small fee you can rent tools, equipment, and work space. Unless you have a professional mechanic in the co-op, you should probably farm out major repair work. You may be able to take out the transmission yourself, thus saving some money, before you send it to the shop for repair. For any repair collective, a friend at an auto parts store is a valuable ally.

THE LONG HAUL

NEPCOOP, the federation of seven Vermont co-ops, rented a tractor-trailer to bring grains into northern Vermont because no commercial trucker would do it. Eventually, a member bought a used rig, and started the Loaves and Fishes Trucking Company, which now makes monthly runs to Boston and New York, and occasional winter runs to Florida.

A tractor-trailer or "semi" (so-called because its trailer is semi-supported by its tractor) is the ultimate vehicle for transporting food by highway. Costing about $50,000 new, this mammoth may inadvertently terrorize Volkswagens but it's awfully efficient in moving foods long distances. As co-op federations do more of their own transportation and buy closer to the sources of production, their need for control of long-distance trucking will increase.

The advantages of long-distance interco-op hauling are illustrated by Intra-Community Co-op (ICC), a regional trucking operation formed in Madison by the 2800-member Common Market preorder, the Mifflin Street co-op store, and Sunflower Kitchen, a cooperative restaurant. The nearest terminal produce market was in Chicago, so the three co-ops set up ICC with its own staff and a 37,000-pound truck — the biggest, short of a semi. Soon ICC expanded its route to include stops at Minneapolis, Ann Arbor, and some spots in between. Produce from the Chicago market and cheese from Wisconsin are delivered by ICC to the Minneapolis and Ann Arbor warehouses, while grains from Minnesota mills are delivered to Wisconsin, Michigan, and Illinois. Stops are often made at farms and dry goods wholesalers. Not only is the ICC controlled by its member co-ops, but its rates are considerably lower than those of commercial truckers, who often charge markups of 40%.

The Dick-Freeman Trucking Company in Bloomington, Illinois, does cross-country hauling for both co-ops and capitalist customers. Co-op business does not yet keep the group's tractor-trailer busy enough to make it an exclusively co-op operation. Dick-Freeman did occasional runs from California to Minneapolis to Rochester, New York, to Boston in the winter of 1974–1975. Aside from logistical problems, the main drawbacks of the operation so far are the still inadequate co-op warehouse facilities and the relative lack of goods that can be backhauled from New England out west, leaving the truck partially empty on the return trip. The Dick-Freeman collective hopes to become an exclusively co-op operation and invites interested co-op truckers to link up with them to form a fleet. (See below for address.)

Aside from its other advantages, co-op trucking can begin to break down the rigid role definition of the capitalist economy. Co-op truckers often become buyers when they get to the market; they can take advantage of bargains or exercise their judgment about bad deals. Long-distance truckers are important news carriers and contact people; there's invariably a party when they arrive in town.

For tractor-trailer and other long-distance hauling you'll need some detailed, expert advice plus lots of careful planning. For-hire truckers can only haul unprocessed agricultural goods and other specific commodities like newsprint unless they have Interstate Commerce Commission licensing. Be sure you know the I.C.C. regulations, the licensing requirements, and the length limits for semis in the states where you'll be operating.

Sources

Each preorder handles its logistics slightly differently. Your best guide will be a self-amending booklet to which all co-op members can contribute their experiences and opinions. At the end of Chapter 5 we've listed some guides that co-ops around the country have published. One that deals specifically with logistics, and may be useful to block-style preorders, is the Broadway Local Food Co-op's handbook. Write to them at 95th and Columbus, New York, New York 10025.

The Office of Economic Opportunity, Washington, D. C. 20506, and the Cooperative League USA, 1828 L St. NW, Washington, D. C. 20036, have publications on store management; you can find others in the library and especially in the libraries of business administration schools. Any good library should also offer a choice of books on what to look for in industrial buildings.

For information on co-op trucking, write to Dick-Freeman Trucking Company, 1004 A W. Washington, Bloomington, Illinois 61701 or the Intra-Community Co-op, 1335 Gilson, Madison, Wisconsin 53715.

12. Finances

BUSINESS SYSTEMS need not conjure up visions of dumpy bald men with green eye shades slaving endless hours in a corner. Behind all other aspects of co-op operation lies the assumption that the money is there to operate. An accounting system should enable you to keep track of your money and to make decisions based on your financial history.

The most important principle is that your members must know what is happening in order to decide how they want their co-op run. If every transaction is recorded, members can assess the relative wisdom and productivity of all expenditures. That's why you keep books; the purpose of accounting is accountability.

There's nothing unreasonably complicated about the record-keeping needed to provide your co-op with useful information. This chapter attempts to explain some basic concepts and describe some simple accounting procedures. We're not going to present a complete course in standard textbook accounting.

Your financial system will reflect the size and sophistication of your co-op; if it becomes a large business, a professional accounting system may be necessary. By all means seek skilled assistance if you're having trouble, and tap any skills your own members may have. There's a big difference, though, between a few co-op bookkeepers and a professional accountant. At times your co-op may need a professional accountant just as it may need a professional lawyer. But don't let anyone set up a system for you that you don't understand. If you don't understand it, it won't work for you.

Every co-op must have a person or committee to inform the members about what's happening with finances. Almost anyone can be co-op treasurer who is meticulous about details, not afraid of numbers, and willing to learn by doing. The treasurer's basic responsibility is to keep the members informed.

A necessary corollary is the members' responsibility to get accurate information before they make a decision. Business decisions should not be the sacred turf of a few heavies. Decisions will be based on many factors besides financial information, though. The numbers don't tell you which alternative is better for your co-op, but they should describe the financial impact of different alternatives.

Primary records

A small preorder will probably need both primary and secondary records. Primary records are the first things you write down. The information is recorded as you go along, not at the end of the week or month. The quality of the information in your primary records determines the quality and reliability of the rest of your figuring. You'll have primary records of money going out (purchases, operating expenses, and capital outlay) and of money coming in (operating income and capital investment).

Primary records furnish important information. If a membership fee is charged, they tell how many people are joining at any given time, and how that compares with other times. From the sales information you can gauge how much people will buy during the spring as opposed to the winter or summer.

Money going out: Your primary record of money going out is your checkbook. If your co-op is larger than ten or so families, open a checking account. Make it a firm rule that all expenditures, however small, will be made through the checking account if possible. There may be one or two suppliers who insist on being paid in cash, but after you've dealt with them for a while, they should change their minds.

A checking account means that only a certain number of people can spend money (by signing checks); and changing the authorized signatures, although a simple procedure, is probably not done very often. The result is a centralization of at least some of the work and decision-making power. In some co-ops, there may be no one who wants this responsibility, or there may be people who feel that no one, or no group, should have this job.

Their reservations are valid, but, we think, unrealistic. One of the big block preorders in Cambridge has grown so large that more than $1000 in cash accumulates in one house on master-order night — in a coffee can. This cash is not spent till two days later. The bump, which hovers around $100, remains in the coffee can all week. Since all payments for food are made in cash and receipts are sometimes misplaced, the person who writes the weekly financial report is frequently frustrated. When the one supplier who took food stamps stopped doing so, this co-op could no longer accept food stamps from its members because it didn't have a bank account in which to deposit them. This caused at least one household to drop out.

There are many advantages to paying by check. It provides a record of where money has gone: to whom, for what, and when. A cancelled check is legal proof of payment. A checking system minimizes losses. Amounts are made out to the penny and can't be shortchanged in transfer. In the event that a check is misplaced or lost, it can be cancelled at the bank. Finally, a checking account helps maintain financial accountability. Only a few people can sign checks, and these people will be accountable to the membership for accuracy and proper business dealings.

Whether or not you have opened a checking account, you must record every expenditure. If you're paying in cash, be sure to get receipts. (You should get receipts when you pay by check too.) If you have a lot of very small expenditures (39¢ for pencils, for instance), you can have a petty-cash box. Write a check to "cash" (the only time you should do that), cash the check at the bank, and deposit the cash in the petty-cash box. Pay people for their small expenditures out of the box and have each person leave a receipt that indicates the amount, date, and purpose of the expenditure. When the petty-cash box is nearly empty, write another check for cash to replenish it, equal to the total of all the receipts in the box, listing as the purpose of that check the various purposes and amounts of the individual expenditures. That way the petty-cash box always contains the amount of the first check, either in cash or in receipts. Another help in handling small expenditures is to get credit at the businesses where you make most of them, and have them send you bills once a month.

In your primary record of expenditures, include date of expenditure, name of payee or recipient, amount, and purpose. In a weekly preorder, your payment to your egg supplier might have as its purpose "eggs" — that seems clear enough. But if your egg supplier sometimes lets you pay a week late, the purpose of the egg payment of September 16 might be "eggs for September 9." The usual presumption in a preorder co-op is that every check dated, say, September 16 is for food purchased, and most likely sold, in the same week. Whenever this isn't the case, say so in your primary record of expenditure.

Purpose of expenditure should conform to a set of categories that you establish in advance. If the checkbook is turned over to the bookkeeper with a notation like "Sept. 16, Stan, $75," she or he should yell and scream until not only is that entry clarified, but the checkwriters are consistently entering enough information to describe every check fully. Stan who? And what for? How about "#324, Sept. 16, Stan Mikulski, $75, onions." That's O.K. if it's understood that the onions are just for that week. If you're paying for two weeks' worth of onions at a time, the entry should say, "Onions, Sept. 9, $35, Sept. 16, $40."

What are some categories of money going out? First is purchases for resale. Next come operating expenses, which might include transportation of goods, supplies, salaries, taxes, rent, phone, utilities, and miscellaneous. Then come capital outlays: equipment, leasehold improvements, deposits repaid, loans made. You can add categories as you need them.

Before we go any further, an explanation of *capital* is required, since it's often misunderstood. If you receive money that's meant to be used by the co-op while retaining its dollar value, that money is not income but capital. It's invested in the co-op, whether in the form of membership deposits, shares, or loans, with the idea that the co-op will use it to carry on its business. Inherent in capital is the notion of retention of value. Capital belongs to the investors, not to the co-op. Whether the money is technically returnable (deposits, loans) or not, its value is supposed to be maintained. *Breaking even* means maintaining the value of the capital invested. *Sustaining a loss* means that you no longer have all the capital that was invested, and *having a surplus* means that you have more than what was invested.

If you do have a surplus, that surplus does not become capital; it is "retained earnings." It represents surplus income that you haven't yet spent, but that belongs to the co-op, not to any individual member or investor.

Just as capital investment is not income, so capital outlays are not expenses. Capital outlays are allocations or transfers of your invested capital from cash into another kind of value, such as equipment, improvements to your rented quarters, loans to other co-ops or individuals, or refunds of capital investments. These outlays aren't counted as operating expenses because some or all of their value is retained. If you lend money to another co-op, you retain ownership of an equal value in a different form. If you buy equipment, only that part of the equipment's value that's used up in each accounting period (depreciated) is considered an operating expense. A general distinction between capital outlays and operating expenses is: purchase of an object that will be used up within a year is an operating expense. Purchase of an object that will last longer than a year is a capital outlay.

In your records of money going out and money coming in, capital items must be kept separate. You'll need separate categories for each kind of investment you receive (deposits, shares, loans). In your records of money going out, capital categories might include repayment or refund of deposits, shares, or loans, purchase of equipment, and expenditures for leasehold improvements.

Money coming in: Your categories of money coming in will vary with the size and complexity of your co-op. Do you charge a membership fee? If you receive the fee and money for food at the same time, you should keep separate track of money for fees and money for sales. Records of money collected for refundable deposits or refunds from suppliers must be kept separate too.

There's no need to keep money physically separate just because it falls into different categories. That's why cash registers have separate subtotals, so all the money can be kept together while it is separated into categories on paper. You can forgo the cash register until you need it, which is when the labor required by the previous system becomes a burden. Any small preorder can keep its records straight by hand.

Let's say your small preorder has three categories of money coming in: sales, membership deposits, and membership fees. Write down on a sheet of paper with the date at the top the amount each member pays into each category, plus the total. This can be a permanent record of who paid what, in what category, on what day.

The information can be entered in a card file or other permanent record, but always keep the original sheet.

If your cashiers feel hassled keeping track of all this, that doesn't mean you don't need the information; it just means you need more or better cashiers, or a more streamlined way to record the information. Try preparing income sheets with members' names on them in advance.

Your primary record of money coming in must show how much money falls into each category that you establish to describe your operation. You need not record each separate transaction, as you do with money going out.

Bank records: Your primary record of income isn't complete without a receipt for the deposit from the bank. The amount deposited in the bank will be the amount entered in the "secondary records" (see below), so it must agree with your cashiers' totals or you must be able to reconcile the difference.

Some suggestions about your checking account:

Verify your bank statement against your checkbook every month. Your statement corroborates your primary records. If it doesn't balance, get upset and find out why. Have deposits been made or checks written without being recorded? Are the amounts of checks and deposits being recorded erroneously? Are you recording all bank charges in the checkbook? Are there arithmetic errors? If you don't know how to handle your bank statement, or if it's consistently giving you trouble, don't let it slide. If none of your members can help, the bank will show you how to deal with it. Save both the statements and the cancelled checks for several years. They are the only sure defense against false claims that you haven't paid one of your creditors.

Number all checks, both on the check and in the check register (stub). If you don't, you'll drive your bookkeeper up the wall.

Don't rip up voided checks; save them. They give you a complete record of where all your numbered checks went. Someday the Internal Revenue Service — or an angry member — may want proof that your books are accurate.

If you accept checks from your members in payment for food, sooner or later one will bounce. The bank will return the check and deduct the amount, which was included in a previous deposit, from your account. Be sure to deduct this amount in your checkbook with an explanation. When you deposit the check again, or the cash with which the member may have redeemed the check, you might make it a separate deposit to balance the deduction. Check with your bank about procedures. Usually you can redeposit the check after it has bounced twice, but not after the third time.

Secondary Records

The secondary records, or "books," are an arrangement of the information in the primary records to make this information useful, easy to extract, and easy to corroborate. Your books may be kept in an accountant's ledger or on any kind of accounting paper with adequate space for the information you need to enter. Most preorders will need only two different pages for each accounting period: one for income and one for expenses. Stores and large preorders may need four separate pages: for capital outlays, operating expenses, capital income, and operating income.

At the end of each accounting period (usually a month), you should enter all your expenses on the expense page, and all the income on the income page. Most accounting paper provides a wide space on each line to describe the payee or the source of income, and two small spaces that can be used for the date and the number of the check. These will be followed by a series of columns in which you can enter the amount of the income or disbursement twice, once in an amount column and once in a category column. Categories in a simple expense journal would include Purchases for Resale, Operating Expenses, Capital Outlays, and Miscellaneous. Here's a sample of an expense page:

45-605 EYE EASE NATIONAL Made in U.S.A.

PEOPLE'S PREORDER COOP
EXPENSE JOURNAL

DATE		DESCRIPTION, CHECK NO.	AMOUNT (1)	PURCHASES FOR RESALE (2)	OPERATING EXPENSES (3)	CAPITAL OUTLAY (4)	MISCELLANEOUS (5)
1	2	EQUAL CARROT CO. 340	15–	15–			
1	2	JOE LANDLORD 341	40–		40–		
1	4	BILL COUGHLAN (GAS) 342	5 25		5 25		
1	4	TERMINAL BANANA 343	23 –	23 –			
1	5	ICM MACHINES 344	20–			20–	
1	5	NEWTOWN TRASH PERMIT 345	5–				5–

If a check has been voided, enter the number in the space for this and write *void* in the space for payee. If a check includes money for two or more categories, each amount is entered in the appropriate column so that the total equals the sum in the Amount column. The Amount column will always equal the sums in all the other columns on the same line.

When you've made an entry on every line except the last on the first page of your journal, add up the totals in each column. The total of the Amount column must equal the sum of the totals of all the other columns. If it doesn't, *go back and find your error before you move on.*

When your first page balances, go on to the next one, entering on the first line the totals from the bottom of the previous page. These will be added to the entries on the second page to form the second page totals. After you've entered every check written in the accounting period you're using, you'll have an accurate summary of expenditures for the month.

The principles for entering incoming money in a journal are the same. The amount entered in the first column must equal the sum of all the other columns. Here the amount in the first column isn't that of a check paid out, but that of a bank deposit. Your categories, as in the records of money going out, describe your operation; they may include Sales, Fees, Deposits, Repayment of Loans, and, of course, Miscellaneous.

In many preorders, you'll need no further information beyond what is in the secondary records, and an occasional financial report based on these records, to tell you how you're doing. Such preorders maintain no inventory, give no credit, pay all suppliers when they deliver, have no insurance or taxes, own very little equipment, and pay no salaries from which to withhold taxes. If all that is true of your co-op, then you're ready to interpret your books. You simply compare operating income (sales plus fees, but not deposits or shares — these are capital) with purchases for resale plus operating expenses (excluding capital outlays). If income is greater, you're making money; if smaller, you're losing money.

If you don't have that simple operation, you'll need additional accounting tools to show members what's happening. These usually include a variety of "schedules" to describe at a given time the state of your inventory, accounts payable, taxes payable, accounts receivable, depreciation, amortization, etc. (These terms will be explained shortly.) When the information on these schedules becomes too complex and abundant to fit into separate sheets, it's usually integrated into the books.

At some point during your co-op's growth, you may decide it's time to move from a simple cash accounting system to an accrual system. These two systems differ in the way entries are posted. The cash method acknowledges a receipt of money (income) when you have physical possession, and acknowledges an expenditure when a bill is paid. This is the way most people operate their personal finances: cash in hand versus wolf at door. Accrual is the more sophisticated method of accounting. It acknowledges receipt when there is a legal right to the money, regardless of its possession or whereabouts. Expenditures are acknowledged upon receipt of the merchandise or services purchased, regardless of when the seller gets around to mailing the invoice. This may appear to be a more paranoid method of accounting, which it is. In large enterprises where one hand doesn't necessarily know what the other is doing, this conservative approach is almost a necessity. It provides a more precise evaluation of how many goods you have or how much money you owe.

How do you decide when your co-op is complex enough to need the accrual system? Basically, it's when cash accounting is not giving you accurate enough information on which to base decisions. If you've been overordering but haven't yet paid up, the cash method wouldn't warn you to revise your policy because it wouldn't reflect the mounting debt until the bills were actually paid. In the accrual method, all unpaid bills would be considered part of current expenses, and your monthly journal would reflect your mounting debt. With an accrual system, you can describe exactly the costs and expenses of running a business in a given time period.

If you only have a few accounts payable or only prepay a few expenses, such as insurance or rent, your cash accounting system won't reflect a great imbalance, but if you have many accounts payable or prepay a lot of expenses, the accrual system will give you a much more accurate month-to-month accounting. A full service store will almost surely need an accrual system, and a small store or large preorder dealing with 30 to 50 other businesses might begin to think about making the change.

Accrual accounting involves adjusting your monthly figures for income or expenses incurred in that month but not physically received or disbursed. If you paid a $200 insurance bill in January and were using the cash method, your books for January would reflect a big loss. In an accrual system, the insurance expense would be adjusted, or spread out over the course of the year, as an expense of $16.67 per month. If you bought some food in November but didn't pay for it until December, it would be considered a November expense under the accrual system and a December expense under the cash system. For a complete picture of an accrual system, see Sources at the end of this chapter.

Financial Reports

The statement of income and expense and the balance sheet are the two major financial reports that small co-ops may wish to issue from time to time and large co-ops should issue every month. The income and expense (or profit and loss) statement is a comparison of income with cost of merchandise and overhead. The purpose of the statement isn't to show how much money there is in the bank but to indicate if the business is operating efficiently or not: where income is coming from, where expenses are going, if income is outdistancing expenses. If you're using the cash method, the time period covered by the statement should be long enough to give more than a six-inch perspective. If there's a cyclical nature to the buying habits of your co-op, the statement should cover an entire cycle. If grains are ordered and distributed in bulk only once every two months, then a monthly statement would give a distorted view of the co-op. One month would look exceedingly lean and the other excessively lush.

The form of the income and expense statement is essentially an itemized subtraction:

Sales
minus Cost of Goods Sold
equals Gross Profit
minus Operating Expenses
equals Net Profit or Loss

Figures are taken from the operating income and operating expense journals. The capital account doesn't enter into the figures at all.

NATIONAL 45-605 EYE-EASE

PEOPLE'S FOOD COOP
INCOME & EXPENSE STATEMENT
JANUARY 1, 1975 to FEBRUARY 1, 1975

	1	2	3	4	5
INCOME					
GROCERIES			2567 45		
PRODUCE			2605 90		
DAIRY			3400 11		
MEAT & FISH			3015 55		
BREAD			990 11		
SURCHARGE			1257 91	10 %	
MISC. INCOME			141 44		
(LOSSES)			(20 —)		
TOTAL SALES INCOME			13958 47		
COST OF GOODS SOLD					
MERCHANDISE					
BEGINNING INVENTORY (12/1)		10101 99			
PURCHASE:					
GROCERIES	3389 59				
PRODUCE	2710 51				
DAIRY	3695 03				
MEAT & FISH	3110 70				
BREAD	1050 31				
NET PURCHASES	13956 14	13956 14			
GOODS AVAILABLE FOR SALE		24058 13			
LESS: CLOSING INVENTORY (12/31)		11368 33			
NET COST OF MERCHANDISE		12689 80	(12689 80)	100 %	
SURPLUS ON SALES			1268 67		
OPERATING EXPENSES					
OFFICE SUPPLIES	27 15				
UTILITIES	100 40				
RENT	300 —				
MAINTENANCE	20 50				
TELEPHONE	50 45				
PAYROLL	500 —				
BAD DEBTS	20 —				
SPOILAGE	30 17				
INSURANCE	30 —				
EDUCATION	20 —				
MISCELLANEOUS	10 67				
PILFERAGE	15 90				
DEPRECIATION	100 16				
	1265 67		(1265 67)	10 %	
NET SURPLUS OR LOSS			3 —		

If you have no inventory, your figure for cost of goods sold can come right out of your books, but you may need some adjustments in your operating expense figure. These adjustments will be based on depreciation and amortization.

When you buy a piece of equipment, the purchase price is not an operating expense but an investment, an allocation of capital from cash into another kind of value. Through the formal accounting procedure of depreciation, you can show a portion of that investment as an operating expense every month, six months, or year — however often you do a statement of income and expense. Depreciation continues until you reach the "salvage value" of the equipment, or until you have reached zero or scrap value. The sum of all the depreciation you claim each month should be added to the other operating expenses in your books.

You can assign a "useful life" to every piece of equipment you buy. Theoretically, this is the time the equipment will be of value to you; in practice, useful life is often determined by accounting considerations. If a business is making a large profit, it will assign the shortest possible useful life to new equipment, so that a large amount of depreciation will occur in the first year to offset the profit for tax purposes; if the reverse is true and money is being lost, a longer useful life may be assigned, so that more of the depreciation will occur in later years to offset possible future profits. You must be aware of these considerations, since if you show a profit at the end of the year, you'll owe taxes on it.

Try to base the useful life of your equipment on an objective evaluation, keeping in mind that you can't change the useful life once you set it. You can, of course, depreciate the remaining value of a piece of equipment all at once in the year in which it unexpectedly goes to pieces.

Let's say you decide that the adding machine that you bought for $48 has a useful life of four years. You can then show $1 per month for four years as an operating expense for depreciation. Keep a schedule of depreciation for all equipment, with columns headed Purchase Price, Date of Purchase, Check Number, Useful Life, and how much depreciation is being taken as an expense in each accounting period. If you buy that adding machine on June 30, you can only show $6 depreciation between then and Dec. 1. This is "straight-line" depreciation; other kinds are explained in IRS publications and accounting texts.

Amortization is similar, only it applies to different types of investment, usually "leasehold improvements," which are not portable like equipment but are made at your expense at the property you rent. Examples: you put in plumbing to comply with health regulations, or you install a new concrete floor. You amortize (depreciate) these expenses over the length of your lease; any value left unamortized when you move is amortized then. As with equipment, leasehold improvements are valued at their original cost to you. The amortization you claim each month or year is another operating expense.

The balance sheet is the other half of the financial report. Combined with the statement of income and expense, it describes your co-op's financial state. However simple your operation, you have to do a balance sheet to see where you stand.

The balance sheet is static like a snapshot; it shows the state of your finances at a given time. It doesn't describe what happened between balance sheets; that's up to the statement of income and expense. The balance sheet tells the co-op: this is what we have, this is what we owe, and this is what our investment is worth. Most of the information for the balance sheet will come from your capital income and outlays columns in the journal.

The balance sheet has two principal categories, assets and liabilities. Assets are what you own or are holding temporarily: cash, equipment, claims on money owed to you, inventory of food or supplies. The list of assets describes how the investors' (members') money is being used. Assets are valued at "fair market value" at time of purchase. This is usually the price paid, unless you got a deal or the item was donated; under these circumstances the retail price is used. Substract from this the depreciation the asset has taken.

Liabilities are what you owe: bills due, loans you've taken out, refundable deposits taken from your members, shares invested in the co-op. The two latter items of capital are listed as liabilities because they're owned by the investors or creditors and are therefore owed to them by the co-op.

If your assets equal your liabilities at a given time, then you have broken even up to that time. If assets are greater than liabilities, you've got a surplus, and if liabilities are greater than assets, you've lost money. If this continues to happen, the deficit will eat away at the capital until the members have lost their investment and the co-op is bankrupt.

The balance sheet can tell you how stable the co-op is at any given time. Members can see where and in what assets their money has been invested, as well as what long-term debts their co-op is liable for. This provides an element of accountability concerning the wisdom of investment, the use of credit, and the projected life of the co-op.

Let's say you start a preorder with 20 families who put in deposits totalling $200. Before you buy your first cabbage, and before you deposit the money in the bank, your balance sheet looks like this:

1. Assets		Liabilities	
Cash on hand	$200	Members' equity (deposits)	$200

You open a checking account and operate for a few weeks. You keep $20 in change outside the bank. You get more members. Your next balance sheet might look like this:

2. Assets		Liabilities	
Cash on hand	20	Members' equity	$300
Cash in bank	280	(deposits)	
	$300		

At the time of the next balance sheet, you have $10 worth of food left over, which you plan to sell the following week:

3. Assets		Liabilities	
Cash on hand	20	Members' equity	$300
Cash in bank	270		
Inventory	10		
	$300		

As you go along you may find that once in a while someone can't pay for his or her food one week, but pays for it a week late. If you allow this, your balance sheet might look like this:

4. Assets		Liabilities	
Cash on hand	20	Members' equity	$300
Cash in bank	255		
Inventory	10		
Accts. Receivable	15		
	$300		

Your co-op gets bigger, your inventory gets bigger, and you decide to buy scales. You invest $36 for two hanging scales, and you figure their useful life at 36 months. After you've had the scales for one month, your balance sheet might look like this (the parenthesis means a negative number):

5. Assets		Liabilities	
Cash on hand	20	Members' equity (deposits)	$400
Cash in bank	270		
Inventory	50		
Accts. Receiv.	25		
Equipment	36		
less accumulated depreciation	(1)		
	$400		

Although the size of members' deposits increased by $100 between balance sheet #4 and balance sheet #5, the amount of money in the bank only increased by $15. Where did the rest go? The balance sheet tells you: some went to increase inventory, some was loaned out as credit, and some went to buy scales.

When you do your next balance sheet, you have received and sold your week's supply of eggs, but somehow the egg supplier hasn't been paid yet. You owe him $50:

6. Assets		Liabilities	
Cash on hand	20	Members' equity (deposits)	$400
Cash in bank	326		
Inventory	50	Accounts payable	50
Accts. Receiv.	25		$450
Equipment	36		
less accumulated depreciation	(2)	Retained earnings (net worth)	5
	$455		$455

What else has changed? For one thing, your scales are a month older, and worth a dollar less. Also, your careful management has begun to produce a surplus — $5 so far. But don't panic; it may be only temporary.

After you've added up all your assets and liabilities, compare them. The difference between them is Retained Earnings or Net Worth. If the assets are greater than the liabilities, the Retained

Earnings figure will be positive; if the liabilities are greater, the figure will be negative. The figure for Retained Earnings, whether negative or positive, always brings the balance sheet into balance, making the left hand column (Assets) equal the right hand column (Liabilities plus or minus Retained Earnings). It is the only figure in the balance sheet that you don't get from your secondary records.

When you compare two successive balance sheets, the difference between the Retained Earnings figure in the first one and the Retained Earnings figure in the second one will be the same as the Profit or Loss figure at the end of the Statement of Income and Expense that covers the period between the two. If it isn't, you've made a mistake.

Making Financial Decisions

The Statement of Income and Expense and the Balance Sheet constitute a financial report. You'll consider the information in this report and use it to plan for the future.

You may decide to change your markup or bump. How much your bump should be depends on your operating expenses, your sales, and your shrinkage. Let's say the Utopia preorder co-op is now charging a markup of 10%, and its monthly Cost of Goods Sold is $1850. The markup is producing $185 a month. Let's say that monthly expenses — rent, trucking, depreciation, etc. — are $180. Therefore, Utopia should have a small surplus or at least be breaking even. And it would be, if it were perfect and didn't have any shrinkage.

Shrinkage is the umbrella term for all the unrecorded things that go wrong and cost you money. Examples:

You buy a 40-pound wheel of cheese for $48. You cut it into forty pieces, weigh each piece, and put prices on them based on $1.20 a pound. If you lost some crumbs in the cutting, or if your cheese-cutter nibbled, those 40 pieces won't add up to $48. The difference is shrinkage.

You buy a crate of 100 juice oranges for $5. You charge 5¢ apiece for them, plus your markup. At the bottom of the crate are five rotten oranges. That's shrinkage.

Other things that go into shrinkage are ripoffs, shortweighing, underpricing, and cashiering mistakes. Shrinkage will vary between 1 to 5% of Cost of Goods sold. As your co-op grows, your shrinkage, as a percentage, will probably grow. Some large co-ops have shrinkage of 5% and still thrive.

What does this mean for the Utopia Co-op? Let's say the Statement of Income and Expense looks like this:

Sales	$2000
Cost of Goods Sold	− 1850
Gross Profit	= 150
Operating Expenses	− 180
Net Loss	= (30)

The 10% bump should have produced $185 if all the goods purchased had been paid for by members in sales. But shrinkage is made up of goods that never made it to the cash register or else were short-weighed or underpriced, so the co-op was unable to realize its full markup on them. Operating expenses were $180, for a theoretical surplus of $5. Instead, Utopia realized only $150 more than Cost of Goods Sold, and had an actual loss of $30. The difference between potential sales and actual sales is shrinkage. In this case, shrinkage was $35, or about 1.9% of Cost of Goods Sold.

What does Utopia do now? Obviously, one idea is to try to cut down on shrinkage by eliminating or counteracting the many shortcomings that produce it. But every well-run food co-op has a natural level of shrinkage that can never be eliminated; it's part of being in the food business. Try hard, but don't be frustrated if your shrinkage doesn't shrink as much as you'd like.

If you can cut any expenses, try that. But most co-ops spend only what they absolutely have to for operating expenses; there may not be much flexibility there. The answer may be that Utopia cannot operate on a 10% bump.

Don't be frustrated by reports that some other co-op has a 10% bump and is doing fine. It may be that the other co-op is really losing money but hasn't figured it out yet. Many co-ops charge considerably more than 10% and still save their members substantial amounts on their food bills. Analyze your co-op's situation and charge what you must to make ends meet. When your shrinkage shrinks or your sales rise enough to make a 10% bump feasible again, you can change your policy.

Don't rush to lower the markup or bump until you've considered several things. Are you exploiting any of your members or workers by not paying them enough? (What is enough is of course for the co-op to define.) Do you expect any increase in your expenses in the near future? Are some members contributing money — by buying supplies, paying for gas, or making phone calls — without reimbursement? Have you been deferring certain important expenses, such as liability insurance or a newsletter, because you thought you didn't have the money? Have you included in your operating expenses taxes, depreciation, and amortization? Don't underestimate your true expenses; it's fine to skimp at the start, but when your skimping produces a surplus, don't force yourself to skimp forever by lowering the bump instead of paying for what you're getting.

Another financial decision that can come out of your records is to increase capitalization. If you find yourself without enough cash to buy the food or to pay bills, one of two things has happened: either you've lost money or you're undercapitalized. If you've lost money and have read this far, you know what to do about it. Raise your bump, increase your sales, or reduce your expenses so that you're breaking even. If the members want to, you may increase the bump to a level above breakeven, until you've made a surplus that balances your previous loss. If you're sure you're breaking even or making a small surplus and are still chronically short you may just not have enough capital to operate on your present scale. Ask members to increase their investment in the co-op by increasing the value of their deposits or shares. Or try to raise capital from another source. The alternative is cutting back the scale of your operation, which, if the members want it, is just as good.

There are other types of decisions that can come out of financial reports. Decisions on whether to expand or limit growth will be based, in part, on financial information. Your accounting system will provide a historic perspective on how expanded volume or variety of goods has affected the co-op in the past. Chapter 14 discusses some of the ramifications of growth.

Specially for Stores

Many of the principles and practices we've discussed apply to both preorders and stores. Because stores usually carry more foods and have more complex operations than preorders do, many modifications are necessary for them. Stores will probably find it more convenient to have separate journal pages for operating expense and capital outlay, operating income and capital income. These can be done just like the example on page 224, with as many columns and as big a journal book as you need to describe your operation.

The heart of the store income journal will be information taken from the cash registers. Besides providing key fundamental data about sales, the cash register is the primary way of assuring efficient exchange of money. This protects the interests both of individual members and of the co-op. All those who operate the register should be familiar with the machine and the accounting system into which sales data are fed.

The cash register should have enough keys to record all the major categories of food sold. If the co-op bumps total sales, a separate key should record the bump. The register should have enough drawers to provide a separate drawer for every worker operating the machine on a given day. And it shouldn't contain any money when the store isn't open for business. Money should come from the bank at the start of every business day and be redeposited at the end of the day. During the day, if large quantities of money accumulate, don't tempt fate. When more money accumulates than is necessary for making change, remove it and deposit it in the bank.

The bookkeeping system is a way to get information from the machine to the membership. Begin with a register cash-out sheet that reports the amount of business done. The dollar amount on the register tape should equal the dollar amount in the drawer, with the following adjustments:

Add to the cash total the amount expended from the register for petty cash, refunds to members, or bank deposits earlier in the day. Have a petty cash voucher and receipt for each petty cash withdrawal; the voucher should indicate the name of the person drawing the money, the purpose of the withdrawal, and the amount. Refund vouchers should record the person to whom food credit or cash was given, the reason, and the name of the register operator.

Subtract the amount of cash with which the operator started the day.

Record any overrings and either subtract them from the tape total or add them to the cash amount.

AGENDA
FOR NEXT
MONDAY'S
MEETING
36
Marstall 75

REGISTER CASH OUT SHEET

Person on Register J. L. Register # 1 Date 1/15/75

Drawer A or B A

Final Cash Out

Cash:	No.	Amt.
50's	(3)	150.00
20's	(10)	200.00
10's	(15)	150.00
5's	(30)	150.00
1's	(85)	85.00
H	(10)	5.00
Q	(100)	25.00
D	(150)	15.00
N	(110)	5.50
P	(65)	.65
Total Cash		786.15
Total Checks		756.48
TOTAL I (Deposit)		1542.63

Corrections #1

Refunds	4.18
Petty Cash	8.75
Welfare Vouchers	48.00
Misc.	0
TOTAL I Plus Corrections	1603.56
Deduct Opening Bank	50.00
TOTAL II (Actual Amount Taken in)	1553.56

Corrections #2

Overrings	2.15
Plus Shortages or Minus Overages	+ .86
TOTAL III (Equals TOTAL II Plus Corrections #2)	1556.57

TOTAL SHOWN ON TAPE 1556.57

Difference Between TOTALS III and IV 0
(Amount Over or Short Due to Operator Error)

Attach Adding Machine Tape and Petty Cash Receipts

Once the register and cash information are collected, they can be consolidated onto a single form, the closing statement. This is especially helpful if there's more than one register or operator. The closing statement determines the total bank deposits for a given day.

DAILY CLOSING STATEMENT

I. (From TOTAL I on Register Cash Out Sheet)

Register #1	1542.63
Register #2	1235.45
Other	0
TOTAL "A"	2778.08

Refunds	8.20		
Welfare Vouchers	95.65		
Petty Cash	16.51		
Other	0	TOTAL "B"	120.36

Total of Opening Banks 100.00

CASH VOLUME: TOTAL "A" PLUS TOTAL "B" MINUS OPENING BANKS 2798.44

II. Grocery Sales (less overring)

Register #1	351.08	
Register #2	230.81	
Total Groceries		581.89

Produce Sales (less overring)

Register #1	256.94	
Register #2	230.11	
Total Produce		487.05

Dairy Sales (less overring)

Register #1	291.57	
Register #2	275.00	
Total Dairy		566.57

Meat & Fish (less overring)

Register #1	286.46	
Register #2	254.58	
Total Meat & Fish		541.04

Bread Sales (less overring)

Register #1	216.34	
Register #2	151.15	
Total Bread		367.49

TOTAL SALES	
Plus 10%	254.40
SALES VOLUME	2798.44

(Equals Cash Volume Above)

III. MONIES FOR DEPOSIT:

Register #1 (TOTAL I)	1542.63
Register #2 (TOTAL I)	1235.45
TOTAL CASH FROM SALES	2778.08
MEMBERSHIP FEES	50.00
SALES TO OTHER CO-OPS	165.32
DONATIONS	2.25
REDEPOSITED CHECKS	7.19
MISCELLANEOUS	0
TOTAL EQUALS DEPOSIT	3002.84

Attach Deposit Slip Carbon to this Sheet!

45-605 EYE-EASE NATIONAL Made in U.S.A.

PEOPLE'S FOOD COOP
OPERATING INCOME JOURNAL
JANUARY, 1975

DATE		COMMENT	1 TOTAL SALES	2 GROCERIES	3 PRODUCE	4 DAIRY
1	1	CLOSED- NEW YEAR'S	—	—	—	—
1	2		1416 89	290 61	252 61	309 30
1	3		1278 50	241 00	235 90	290 10
1	4		1176 82	200 78	211 15	255 91
1	5		1231 76	220 00	235 16	261 80
		TOTAL, JAN. 1-5, 1975	5103 97	952 39	934 82	1117 11

The results of each day's operation are recorded in the Operating Income Journal. In co-op stores this journal should be filled out either every day or every week. The Total Sales figure comes from the Closing Statement items marked *cash volume* and *sales volume*, which should be equal. Human failing does make a rare appearance and these figures can differ. If sales volume is greater than cash volume, enter the difference as a loss in a separate column of the journal. If sales volume is less than cash volume, enter the difference as miscellaneous income in a separate column.

The store's disbursement or expenses journal can be brought up to date every week; a convenient time is just after you've paid your bills. The disbursement system is keyed on your checking account just as the income journal is keyed on your cash register.

Stores may want more than one checking account. You may have one account for expenditures over $200 and another for expenses under $200. The large-sums account may require more than one signature. If there is paid staff, the store should have a separate payroll checking account. Checks of this type are printed with spaces for payroll accounting (hours worked, gross pay, state and federal tax deductions). The IRS booklet, *Mr. Businessman*, will tell you how to do payroll accounting in addition to many other procedures you'll need for tax purposes.

Your store journal can tell you what items sell best — produce, groceries, etc. — and which expenses are hurting most — utilities, rent, payroll, etc. This kind of information leads to decisions on policy questions: Is it worth the time and energy to stock gro-

MEAT & FISH	BREAD	SURCHARGE (10%)	MISCELLANEOUS	(LESS LOSSES)	
—	—	—	—	—	
280 01	155 55	128 81	—	—	
251 25	144 02	116 23	—	—	
260 40	131 60	105 98	11 00	—	
270 05	140 50	112 75	—	(8 50)	
1061 71	571 67	463 77	11 00	(8 50)	

ceries? Should the co-op move to a more efficient building? Is the staff being paid too much or too little?

Like a preorder, a store can best communicate financial information to its members in summary reports. This saves members the rather time-consuming and perplexing task of poring over pages of journal entries. Income and Expense Statements and Balance Sheets have already been described. Stores usually have more assets than preorders do, so their Balance Sheets are longer. The inventory of most preorders can be easily calculated; for stores it's not so simple. And stores may not want to take a complete inventory every time they need a balance sheet.

To keep track of how much inventory is on the floor at any one time, you can keep a catalogue of transactions in inventory in a ledger book. The ledger is also used to keep track of the value of your equipment and other assets and liabilities.

Keep similar accounts for produce, dairy, meat, fish, etc. Also keep accounts on all assets. In the sample below, the office equipment account includes only an adding machine. Usually there would be many items listed with different depreciation schedules.

In addition to the Balance Sheet and the Income and Expense Statement, stores are well advised to write periodic budgets. If the two previous reports are considered indicators rather than precise statements of fact, the budget is the crudest indicator of all. It depends on past performance, present needs, future expectation, and the budget creator's cosmic sense of what's happening. Often the budget is little more than a guess. Past performance may be

PEOPLE'S FOOD COOP
LEDGER BOOK

	DATE			DEBIT	CREDIT
①			GROCERIES		
	1	12	A&G GROCERIES	1234 56	
	1	12	SALES, 1/12		234 —
	1	13	SALES, 1/13		1000 56
	1	13	INVENTORY, 1/13	900 —	
	1	14	SALES, 1/14		345 61
	1	15	SALES, 1/15		254 39
	1	16	A&G GROCERIES	1123 89	
	1	16	INVENTORY, 1/16	1423 89	
②			OFFICE EQUIPMENT		
	12	1	ADDING MACHINE	125 —	
	1	1	DEPRECIATION		2 08
	2	1	DEPRECIATION		2 08
			CLOSING BOOKS, 2/1	120 54	
③			LONG TERM LOANS		
	1	1	LOAN FROM BANK		8000 —
	2	1	MONTHLY PAYMENT	100 —	
	3	1	MONTHLY PAYMENT	100 —	
			CLOSING BOOKS 3/1		7800 —

meaningless because of new factors like carrying more types of food or changes in membership.

The utility of the budget is that it provides a starting point. It's also another form of accountability, since people in responsible positions must justify their performance in relation to the budget. Finally, the budget allows the co-op to allocate parts of its income for specific projects — painting the store, expanding services to members, buying new equipment, starting an education program. The main problem with a budget is that it may be taken too literally. When people forget that it's a crude device and demand precise compliance, the budget becomes an instrument that controls people rather than a tool to be used by people.

To create a budget, the co-op should consider a relevant time frame, a complete cycle of co-op activity. Then, in a manner similar to the Income and Expense Statement, devise an extended subtraction:

PEOPLE'S FOOD CO-OP BUDGET

	This Month			Cumulative		
	Budgeted $	Actual $	Difference	Budgeted $	Actual $	Difference
Sales	55,000	50,000	-5,000	110,000	112,500	2,500
Cost of Goods	50,000	47,500	-2,500	100,000	100,000	0
Gross Margin	5,000	2,500	-2,500	10,000	12,500	2,500
Expenses:						
Rent	500	500	0	1,000	1,000	0
Payroll	2,000	2,000	0	4,000	4,000	0
Insurance	50	50	0	100	100	0
Utilities	200	200	0	400	400	0
Maintenance	250	250	0	500	500	0
Total	3,000	3,000	0	6,000	6,000	0
Surplus	2,000	- 500	-2,500	4,000	6,500	2,500
Allocation of Surplus:						
Education	500	500	0	2,000	1,500	500
Office Equipment	250	250	0	250	250	0

Allocation of surplus, real or projected, involves basic policy questions. Of course, some money should be allocated to operating expenses like telephones and stamps. The rest should be spent according to the collective wishes of the members. Here's where accounting and democratic decision making finally come together.

Sources

Anthony, Robert N. *Essentials of Accounting*. Reading, Massachusetts: Addison-Wesley, 1964 (Also available from NASCO.)

Danforth, Art. *A Primer of Bookkeeping for Cooperatives*. Washington, D. C.: Cooperative League of the U.S.A., 1970.

Johnson, Glenn L., and James A. Gentry, Jr. *Finney and Miller's Principles of Accounting; Introductory*. Seventh Edition. Englewood Cliffs, New Jersey: Prentice-Hall, 1971.

Miller, Herbert E. *The Accounting Process* (a Programmed Adaptation of *Finney and Miller's Principles of Accounting*). Prentice-Hall, 1971.

The Internal Revenue Service provides detailed manuals for all your tax operations. Their booklet, *Mr. Businessman*, will tell you how to do payroll accounting and perform other procedures. Ask for it at your local IRS office.

The best resources, if you're in trouble, are accounting wizards within your co-op, or friends in neighboring co-ops.

13. Legal World

As a food co-op grows, it will begin to come into contact with the law, that amalgam of rules, interpretations, and enforcement procedures by which society attempts to regulate human activity. This chapter will describe some common laws with which co-ops may have to deal. But it's not a substitute for good legal advice, and since laws vary from state to state and city to city, it won't usually be possible for us to say exactly what your co-op should do. A portion of the preamble to the bylaws of the North Country People's Warehouse, we think, is a good expression of what the law really means:

> The People's Warehouse at the time of incorporation . . . is a living, functioning entity which has come to be what it is thru an organic process of growth, and has changed and adapted itself to the needs of its community . . . Thus there exists a common law — a knowledge and a feeling in the minds and hearts of the people who are or have been associated with the People's Warehouse. This incorporation charter and these bylaws are only extensions and clarifications of this common law; they are in no way a replacement for it.

Most laws affecting co-ops are reasonable. Co-ops shouldn't be averse to complying with legal standards of sanitation in food handling or rules for accurate reporting of sales and wages. These laws regulate many small businesses whose owners have no more legal experience than do the members of your co-op. For this reason, government agencies usually provide directions that tell, in everyday language, what you are required to do and when and how to do it. If you hire staff and apply to the Internal Revenue Service for the required Employer Identification Number, you will receive, along with the necessary reporting forms, several pamphlets containing step-by-step instructions on how to compute, withhold, and report payroll taxes.

In addition, most agencies have employees whose job it is to assist people in complying with the laws. Many health inspectors, in addition to telling you if your co-op meets local sanitation requirements, can suggest cheap and easy ways of correcting any violations. Government agencies usually view co-ops favorably and will give them a friendly reception.

Some of the people involved in food co-ops have had experience in the radical or civil rights movements, and bring from these experiences a deep distrust of all government agencies. They forget that the cooperative movement has a long and respected history. Co-ops are seen by most people as an example of mutual assistance among neighbors. This isn't to suggest that you'll never encounter hostility or harassment. At the end of the chapter you'll find some suggestions on dealing with this. But we think you'll find that hostility is the exception rather than the rule.

How do you know when you need a lawyer? If an individual or government official tells you that you need legal help, he or she is probably being honest. If his or her intentions were hostile, he or she could simply take action adverse to you without even letting on that you needed help. If your co-op is threatened with any penalty or fine more serious than a parking ticket or a small surcharge for late tax payment, it's best to know the risks and alternatives from a lawyer before you decide what to do.

If somebody sues you, you'd better find a lawyer. Usually you'll get a full and fair hearing in court or a fair settlement out of court only if you're represented by counsel. The same is true if you want to sue someone else. The one exception is small claims court. A good general introduction to small claims court can be found in the 1975 *Consumer Reports Buying Guide*.

If you don't understand any contracts, or the instructions for any legal paperwork, check with a lawyer. A lease, purchase order, credit agreement, or tax return is binding on you and your co-op when you sign it, even if you didn't understand what you were signing.

You may also want a lawyer to help you incorporate, although it isn't necessary. A lawyer can explain some of the different ways of setting up your corporation and can help you put your ideas into proper legal form.

If your co-op wants to do its own trucking across state lines, you'll have to check with the Interstate Commerce Commission, which has a complex scheme of licenses and regulations, enforced by substantial penalties. It's probably best to consult a knowledgeable attorney here as well.

Lawyers may be useful in zoning matters, which can be both highly political and highly technical. If your co-op's problem has to do with its legal rights and duties, its business relations, or its relations with its neighbors, a lawyer may be able to offer help, or may just be able to intimidate the right people.

All this isn't to say that lawyers are *required* for any specific jobs. But like any other expert, be it an accountant, a buyer, a truck-repair person, a butcher, or a store manager, a lawyer can be awfully useful at certain times. Sometimes elected officials, government bureaucrats, or other co-ops that have encountered similar problems can also help.

Most food co-ops can't afford to pay the going rate for a lawyer's services, which may be $50 an hour or more. One source of cheap legal services may be within your co-op or other neighboring co-ops whose lawyer or law student members would be willing to volunteer their time.

Some legal aid organizations have the staff and authorization to help co-ops, especially if the co-op members would be individually eligible for legal aid. Many lawyers in private practice and some employed by private businesses volunteer a portion of their time to *pro bono publico* (for the public good) projects. If you can't find a lawyer in any of these ways, just call one you think might be sympathetic and ask. Most local bar associations provide referral services that can be located in the Yellow Pages under "Attorneys."

Since most lawyers specialize, every one will not be familiar with your particular co-op's problem. For this reason, be sure that your lawyer is familiar with co-ops or is willing to take the time to become informed.

Incorporation

A corporation is an artificial entity created under the laws of a state or national government. It is composed of a number of people but is permitted by law to act as if it were an individual, separate from all of them. The only way to incorporate is to take the steps required by the state in which you wish to incorporate.

Most small preorders would not think of incorporating. Many

large preorders and stores that probably should incorporate do not. There are several advantages to incorporation:

Your co-op will become a "legal person" that can make contracts, sign leases, and own property in its own name. Actions taken by the co-op will bind the co-op but not its individual members.

Individual members will not be personally liable for acts of the co-op. In an unincorporated co-op, individual members may be held liable for the acts of the co-op or of other members engaged in co-op activities. If a co-op member causes an accident while trucking crates of vegetables, a person injured in the accident can sue other members of the co-op to recover damages. Even if the suit were unsuccessful, it would be a great nuisance to the co-op members who were sued. If the co-op were incorporated, the injured person could sue the co-op, but not its members. Even if the person won, his or her recovery would be limited to the assets of the co-op.

State corporation laws require that the structure and decision-making procedures of the corporation be set out in its certificate of incorporation and bylaws, and that the bylaws maintain minimum standards of fairness in the election of officers. The democratic nature of a co-op is best preserved if the rules are understood in advance. Preparing for incorporation means a co-op has to define its goals and structures, and this can be a useful process.

Incorporating gives the co-op continuity. Unless you limit its duration at the time it is formed, a corporation will continue until its members or shareholders vote to dissolve it.

One of the most practical advantages of incorporating is that many people with whom you do business will take you more seriously. Before the Boston Food Co-op could lease its present building from Boston University, the university insisted that the co-op incorporate. Many co-ops in Connecticut have found it possible to get food-stamp authorization only after they incorporated.

There are also some disadvantages to incorporation. Corporations must observe certain formalities, such as filing annual reports with the state. The thinking that goes into these reports may be productive, but some co-ops may find it a waste of time. Probably more important are corporate income taxes, filing fees for incorporation, and possible lawyer's fees. Nature's Bakery in Madison decided to dissolve its corporation and become a partnership because, as one member of the collective explained,

Being incorporated means you've created a legal entity. If that corporation pays people, then it's got to pay unemployment taxes. If you're a partner, you're self-employed. You're not an employee, so your business won't be paying unemployment taxes. Everyone in Nature's collective is a partner, so we have no employees.

An employee's social security tax paycheck deduction is matched by an equal "contribution" by the employer. A partner's social security tax is less than the employee-employer total [7.9% as opposed to 11.7%].

All in all, partnerships pay less to the government than corporations do, and there's a lot less paperwork. But there is personal liability. If someone gets sick from your bread, you get sued, not a corporation.

We'll talk more about paying employee taxes later in this chapter.

Finally, state corporation statutes place certain limitations on the type of decision-making structure a corporation can adopt. Many state laws require that a corporation have an elected board of directors, a president, a secretary, and a treasurer, and that the board make its decisions by majority vote. These requirements may conflict with the collective, decentralized decision-making procedures followed by many food co-ops. While some state corporation laws are flexible enough to cover innovative co-op structures, a co-op opposed to all hierarchies may find it impossible to meet incorporation requirements.

Even if you don't wish to incorporate, it would be useful to set down the structure, bylaws, and rules by which you intend to operate.

Co-ops that don't wish to incorporate but are concerned about the individual liability of their members can get insurance to cover liability for injuries to others. While the insurance won't legally prevent suits against individual members, as a practical matter the existence of the insurance as a fund for the compensation of injured parties will make such suits unnecessary.

The two principal documents creating the legal structure are your certificate of incorporation and your bylaws. In these two, you should set out the purposes of your co-op, the rights and duties of members, the powers and duties of directors and officers, the procedures for making major decisions, and other basic operating rules. Review carefully the law under which you intend to incorporate to be sure that your proposed certificate of incorporation and bylaws fit within its limitations.

One of your decisions when you incorporate is whether you're going to be a stock co-op or a membership co-op. In a stock co-op, the members invest money and shares are issued to them. The co-op pays either limited or no dividends on the stock and each shareholder has only one vote at meetings, regardless of the number of shares owned. At the end of the year the co-op's surplus is either reinvested or returned to the members in proportion to the amount of their purchases, in classic Rochdale fashion. Members who withdraw can usually sell their stock back to the co-op.

In a membership co-op, persons or households wishing to participate pay a membership fee annually or upon joining. No stock is issued. Although there's nothing to prohibit nonstock co-ops from paying patronage refunds or rebates, in practice most of them pass savings on to their members by setting prices as low as possible. Since the membership fee is usually small, the co-op raises much of its capital from grants, loans, contributions, and operating surplus. Most of the traditional co-op stores founded before 1965 are stock co-ops; most of the newer preorders and stores are membership co-ops.

The Cooperative League of the U.S.A. in its booklet *Time to Organize?* offers sample articles of incorporation and bylaws, and suggestions on where and how to incorporate. This and other publications can give you an idea of what other groups have done, but you shouldn't follow their suggestions blindly. What may have been appropriate for one co-op may be entirely wrong for yours. *Time to Organize?* recommends incorporating under the law of the District of Columbia and furnishes an excellent set of articles and bylaws for forming a stock co-op. But if your co-op is a preorder operating out of somebody's garage and wants to incorporate only to be eligible to take food stamps, these bylaws would be inappropriate.

Here are some of the topics you should include in your certificate of incorporation and bylaws:

Purposes and powers. In most states you must state the purposes and powers of your co-op. Be careful not to limit future growth unintentionally. A co-op whose stated purpose is to "obtain good quality food at low prices for its members" may have problems when it decides to sell books or hardware. At the same time, you do want to bind your co-op to generally recognized cooperative principles. A good compromise is to state that your co-op may do anything permitted by law which is also consistent with cooperative principles. You might find it useful to list these principles in the bylaws.

Admission of members. This section should state who may become a member and what he or she must do to join, including paying membership fees, agreeing to abide by the rules and regulations, and participating in co-op activities.

Resignation and removal of members. There should be some procedure by which a member can notify the co-op that she or he is resigning. You might also want to adopt a procedure for removing people whose conduct disrupts or is detrimental to the co-op, along with some sort of fair hearing for them.

Rights and powers of members. The members usually have the power to elect the board of directors and should, as a group, either be the only body in the co-op with the power to make major policy decisions or should have the power to reverse decisions made by others.

Meetings of the members. The certificate of incorporation and bylaws should outline the procedures by which members may exercise their powers. It's usually a meeting, although in some cases ballots and referenda are also used. Provide for a regular or annual meeting and for the calling of special meetings when members or officers feel the need.

Quorum at membership meetings. A quorum is the number or percentage of the people eligible to participate in a meeting who must actually be present for the meeting to exercise its powers. Set the quorum too low and a small band of fanatics can take over your co-op. Set it too high and you'll have trouble getting a quorum at all. If your co-op has more than 100 members, a quorum of more than 20% of your membership may be unrealistic.

Notice of membership meetings. Takeover by a minority because of low quorum requirement may be partially prevented by requiring that written notice of meetings be mailed to each member or household. This notice should state the date, time, place, and agenda of the meeting, so that if a controversial issue is to be discussed, the members will be more likely to come. In smaller co-ops you can convey notice of meetings by telephone.

Board of directors. Most corporation statutes require that general supervision of the corporation's activities be given to a board of directors or similar body. As a practical matter, this is probably a necessity in a large co-op. The general membership can't be expected to turn out once or twice a month to discuss whether or not to open a second checking account or participate in a bulk order of organically grown oranges. The board usually has five to twenty directors elected by the membership.

In some co-ops, the holders of certain offices like manager may be *ex officio* members of the board. Often *ex officio* directors can participate in meetings but can't vote.

Selection of directors. In a co-op, the board will be elected by the members. You can have elections each year or every six months, or can provide for staggered one-, two-, or three-year terms. Since many new-style co-ops experience a fairly high turnover of people, ideas, and enthusiasm, they may prefer to vote for an entire new board every year.

If lots of co-op members are interested in serving on the board, you'll have no trouble finding enough qualified candidates. But if you think this may be a problem, consider establishing a nominating committee. Its function isn't so much to screen potential candidates as to persuade qualified people to serve.

Directors' meetings and quorum. Usually the quorum requirements are higher in directors' meetings. In most co-ops it takes a majority of the directors to hold a valid meeting. Frequently the bylaws call for directors' meetings once or twice a month and establish procedures by which special meetings may also be called. Under most state laws, a board meeting isn't valid unless all the directors are notified of the meeting in advance. Many co-ops require that all board meetings be open to the members. It's useful to post agendas and minutes.

Resignation, removal, and vacancies. Obviously, a director who wants to resign should be free to. Since directors are elected by the members, most co-ops make them removeable only by the members. Some allow the board to remove its own members, but only in certain situations, as when a director never comes to meetings. Many bylaws provide that a director be given opportunity to be heard before any vote is taken on his or her removal. The board is often given the power to fill its vacancies until the next regular meeting or election.

Officers. Usually, state law requires that each corporation have a presiding officer, a recording officer, and a financial officer, and permits the corporation to appoint such other officers as it sees fit. Many co-ops provide in their certificates of incorporation and bylaws for a president, secretary, treasurer, and general manager or managers, and leave the creation of other offices to the board. With a little careful wording, most forms of collective management can be set out in a co-op's bylaws. The bylaws should outline the powers and duties of each of the major co-op officers.

Selection and removal of officers. The officers are usually elected by either the board or the members. In a large co-op it may be better to have the manager(s) chosen by the board, which is in a better position to supervise and hold them accountable. Some co-ops have subcommittees of the board, open to any interested co-op members, that look for and screen potential staff.

If an officer is elected by the members, only the members should have the power to remove him or her. If the officer is elected by the board, he or she should be removeable by either the board or the members. As with the removal of directors, fairness requires that any officer whose removal is sought be given advance notice and an opportunity to speak in his or her defense.

Amendments. The procedure for amending the certificate of incorporation, which is filed with the state, is usually set by state law. The procedure for amending the bylaws, which are not so filed, is usually set out in the bylaws themselves. By amending the certificate and bylaws you may change the nature of your co-op. For this reason, many co-ops permit their bylaws to be amended only at a membership meeting, after members have been notified of the nature of the proposed amendment.

But in many co-ops it's difficult to call and hold membership meetings during much of the year. During the first weeks and months of operation, many changes may be needed in your bylaws. You can solve this problem by permitting the board to amend the bylaws, but only after notice is given to the members. If there's sufficient member concern, a general meeting can be called.

Miscellaneous. Some other topics you may include in the bylaws are: setting the co-op's fiscal year, providing for a corporate seal, requiring bonding for cash-handling employees, limiting the accumulation of reserves, and specifying whether the co-op will sell to nonmembers.

Most states have several different incorporation laws, each designed for a different kind of corporation. Before deciding where and under what law to incorporate, examine each of the laws carefully. Many states have specific cooperative corporation laws, but they're often designed for stock or producers' co-ops and are inappropriate for the new food co-ops. A membership co-op may be better off incorporating under a general membership or nonstock corporation law than under the law specifically designed for co-ops. If you do this, though, check to see if your state law limits use of the words *cooperative* and *co-op* to corporations organized under co-op statutes.

If you find your own state law unsatisfactory, you can usually incorporate in another state and register to do business in your own state. This involves appointing an agent for service of process, furnishing certain information about your co-op, and paying a filing fee to the corporation office in the state in which your co-op is located.

Some co-ops can obtain some of the advantages or legitimacy of being a corporation without incorporating, if they establish themselves as part of an existing incorporated organization like a church or community renewal agency. The drawback is that members' control over their co-op may be limited by the needs or interests of the sponsoring organization.

Law requires that all corporations observe certain formalities. Notices of meetings must be given and minutes kept. Annual reports must be filed with the state corporation office. Resolutions must be passed to open bank accounts or enter into leases. Many of these formalities seem stuffy and unnecessary in the casual co-op atmosphere, but failure to observe them may cause the co-op to lose its rights and powers as a corporation or may render some of its acts and agreements void. A little attention to form as well as content is important.

Contracts and Leases

It's usually to your co-op's advantage to have the terms of any agreement you make set out in writing. When you sign any written document on behalf of the co-op, be sure you have the authority to sign, and indicate with your signature that you're signing for the co-op and not for yourself; e.g., "Charles Fourier, for the Utopia Food

Co-op, Inc." Most important, before you sign any written agreement, be sure you've read every word in it, that you understand exactly what each word means, and that the document says exactly what you want it to say. If you don't understand something, ask. If you're told that a sentence that appears to mean one thing means something else, have that something else written down and added to the contract. If you're not satisfied with the explanation, seek legal help. Making a contract you didn't intend to make can be costly. In court, it's no defense to say you didn't read or understand what you signed.

One typical contract is a lease. If the lease is written, its terms will set out the rights and duties of the co-op and of its landlord. If it's not in writing, a tenancy at will in other words, these rights and duties will be determined by local law, which usually requires that the tenant pay the rent on time and not damage the building. If the rent is paid monthly, a month's notice is usually required for the landlord to raise the rent or for either party to terminate the relationship. The landlord may or may not be required to make repairs.

Some types of credit, such as loans and time payments on equipment, involve the creation of a security interest, under which the lender reserves the right to seize or repossess the property of the borrower if the loan isn't paid. These security arrangements are always in writing and should be read with some care, as should all other contracts.

Licenses and Inspections

Most state and local governments regulate the cleanliness and handling of food, the accuracy of weights and measures, and the adequacy of plumbing, wiring, and fire exits. They publish standards and enforce them through a system of inspections and licenses. If your co-op is a small preorder, chances are that these regulations may not apply to you, or if they do, that the local authorities won't bother enforcing them. Nevertheless, you might want to look at them just to get an idea of what is considered clean, safe operation.

If your co-op is operating a store or warehouse, you can expect to see the health inspector. Although it can be argued that a co-op isn't a retail business because it sells only to members, it would be embarrassing for a co-op, which claims to be serving the needs of its members, to insist that it's not required to live up to the standards established for profit-making stores.

At your city or town hall, you may find out what licenses you'll need and how to get copies of the regulations that apply to you. The fee for licenses is usually small; the main purpose of licensing in most places is to provide the government with a list of the stores selling a particular product or line of goods.

You will not ordinarily receive advance notice of an inspection. The inspector usually announces him- or herself when he or she arrives, and, if asked, should be able to produce identification. When the inspection is completed, you should get a written or oral summary. If there are any deficiencies, you'll usually have a reasonable time in which to remedy them. Inspectors are often the best sources for cheap repairs or ways to fix violations.

Zoning

Zoning is the system by which local governments limit certain activities, such as manufacturing and retail selling, to particular sections of town. Exceptions, called variances, may be made in cases of hardship. Before your co-op rents or buys any store or building or invests money in one, check with the local building or zoning inspector to be sure that the building is zoned appropriately. Don't take the word of the landlord or rental agent. For zoning purposes, a food co-op is in the same category as a supermarket.

It's possible to obtain a variance through public hearings, but the procedure can be both costly and difficult, and should be avoided if possible.

Food Stamps

The Food Stamp Program was established by the federal government to increase the food-buying power of low-income families. Those eligible buy food stamps for less than face value, then use them at full face value to buy food at any authorized store. The store then deposits the food stamps in its bank account and receives credit just as if they were cash.

Food co-ops, including preorders, can be authorized to take food stamps. A call or letter to the nearest Food and Nutrition Service

Field Office of the U.S. Department of Agriculture will bring the necessary application. After you fill out the form, you'll be interviewed by a food stamp representative.

Federal law gives the Department of Agriculture some discretion in authorizing retailers to accept food stamps. One criterion is whether or not the retailer is financially responsible. In the case of food co-ops, the USDA may equate financial responsibility with incorporation, though this is by no means always the case. If many of your members use food stamps, though, you should take whatever steps are necessary to get authorization.

Insurance

There are several types of insurance your co-op may want to have. Liability insurance protects the co-op by paying claims against it for injuries caused to others. In most states, liability insurance is mandatory on any vehicles you own. Since the co-op could also be held liable for injuries caused by a co-op member's private car while the member is on co-op business, insurance against these accidents is also advisable. A third kind of liability insurance protects against claims of people injured at the store or distribution center.

The co-op can also get insurance coverage for damage to its own property because of theft, fire, flood, and other disasters. If your co-op has full-time paid staff, you should carry workmen's compensation insurance. It pays to check on how the insurance company has classified the staff. It costs a lot more to insure someone classified as doing heavy labor than someone classified as a clerical worker.

Some agents have difficulty writing insurance for the new co-ops because these co-ops don't fit neatly into any of the insurance companies' conceptual pigeonholes. However, the insurance your co-op needs is available, so if the first agent you see can't give you what you want, shop around. You may also find better prices that way.

Taxes

The reasoning of the Nature's Bakery folks quoted earlier, that co-ops shouldn't have to pay unemployment or social security taxes for their staff, is quite common. Some co-ops avoid payroll taxes altogether by classifying their employees as consultants or independent contractors. The employees then report their income and pay their taxes individually on or before April 15. Although this does have the advantage of allowing the employee use of tax money for up to a year (rather than having it withheld), there are problems with this system.

If your independent contractors are really full-time permanent employees, the IRS may catch you and demand thousands of dollars in back taxes. The wheels of the Internal Revenue Service grind very slowly, but they grind exceedingly smooth. If you want your co-op to survive, we advise you to pay the payroll taxes. It may be a good idea to set this money aside in an escrow account so that you'll have it when it's due.

Under the independent contractor system, the employee has to pay the entire 7.9% social security tax him- or herself. Under the payroll tax system, the employer pays 5.85% and another 5.85% is withheld from the employee's wages. Although this adds up to more money for the government, it also adds up to less of a burden for the individual taxpayer. That 7.9% can amount to several hundred dollars even on a very modest income. As businesses that turn over hundreds and often thousands of dollars each week, co-ops are far more able to shoulder their tax burden than most of their subsistence-income employees are.

Employer contributions to unemployment insurance, workmen's compensation insurance, and medical plans, are also responsibilities that a co-op owes to its staff. Co-op staff members often work for very low wages and have no financial reserves or medical insurance of their own; in case of injury they may really be up the creek. Broken arms and severed arteries are not accidents unknown to co-ops. The least a co-op can do to acknowledge the financial sacrifice staff members are usually making is to take fundamental precautions in their interest.

Other kinds of taxes you may have to deal with are business income and excise taxes and sales taxes. In many states, sales tax isn't collected on food, but if it is, or if you carry nonfood items, keep careful track of sales tax collected. Again, an escrow account is advisable. It can even earn interest until the money's due.

Some states impose income or excise taxes on businesses. You may be subject to these taxes even if you're a nonprofit organization. Whether you're incorporated or not may be a factor. Call, visit, or write to your state tax agency for copies of tax returns and instructions that might apply to your situation.

If your state has a minimum tax per year on nonprofit corporations, you should know about it at the beginning of the year so you can budget for it. Don't be timid about asking for information or about considering yourself a business. If the state considers you a business, you'll have to deal with it on their terms.

Finally, there's the possibility of corporate income tax. Although co-ops are technically incapable of making a "profit," you may accumulate some surplus, which, if it's not spent or returned to members, can be taxed. Plan carefully to make sure this doesn't happen to you.

Defense

Sometimes a co-op discovers that, in addition to the various natural disasters that loom from time to time, there are difficulties that have been intentionally created by hostile people or organizations. This hostility may come from a variety of sources.

Co-op members don't buy as much, if any, of their food from profit-making stores. As the co-op movement grows, the retail food trade as a whole will begin to feel the threat.

In addition, some cities tax businesses, not only on their sales, but on their profits or their gross incomes. A medium-sized preorder of 100 families can easily consume $100,000 worth of food per year, at wholesale prices. The same food might cost $130,000 to $160,000 at the local supermarket. The tax lost on this market can be considerable, and local authorities may try to get preorders to pay business taxes. Or they may try to harass co-ops out of existence.

Some people may even object to the social aspects of cooperation or to the lifestyle of some co-op members. Student co-ops in areas with uneasy town-gown relations, or hippie co-ops that don't include the other people in their neighborhoods may be the objects of social hostility.

Many co-ops consider it a major goal to organize their community, or at least to create a sense of community among their members. Most co-ops have such a goal, whether it is explicit or not. All co-ops, to one degree or another, do in fact increase the organization of their community. Community organization isn't always seen as a good thing by those who benefit from its disorganization.

This group includes not only those profit-making businesses that exploit the community economically but also those people in and out of government who exploit the community politically.

So it's wise, while avoiding undue paranoia, to prepare for defense against aggression. There are several things you can do, both before and during an attack on your co-op.

One cardinal rule is: don't unnecessarily antagonize. Be friendly to outsiders and be courteous and helpful if asked what you're doing. If the co-op is in a conservative neighborhood, you might consider asking members to respect the standards of dress and speech that predominate. Don't make undue noise, paint rude signs, or leave messy garbage on the street. Always let neighbors know they're welcome to join. A low-key canvassing campaign, or leaflets left on doors or windshields or tacked on bulletin boards and telephone poles, can help.

Make sure there's adequate parking at the distribution site. This can become a real bone of contention, and disgruntled neighbors may easily harass otherwise neutral city authorities into hitting you with a zoning ordinance. In Venice, California, a part of Los Angeles, police started ticketing cars outside one of the Free Venice Co-op's three distribution points — even when there were people inside the cars. The neighbors had complained about the traffic. The co-op eventually had to move to a new site, but the city continued to harass it.

Some basic rules are: don't park in, or in front of, people's driveways. If there isn't adequate parking near your distribution site, stagger distribution hours or consider dividing into branches or blocks. If there's an insoluble problem, move before things get worse.

One of the best ways to avoid harassment is to make it hard for your enemies to find excuses to harass you. Learn what the local licensing and inspection codes are and follow them. Most inspectors are not enemies of co-ops; some may even be sympathetic.

If you've done all you can to avoid harassment, all to no avail, there are a number of legal or law-related steps you can take. The initial decisions of most government agencies can be reviewed on appeal, first higher up in the agency and then in the courts. If the agency has acted arbitrarily, its decision can be reversed. The lawyer for the Free Venice Co-op went to the tax board to protest the

1% business tax on gross volume that other preorders in town had been paying. She won her case, all preorders were exempted from the tax, and her efforts fulfilled her co-op work requirement several times over.

In St. Louis, the Midwest Cooperating Consumers Association, a federation of preorders, got the Legal Aid Society to help them fight the local sales-use tax. They won a slight concession when the authorities agreed that co-op members who were getting state welfare (but not those who were getting federal food stamps) were exempt from the tax. The co-op also fought a merchant's license tax by writing directly to a city councilor asking for an opinion on whether preorders were really merchants since they were not reselling goods but purchasing collectively. The councilor agreed that preorders were not merchants and they were therefore exempt from the tax.

Whenever you go to court, to a hearing, or even to an interview with a bureaucrat or politician, take as many people as you can without turning it into a mob scene. A lawyer arguing in a vacuum isn't nearly so effective as a lawyer arguing in a courtroom or hearing room backed up by fifty supporters, by posters and leaflets in the community, and by articles in the local press.

Agency determinations are often affected by elected officials who show an interest. A letter from a senator or a mayor may cause an agency to think twice before turning down a legitimate request. With the growing membership and popularity of food co-ops, many elected officials may be sympathetic.

Some organizations in this country have political influence out of proportion to their numbers simply because they organize good letter-writing campaigns. Letter-writing campaigns to local and national officials are easy to organize, especially if you provide the paper, the pens, and the suggested text. (You can also provide addressed stamped envelopes with a box for mailing.)

An essential part of political organization is publicity, and here your media committee can help. If you're fighting a legal or political battle, it's a good idea to have press conferences — but not too many or the press will stop coming. Send out press releases and try to get co-op spokespeople on radio talk shows. (See Chapter 9.)

Occasionally, co-ops have trouble with wholesalers who have been pressured by their capitalist customers not to deal with co-ops.

In Vermont, NEPCOOP was getting wood-burning stoves directly from the factory and selling them at almost 50% below retail prices. The local stove retailers successfully pressured the supplier to stop selling to co-ops. NEPCOOP got a lawyer, who said the company could be enjoined to sell to the co-ops, but the company explained that, injunction or no, they could make the stove deliveries extremely difficult and inconvenient. NEPCOOP gave up selling stoves — temporarily.

Such problems are rare, but may become more common as co-ops begin to make a dent in the profits of local merchants. Sometimes a little community pressure, a little publicity, or a stern letter from a lawyer may help to change a wholesaler's point of view. If only one co-op is being discriminated against, it can try asking other co-ops that deal with the same wholesaler to use their combined buying power to change his or her mind. The New Haven Food Co-op was having trouble with a local wholesaler until co-ops in Boston asked their wholesaler, who supplied the New Haven wholesaler, to speak to his friend. This seemed sufficient to straighten things out.

If your co-op is being harassed or interfered with by a private business or individual, you may, upon consultation with your friendly lawyer, decide to go to court for help. There are many state and federal laws forbidding various types of unfair competition. These may be enforced by public or private suits. The results of such suits may be money damages awarded to your co-op, a court order to the other party to cease its improper activity, or even criminal penalties. Sometimes just the fact that your co-op is willing to go to court is enough to make the other party stop.

Co-ops that have accumulated significant amounts of equipment and food may be subject to theft. The problems range from professional burglars to local toughs to unscrupulous member or nonmember shoppers. Here are a few remedies you might consider:

You can prevent or cut down on burglaries by installing a burglar alarm system. Alarm systems need not be expensive and can be constructed by a talented co-op member. You may want to have your system connected to police telephones, but usually the burglar is gone long before the police arrive.

Having members guard the premises may be useful if you're experiencing a crime wave. But it probably won't be too agreeable to the members on a long-term basis. Scheduling activities at the co-op almost round the clock may be a workable idea: deliveries start early in the morning; meetings and social events can go till quite late, and some members with unusual schedules may even be willing to stay in the store in the wee hours of the morning to do co-op jobs.

Vandalism is usually a result either of random destructiveness or of neighborhood antagonisms. It's extra important to nurture good community relations both to prevent vandalism and to motivate the people living near the co-op store or distribution center to watch and protect it. In most urban neighborhoods, there are some people who spend a lot of time watching the street; cultivate their friendship.

Some vandalism simply can't be helped. You can ask for police protection, but it's doubtful that the squad cars can come around often enough to provide it. You can look into insurance, unbreakable glass, or gates. Generally, spontaneous vandalism doesn't last for long, and just when you're getting desperate and thinking about putting up those depressing gates, it may end.

Theft by members is rare. If nonmembers shop in the co-op, they may be the culprits, and you might want to reconsider your policy. In your educational programs, try to impress on members that they *own* the co-op. Mill City Foods, one of the ten co-op storefronts in Minneapolis, at one time had a severe ripoff problem and suffered heavy losses. Some of the theft was probably not deliberate since people using the store did their own bagging and weighing and probably erred in their own behalf. When faced with a financial crisis, Mill City raised $2000 from its neighborhood to cover losses. It's a good idea to put out "munchies jars" for members to drop change into when they eat something in the store.

Sources

Matt and Ronnie Perlstein, who wrote most of this chapter, are compiling legal resource materials for co-ops. You can write to them at 16 Maplewood Avenue, West Hartford, Connecticut 06119. Ask for a copy of the Down to Earth Food Co-op's bylaws and articles of incorporation.

You may want to send away for two publications of the Cooperative League of the U.S.A., 1828 L St. NW, Washington, D.C. 20036: *Time to Organize?* and *Taxes – Cooperatives Have Them Too.*

14. Growth

Co-ops can have two kinds of growth. External growth means more members, more kinds of food, and more volume. Internal growth means new levels of participation, new systems for making operations more efficient, and higher food consciousness among members.

External and internal growth often complement each other. The Friends Co-op in Freedom, Maine, grew from a small group of friends to a 500-member preorder in four years. The growth in their membership and that of other Maine co-ops led to the creation of Coordinated Produce to handle buying from the Boston terminal market.

But internal growth doesn't require external growth. In Laramie, Wyoming, the mainly student membership of the Laramie People's Market has remained stable, but the co-op decided nonetheless to have a general coordinator to handle the problem of student transience.

External growth, especially if it isn't accompanied by internal growth, may not be a good thing. Growth and profits are two primary capitalist values. Co-ops have done away with profits; and many are re-examining growth.

Ecology of Size

If democratic control is what co-ops are striving for, then the larger the co-op, the less control each member has. Moreover, in any organization of more than 500 people, there will be alienation because no one can remember 499 other faces. Co-ops that emphasize direct democracy or personal cooperative experiences may want to limit external growth for these reasons.

Instead of assuming that more is better, it's helpful to look for the ecology of size. Ecology of size is a tool for analyzing the input of people in any economic operation. It's a way of determining the quality of an individual's experience. In a food co-op, ecology of size is achieved when you have a reliable means of delivering food to people, and when the work necessary to do this is distributed equitably. Co-ops need to analyze their work situations and decide on the best combination of time and people for each. It may be better to have two people cutting cheese even though one can do the job. Having two people makes for a more cooperative experience. At a large distribution center we know, the work of filling orders gets so hectic that volunteers don't have time to talk to their friends when they come in to pick up their food. Ecology of size here means that maybe distribution should be decentralized.

In addition, economies of scale only work to a certain point, after which more energy, time, and even money may be involved to maintain your operation. An economy of scale is a savings achieved by operating at a certain volume or ordering in certain bulk quantities. Co-ops that buy grains together through a federation get lower rates because they're operating at a greater economy of scale. The most elementary economy of scale is a small group of families, a simple co-op, buying together in wholesale sizes to get wholesale prices.

Once a co-op has achieved a volume at which it can get good discounts from wholesalers, there may be no point in going further. The real cost in terms of energy, time, and even money, may increase with further expansion. At a dollar volume of, say, $10,000 a week for a store, a certain number of problems occur. At $20,000 a week, problems don't necessarily double; they may increase geometrically.

One good way to assess your co-op's economic optimal size is to look at the books. Find the number of errors generated by a set dollar volume. You may note that your preorder, spending $350 a week, was able to keep its bump at 5% most of the time. At $500 a week you find that errors in buying result in larger losses or that refunding problems are more complicated, and it becomes necessary to raise the bump to 10%. Since the books are a partial record of your past, they should give some clues about the problems that growth may intensify.

Unfortunately, many co-op people don't understand what this

financial information may mean. The result is that members sometimes divide into two camps — the business heads and the philosophical heavies. The difference in approach is not bad in itself, but financial information should be demystified and understood by everyone so that people's natural biases will be clear.

Both economic and cooperative values, then, point to a limit to external growth. But they won't always lead to the same decision on optimal size. Usually, economic and cooperative values have to be balanced, and for each co-op, the balancing act will be somewhat different.

Some of the important cooperative values are participation, member control, education, group process, individual growth, and cooperation with other co-ops. The economic values include financial strength (buying power, decent wages), savings (capital availability for reinvestment or fronting large deals), accounting, fiscal planning, and the efficiency and reliability needed to deliver the goods.

In balancing these values, a co-op must look at its structure in depth, and see how all the above factors influence each other. If, for example, you hire an accountant to do the books, you may create a bookkeeping system incomprehensible to the membership. You might resolve this problem by having your accountant work with a finance committee of co-op members. Here, economic and cooperative values can complement each other, and you may end up with a better system than you'd have with one expert working alone, or with a committee of amateurs.

A supermarket-sized store may be incompatible with cooperative values, both of social interaction and of neighborhood-based business. In 1973 the Boston Food Co-op, after some harrowing debate, rejected a plan to move into an abandoned supermarket. The majority of board members preferred to keep the co-op medium-sized and help other neighborhood co-ops get started. The larger store would have made BFC too much the granddaddy among Boston co-ops, would have created resentment, and would have drawn more members from far-away neighborhoods.

Alternatives to External Growth

The Allston-Brighton Food Co-op in Boston started as a unified preorder in 1971. By the fall of 1973 it had quadrupled its membership and had to deal with the resultant logistical problems. The co-op decentralized by splitting into four blocks.

Co-ops can also split their operations in two. The Broadway Local Food Co-op in New York City went from a unified preorder to a block preorder to two separate block preorders that use the same distribution center but buy and pick up food on different days. They share equipment and set policy together but otherwise operate like two separate co-ops.

Along with decentralizing and splitting in two, overcrowded co-ops can start new co-ops or refer people to already existing ones. In Austin, the Woody Hills Food Co-op was the only storefront in town until the fall of 1974. Members who had to drive all the way across town to use the co-op organized Avenues Food Co-op in their neighborhood. The Austin Community Project, of which Woody Hills is a member, loaned the new store $2500. The North Country Co-op in Minneapolis grew so fast in its first year that its facilities soon became overcrowded. Within four years, fourteen other stores opened in Minneapolis-St. Paul.

Often the most obvious way of dealing with external growth is simply to close membership. The debate over this may be painful but shouldn't be avoided if you want a co-op and not a zoo or merely a cheap-food business. In making this decision, you'll need all the relevant information, fiscal and social, as well as the input from people representing other co-ops. Closing membership may be restrictive for the co-op, but it can also be a boon to the movement in the area.

If you close membership, then a waiting list doesn't seem to us to be a sound idea. A waiting list, unless there are provisions that the co-op will be open to a group of new people in the immediate future, may make the co-op seem like a very exclusive organization.

A better strategy is organizing a group of co-op activists to help new applicants start their own co-op. Don't assume that they'll do it on their own. Or, if there are co-ops in the area that need members, be a referral service for them. If there are reasons why they don't have full membership, they might welcome some help in ironing out their problems.

If, because your co-op is better organized than the others nearby, it starts drawing their members, you should be careful that you don't end up hurting other co-ops. Growth brings up the important question of co-ops' responsibility to one another. If we focus all our energy and all our best organizers on one food co-op in the area, then we can expect unequal economic development. This may seem unimportant initially, but after a while other co-ops will begin to resent the larger co-op and tension will build.

Finally, if you're closing membership, explain carefully to people why you had to make such a decision. Most people in our society assume that more is better, and if you can convince them that this isn't always so, you may avoid bad feelings. Explain the open membership doesn't mean that one co-op is capable of feeding everybody.

A co-op can close membership unintentionally. If the co-ops' facilities become so crowded, or its operations so hectic, that members start dropping out, the effect is the same as formally closing membership. The disadvantage is that this produces many exmembers who may be turned off to co-ops. Never underestimate the seriousness of this situation. Co-ops like this have membership flows. As the facilities become overcrowded, members drop out. Once enough members have left and the facilities are no longer overcrowded, the co-op again becomes attractive and new people join. And the cycle goes on. This may also occur in co-ops that have no membership requirement and are open to the public.

Nuclear Cooperative Forms

In any organization there are certain reproduceable forms that are the organization's motor force. In a factory, the nuclear form may be a group of several workers who collaborate on a particular stage of production. In a co-op, nuclear forms exist both formally as work teams and study groups and informally as groups of co-op members who are also friends.

In a small preorder, the whole group may comprise one nuclear cooperative form. As preorders grow, individual neighborhoods, branches, or blocks may be the nuclear forms. These small groups are essential for accomplishing both the co-op work and the co-op goals of community and interdependence.

You should be able to identify and reproduce the nuclear forms in your co-op. When unexpected and unplanned growth comes, and that's the way it usually does come, it's essential to know how to deal with it. Many people assume that new members should simply be added to existing groups. This will only work to a degree. Adding twenty new people to a small bookkeeping collective because there's no place else to put them will frustrate the new members and disrupt the collective because it can't handle, nor does it need, so many bookkeepers.

A better strategy is to divide up work so that if many new members join at once, new small groups containing a few experienced members can be formed. This may mean creating new types of groups and spinoff activities such as daycare, research, or media committees.

The larger an organization is, the more difficult it becomes for people to represent the viewpoints of their fellow cooperators. If you are aware of the participating nuclear forms, it's possible to get people together from these various groups to get a sense of what's happening to the co-op as it grows.

If growth alienates members or causes them to drop out, co-ops need to know this and to plan their growth in a direction that won't end up excluding people. One suggestion is to solicit alienated members to help in shaping the co-op. If you look at your co-op's history and see that it has as many exmembers as current members, try to figure out why. Some reasons for a high turnover may be related to excessive growth while others may be unavoidable and even healthy. If your co-op has grown to several hundred members and some of the original people have dropped out to form smaller co-ops and try to recapture the old intimacy, that's healthy because it leads to a proliferation of co-op types and sizes. If members have left a preorder to join a new co-op store, that's O.K., too; there are enough people who prefer the unique advantages of preorders to keep both models thriving.

Preorder Growth

As a preorder grows it faces certain choices. Choices made when a preorder has forty households may influence the structure of the co-op when it has a hundred households. Some choices may even influence whether the preorder will grow into a store or remain a preorder within a federation.

As a small preorder grows, the major change may be moving the distribution site from someone's house to a permanent center. The size of this center, and its availability at other times of the week, will influence the co-op's future structure. If the distribution center is small, the co-op will quickly outgrow it. If a larger space isn't available, the co-op may develop into a block or branch type preorder, or split into two co-ops.

The size of the distribution center will also influence the variety of food the co-op can carry; the bigger the center, the more you can handle. Sources of electricity and water will also determine what is carried. Just try distributing fresh fish without a sink.

The more food you carry, the more jobs you create. A wide assortment of food is often an impetus for the development of a job-specific work system. This structured, efficient type of work system can lead a co-op in the direction of becoming a store.

As the preorder grows larger, and distribution becomes more crowded, the co-op may institute time-saving systems like prebagging. Order forms grow larger, and collating can become a problem. Two possible responses are to develop an experienced job-specific collating team, or to split the co-op into smaller ordering groups, which can be a first step toward branches or blocks. In this case, collating, not distribution, is the impetus.

Other logistical changes create specialized jobs. To get a better deal on produce, the co-op may hire a buyer. The number of vans or pickup trucks available to the co-op is usually limited, and the same people can't be expected to donate their vehicles all the time, so the co-op may start renting a truck. Or a trucking collective, paid by the co-op, may be formed.

A preorder of this size starts to create a surplus job pool. It can choose to reduce the work requirement or it can create new jobs. The first alternative isn't advisable because it weakens the members' responsibility to the co-op. It's hard to maintain that commitment if you only work a few hours every few months. Most co-ops choose to expand the range of jobs. They can create new job-specific work teams to handle newsletters, nutrition programs, small-scale food production like baking or yogurt-making, daycare during distribution hours, and so forth.

All this added complexity shouldn't scare people away from a large co-op. When a co-op can afford to branch out into new programs, it should do so, and bring its members new rewards. The right kind of infrastructure can maintain the personal contact the co-op needs. But for many people, large size and cooperative values don't mix well. For preorders one available alternative is decentralizing into blocks or branches.

As discussed in Chapter 3, the difference between blocks and branches lies in how the work of the central co-op is handled. In a block preorder, the individual blocks run the co-op once every rotation cycle. Branch preorders have central committees to handle this work, and only ordering and distribution are decentralized.

If the unified preorder has already divided into work groups that rotate doing the work of the whole co-op, then it will probably develop into a block-style co-op. If the unified preorder has already developed a job-specific system, these job-specific teams can easily grow into the central committees that are responsible for basic operations in a branch-type preorder.

The block structure is more decentralized than the branch, and may appeal to the political values of some members. It also appeals to people who feel that every member should know how to do every job. The branch structure may appeal to people more concerned about efficiency and the development of expertise.

Preorder growth doesn't necessarily stop at the block or branch level. Preorders can take the further step of creating a federation of co-ops that buy, transport, and warehouse food together. Although federations will be discussed in the next chapter, we want to point out how some of the decisions made at the block and branch level may influence the structure and operations of a federation.

The different work structures of the block and branch types may influence the political development of the federation. The block orientation may encourage more decentralized and participatory ways of doing federation jobs. The branch orientation may encourage centralization of work responsibility, leading to paid staff collectives for various federated operations. The expertise and continuity needed for these jobs may require paid staff in any case, but the orientation of the member co-ops will influence how much work is centralized and how much is left open for member participation.

Federations of preorders can be an effective solution to the contradictory goals of staying small and cooperative, and having an influence on the food system. Federations can centralize the ordering, buying, shipping, and warehousing of food, enabling a small preorder to exercise some financial power and carry a wide variety of foods. The federation can contract with farmers, buy railcar-loads of rice, get cheaper prices on groceries, butcher meat, bake bread, and run education programs. The member co-ops can stay as small and personal as they want, without giving up economic clout.

This is one possible path of preorder growth; the other is turning into a store. Many large unified preorders have chosen to grow into stores rather than breaking down into branches or blocks. This may be a common path, but it is by no means the only way a store can begin. Glut, of Washington, D.C., began as a preorder in the late 1960s and quickly grew until it was operating out of several different distribution centers in neighborhood schools and churches. The need for a central distribution point led the co-op to a storefront in Mt. Ranier, Maryland, which was called "the warehouse." Monday, Tuesday, and Wednesday mornings were spent setting up for an all-day distribution on Thursday. By the fall of 1972 they decided to open their doors to people in the neighborhood on Friday, Saturday, and Sunday, so that the surplus from Thursday's distribution could be bought. By fall, 1973, the Glut storefront stopped preordering and opened as a collectively run community store without a membership.

The first step in the growth from preorder to store is securing a large distribution center, available more than one day a week. If the preorder plans to go to a store, it's important to have a safe site. This usually means renting or owning a place. If the distribution center is donated, it can just as easily be taken away. The co-op should have some contractual rights to the place.

When the preorder has outgrown this space, it can split into two distribution days. This means separate orders, purchases, distributions, work teams, and books. The co-op's overall coordination can remain centralized, with capital equipment, education, communication, and decision-making still shared. To maintain even more cohesion, work responsibilities can also be centralized. You may pick up your food with the Monday group, but be working this month distributing food for the Wednesday group.

The next step is to set up a day for distributing any surplus. Having a surplus day makes it possible for the preorder to buy too much and never have to short its members. The surplus is sold to members or nonmembers. Surplus days can be a good way of recruiting new members, which is usually necessary if you want to turn into a store.

The big step in moving from a preorder to a store occurs in ordering. When the volume is high and stable enough, and if there's adequate storage space, the co-op can start maintaining an inventory of nonperishables. This can be a logistical choice on the part of the people doing ordering, without changing the co-op's structure. Members can still be expected to order all their food. It just becomes easier to fill the orders from an inventory than to compile a master order each week. Common Market in Madison maintains an extensive inventory of nonperishables, but is not planning to become a store.

The next change, to a mixed system of preordering perishables and picking up inventoried items, is an easy one. As this happens, the co-op membership may have grown some more, requiring the addition of another distribution day. The co-op may set aside another day for selling surplus. This can now be combined with the sale of stocked items. By this point the preorder has turned into a store, even if it's only open four days a week, and still preorders its perishables. The final modifications just flow by themselves.

Old habits die slowly. The structures and systems of the parent preorder will influence the new store. The Boston Food Co-op went from a small preorder to a 3500-member store in less than four years. Thursday is still its biggest volume day; it was the day that the original preorder did distribution.

Store Growth

Not all stores grow from preorders, nor are preorders necessarily smaller than stores. In many parts of the country, small neighborhood stores seem to be the primary co-op structure.

The problems of growth faced by stores are very different from those faced by preorders. Obviously, neither location nor work can be decentralized, although there are ways to prevent overcentralization of work or decision making. Two major growth-related concerns of stores are hiring staff and building infrastructure — that is, finding new ways for members to participate.

STAFF

Some co-ops may decide that they've reached optimal size when they foresee that any more growth will lead to the need for paid staff.

But staff need not mean alienation; for some members, staff may be the people they know best in the co-op. A salaried manager or management collective gives continuity and coherence to the store, cutting down on communications snafus. In a large store, chances are that one and perhaps several people work at least a few full days each week. These people should be paid a living wage, if at all possible. Having paid staff provides a few people with a livelihood in the alternative economy.

On the other hand, a paid staff costs money. More important, it can assume too much responsibility, leading to a decline in member participation. Members may no longer see the need to participate once staff is hired. You can guard against this if you maintain your volunteer job allocation system, build up a store infrastructure of people participating in spinoff activities, and reserve important policy decisions for general meetings or for debate during election campaigns for board of directors.

You can also encourage member feedback. The Boston Food Co-op, which has a nine-member collective staff, keeps a log of minutes from staff meetings at the front desk, alongside a suggestion book. There are two columns on each page of the suggestion book: on the left for the suggestion and on the right for remarks by the staff on how they're responding to it. Entries in this book are read at every staff meeting.

If you're considering hiring staff, you might ask yourself the following questions:

1. What exactly do we want this person to do? To whom will this person be responsible?
2. Are we hiring somebody without first considering how we might reorganize our job allocation system?
3. Can we afford it? How will paying salaries affect our food costs?
4. Is this a permanent move or can we expect this person to organize him or herself out of a job?
5. Will this result in our growth? (Do we want to grow?)
6. Will this preclude having more volunteers? How can we make sure it doesn't?
7. What support will we give this person after hiring?

Paid staff will change your co-op. You'll be entrusting more day-to-day decision-making power to the paid members. Be sure you look for people who exemplify your cooperative values and experience; hire co-op members if possible. Try to make sure that anyone you hire can stay for a while; we suggest a minimum of one year. High turnover is disruptive, inefficient, and often costly.

A co-op staff person should have plenty of energy; staff frequently work 14-hour days. But try not to let staff members overwork consistently, even if they're willing to. There's a tendency to set superman -woman theories of staff. Certainly competence, high energy level, and commitment to cooperative values are requirements. But like very active volunteers, staff members can burn themselves out. In this sense it's important to find people who know how to organize and don't try to do all the work themselves.

Another principle is to pay a living wage. A living wage means different amounts in different parts of the country, and it's a lot less for a single person than it is for someone with a family. Long-range fiscal planning is needed to be able to hire a wide range of people and make your staff representative of your membership. Many co-ops pay staff according to need. In Urbana, Illinois, twelve workers at the Earth Foods Co-op get paid in cash while another twenty get paid in food.

The subsistence wages that staff in many new-style food co-ops receive should not continue indefinitely. The low wage limits staff to primarily young people without family responsibilities. As these folks get into their late twenties and early thirties, many of them will need to earn more money to provide a minimum of comfort for their families. The long-term commitment the co-op movement needs may not be forthcoming if co-ops can't find some way to pay better wages.

The whole salary dilemma revolves around the competing goals of maintaining the lowest possible prices and giving workers a living wage. Many full-time co-op activists are underpaid or not paid at all because they're dedicated to selling food at wholesale prices, and every markup seems a violation of the nonprofit principle. Obviously, some compromise must be reached. The burn-out rate is too high in the co-op movement, partly as a result of overwork, lack of vacation time, and the nervous exhaustion that may result from living on too little money for too long. Each co-op that considers hiring staff will have to deal with this dilemma according to its own values. We want to caution you, however, against the notion that accepting low pay is a necessary sign of dedication or that insisting on decent pay is mercenary. The best co-op worker isn't necessarily the one who will work for the lowest wage.

How will you organize your staff? A store manager with assistants creates a hierarchical situation that some people feel contradicts the democratic ideals of cooperativism. Many co-ops have moved from manager to management collective successfully. Some stores have a "manager" for legal purposes, or just because the board wants to know that someone is in charge; but actually they are collective operations, with equal decision-making power and equal pay. The Washington, D.C., warehouse will not sell to stores with hierarchical staff.

BUILDING INFRASTRUCTURE

What is the optimal size for a co-op store in terms of cooperative values? The answer, we think, lies particularly in nuclear cooperative forms. Is your co-op really an organization in which there's more than token participation? Are there lots of small groups working for and with each other? Is there feedback from the membership? Are people taking initiative? Are co-op activities creating spinoffs where people get together just to enjoy themselves or to express their other interests? If the answer to many of these questions is no, then external growth many not be the right direction. Instead you might want to concentrate on building up your store infrastructure. Six complementary approaches are:

1. Start communication and education programs.
2. Have social activities — picnics, potlucks, etc.
3. Organize job-specific work teams.
4. Organize spinoff activities related to member needs.
5. Organize support for community struggles.
6. Develop interco-op cooperation.

Work teams, spinoff activities, communication programs, and social events have all been described in Chapters 8 and 9. How and if you organize support for community struggles will depend on the community itself. In Cambridge, Massachusetts, food co-ops took part in a struggle against MIT's redevelopment plans. In a co-op area of Minneapolis, a tenants' union struggle involved over 50% of the residents, and in Madison, the co-op community was partly responsible for the political direction of Mayor Paul Soglin. One block of the large Mission Hill preorder in Boston worked with a planner to develop an alternative renewal proposal for the area.

Interco-op cooperation should take place not just among the activists of the various stores and preorders, but among less heavily involved members as well. Events that invite participation from many co-op members, users, or potential members, need to be encouraged. Some co-ops build interco-op solidarity by having harvest fairs or celebrations of the equinox. In Austin, a fair put on by various co-ops drew several thousand people. Try having an organizing group in your co-op whose concern it is to help other co-ops get formed.

One way to build infrastructure might be to form a "Sunday co-op." Membership in the Boston Food Co-op had been closed for several months when the board decided to open the co-op on Sundays to accommodate some new members. A plan was devised to form a Sunday Co-op rather than to open the co-op to members at random, as it operated on the other days of the week. If a small group of people joined the co-op with the understanding that they'd work and shop on Sundays only, the regular staff could leave the lighter responsibilities of running the store to a volunteer co-staff. (No deliveries or orders are made on Sundays.) A mellow, controlled environment might lend itself to experimentation with ideas, in relation both to the mushrooming size of the co-op's membership, and to alternative food-buying structures.

A group of interested co-op members, the Sunday Collective, was assembled, and the Board of Directors approved the proposal in January of 1974. The collective was responsible for running the store on Sundays and for recruiting and educating Sunday Co-op members.

The Sunday Co-op began with 100 people. Because of the smaller group, people could get to know each other. The slower pace of Sunday business and the less hectic atmosphere made personal communication easier. Members also got to know the different aspects of store operation. When they became integrated with the larger membership, they were usually the first to sign up for work teams and get actively involved in the store.

15. Federations and Warehouses

> "The fact that federation enables members to pass from one settlement to another . . . is in reality only one among its many favorable results; the vital thing is federation itself, the complementing and helping of each group by the others, the stream of communal life flowing between them and gathering strength from each. No less important, however, is the fact that the settlements stand in some relation . . . to society at large — not merely because they need a market for their surplus production . . . but because the settlements must . . . influence the surrounding world in order to live at all."
>
> — Martin Buber, *Paths in Utopia*

A FEDERATION is a co-op's co-op. It accomplishes for the co-op what the co-op accomplishes for its individual members. By consolidating the economic strength of its member co-ops, a federation can get better quality and prices. It can bypass wholesalers and get food directly from farms and producers. The Michigan Federation of Co-ops contracts directly with farmers to get the cheapest prices and best quality on the grain it carries.

Federations accumulate capital and organize markets that make possible the development of a viable alternative economy. They actively support vertical growth: the control of our food from compost to co-op. Federations may include collectively run farms, mills, bakeries, granola factories, apiaries, and restaurants. They may also cooperate with collectively run nonprofit industries, encouraging the horizontal growth of co-op garages, bike shops, housing, credit unions, insurance, health clinics, daycare centers, clothing, hardware, and book stores.

Although their primary reason for being is economic, federations also promote political and educational cooperation among their members. Federations often set policy at meetings attended by people from member co-ops. The Policy Review Board of the North Country People's Warehouse meets for an entire weekend every few months to make decisions affecting the warehouse, give people a chance to see each other, and have a Saturday night boogie. Regional newsletters contain information about food sources, education programs, organizing experiences, and technical and logistical developments. In both meetings and newsletters, the emphasis is on mutual problem-solving. In New England, NEFCO has an education and resources committee to help start new co-ops and assist ongoing co-ops. The alternative to this cooperation may be seen in the isolation of the average corner grocery store.

Some federations also coordinate regional food boycotts and protests. One of the major reasons for the organization of the Washington, D.C., Food Federation was the difficulty an individual store had in trying to build a citywide protest of the local food tax.

At present, co-op federations operate several different services for their members. There are buying services on the produce market, large joint purchasing deals, grain and staples warehouses, trucking and delivery operations, collective production shops, and interfederation trading.

Buying services are a way to consolidate the buying power of co-ops on the market so they can enjoy the same advantages that large stores do. They centralize the necessary expertise of buying and of developing contacts with local farmers. Joint purchasing may be a first step in the development of a warehouse. The member co-ops order anything from 10,000 pounds to 40,000 pounds of grain, beans, or staples, and pick it up off the back of the truck when it comes to town. When the Dick-Freeman collective arrived in Boston with 40,000 pounds of oats and honey, about thirty representatives from NEFCO co-ops throughout New England came to unload the truck, which occupied one third of a narrow Dorchester street. Federations also trade with each other; the warehouses in Minneapolis and Ann Arbor often trade Minnesota wheat for Michigan beans.

Organizing a Federation

All a co-op needs to start a federation is one other co-op. It can begin with simple sharing of information about sources and logistics.

In Boston, the Jamaica Plain Co-op has the volume to help the Roxbury-Dorchester Co-op get a better deal on groceries, while Roxbury-Dorchester's meat expert helps Jamaica Plain improve its meat operation.

If you want to start a federation in your region you can take several simple steps. Personal contact is essential. Visit as many co-ops as you can. Even if others aren't ready to join, your presence will encourage them. Send a questionnaire around to the other co-ops in your region. Make it clear and leave enough room for detailed answers. Compile information on what they carry, how they operate, how many people they feed, and what they might want out of a federation. This information can help you identify economic priorities. Bring it to an initial meeting to help you decide what you want to do first.

Meetings should be held at least monthly to start. Encourage member co-ops to bring along other co-ops in their area. Broaden the base to include as many participants as possible. Rotate the place of the meeting throughout the region to allow distant co-ops greater access to the federation. This breaks down the tendency to centralize everything in the city, gives people a chance to see other co-ops, and allows urban members the opportunity to enjoy the pace (and sometimes the rigors) of country living.

When the number of participants exceeds 100 and you find the meetings unmanageable, set up subregional meetings as well. These will encourage subregional autonomy and problem-solving, and free up time at the larger meetings for broad policy and logistical decisions. Subregional meetings can be held in three or four areas simultaneously, and can decentralize decision making and encourage the participation of small co-ops. NEFCO includes subregional federations in Maine, Connecticut, and western Massachusetts.

Each member co-op may want to set up a group within itself to do its share of the federation's work and to inform members of the federation's activities. This can decentralize some federation work, bringing it down to the level of the member co-ops, where it belongs. Another way to maximize participation is to have separate collectives within the federation for grains, cheese, produce, etc.

The structure of the federation will be influenced by the structure of the member co-ops. A federation made up predominantly of preorders will probably maximize the participation on which preorders depend for their survival. As each member demands accountability from his or her co-op, so member co-ops can demand accountability from their federations. As federations can centralize buying power to be effective economic institutions, they can decentralize member control to be real cooperative institutions. Without a strong member base, a federation can become merely a nonprofit wholesaler selling cheap food.

How a federation chooses to capitalize its operations directly determines how much control co-ops will have over those operations. NEFCO finances most of its purchases by asking each member co-op to pay either when it orders or when it picks up. Each co-op must make the conscious decision to support each venture by raising its share of the money. If the money isn't raised, the purchase isn't made.

A second common method of raising capital is the front, or deposit, system. The federation requires its member co-ops to have on deposit at all times a sum usually equal to an average week's or month's purchases. The People's Wherehouse (*sic*) of Ann Arbor asks its member co-ops to front two thirds of an average month's purchases. A co-op paying up front isn't voting with its spending power for each purchase the federation proposes. Since the money has been collected in advance of the decision of what to order, co-ops have little veto power over specific purchases, although they may have considerable control over general policies. (For more explanation of a front-money system, see pp. 289–90.)

All federations to one degree or another use or would like to use low-interest loans from their member co-ops and individuals in the community. But federations must be especially conscious of the centralizing tendencies of getting large sums of money without granting control over these funds to member co-ops. Being independent of the need to approach co-ops for capital may soon mean being independent of the need to consult co-ops on purchasing policy. One way to mitigate this might be with democratically controlled sustaining funds for the co-op community. (See pp. 298–300.)

Joint Purchasing

Once you've set up a federation you're ready to buy food together. Buying on a federated level is very different from buying as an individual co-op. The economy of scale is much larger. The economic clout is real and you can make demands that individual co-ops cannot. You also have to take into account a much larger and more heterogeneous membership base.

1. Find as many sources as possible. Determine what quality and price choices are available.

2. Learn what demand from member co-ops is. Help them determine how much they want by studying their volume figures. Remind them that small volume items, or those previously hard for them to get (ginger root, for example) may now be available.

3. Find out what the minimum order is.

4. Evaluate the amount of energy people must expend to do the deal. Are co-ops committed to helping unload the truck and store the food?

5. Consider transportation: proximity of sources, quality of communication, cost and date of delivery.

6. Weigh the political considerations. Do you want to buy from outside your region or would you rather make a determined effort to boost the local economy? Are you boycotting certain products? Are you trying to support small organic farms?

Now you're ready to compile an order. Here are some logistics for handling a joint purchase:

1. Set a time by which all orders must be in. Give member co-ops adequate time to compile their orders, collect their money, and give it to the federation.

2. Have people available at publicized telephone numbers at specific times to handle calls from member co-ops.

3. Encourage payment by cashier's check or money order so you don't have to wait for checks to clear.

4. Order the food.

5. Distribute the food when it arrives.

(a) Where is the truck delivering the food?

(b) When is it going to arrive?

(c) How are people going to pick up their orders?

(d) Who is going to be there to help unload?

(e) Who can you call at a member co-op if someone doesn't show up?

Joint purchasing is a simple way to handle federated orders and is good practice for eventual warehousing. The participation it demands from member co-ops will lead to a more participatory warehouse later on.

Warehousing

In the past, warehouses have often preceded federations. Now there are several federations actively doing joint purchasing which do not yet have warehouses but are planning them. These federations have a unique opportunity to discuss several important policy issues before opening their warehouses.

A federation that has regional representation may find it difficult to agree on where the warehouse should be. Warehouses in a major city may be nearest to the greatest concentration of federation members and wholesaling houses, but rural and suburban co-ops may be justifiably reluctant to battle long distances and city traffic each time they need a bag of rice. Warehouses in rural areas will seem inefficient to city dwellers, and property in the suburbs is often priced if not zoned out of consideration. Most warehouses in fact wind up in cities.

A possible solution might be setting up several small warehouses throughout the region. The Minneapolis People's Warehouse has encouraged groups of co-ops in its region to set up their own warehouses if they have the volume. The People's Warehouse also has a policy of putting small coffee grinders, nut grinders, flour mills, and juicers into member stores on an experimental basis. The warehouse bears the initial cost and the store can buy the machine if it proves popular. If not, the warehouse can transfer the miniature production unit to another store.

A region that has a strong interest in participation should consider organizing a warehouse with as much volunteer labor from member co-ops as possible. Warehouses should be organized to reflect the regional uniqueness and political focus of the region. Areas with a tradition of community service stores will have a warehouse organized on that basis, as does the Washington, D.C., area. In other words, to reflect the values of your co-op community, the warehouse should also be a co-op. Some warehouses are not. The folks at Cooperating Community Grains in Seattle write: "CC Grains is not a co-op. It is a mill and warehouse that supplies co-ops. We are a worker-owned and -operated business."

Rural federations have usually organized trucking long before they're ready to consider warehousing. It may be best in these cases to organize the warehouse around the needs of the existing trucking, and possibly to merge the two. The Intra-Community Cooperative in Madison started as a trucking collective and then developed a warehouse.

There is a distinction between practicing warehousing and actually leasing a warehouse. Warehousing means keeping an extra supply on hand for more than one co-op; this can be done in an existing storefront, an empty garage, a basement, or any other available space. A region knows it's ready for a warehouse when it's already warehousing on such a large scale that it needs a separate space. Our friends in Minneapolis offer an excellent guide:

> There is a lot of bozo thinking about warehouses. Some places try to establish a warehouse before they have strong neighborhoods. Then they wonder why their warehouse venture doesn't work out. We suggest you start a wholesale section in your largest or otherwise most convenient co-op store. That is, you could sell full bags to individuals or other co-ops at half of your usual markup. Start small; maybe buy five extra bags of flour and ten extra bags of rice or wheat and ten extra boxes of raisins . . . When, and not before, there are so many co-ops and individuals coming in to buy full bags that it is interfering with the operation of your retail co-op store, then look for another building. You may divide into two separate (retail and wholesale) operations (complete with separate checking accounts, separate collectives, and separate buildings) at any stage. These three (checking accounts, buildings, and collectives) do not have to be separated in any particular order and none of the three should be separated until absolutely necessary.

In other words, acquiring a warehouse is the last step in the development of regional warehousing. The knowledge you'll need about budgeting funds, calculating turnover, locating sources, and making contacts with co-ops in your region will all be learned by wholesaling at the retail outlet.

DISTRIBUTION AND INVENTORY WAREHOUSING

Distribution warehousing has grown out of the need some regions see to make high quality, low-cost produce available to co-ops in less than case sizes. Produce is preordered by member co-ops and bought by a produce collective either at the local market or directly from local farmers. It's then brought to the warehouse and set out for the co-ops, which come at prearranged times to pick up their orders. Because the produce has been bought for immediate distribution and is highly perishable, there's no attempt to store it; everything but the hardiest of root crops is dispersed as soon as possible. The warehouse functions more as a distribution point than as a warehouse. The Southern California Cooperating Community (SCCC) warehouse, the Philadelphia warehouse, and the New York City People's Warehouse all operate this way to meet the produce needs of their regions. In fact, so little is actually stored at the New York People's Warehouse that it becomes the Warehouse Coffeehouse and holds concerts most Friday nights.

NEFCO and Austin Community Project (ACP) provide a similar service, but because they don't break up cases, they've been able to do it without a warehouse. NEFCO has its member co-ops come to the terminal market to pick up their produce; ACP, which either buys its produce in San Antonio or grows it on one of the co-op farms, delivers and distributes right off the back of a U.S. Army surplus truck.

Inventory warehousing is no less complex than distribution warehousing, but it's somewhat less risky. It involves buying nonperishables in bulk and storing them so that they're conveniently available to co-ops. Such warehouses offer a variety of bulk grains, beans, dried fruits, oils, pasta, nuts, seeds, nut butters, and honeys. Because there's relatively little spoilage in staples, the close communication with member co-ops that distribution warehousing requires isn't so necessary, and mistakes may be less financially damaging. The Washington, D.C., Community Warehouse still has several sacks left from an inexperienced purchase made last year; had they been dealing in produce they would have been forced to unload the item at a considerable loss. As it is, they sell a sack here and a sack there, and everything works out without spoilage.

But don't underestimate the losses that can be incurred in inventory warehousing. It's a bad idea to tie up capital in slow-moving inventory. Mistakes in staples can be much more expensive than in produce: a sack of rice is worth more than a crate of cabbages. Moreover, some staples do go bad. A member of the Philadelphia warehouse writes, "Anybody want 400 pounds of rancid sunflower seeds, cheap?"

When you decide that a separate warehouse is necessary and that you have the required wholesaling skills in your region, start looking for a building. At a regional meeting, consider how you're going to finance the warehouse. Decide how the work will be done, how decisions will be made, and how eligibility for membership will be determined. If work is to be done by a warehouse collective, set up a means to maintain dialogue between this collective and the regional federation.

Much of what we've said in the section on store layout (Chapter 11) applies to warehouses. You need adequate heating, plumbing, and electrical systems, and if you're going to deal primarily in produce, try to find a place already equipped with a walk-in cooler. Always check with the local health department for warehousing regulations. Rarely will you find a building that conforms to all health code specifications, but the regulations will give you an idea both of what to look for and of what kind of problems to expect from the health department later. Rents on warehouses are often figured on so many dollars per square foot, and will vary widely from region to region.

A loading dock is a necessity that many warehouses have tried to do without. The warehouses in Ann Arbor, Minneapolis, San Francisco, and Philadelphia do not have loading docks but use back power and ramps to move goods in and out of trucks. But even using a ramp, it takes four people a little practice to ease a 600-pound, 55-gallon drum of honey down from a truck without having it torpedo through the warehouse.

The Minneapolis People's Warehouse didn't have a loading dock when they purchased their building in 1973. At that time they wrote, "There is nothing but inertia keeping us from designing and building [a loading dock]." A year later the dock still hadn't been built. Warehouse workers, far from being inert, are very busy. When looking for a building, don't automatically assume that you'll have the time and energy to build all the things you need. Analyze the energy and commitment from co-ops in your region.

Often the best available location, because of either rent or accessibility, isn't a warehouse at all. SCCC in Los Angeles operates its warehouse out of the basement of a professional building on Santa Monica Boulevard. The San Francisco Cooperating Warehouse was formerly a garage; NEPCOOP in Vermont used to store its staples in a residence. If you find a building that wasn't formerly a warehouse, be sure that trucks will have access to it. It's self-defeating to have a warehouse on the wrong side of a bridge that won't hold the twenty-five tons of a fully loaded diesel rig.

Finding a bridge that you can always go over is a lot easier than finding one that you can always go under. The Packard Street Food Co-op in Ann Arbor was once making a cheese run in a rented truck that proved to be six inches higher than the bridge between the warehouse and their storefront. The $600 repair bill was an expensive lesson.

BUY OR LEASE?

Regions warehousing produce might try to find rent-free buildings that have been abandoned or vacated because of urban renewal. The Philadelphia and New York warehouses both operate out of structures "liberated" from city redevelopment agencies. Look into areas that are in the path of controversial, long-range government projects. The distribution warehouse may then serve to rally community resistance to "urban removal" and in turn may gain local support for its demands for legal possession.

Inventory warehouses can't take the same risks. Don't store inventory in any structure that isn't clearly yours.

Initially, look for a place to rent, not to buy. In our economy there are many advantages to owning property, but there's no way to estimate the risks involved unless you're sure how successful your warehouse will be. Unless you're certain of a stable, long-term operation, the chances you'll be taking by investing needed capital in an unproven location are too great.

Only a region with a committed co-op community that has proven capable of supporting a warehouse should consider buying. One community that has done so is Minneapolis. The North Country People's Warehouse, after losing its lease in the fall of 1973, decided to buy a building for $69,000 plus 8% annual interest, payable in five years. After the down payment, they owed $50,000 — or $10,000 a year. The short time they had to pay proved an advantage in two ways: it meant they would be paying less interest than if the payments were stretched out over twenty years, and it meant that they had to get support from the community to the tune of $10,000 per year. So far, the warehouse has been able to raise this money through collection jars in co-op stores and small interest-free loans from individuals. The staff wrote: "If each of the approximately

20,000 people who shop in the co-ops were to donate 50¢ each, this would generate the needed $10,000 per year. $2.50 from each shopper would pay off the building."

Even if your region has the resources to buy a warehouse, you may decide against it. Funds can be raised for only so many causes at once. If there are other, more important causes in the community to which co-op people are contributing, it might be best to wait. Fund-raising also takes people's energy away from other projects.

FINANCING

You'll have to raise money to pay the first month's rent, security deposits, and cost of equipment, improvements, and initial inventory before the warehouse is operating. This is usually done with a loan from the largest or several large co-ops in the region. The San Francisco Cooperating Warehouse was started with a loan of $3800 worth of inventory from its largest co-op store, Seeds of Life. The People's Wherehouse in Ann Arbor got started with the help of a $1600 loan from the Packard Street Co-op. If no one co-op has the money to spare, ask for short-term, no-interest loans from several participating co-ops and from people in the community. Fund-raising events like suppers, concerts, and fairs have also helped start warehouses. Adelle Davis once gave a benefit for the Ann Arbor People's Wherehouse.

Very little equipment is needed to open a warehouse, and much of it can be bought gradually. You'll need wooden pallets to keep stock off the floor, a universal health department regulation. You can often get pallets free with orders or from large commercial warehouses and markets. Also essential are a two-wheeler, a cart or two, and a beam scale for weighing heavy items. Your next long-term investment should be a walk-in cooler for cheeses, dried fruits, oils, and other perishables. Used coolers are frequently available from supermarkets going out of business. After a walk-in cooler, a good investment and the current pride of many warehouses is a pallet jack, which sells new for $300. A pallet jack will enable one person to load, unload, or move pallets fully loaded with hundreds of pounds on them. Other items such as ramps, shelving, oil drum carts, and rollers may be bought or made as needed.

You can purchase initial inventory either with loans or with co-ops prepaying, or fronting, the money. This inventory should be a combination of items that sell quickly, and thus keep your money recycling, and items that provide a considerable savings when bought in sufficient quantity. Remember that the warehouse's operating funds are generated from the markup on sales; items with high turnover will make the warehouse self-sufficient faster.

Once you've raised the money to start the warehouse, you'll have to repeat the process of raising money to keep the warehouse going. The greatest need of most warehouses is capital. To provide co-ops with a variety of foods and offer the savings that come from buying in quantity, you'll have to tie up a lot of money in inventory.

There are two general systems for raising capital. Most warehouses use their own unique combination of the two. The first and more widely used is asking for long-term low or no-interest loans from community people. Local, government, and social action programs are also sometimes sources of loans or grants. Loans can be accepted on a one-year or 18-month basis, after which time the principal is repaid in full or in monthly installments. By continuously seeking out loans, you may keep the capital fund constant or even growing while old loans are being repaid. An example of the monthly cycle of a capital fund is provided by Tucson's People's Warehouse:

LOANS: 1974

Month	*Received*	*Paid Out*	*Balance*
Jan	$4014.33	$ 190.00	$3824.33
Feb	3060.00	155.00	6729.33
Mar	758.89	818.00	6670.22
Apr	2800.61	778.24	8692.59
May	791.24	1315.99	8167.84
Jun	3915.00	510.00	11,572.84
Jul	688.69	2424.72	9836.81

The second system of raising capital is requiring front money from member co-ops. A front-money system means that each co-op lends the warehouse a sum equivalent to the amount of its purchases over a given period of time. The period of time differs depending on whether you're dealing in produce or staples. The Los Angeles SCCC warehouse requires that co-ops buying produce have on deposit the amount of an average week's purchases. Inventory warehouses often require a loan amounting to an entire month's purchases. In reality, few co-ops can raise that much money all at once. The Ann Arbor People's Wherehouse has therefore developed a complex schedule of installments. Co-ops pay toward their front at least 10% of their monthly order. These 10% payments are accumulated until two-thirds of the front money has been received. Once a co-op has paid two thirds, it is only required to pay a 1% charge that goes into the Federation Fund; this isn't a loan but a straight capitalization fee. All front-money loans and capitalization fees are paid over and above the regular warehouse markup.

You may use either system, both systems, or devise one of your own, but there are two requirements of any method used to raise money from other people. First, the money must clearly be used to benefit the community. Second, a comprehensive accounting system must be devised to keep track of funds, and it must be open to the community.

The North Country People's Warehouse recently decided to ask each farmer it dealt with to pay 1¢ per bag for all food sold to the warehouse. The money goes to the Organic Growers and Buyers Association to promote organic farming and establish a certifying system for organic farmers in the area. Farmers are accustomed to paying such fees to operators of grain elevators and other distributors; these fees usually go to promotional and lobbying groups like the National Soybean Growers Association.

In participatory warehouses, penalty fees or higher brokerage fees for co-ops that don't send voluntary labor are other possible sources of funds. Some warehouses also charge delivery fees, which encourage co-ops to pick up their food. All these fees are small, calculated to cover the cost of the service. Penalty fees are applied to a salary for someone who's doing the job in place of the absent co-op volunteer. Says a Philadelphia warehouse worker: "Our credo is work or pay. Most co-ops choose to send labor."

WAREHOUSE WORK SYSTEMS

Warehouse work systems range from collectives that ask little regular participation from member co-ops to small produce buying collectives that rely on committees of volunteers to do most of the work of the warehouse. Distribution warehouses use more volunteer participation than inventory warehouses do because of the logistics of dealing in produce. Preordering and distributing perishables requires the warehouse collective to work closely with co-ops and requires co-ops to share in ordering and organizing pickups.

It's best to have volunteers organized into committees or work teams with clearly defined tasks. SCCC requires every member co-op to supply either 10% of its membership or at least eight people, whichever is larger, to one of seven warehouse work teams. The New York People's Warehouse has divided labor into eight committees, and insists that each co-op "take responsibility to see that the committees function and that work commitments are met by those who made them."

Distribution warehouses should use volunteer work teams to assist but not to replace the produce-buying collective. The ability to deal with wholesalers, recognize quality produce, and understand the workings of the market can only be acquired with experience. Even NEFCO and Austin Community Produce, which provide a buying service without a distribution warehouse, see continuity as the key to quality buying, and each has a small, stable collective that is assisted by volunteers from member co-ops.

Inventory warehouses are usually run by permanent collectives with no regular volunteer labor. Most inventory warehouses don't seek regular participation by member co-ops for the same reason that distribution warehouses don't use volunteer labor for their buying collective. The need for continuity and stability has so far outweighed the educational and cooperative benefits of participation. Collectives in inventory warehouses often feel that finding sources, ordering from brokers and producers, arranging trucking, receiving goods, keeping inventories, making deliveries, and keeping books are beyond what can be expected of rotating volunteer committees. Whether these warehouses can remain responsive to their member co-ops without at least some regular volunteer participation is an open question.

Worker collectives are becoming more sensitive to the political and educational need to encourage participation as a prerequisite to knowledgeable control. A worker in the Minneapolis warehouse writes:

> We do encourage people to visit us and work with us for the day to learn about the sources and movement of their food . . . We discourage extensive use of volunteer labor because we feel it does not apply as a long-term strategy when we extend control over areas other than food distribution and because we place a high priority on providing employment within alternative institutions.

DECISION MAKING

The question of participation becomes critical when you consider how decisions will be made. Decision making in a warehouse should occur on two levels: all major policy decisions should be brought before regional meetings, and day-to-day operating decisions should be made by the staff.

If there's no federation in the region of your warehouse, you might organize one. If warehouse business begins to take up too much time at federation meetings, other policy-making boards or committees can be set up. Take care that members of the decision-making body are neither outnumbered nor overpowered by the warehouse collective. In the Philadelphia warehouse, no member of the board of directors can simultaneously be employed by the federation. Equal care must be taken that representatives to the decision-making body don't reflect only the attitudes of the paid staffs of co-op stores. Understanding this, the Minneapolis warehouse asks each of its thirty-seven participating members to send two representatives to its Policy Review Board, and strongly urges that at least one not be a paid staff member and that at least one be female. Cooperative farms and cafés are also part of the Policy Review Board, which represents co-ops in Minnesota, Wisconsin, North Dakota, South Dakota, and Iowa.

The quality of decision making on policy boards is a function of how much board members know about the warehouse operations. If co-op representatives aren't encouraged to work with warehouse staff, they won't be able to make independent, confident decisions on where the warehouse should be headed. They'll only be able to veto or rubberstamp.

The warehouse collective should be guided by policies set by the federation, but otherwise must be free to decide operational questions. Regions define the jobs; collectives decide how to do them. Unfortunately, this doesn't always happen. Policy decisions often have to be made before the region has time to arrive at a consensus. A policy-making body is nonetheless a necessary vehicle for promoting warehouse accountability.

MEMBER ELIGIBILITY

The best selling policy is one that clearly reflects the consensus of your region. Several basic questions are: 1) Will the warehouse sell to capitalist retailers? 2) Will it sell to nonco-ops? 3) Will it sell to individuals? 4) Will it refuse to sell on certain political grounds?

You may choose to sell to capitalist retailers for two reasons. The first is simply to increase your volume to help make ends meet. The second is to make contacts with noncooperative businesses to spread the co-op philosophy. Seattle's Cooperating Community Grains sells to capitalist retailers for both these reasons.

But there are drawbacks to dealing with capitalist retailers. Most co-op workers accept low wages as an investment in the future or as a subsidy to the low-priced food co-ops offer. Providing capitalist businesses, which have no interest in the co-op movement, with a lower cost item from which to extract profits may be demoralizing and self-defeating.

You should probably limit your membership to community organizations that share the spirit if not the form of cooperation. The Community Warehouse of Washington, D.C., allows a formally profit-making but community-conscious group to bottle honey in its facility. San Francisco's Cooperating Warehouse provided food for a recent Allen Ginsberg reading. Tucson's People's Warehouse asks community groups wishing to buy from it the following questions:

How do you serve the community?
What is your markup system?
What are your motives for doing business?
How do your workers' wages compare with income?
How much input do the workers have in decision making?

The Washington, D.C., warehouse will sell to any community group or individual as long as they're buying the food for themselves and not for resale; if the group intends to resell the food, the operation must be "collectively run and community owned (no private ownership or stockholders)."

If your co-op decides to sell only to co-ops, you'll have to define what a co-op is. The membership clause of the North Country (Minneapolis) People's Warehouse bylaws is instructive:

> Members of the People's Warehouse are organizations which democratically distribute whole foods. Members must meet the following criteria:
>
> a) Any group of people who have organized to distribute food to themselves for no profit . . .
>
> b) The organization must actively solicit the participation of all its consumers in decision-making . . .

> c) Any salaries shall be determined in a public democratic manner based on the principle, each according to his/her needs.
>
> d) Organizations which make a distinction between salaries of ordinary workers and managerial personnel will not be considered. This distinction does not apply to voluntary help.

Whether or not this is an adequate description of the co-ops in your area, you may want to use this checklist when your region attempts self-definition.

Each warehouse must also decide if it will sell to individuals. The Ann Arbor and San Francisco warehouses don't. They not only want to encourage collective buying, but they oppose hoarding. An executive of the Glide Foundation, a local nonprofit group, came into the San Francisco warehouse one day explaining that he had been reading of the protein shortage the world may soon face and wished to buy a 55-gallon drum of peanut butter to adorn his game room. He was refused.

The Minneapolis warehouse folks are equally conscious of the importance of collective buying but they also see advantages to selling to individuals:

> We sell to individuals who come in off the street because (1) if we made people go to the co-op store then we would be setting the store up as an unnecessary middleperson. This is contrary to our basic purpose; (2) Most individuals come here because they were sent by a neighborhood co-op store to buy (say) one bag of milk powder. When they feast their eyes on our many 50-pound and 100-pound bags and 5-gallon tins of goodies, wheels start to turn in their heads. In about one week we see the same individual back with 3 or 5 of his/her neighbors —
>
> and ta da
>
> — a buying club is born. This happens to us about once per week . . . If we didn't sell to individuals or if we made it difficult thru some complicated bureaucratic maneuver for them to buy thru us then these buying clubs would not emerge.

Some regions include as a requirement for membership in the warehouse that co-ops be neither sexist nor racist. The Southern California Cooperating Community wrote in its bylaws:

> Co-ops which have racist or sexist practices, or which otherwise violate the dignity of people . . . and who persist in these practices after discussion by the community will be subject to expulsion by a ¾ vote of the co-ops.

The San Francisco warehouse is also concerned that co-ops may be sexist. Before the opening of the Potrero Hill co-op store, the warehouse staff had a meeting with store organizers to register its displeasure that the store staff consisted of seven men and only two women.

LOGISTICS

The best information on warehouse logistics may be found at the warehouses themselves. Visit the co-op warehouse nearest you (see Appendix I) and spend a few days working with its collective. Warehouses are very open and generous to any visitors but are especially happy to see someone wishing to learn by sharing experience as well as by asking questions.

Sources of food are constantly changing, and can best be learned from the warehouse nearest you. Attend co-op warehouse conferences and share notes. Both the San Francisco and Minneapolis warehouses have printed source lists and these are worth writing for. Talk with warehouses that use particular sources about the best way to approach them. See Chapter 10 and 11 for information on dealing with wholesalers, taking inventory, and negotiating terms and credit. Some warehouses will be able to give you credit references for suppliers they deal with, but you'll probably have to pay at pickup or even in advance on the first few orders.

You must decide in many cases whether you're better off paying higher shipping costs on a shipment of one or two items from a direct source, or paying lower shipping costs on a large mixed order from a less direct source that charges higher wholesale prices. The more pounds you have shipped from one place, the cheaper the shipping cost; freight rates are determined by weight bracket: 500 pounds/ 1000 pounds/ 5000 pounds/ 24,000 pounds/ 40,000 pounds (a semi).

What distinguishes the new movement in regional warehousing from the 1930s and earlier co-op warehouse ventures is the new movement's consciousness that centralization may be good economics, but it can be lousy politics. Warehouses that exert too much influence in a region by the simple weight of their economic concentration may end up engaging in the same top-down power politics that the new co-op movement is trying to avoid. The example of Cornucopia is a case in point.

CORNUCOPIA, A WAREHOUSE FAILURE

Cornucopia, a warehouse in Chicago, folded during the summer of 1974 after two and a half years of problem-filled operation. Cornucopia started as a task force in the winter of 1970–71. About sixty preorders were buying from one wholesaler who, with the help of the Lutheran Church, had begun a service called Feed the Hungry. Some co-op people created the task force because they were dissatisfied with the paternalism of this wholesaler. The task force decided that the Chicago co-ops needed a warehouse and an independent buyer on the market. Despite the fact that many of the co-ops surveyed said they were pleased with their present wholesaler, the task force decided to go ahead with its plans.

It got encouragement from the Cook County Office of Economic Opportunity. The OEO was trying to organize preorders in Chicago's poor neighborhoods. It funded a marketing survey, which estimated that 100 co-ops would use a warehouse if it existed. The survey overestimated the ability of the OEO to organize preorders for the poor, and mistakenly reported that Self Help Action, a private assistance project, had 50 co-ops ready to buy from a warehouse.

On the basis of its survey, the OEO promised the task force a grant of $30,000 and helped it raise another $30,000 from W. Clement Stone and the American Freedom From Hunger Foundation and various Chicago department stores. A core group on the task force worked throughout 1971 with the OEO, raising the money and making plans for the warehouse.

They rented a 16,000-square-foot warehouse on the west side of town. Based on their projections, this wouldn't be too big, nor would the $1250 a month rent be too expensive. They spent nearly $10,000 on rent and capital equipment. By March 1972, Cornucopia was stocked with fresh produce, flour, grains, beans, nuts, dried fruits, and cheese. The markup was set at a reasonable 8% for entire cases and 11% for partials.

Instead of the anticipated 100 co-ops, there were 5. In the next six months the number of affiliated co-ops grew to more than 50, but the increase in volume couldn't keep up with the cost of running the warehouse. The staff doubled from the original five. Full-time staff earned $500 per month and part-time, $250. Labor, rent, taxes, union dues, interest on loans, and ripoffs added up to a monthly operating expense of close to $5000. The expanding volume couldn't cover the costs and by the end of the first summer the warehouse had to double its markup to try to get out of the red.

Some of the increased markup was put onto the price of the products instead of being added on at the cash register. One former staff member explained that part of the bump was hidden "in the best interests of the people." The staff was willing to "tell a little lie to keep the people buying."

Twice in the fall of 1972, the OEO came to Cornucopia's aid. In October, it gave the warehouse the free use of a refrigerated truck to enable it to carry meats. It was hoped that the new product, sold at a 10% markup, would increase sales and get the warehouse out of trouble. It didn't. The next month Cornucopia had to close because it couldn't pay its bills. OEO bailed it out with a loan.

The affiliated co-ops met during this crisis and agreed that Cornucopia should charge whatever markup was necessary to cover its operating costs. Member participation increased at this time because of the crisis atmosphere. Cornucopia was able to reopen in December, and things started looking up.

At the start of 1973, the higher markups and increased volume led to a money-making operation. Summer brought a reduction in volume and the books again went into the red. In the fall, the operation once more got off the ground. New staff members, with new energy and dedication, worked hard to make the warehouse a success. Many of them worked overtime for no extra money, but their efforts weren't enough. At the end of 1973 the books showed a $20,000 loss.

The actual situation wasn't so bad as the paper loss indicated, but member co-ops became discouraged when they heard about it. This sentiment, coupled with constant increases in markup, drove many co-ops out of Cornucopia. As volume fell in 1974, the markup rose to 35%.

By summer 1974, Cornucopia was again seriously in debt. Its operations were running at a loss; it owed money to the IRS, the landlord, the staff, and numerous creditors. It took the assets it had, paid off the government and staff, defaulted on its other creditors, and closed its doors. Cornucopia reorganized into a buying and trucking operation and is still serving some co-ops in this manner.

When Cornucopia folded, its staff suggested that co-ops should find their own distribution centers. Some co-ops found centers immediately but others didn't. One organizer remarked: "The financial crisis brought people out of the woodwork and pulled us together."

The organizers of Cornucopia substituted fund-raising and planning for organizing. They relied on a marketing survey done for OEO instead of working with the area's co-ops to determine how much business they would have. They raised a great deal of money from OEO and other outside sources rather than trying to tap the resources of the co-ops that would be using the service. Instead of spending what the base could afford and setting up a small operation at the start, they spent whatever they wanted to and created a structure that their base could not afford. Their nonparticipatory structure lost them the commitment of the people they were serving and added the cost of ripoffs to their already bloated operating expenses.

Cornucopia was set up on too grand a scale to be supported by a reasonable markup on sales. Instead of trying to cut back its $5000 per month operating expenses, it kept increasing its markup and going to OEO for loans to pay its debts. Although the staff was dedicated, the warehouse suffered from top-down organization. An alternative is bottom-up organizing, in which the base of co-ops creates a federation or warehouse to meet its needs.

Sustaining Funds

In many centers of co-op activity, alternative businesses have formed sustaining funds to support worthy community projects or to generate needed capital for themselves. In Madison, Wisconsin, a sustaining fund was created in late 1970, mainly by nonrevenue-producing organizations like the local tenants' union and women's counseling center. By October 1971, it was bringing in almost $1000 per month. Part of this money came from voluntary deductions on the paychecks of city and university employees. The emphasis on supporting political projects and the apparent lack of emphasis on investing any significant portion of the money in viable alternative businesses helped to create a highly charged political atmosphere that eventually killed the fund. Its decision-making structure allowed for consensus, but because the spirit of consensus was lacking, it ended up, according to one observer, "a tyranny of the minority where 2 or 3 groups could, and often did, block any action."

But the Madison experiment legitimized the idea that an alternative community can generate and control its own funds. Members of Denver's Common Market Food Co-op recently voted to tax themselves 1% of purchases to support a sustaining fund that emphasizes its responsibility to poor people, women, and minorities. In Minneapolis, the Building Fund has raised more than $10,000 per year to enable the People's Warehouse to buy its own building. Most funds, like the one in Minneapolis, collect contributions through coin cans placed prominently in food co-ops and other alternative businesses.

Eligibility for membership in, or grants from, sustaining funds, and decision making in these funds, are perhaps the two major problems. We think the guidelines suggested by fund organizers in Washington, D. C., are useful:

> Any group receiving money from the Fund [must] be a member. Membership means the group is each of these things: 1) anti-profit; 2) non-hierarchical; 3) providing a direct service to the community; 4) having open finances and open meetings . . .
> One way to reduce factionalism is to restrict the use of Fund money to equipment, tools and buildings. Money spent on salaries, telephone bills, etc. is gone for good; it cannot be recovered. In other funds this has led to interminable arguments over whether a group has "correct" politics in the way it uses irrecoverable money. In our plan, the tools, equipment, or building belong to the community in the event a project should fail, and the tools can be used by any member of the community at any time, within reasonable limits . . . Groups receiving grants or loans [should] be agreeable to the proposition that if their organization is dissolved, its assets will not go for private gain but will instead by recycled back into the community. In this way the total share of community wealth grows, encouraging further economic development. This will reduce factionalism by eliminating irrecoverable drains and encouraging the idea that we are working together to build something that will benefit us all.

Democratic decision making must be built into a sustaining fund's structure. This means frequent open meetings, ample publicity about meetings, information about fund activities readily available at co-ops and other places where fund members gather, frequent election of boards or officers, and adherence to the one member-one vote principle. Consensus decision making, which is a skill gained over time, should be used only when participants understand its conciliatory spirit and even then should not be used to the total exclusion of voting.

Although they are a step in the right direction, sustaining funds are by no means the ultimate answer to the financial needs of an alternative economy. As long as co-ops or their sustaining funds keep their money in corporate-controlled banks, they lose a measure of control over their resources, and may in fact be investing in their own destruction. Banks, through their loan and investment policies, decide how a community will or will not develop.

Depositor-controlled community banks may be a way for an alternative economy to control its own finances. Decisions on bank loan policy for economic development of a community could be made by depositors on a one member-one vote basis instead of by directors whose power depends on how many shares they own in the bank. Loan policy could then reflect the interests of community residents and small businesses instead of the interests of shareholders who often don't even live nearby.

Depositor-controlled commercial banks would be more useful than credit unions or cooperative banks in building an alternative financial structure. Credit unions and co-op banks, though fine for personal savings and loans, are limited by law from lending money to commercial enterprises. Commercial banks, by contrast, can apply a good deal of their money to commercial loans, and, according to one study, "they can be owned by holding companies which in turn can be controlled by bank depositors on a one person, one vote basis. In addition, the ability of banks to accept 'demand deposits' (checking accounts) makes them desirable since this service is obviously needed by residents."

Banks can be chartered by either the state or the federal government. Regulations vary, but in most places a nonprofit corporation can own a controlling share of a bank's stock, and this corporation can in turn consist of all the depositors in the bank. It's theoretically possible for such "people's banks" to be formed, although many obstacles would present themselves, not the least of which is the relative lack of financial expertise in the co-op movement.

Horizontal and Vertical Growth

Federations are not only effective tools for co-ops seeking better sources, but they can also support the development of cooperative producers and services in and out of the food business. Horizontal growth is the expansion of nonfood co-op enterprises. Vertical growth is the creation of food producing, processing, and storage facilities within the cooperating community.

Several types of consumer co-ops in Minneapolis-St. Paul have patterned themselves after the food co-op stores. The past and current line-up of nonfood consumer co-ops includes North Country Hardware, North Country Drygoods, and North Country Bookstore and Reading Room, all housed in one building; Free-wheel Bike Shop, repairing and selling both new and used bicycles; three cafés; the Art Supply Sellar; a garage which requires membership to help pay for tools; a collection or guild of miscellaneous artisans such as plumbers, glazers, woodworkers, roofers, and masons; and Christopher Robin Press, which prints for both co-ops and a nonco-op groups. The bike co-op recognizes membership, defined in terms of volunteer work, in other parts of the co-op system as equivalent to membership in the bike shop.

All these groups will instruct the people they work for. Their idea is to democratize and demystify the knowledge needed to maintain and repair the machines and buildings we use.

Vertical expansion in the co-op movement can include any part of the food production or distribution process. The capital, expertise, and licenses needed are different for each operation, and vary from one region to another. In most parts of the country, but by no means all, it's easier to produce yogurt cooperatively than to start a mill or keep bees. A juicing collective may consist of two people, a juicer, some fruit, and some imagination. An herb producer may be one person in a city apartment.

Most food production shops are run by collectives. The skills, commitment, and continuity required make this a logical mode of operation, though volunteers often help out with deliveries, cleanup, and other jobs. Volunteer work in a production shop can easily satisfy a member's co-op work requirement.

BAKERIES AND MILLS

Probably the two major areas of vertical co-op growth are bakeries and mills. In Minneapolis, the People's Company Bakery, which has been operating since 1971, produces five hundred loaves a day of over a dozen different kinds of bread, including raisin, apple cider, date nut, and Russian rye. They also make four hundred pounds of granola a day and two batches of cookies, cakes, and pies a week. Nature's Bakery in Madison makes two hundred loaves a day as well as two or three trays of sweets daily, bagels (ten flavors), and peanut butter three times a week. The Bread Shop in Chicago makes whole-wheat pizza which is sold by the slice as well as by the pie.

The initial costs of setting up a bakery vary. Nature's Bakery got all its equipment at auctions or from bakeries going out of business. Their Middleby-Marshall 18-tray rotating oven, 7′ × 7′ × 10′, which would sell for $10,000 new, was purchased for $150 from a baker who was going out of business and was pleased to have someone take it apart and move it for him (a considerable task). Nature's Bakery later went to an auction and found a perfectly good Middleby-Marshall that couldn't be sold and was eventually dismantled for junk. This bakery's total equipment expenditure came to less than $1000. This included stove, mixers, refrigerators, bread table, bowls, pans, and trays.

Most co-op mills are run by small autonomous collectives that supply flour both to bakeries and to preorders and stores. A collective is particularly advisable here, since the machinery is delicate and expensive, and, as some co-ops have discovered, there is more than one way to mess up a mill.

The most common source of mills for co-ops is the Meadows Mill Company in North Wilkesboro, North Carolina; their smallest stone mill (8-inch) can grind about 75 pounds of flour an hour. These 8-inch mills are now operating in co-ops in Vermillion, South Dakota, Iowa City, Iowa, Fayetteville, Arkansas, and many other communities. The Washington, D. C., warehouse has a 20-inch Meadows, and the San Francisco warehouse recently acquired a 30-inch Meadows that produces 700 pounds of wheat flour an hour.

Seattle has by far the most extensive milling operation of all co-op centers in the country: two stone mills, one for wheat and the other, a hammer mill, for soybeans and other coarse grains. Soybeans cannot be ground on a regular mill, as the Ozark Food Co-op discovered; the soybean oil badly gummed up the stones, which then had to be resurfaced.

Grinding stones must be resurfaced or "dressed" periodically. That is, they must be sharpened and shaped for optimum milling. If the stones develop smooth spots, the efficiency of the mill is decreased tremendously. When stone mills were more common, people would spend their lives dressing stones. It is an art that took years of apprenticeship to learn. Some co-ops dress their own stones — but this should be attempted only with extreme care. The folks in Ann Arbor tried and nearly destroyed their stones; it took a skilled person far longer to get them into shape afterward. Recovering this art is something a few people could do for the co-op movement.

Setting up a mill or a bakery is a complicated business. You'll need expert advice and full knowledge of local health codes. You'll also need a dependable buying community and a committed group of bakery or mill workers. Visit the co-op bakery or mill nearest you, write to the Ann Arbor or Minneapolis warehouses for advice, and learn all you can from friendly local bakers and millers. Keep your eyes open for small shops that are in trouble and might consider going cooperative.

OTHER TYPES OF PRODUCTION

There are many other areas of food production that a small group in your co-op might explore. Yogurt making may be done on a large scale in someone's house — but be sure you check local regulations. Beekeeping can be a good part-time occupation for members of rural and suburban co-ops, and even city folks can do it if they arrange to locate their apiary on a farm or orchard outside of town. You can grow herbs in a city apartment and supply them to the co-op fresh, dried, or frozen. Sprouts are even simpler to grow and take only a few days. Some co-ops have community gardens in which a member with some uncultivated land invites others in the co-op to stake out plots and share the cost of tilling, watering, and fertilizing. Sometimes municipalities set aside land for community gardens. There are several farms that deal mostly with co-op federations; Wiscoy Valley Community Farm in Winona, Minnesota, and

Winding Road Farm in Boyceville, Wisconsin, regularly contract with the North Country People's Warehouse. A fair price is determined on the basis of expense statements submitted to the co-op newsletter, *The Scoop*.

Co-op restaurants are thriving in many regions; they provide congenial gathering places as well as high quality food at low prices. The New Riverside Café in Minneapolis has survived for years without any set prices; people pay what they can. This has resulted in many free meals but also in the receipt, once, of $200 for a dish of rice and vegetables and $30 for a cup of tea. Most co-op restaurants are run by collectives; Seward Café in Minneapolis and Kosha Kitchen in Washington, D. C., also have open community meetings.

A group of co-op members might look into canning, freezing, jam and jelly making, or mayonnaise production.

Drying fruits is another possibility. Farmers in your area may be willing to sell you odd-sized fruit for very little. The San Francisco co-op community recently contracted with a local organic farmer for figs that they picked and dried themselves.

Then there's the Loose Azza Goose juice-making collective in Tucson, which provides fresh fruit and vegetable juices in dizzying variety to the local Food Conspiracy, Oblivion, and Tao co-ops. In areas where maple syrup is tapped, a co-op group might get into producing that commodity; it takes a few months of intensive work in the spring. In Minneapolis, some people associated with the Red Star Apothecary, which is housed in the People's Warehouse building, have begun to distill oils. The North Country community can also boast Jan and Mary's Organic Ice Cream. The opportunities for expansion are limited only by the energy and imagination of your co-op community.

Sources

Regional co-op newsletters are a good source of information on federations. Contact the federation or warehouse nearest you. (Addresses are in Appendix I.) News about joint purchasing is shared at frequent co-op conferences. The Minneapolis and San Francisco warehouses, and Kokua Country Foods in Hawaii, will send their lists of wholesale sources if you write to them.

A good pamphlet on sustaining funds is C. Simpson's "This is not a history book: some information about sustaining funds in the U. S.," *Common Sense*, 1802 Belmont Road NW, Washington, D. C. 20009. A rationale for depositer-controlled banks is "We Can Do It Ourselves: a report on a depositer-controlled bank as a step towards commercial redevelopment of Model City," by the Southside Planning Council, Minneapolis. If you're interested in forming a credit union, see:

Croteau, John T. *The Economics of the Credit Union*. Detroit: Wayne State University Press, 1963.

Dublin, Jack. *Credit Unions, Theory and Practice*. Detroit: Wayne State University Press, 1966.

Also, write to the Credit Union National Association, Box 431, Madison, Wisconsin 53701, or your state credit union league.

The first draft of this chapter included sections on yogurt making, herb and sprout growing, and cooperating with bees. They were deleted to keep the book's length and price reasonable. The New England Federation of Co-ops will be printing them as separate pamphlets, so if you're interested, write to NEFCO, 8 Ashford St., Allston, Ma. 02134. Meanwhile, a good cookbook like *The Joy of Cooking* can get you started on yogurt, and for apiaries, the standard references are:

Root, A. I. and E. R. *ABC and XYZ of Bee Culture*. Medina, Ohio: A. I. Root Company.

Grout, Roy A. *The Hive and the Honey Bee*. Hamilton, Illinois: Dadant & Sons.

Both Root and Dadant also publish pamphlets and journals and supply beekeeping equipment.

You can get advice on starting community canneries from the Ball Corporation of Muncie, Indiana, or from the U. S. Department of Agriculture or local university extension services. The Natural Organic Farmers Association (address in Appendix II) publishes a newsletter with information on canning and storing fresh food. Write to them for back issues. Or get:

Rodale Press. *Stocking Up*. Emmaus, Pa., 1974. A guide to storing, canning, and preserving.

16. Politics

IF you've read this far you know that we don't think food co-ops can or should be politically "neutral." Nor do we think the Rochdale Pioneers intended them this way. For the Pioneers, political and religious neutrality grew out of a situation in which one sect wanted to take over the society, thus violating the principle of open membership.

But the Rochdale Society *was* political; its founders were radicals, blacklisted from their trade because of strike activities. Consumer cooperation grew out of the nineteenth-century utopian socialist and radical reform movements. The Rochdaleans certainly recognized that taking control over the distribution of consumer goods was a political act.

This is even truer today, when economic control is far vaster and more centralized than it was in the days of Rochdale. The concept of cooperativism is political because it eliminates profit, spreads social wealth, and substitutes cooperation for competition in economic affairs. A co-op that refuses to act politically in some situations may essentially be supporting the *status quo*, saying that nothing needs changing. The important distinction is between broad political commitment and sectarianism. Co-ops should be nonsectarian in their membership requirements. But this doesn't mean they should abandon their social vision.

Co-ops are political for other reasons. They develop organizational and financial skills within a community that can enhance organizing around other issues. The level of trust and the lines of communication that co-ops build can, and often do, help a community fight political battles.

Democratic decision making is an exercise of political muscles, which in most Americans are almost atrophied. Mere exercise of these muscles will make them stronger. Thus, participants in democratically run co-ops are likely to become more active citizens who demand responsiveness from the larger political structure.

The experiences and interactions that go on inside co-ops also make them political. Many people are beginning to recognize that politics includes not only public but private power relations. The now-familiar term *sexual politics* refers to the ways that members of one sex maintain power over members of the other in social and personal relations. In fostering cooperative values, sexual equality, and collective experiences, today's food co-ops are adding a further dimension to our understanding of politics.

Women's Liberation in the Co-op

In most nuclear families, men are the breadwinners and women are the housekeepers. Even if the women are working, they're usually paid less than the men are, and are responsible for the family's domestic welfare in addition to their 9 to 5 jobs. Two of the co-op movement's goals should be: to help men take an equal share in family welfare responsibilities, and to build up women's business skills and self-confidence.

Although we feel that an all-woman or "housewife" co-op is a contradiction of cooperative values, we acknowledge that many such co-ops exist and do play a role in the movement for sexual equality. Many women have specific needs that support a participatory co-op structure. If they're around children most of the time, they need purposeful adult associations. A housewife co-op can grow into an efficient operation in which the women participating develop self-confidence and skills. If these women get the necessary psychological and political support as they move out of dependency, they will eventually stop tolerating second-class status in their private lives.

An organizer of a predominantly women's co-op in Holyoke, Massachusetts, writes,

> As quickly as the men were running from us, the women were joining our struggle. We took our meetings to their own kitchens, and purchasing decisions were often made while toddlers climbed on our laps and spilled

> juice on our precious position papers. These women's combat training in the supermarkets proved to be invaluable, particularly to co-op organizers who had never had to cope with feeding a family. The women, innocent of the rules of "good business," did not know that a co-op could not succeed, so they made it succeed. Never having been lauded for individual achievement, they saw nothing demeaning about collective effort.

If women haven't worked since marriage, or since having children, they need the opportunity to hold responsible positions without previous credentials or work experience. In Holyoke, women found this opportunity. A struggling co-op's need for committed people renders absurd the insistence on impeccable education and employment records. When time, energy, and willingness to learn became defined as assets, a truly incredible amount of womanpower was liberated in the Holyoke Co-op.

Co-ops can serve as a testing ground for women attempting to make the transition from home to job. They may lead to full-time jobs in the alternative economy. Or they may engender the self-confidence and initiative that leads to higher career aspirations or further education. Two women in the Holyoke Co-op, while involving themselves in co-op work, also found the energy to seek employment and go back to school.

There are, of course, many problems with an all-woman co-op. For one thing, women may be growing, socially and politically, much faster than their husbands are. As husbands realize that the co-op is not just another social club, they may begin to perceive it as a threat. Or conversely, they may refuse, either from ignorance or from insecurity, to give credence to the valuable co-op work their wives are doing. This can undermine the women's self-confidence. Since most co-op work is voluntary, it's easy for men to ridicule it.

To counteract some of these problems, housewife co-ops need to develop conscious support mechanisms on both individual and organizational levels. Emotional support from other women is vital in helping women deal with both direct and subtle attacks by their husbands and other men (sometimes including wholesalers). Financial support may be important for those who are very active. Sometimes social agencies or foundations will finance programs that qualify as job training for women, especially in low-income areas. Financial support from within the co-op is preferable, though, as it has the twin advantages of educating co-op members to the importance of the activists' work, and of maintaining the co-op's independence. Technical support can include training programs in buying, accounting, inventory, etc.

In Holyoke, a husband who began to perceive the co-op as a threat eventually forced his wife to drop out. The co-op members themselves didn't understand what was happening, and as a consequence didn't provide the support this woman needed. Since then, they have been more sensitive to these kinds of pressures. One member, who faced condescension at home for her "nice," not-too-serious little co-op hobby, became extremely confused as she tried to reconcile the hours of hard work she had been putting in with her husband's attitude. Support from other women in the co-op averted the loss of another valuable member.

Co-ops should be aware of the difficult road some women travel when they begin to move out of dependency. There will often be setbacks, and women whose co-op activity is beginning to conflict with demands from home may temporarily renege on co-op responsibilities. As aggravating as this may be to the person left holding the bag, it's important to avoid an enraged "you're fired" attitude. This reinforces the misconception that married women are unfit to hold positions of responsibility. An alternative is to educate women to the importance of meeting co-op responsibilities and to develop resources to help meet these responsibilities — car pools, child-care co-ops, etc.

The day-to-day hassles of running a co-op often preclude paying adequate attention to support mechanisms for women. Women's needs, which aren't by any means a side issue, often have to be postponed by the women themselves to keep the co-op functioning. This will probably keep happening until a sufficient amount of energy has been expended by the co-op movement as a whole to generate a body of women's support mechanisms that can be brought into play at the very beginning of a new co-op. The Cambridge Food Co-op store, for instance, has a child-care space for parents shopping or doing work hours.

In the long run, co-ops won't solve the problem of sexism until work is equally divided between women and men. This was brought home to a Holyoke organizer by her three-year-old son when he informed her one day that the "co-op was for women." Was the co-op, in fact, creating a new stereotype of co-op as "women's work"? Other co-ops in the region served primarily university-oriented communities and had strong male participation. Thus, it had been easy to view the Holyoke situation without dismay because of the larger co-op picture. But once this balloon was burst by the chauvinistic toddler, his mother realized that for most of her co-op's membership, cooperatives did not go beyond the borders of Holyoke. It became important, then, to broaden the other women's view of the co-op movement, and to bring men into the Holyoke co-op. The first of these objectives was easily accomplished by joining a regional co-op federation. The second has still not been dealt with satisfactorily, and poses a continuing problem for Holyoke and many other communities.

Much of what's been said here applies to co-ops with both male and female participation. In the decision-making bodies and work teams of these co-ops, women's caucuses can often supply needed support. Emotional and financial support mechanisms must be developed and feminist consciousness must not be the exclusive property of the female members. In the San Francisco warehouse, feminism is equally important to women and men; the result is a five-man, five-woman staff.

Community Organizing

The Listen Food Buying Club in Lebanon, New Hampshire, not only orders food but operates a resource center, thrift store, and summer gardening program for its mostly poverty-level membership. The co-op organizes workshops for women on careers, ageing, divorce, and poverty. Co-op people are actively working for social reform in housing, food, and welfare policies.

Many people active in food co-ops are like those in Lebanon, concerned with the total welfare of their neighborhoods. They see themselves as community organizers more than just co-op organizers. Poor or even middle-class people have little power individually, but a well-organized community can exercise a lot of power. Community organizing is a process of building power through collective action.

The battles that people fight differ from one community to another. One neighborhood may fight for an end to police brutality and the adoption of a civilian review board. Another may fight for more police protection and a crackdown on crime. One community may use a rent strike to attack absentee landlords. Another community of small homeowners may fight for zoning changes to protect the residential quality of a neighborhood. Though the politics behind the fights may differ, the politics of most community organizers are the same; they want to help people gain the power to control their own communities and lives.

Neighborhood-based food co-ops, or co-ops with blocks, branches, or storefronts centered in a neighborhood, are very useful for community organizing. A food co-op rooted in a specific neighborhood usually represents a cross-section of the local population: old as well as young people, single people, couples without children, and families; homeowners and tenants; and people of different races, religions, and ethnic backgrounds. If certain groups aren't in the co-op, actively recruit them. A co-op with representatives of all parts of the community can help an organizer reach everyone in the area.

The co-op not only brings different people together, but does it in a way that can be an invaluable resource for organizers. The trust that members have for organizers based on their co-op work can help the organizers' credibility when they approach members about other issues. The more participatory a co-op is, the more valuable the level of trust that can develop. If a group of organizers runs the co-op for the community, the members may learn to trust them, but they won't have the experience of trusting each other. This trust is even more important than their trust for the organizers. If they don't trust each other, they'll never be able to create the strong common effort necessary to win power from those who now monopolize it.

Co-op members also learn how to control their own organizations, to make decisions, and to handle money effectively. All these lessons can help in organizing the community to take control of its future.

Leaders emerge naturally in a participatory co-op. Organizers should be aware of what people do in the co-op, so they can identify potential activists and opinion leaders. Organizers should work with these community residents to establish good rapport before trying to recruit them into another organization. If people are working and talking with you in the co-op, they're going to learn about your other community activities, and may volunteer before you even ask them.

It's good to keep in mind the distinction between community activists and opinion leaders. The activists are necessary for the work they do. The opinion leaders are important for the influence they have over others. It's not worth losing the support of an opinion leader by demanding that he or she work as much as an activist. Activists, for their part, shouldn't be expected to influence others, unless they are also opinion leaders.

A food co-op is not only a learning experience but a means of communication. Organizers have to be able to get in touch with a community and co-ops have already established means for communicating: newsletters, signs, telephone trees. A distribution center or store is a central place in which to make the face-to-face contacts upon which good organizing depends. Interested co-op members can get the word out to the rest of the community much more effectively than can a leaflet canvassing the entire neighborhood.

A food co-op can be a financial resource. Some large preorders in Cambridge have a standard "social action bump" to which members may contribute. (There's no pressure to do so.) The fund goes to a different community group each week — the tenants' committee, the women's health center, etc.

In most cases, it's probably not a good idea to use the economic resources of a co-op for community organizing. Most co-ops are run on tight budgets and can't afford to support political activity. This way of politicizing a co-op can create resentment. Only if a co-op is established specifically as a financial support group for political activities or if contributions are completely voluntary should it be used this way.

But a co-op can support political struggles in other ways. It can take a public stand or simply recommend that the membership become involved. It can use co-op facilities for meetings or work projects. Members can turn out at demonstrations, hearings, or city council meetings. They can sign petitions, write letters, and contact their friends to do the same. They can make individual financial contributions. In Venice, California, several years ago, co-op members participated in an organizing drive that stopped plans for a $26-million redevelopment project that would have made the funky canals area, where many members lived, into a yacht harbor. Remember, though, that food co-ops exist for a specific purpose. They can't be used to fight city hall, university expansion, unscrupulous landlords, or state highway plans. Other committees have to be established.

Crisis organizing, which makes short-term demands on people's time, doesn't create so much of a problem for a co-op as ongoing community organizing does. If all the co-op activists are recruited into other organizations which make big demands on their time, the co-op will suffer. Co-ops, for their part, must continually be creating new activists and must accept their responsibility to the rest of the community not to monopolize all the talent.

A co-op has to put its own survival above the needs of community organizers. If something comes up that is really a threat to the entire community, the membership will probably force the co-op to act. But if a membership isn't ready to act, it's better not to force it. Good organizers don't confuse the co-op with the community, and usually won't make demands on the co-op that would put it in a difficult position. Smart co-ops don't let themselves be put in difficult positions by bad organizers.

Boycotts

In 1973 the Ithaca (New York) Food Co-op, a large rebate-type store, underwent an agonizing political experience. The board of directors voted to carry both Teamsters Union and United Farm Workers Union lettuce and to allow members to choose between them. Supporters of the United Farm Workers vociferously opposed this decision. They argued that the battle between the Teamsters and the UFW was not really an interunion jurisdictional dispute but a dispute between a union that truly represented the workers, the UFW, and an intruder in the fields, which had no roots in the largely Chicano farmworker communities, and whose essential loyalties were with the growers. Comparison of the Teamster contracts with those won by the UFW in the late sixties seemed to bear out this claim. With the Teamster contracts came a return of the despised labor contractor system and of a looser regulation of pesticide use. The UFW was fighting for its life and its supporters felt that even recognizing the Teamsters as serious claimants to the role of representing farmworkers was a betrayal.

The co-op board held to its position and supporters of the UFW began to picket the store. Eventually the co-op sought and got an injunction against the picketing. Feelings ran high as Ithacans watched the co-op behaving very much like a profit-making establishment. One older member said: "In the last few years we've seen very little of goals other than strictly commercial ones. The test of the co-op at the moment seems to be what makes the most money, and the consideration of human needs seems to have been forgotten. As far as I'm concerned, the behavior of the management and the board of directors . . . [has been] absolutely abhorrent. I for one feel that it's almost a fraud to continue to be a member." The co-op's sales were off and it failed to pay a rebate for the first time in many years.

The Hyde Park Co-op in Chicago, also a rebate store, had a similar experience. The co-op had voted to carry only UFW lettuce, but the local UFW support committee learned from some truck-drivers that they were bringing in Teamster lettuce. One observer wrote, "Two men from the support group went down to the loading-storage area in the co-op's basement to see the crates, but were stopped on the way down by [the] manager." After some pushing and shoving, they discovered that Teamster lettuce was being repacked and sold in crates decorated with the UFW symbol, the Aztec eagle.

The question of supporting boycotts can be a difficult one for co-ops. In the farmworkers situation, the Teamsters Union went into the struggle with the approval of the growers who wanted to avoid signing tough UFW contracts again, as many of them had to do in the late sixties. Most new-style co-ops respect UFW boycotts; Tucson's Food Conspiracy donates staples to UFW strikers.

The Lynn, Massachusetts, co-op split over the farmworker issue, with one group of more politically conscious members supporting the boycott of Teamster lettuce and another group insisting on political "neutrality." In Wrentham, Massachusetts, the Trinity Church Co-op membership favored buying non-UFW lettuce and grapes; the buyers absolutely refused to get grapes but, according to one member, "compromised on lettuce at the group's insistence."

The UFW-Teamster dispute is only one example of the kind of boycott decisions co-ops face. Some federations boycott bananas, pineapples, and other tropical fruits that are grown in countries where labor conditions are abhorrent or cash-crop economies prevent the development of self-sufficiency.

If a majority of co-op members firmly opposes a boycott, it makes little sense to try to force them to participate. Such a political stance may alienate current members or discourage potential ones, just as a too-pure stance on nutritional or organically grown food can limit membership. We think it's preferable to make a co-op attractive to people of as many political persuasions as possible, and, once people are in the co-op, to try to educate them about political and economic struggles.

Of course, co-op staff or workers in federations may refuse to handle a boycotted product. This is a valid position for a staff to take, considering the natural affinity between the interests and goals of co-ops and those of struggling workers. If the membership overwhelmingly desires *not* to support a boycott, it can, through its general meeting or board of directors, fire the staff or withdraw from the federation.

An effective boycott has three components: the boycott itself, education about why it is happening, and publicity to let people know about it. For education, a special committee may want to find out all it can about the boycott and communicate this to co-op members. The best source of information is the group or coalition calling the boycott.

The next step is to determine how much energy your co-op wants to put into this boycott. If members only want to express their support by not buying, without taking more positive action, that may be the most your co-op can do. However, if there's a committed group of people ready to do more in support of the boycott, their next step is to visit the stores still carrying the boycotted product. First, find out how much the store depends on the boycotted product. If it's a minor part of the total sales, then it will be much easier to get the product removed from the shelves. If it's a major part of the business, it may be impossible or nearly so. Also, find out if there are alternative places to shop nearby, in case a picket line becomes necessary.

Present the owner or manager of the store with your case. If she or he appears friendly, you should attempt persuasion. The threat of picketing doesn't have to be made explicit. If approached by a delegation, the owner will get the idea. If persuasion doesn't work, consider a picket line, but make sure you have the people for it.

Before organizing a picket line, consult a sympathetic lawyer and be sure you can contact him or her if necessary. Prepare a flyer listing your legal rights and the phone number of the lawyer or a coordinator. This will prove useful in dealing with police; when they see you are prepared, they will be less likely to round you up. Prepare leaflets to hand out to shoppers.

Before going out, hold a meeting of those who will be picketing or leafletting. Agree on how you'll handle possible arrest situations. Also agree on general picket-line tactics. Select two or three picket captains who'll be responsible for maintaining discipline on the line and serving as spokespeople to the police and management. On the line itself, beware of crazies — people who want to push a separate political issue or who might get violent and provoke unnecessary arrests.

If your co-op doesn't have the energy or commitment for leafletting and picketing, it may still be able to send petitions, personal letters, or delegations to the business being boycotted. If you don't let them know you are boycotting them, your effect will be considerably more limited.

If you can form coalitions with other co-ops, or if you are large enough, you might consider initiating boycotts or using the threat of them to improve product services. This is only possible if you're dealing with small producers to whom your business will make a difference. For instance, the unnecessary use of sugar in all sorts of products is one of America's worst eating habits. By dealing with small producers you could begin to change this. You don't have to be threatening about it. Providing that it doesn't drastically raise their own costs, they might be glad to reduce the amount of sugar they use. A coalition of co-ops and consumer groups is the most effective way to carry this out.

Co-ops, as institutions concerned both with food and with bettering economic conditions, are well suited to organizing boycotts or participating actively in them. If the membership desires it, and the co-op's work system can support it, boycott activities may count toward a member's work requirement. In the end, boycotts depend for success on widespread public support. By helping to mobilize this support, co-ops can give people a sense of their economic power.

Land Reform

Say "land reform" and most people think of Asia, Africa, or Latin America — anywhere but the United States. In reality, land reform is at least as necessary in the United States as in the developing world. Eight oil companies alone control 64.6 million acres of land in the U.S. South Vietnam's total area is only 42.4 million acres.

Say "big business" and the response might be "automobiles" or "defense," but America's biggest industry is agribusiness; at $150 billion a year, it accounts for 20% of our Gross National Product and employs 30% of nongovernmental American workers. And in spite of the size of that industry, 2000 American farms are forced out of business every week, with most of the small farms being absorbed by corporate conglomerates. In California, 45 corporations own 40% of the cropland; in Maine, 12 corporations own 52% of the land. In all, 5% of the population own two thirds of America's private real property.

In the name of efficiency, the U.S. Department of Agriculture boosts agribusiness at the expense of family farms. This should surprise no one, since Secretary of Agriculture Earl Butz came to the Cabinet via a directorship at Ralston-Purina, a major agribusiness corporation. Butz's predecessor at USDA was Clifford Hardin, who is now a director at Ralston-Purina. Recently the Farmers Home Administration refused to grant a loan to the *Cooperativa Campesina,* a small cooperative farm run by former migrant workers in California. Said Homer Preston, deputy administrator of USDA's Farmer Cooperative Service:

> The low-income farmer is not personally my cup of tea. Our conventional co-ops are not exactly enthusiastic about them. They don't have much to offer except labor and it is less important today . . . They're tied in with idealism and civil rights and a lot of romanticism. The purpose of cooperatives is not to keep mass numbers in farming but to help those who remain. You can't go against market trends when everything else points to bigness.

But what mainly points to bigness is government policy itself. Through a wide range of tax and other subsidies, the government helps big farmers while squeezing out small farmers. First, direct subsidies are provided to keep cropland idle. These are designed to keep prices up by limiting supply. Some of the richest companies in the country collect these subsidies, including the huge J. G. Boswell Corporation in California, which controls 110,000 acres of land producing cattle, cotton, fruit, and vegetables.

Another subsidy is government-financed irrigation. The 1902 Newlands Reclamation Act, intended to aid family farms, specified that to receive water a farm must be 160 acres or less, and the farmer must reside on the land or nearby. This law has been blatantly ignored or else interpreted in wildly circuitous ways to benefit agribusiness. Corporations controlling much of the cropland in California now violate this act.

The government also helps agribusiness by funding land-grant universities. Food industry executives dominate advisory committees that set research goals. Our knowledge of biological pest control, of organic farming technology, and of ways to increase small farm efficiency, is still relatively rudimentary because agribusiness is more interested in chemical pesticides, monocropping, and food marketability.

The result of all this government favoritism has been a slow, painful decline for the small farm. In 1950, the U. S. had 5.4 million farms; in 1973, there were fewer than 2.9 million. According to the 1970 census, farm population has dropped below 10 million for the first time in American history. This depopulation has left the countryside, as one writer put it, "scarred by deserted farms, empty stores and padlocked schools."

The trend toward bigness in both agricultural production and food marketing has often been justified in the name of efficiency. But is efficiency really more important than maintaining a prosperous rural population instead of decimating the countryside? And are corporate farms really more efficient? There is important evidence to suggest that they are not. Huge, single-crop fields, mechanized harvests, crowded feedlots, and integrated canning, distributing, and retailing may actually entail more wasted labor in bureaucratic tasks than do smaller-scale operations. Big companies that lack real competition don't try to produce better food for less money.

On the farming level, there's evidence that big corporate farms are less efficient than smaller ones that farmers and their families can manage by themselves, with occasional help. "Size does not always — nor even usually — equate with efficiency," according to University of California researchers. The government's own studies indicate extremely high efficiency for farms of 100 to 160 acres with the optimum size for many crops being 150 to 300 acres.

No mistake should be made about the magnitude of the problem, but there is hope — in the land reform movement and in several partial remedies to current patterns of land ownership and land use. First, there's the concept of the land trust. Similar to the land banks of the New Deal — through which the government bought land and resold it to farmers — the land trust provides a means of preventing small farms from being absorbed by corporations or being used for speculation. Unlike the land banks, land trusts remove land from the market totally. The trust holds all land while those who work it act as trustees for all humankind, present and future. Long-term leases (99 years, renewable), protect the users of the land while the trust insures that the conditions of the contract and trust charter are fulfilled.

A second partial solution to our land problem, organic farming, may spread by necessity as chemical farming digs its own grave. Organic methods suit small farms far better than large ones, avoid monocropping, and produce nutritious food. Organic farms consistently outproduce equivalent-sized chemical farms; it's simply very difficult to run an organic operation of more than 160 acres. Obviously, organic farming can be combined with another alternative to corporate ownership: the farmer-controlled cooperative farm, such as *Cooperativa Campesina*.

Part of the land reform movement focuses on action through legislation and the use of government power. Although the policies of the USDA and other agencies suggest the limit of such hopes, several proposals, if implemented, could stop the takeover of farming by corporate conglomerates.

Simply enforcing laws already on the books that deal with size limitations and demand residency on government-grant lands would be a major step. Farms violating the Newlands Reclamation Act of 1902 should be sold at the original prices to cooperatives and family farms. Unfortunately, the Justice Departments of both California and the United States think that enforcement of the Newlands Act would be a disaster. It would certainly destroy conglomerate farming in California and the Southwest.

Of proposed new laws, the most far-reaching would exclude conglomerates from farming, while permitting families and farmer-operated co-ops to incorporate. Such a Family Farm Act has been part of North Dakota law since the 1930s. Several times, corporations have forced a referendum on the law, but they have always lost. As recently as 1967, 76% of North Dakota voters insisted on retention of the ban at full strength. Recently, several other states have passed similar laws, but a National Family Farm Act, a major thrust of the land reform movement, has so far been defeated in Congress.

The most obvious role for food co-ops in the land-reform movement lies in their use of buying power. This means buying from farmers' co-ops and family farms rather than from distant corporate producers. When no local products are available, food with the lable of a good union is preferable to nonunion or company union brands. In the same way, co-ops can support organic farms by buying organically grown produce whenever possible. Food co-ops thus act as alternative marketing channels that not only lower prices for their members but also help insure a decent life for people living on the land.

Political Dilemmas

Food co-ops, like many institutions in the alternative economy, pay relatively low wages to full-time workers. Because of their participatory nature, co-ops have many activists who work part time for no pay at all. This is a difficult situation for several reasons. People who have families to support usually cannot be employed by co-ops. This generally limits co-op staffs to young people without families. Their outlook and biases are inevitably reflected in co-op policy. As the co-op movement grows, these biases may prevent co-ops from becoming a true alternative food source for some segments of the population.

Co-ops should support their full-time workers decently, and yet the economic realities are such that they often can't afford to do so and at the same time keep their prices low. Rebate-type co-ops do pay decent wages, but their prices are market-level. One reason for this problem is that the individual profit margin on many foods is low, and money is made mostly on volume of sales. As co-ops increase their volume, they may be able to pay higher wages.

A related problem is unionization. Most co-op workers — again, with the exception of rebate co-ops — are not in unions. In many cases when co-ops talk about eliminating the middleperson, they are also talking about eliminating the union wage-earner: the truck driver, the bakery employee, the wholesaler's helper. New-style co-ops and other alternative businesses undercut union wage scales. As co-ops grow, unions may perceive this as a threat.

Co-op staff members themselves often have no desire to form unions or join existing ones — despite the fact that most co-op people support the United Farm Workers and some other unions. This contradictory situation is partly a result of the conservative role many unions play in our economy. After decades of struggle for recognition, unions have achieved positions of power; union leaders earn large salaries, are surrounded by numerous petty officials, and are sometimes consulted on matters of government policy. While there are many radical workers in the rank and file, most union leaders are inclined to defend the *status quo*. Sympathy for unions *per se* is therefore not high among workers in the alternative economy. They distinguish between unions that are worthy of support and those that are not.

The unfortunate fact remains that as co-ops grow they may begin to put ordinary workers out of jobs. It's not these workers' fault that their unions may be complacent and conservative. Yet the argument is sometimes made that extravagant national defense spending should be maintained, or some ecologically disastrous building should be constructed, simply because this will preserve jobs. This argument can become a *reductio ad absurdum*. Obviously, socially undesirable jobs should be replaced with useful ones. In the same sense, workers in capitalist industry who may someday become unemployed because of expanding co-ops should be put to work rebuilding an economy (and an ecology) that has been devastated by profit-making industries. By that time, also, perhaps co-ops can pay union-level wages.

We should also remember that a relatively small proportion of workers earn high union salaries. Many are not in unions at all. Some craft unions are notoriously clannish and discriminatory.

One reason co-op workers are not often interested in unions may be that they are partial owners of their co-ops and participate in decision making. They understand their jobs in a larger framework and they usually participate in all levels of work, from the menial to the purely intellectual. Workers' control makes the union-boss antagonism obsolete.

The potential conflict between co-ops and union labor remains. Co-ops should be aware of it and do what they can do to resolve it.

This means making good wages a real priority and avoiding the notion sometimes found in alternative institutions that poor is good and anyone who wants to be paid decently is not dedicated.

Co-ops can also help unions form co-ops of their own. In the process the two groups may grow to understand each other better. The International Ladies Garment Workers Union in Fall River, Massachusetts, recently invited members of the NEFCO to speak with them about food co-oping. In 1974, employees of a large bookstore chain in Boston formed a food co-op. Combining consumer and producer cooperation is, after all, one of the animating visions of the cooperative movement.

Sources

The information on UFW–co-op conflicts comes from Friends of the Farm Workers in Ithaca, New York, and an article by Paula Giese, "How the 'Political' Co-ops Were Destroyed," in the *North Country Anvil*, #13, October-November 1974. There's advice on organizing boycotts in *The Organizer's Manual*. The Allston-Brighton Food Co-op publishes a monthly Boycott Census that can keep you up-to-date on what not to buy. Their address is 11 Myrick St., Allston, Mass. 02134, and subscription price is $1.50 per year.

You can get a list of groups involved in land reform from the National Coalition for Land Reform, 345 Franklin St., San Francisco 94102. The coalition publishes an excellent magazine, *People and Land*, and can supply you with a bibliography. Get in touch with the two organizations that represent small farmers: the National Farmers' Organization, Corning, Iowa 50841, and the National Farmers' Union, Box 2251, Denver, Colorado 80201. Other sources on land reform:

Barnes, Peter, ed. *The People's Land*. Emmaus, Pa.: Rodale Press, 1975.

Barnes, Peter and Larry Casalino. *Who Owns the Land?* San Francisco: Center for Rural Studies, 1974.

Eat It: *Agribusiness, Farming, Food, and You*. Rifton, N. Y.: *WIN*, 1972.

International Independence Institute, *The Community Land Trust*. Cambridge, Mass.: Center for Community Economic Development. Write to I.I.I. at Box 183, Ashby, Ma. 01431.

Robbins, William. *The American Food Scandal*. New York: Morrow, 1974.

U. S. Department of Commerce, Bureau of the Census. *Statistical Abstract of the United States*. Washington: 1973.

A Parting Word

In the course of writing this book, we had a chance to visit several of the large centers of co-op activity. We went first to Ann Arbor, where the Michigan Federation of Food Co-ops was hosting a conference on warehousing. We met co-op people from many of the twenty-three warehouses in the country, and others from places like Austin who, like ourselves, wanted to learn about warehousing. In the two days we spent talking about practical and theoretical issues, we became aware of our New England biases.

The co-op movement is far from monolithic. The thousands of co-ops in the country reflect different values and priorities. Differences exist because the values of the organizers differ, and the communities they serve differ. Some co-ops are more participatory than others. Some have a stronger consciousness of nutrition than others. These regional differences make for a stronger co-op movement because we can learn from each other how to make our own co-ops better.

Without attempting to cover every region or mention every co-op, we'd like to make some closing observations about the values that are stressed in some of the major centers of cooperative activity. These values exist in all co-ops to some extent, but we'll discuss them using examples from the regions in which they are strongest.

Co-ops in the Northeast are highly participatory. Most are preorders, or had their beginnings as preorders. They are usually able to distribute food at only 5% above the wholesale prices they pay. Participation means few or no staff salaries. Many of the stores in the region work on the same principle. The Cambridge Food Co-op can operate on a 10% surcharge with a paid staff of only five because of the commitment members make to work two or three hours a month in the store.

Member participation is also important in the San Francisco Bay Area. It remains the basis of the Berkeley Food Conspiracy. The decentralized block model of the Conspiracy is mirrored in co-ops in Cambridge, Boston, and New York. These co-ops organized themselves to stay decentralized so that members would not lose control as their co-ops grew larger. On both coasts it was important to co-op organizers to create alternatives to supermarkets that would be controlled by the people who use them. Some preorders were set up partially as vehicles for community organizing. They were viewed as a means of giving people the skills with which they could take control of their lives and communities.

The emphasis on participation has influenced the stores, warehouses, and federations in the Northeast. Both NEFCO and the New York People's Warehouse stress participation. They ask for voluntary labor and political participation from their member co-ops. The San Francisco stores, despite the fact that they have emerged somewhat in reaction to the preorders, also emphasize participation. Seeds of Life is run with no paid staff.

In most large co-ops and warehouses, the desire to increase participation must balance with the requirements of full-time managers or staff. The paid collectives that run these operations usually follow the principles of worker control which can be best seen in Seattle and Washington, D. C. Although the Seattle Workers Brigade and the Washington, D. C., storefronts don't consider themselves co-ops, they relate to the co-op movement and have shared their experience of worker control with collectively run co-ops. While co-ops accept that members have the final say, the Brigade and D. C. storefronts give that power to the workers who run their operations. Food co-ops are learning to balance the ultimate power of their members with the rights of their collectives to make decisions within the policy boundaries set by the cooperating community. As the co-op movement continues to expand into production, processing, and distribution, collective management will become more visible as an alternative to the hierarchical relationships in the capitalist economy.

While traveling in the Midwest, we realized that while we may have something to offer about participation, we have a lot to learn about food. Food co-ops are not just cheap food stores. Quality food is important to all co-ops, but we learned that some co-ops are stricter than others about the food they carry.

In Minneapolis, we ate very well for very little. We were introduced to a diet of legumes, grains, seasonal produce, and dairy. In the Minneapolis-St. Paul co-op storefronts, nutritional considerations outweigh the desire to appeal to a broad base of the population by carrying processed or prepared foods. Our friends in the Minneapolis co-ops talked to us about the politics of food: who gets what from the earth's limited resources, and how we can eat sanely in a world where starvation is common. These politics include developing a rational allocation of land to grow the most protein, protecting the fertility of the arable land we have, and educating people about nutrition. Our friends spend as much time talking about food as they do eating.

Co-ops in the Southwest and Northwest are also concerned about the food they carry. Co-ops in Tucson, Arizona, and Portland and Eugene, Oregon, carry organically grown grains and vegetables and emphasize the safety and wholesomeness of their food. Many of these co-ops developed out of a need to find a reasonably priced alternative to the capitalist health-food industry. Some were the intitial sources of such food in their areas. Co-op people in these regions feel strongly that chemically grown and treated foods are dangerous and are trying to educate their communities to the alternatives.

Those closest to food sources often develop good food consciousness before their city cousins, some of whom may think that rolled oats grow in fields. If you're contracting for a price with a farmer, you can also contract for quality.

The co-op movement is growing both vertically and horizontally. A resident of Madison, Wisconsin, can buy cooperatively baked bread in a co-op store, and ride a bike from a co-op housing project to work at a co-op warehouse. Cooperative farms in Minnesota, Wisconsin, and Michigan grow food for their respective federations. Throughout the Midwest, grains are turned into flour in co-op mills, flour into whole-grain bread in co-op bakeries, and whole-grain bread into that important other kind of bread for purchases in co-op storefronts. Vertical growth includes granola factories, warehouses, produce-buying services, restaurants, regional trucking, and herb and spice apothecaries.

As we visited co-ops throughout the country, we were struck by their different styles and orientations. The co-op movement was broader than we had expected, but wherever we stayed, we were received with friendship. We hope this friendship still exists when there are millions of people in the new co-op movement.

The Ann Arbor conference itself illustrated many of the cooperative principles we've written about. The business of the conference was handled without any rigid agenda. No one ran the meeting, and decisions were made by consensus. The atmosphere was loose and friendly. Even as people argued over politics, they remained considerate and listened to each other. When we weren't busy making deals on beans and cheese, or setting a new rate for cross-country co-op trucking, we talked, ate, and danced together. We even worked together — unloading and reloading the Intra-Community Cooperative truck.

If the spirit of that gathering can continue to grow, we will create something new to contemporary America: humanized, democratically controlled, nonprofit economic institutions. We can build a food distribution system that carries safe nutritious food for reasonable prices based on the necessary costs of production. No one will make a profit or an exorbitant salary from our need to eat.

We'd like to see an end to a system that allows an agribusiness executive to eat filet mignon on his expense account while poor, elderly couples on social-security pensions eat dog food for their quotient of protein. We'd like our children to grow up eating healthful food instead of sweet processed junk. We'd like them to know what fresh peas and carrots taste like. We'd like them to live in a society that contains an alternative to the exploitation and profiteering of monopoly capitalism.

Are we just dreaming? We don't think so. We've been enjoying the advantages of cooperative buying for several years. We've seen the movement grow enormously in the last five years, and it shows every indication of continued growth. We believe that co-ops can create an alternative to the present food industry. We have worked for more than a year on this book to try to help that alternative become a reality. We will be pleased if it generates some debate within the co-op movement leading to new ideas and new directions.

Appendices

Index

APPENDIX I

Regional Contacts

The following is a list, in zipcode order, of regional food co-op contacts and federations.

New England Federation of Co-ops
(NEFCO)
8 Ashford St.
Allston, MA 02134
617/ALIVING

Maine Federation of Co-ops
Box 107
Hallowell, ME 04347

New England People's Co-op
(NEPCOOP)
Box 247
Plainfield, VT 05667
802/426-3878

People's Warehouse
21 Second Ave.
New York, N.Y. 10003
212/477-9685

Clear Eye Warehouse
367 Orchard
Rochester, NY 14606
716/235-1080

Philadelphia Federation of Food
Co-ops/Powelltown Warehouse
3300 Race St.
Philadelphia, PA 19104

Community Warehouse
2010 Kendall St. NE
Washington, D.C. 20002
202/832-4517

Sunshine Cooperative Association
4435 NW Second
Miami, FL 33127

Good Foods Co-op
314½ S. Ashland
Lexington, KY 40502

Common Market Warehouse
Box 8253
Columbus, OH 43201
614/294-0145

Michigan Federation of Food
Co-ops/People's Wherehouse
404 W. Huron
Ann Arbor, MI 48103
313/761-4642

Blooming Prairie Warehouse
529 S. Gilbert
Iowa City, IA 52240
319/338-5300

Intra-Community Cooperative (ICC)
1335 Gilson
Madison, WI 53715
608/251-2403

Scoop/People's Warehouse/Red Star
Apothecary
123 E. 26th
Minneapolis, MN 55404
612/824-2634

Food Co-op Project
64 E. Lake St.
Chicago, IL 60601
312/269-8101

Midwest Cooperating Consumers Association Warehouse (MCCA)
4140 W. Pine
St. Louis, MO 63130

Kansas City Grain Warehouse
4109 Locust
Kansas City, MO 64110
816/561-6301

Cooperation
5423 Druid Ln.
Dallas, TX 75209

Austin Community Project
1602 W. 12th
Austin, TX 78703
512/477-6255

Common Market of Colorado
1100 Champa
Denver, CO 80204
303/893-3430

People's Warehouse
411 N. 7th
Tucson, AZ 85705
602/884-9951

Southern California Cooperating Community
11615 Mississippi
Los Angeles, CA 90025
213/478-1922

San Francisco Warehouse
1559 Bancroft
San Francisco, CA 94124
415/822-8830

Kokua Country Foods
2357 S. Beretania
Honolulu, HI 96814
808/941-1922

Starflower
385 Lawrence
Eugene, OR 97401

Cooperating Communities
4030 22nd Ave. W.
Seattle, WA 98199
206/283-3777

APPENDIX II

Regional Organic Farming Groups

Since 1971, Rodale Press, publisher of *Organic Gardening and Farming* magazine, has operated a certification program for organic farmers. Here is their current list of regional organic farming groups, in zipcode order.

Maine Organic Farmers & Gardeners Association
Mort Mather, President
RD 2
North Berwick, ME 03906
207/998-4580

Natural Organic Farmers Association (NOFA)
RFD 1
Plainfield, VT 05667
802/426-3878

Organic Food Producers' Certification Program
Clarke Langrale, Jr.
RD 1
Box 296A
Pennington, NJ 08534

New York Organic Farmers
Nick Veeder
RD 1
Jordanville, NY 13361
315/858-0729 or 823-0818

Pennsylvania Organic Farmers-Consumers Organization
Paul Hartz, President
RD 1, Box 86
Morgantown, PA 19534
215/286-5268

Southern Agricultural Association of Virginia
Box 734
S. Boston, VA 24592
703/476-2543

Rural Advancement Fund
Jim Pierce, Executive Director
1947 Lansdale Dr.
Charlotte, NC 28205
704/537-6509 or 537-1745

Piedmont Organic Movement Association
Charles Parrott
714 S. Line St.
Greer, SC 29651
803/877-4104

Eastern Georgia Farmers Co-op
Box 35
Waynesboro, GA 30830

Bluegrass Organic Association
Mrs. Jean Warriner
137 Eastover Dr.
Lexington, KY 40502
606/266-6758

Michigan Organic Growers Association
John R. Yaeger
Rt. 1, Box 188
Lawton, MI 49065

Wisconsin Organic Growers Association
Joseph Plesko
10780 S. 92nd St.
Franklin, WI 53132
414/425-4771

Minnesota Organic Growers and Buyers Association
Monica Krancevic
c/o Environmental Library of Minnesota
1222 SE 4th St.
Minneapolis, MN 55415

Illinois Organic Growers
Alexander J. Smith
Route 1
Box 133
Dixon, IL 61021

Tangipaho Organic Farmers' Association
Hurd Hess
P. O. Box 457
Albany, LA 70711

Organic Growers' Cooperative & Extension Service
P. O. Box OGC
McKinney, TX 75069

Family Farmers
Malcolm Beck
RD 13, Box 210 TA
San Antonio, TX 78218
512/651-6115

Colorado Growers and Marketers Association
Jim Fowler
2555 W. 37th Ave.
Denver, CO 80211
303/477-6291

Organic Growers Association
David Rowley
1312 Lobo Pl. NE
Albuquerque, NM 87106
505/268-5504

California Certified Organic Farmers
F.F. Cal Slewing
587 Heather Way
San Rafael, CA 94903
916/337-6305

Northwest Organic Food Producers Association
Pat Langan, President
Rt 2, Box 163
Toppenish, WA 98948
509/865-2697

APPENDIX III

Food Cooperative Directory

This listing of food cooperatives across the U.S. and Canada is adapted from the *Food Cooperative Directory* published by the Food Co-op Project in Chicago. *The list is in zipcode order*. You will find errors here due to production methods as well as the fact that some co-ops change addresses frequently. To obtain the latest and most accurate information send $3 to Food Cooperative Directory, Food Co-op Project, Loop College, 64 E. Lake Street, Chicago, Illinois 60601. This will buy you 2 updated editions of the *Directory* and a 6-month subscription to *Food Co-op Nooz*.

MASSACHUSETTS

AMHERST FOOD CO-OP
24 CHURCHILL ST.
AMHERST, MA 01002

MIXED NUTS CO-OP
HAMPSHIRE COLLEGE
BOX 1229
AMHERST, MA 01002

PEOPLES MARKET
STUDENT UNION
UNIVERSITY OF MASSACHUSETTS
AMHERST, MA 01002

YELLOW SUN NATURAL FOOD CO-OP
23 REAR N. PLEASANT ST.
AMHERST, MA 01002

BELCHERTOWN FOOD CO-OP
PAUL BOURKE
RR1 BOX 56
BELCHERTOWN, MA 01007

BLANDFORD CO-OP
JOY MCKENNA
HERRICK RD.
BLANDFORD, MA 01008

HOLYOKE FOOD CO-OP
ELLEN EDSON
65 PEARL ST
HOLYOKE, MA 01040

ANOTHER DAY CO-OP
42 MAPLE ST---WHSE
FLORENCE, MA 01060

SQUASH FOOD CO-OP
RICH GEFFIN
258 RIVER DR
N. HADLEY, MA 01065

SHUTESBURY FOOD CO-OP
CAROL MIZAUR
BOX 87
SHUTESBURY, MA 01072

SOUTHWICK CO-OP
SHEILA WEBBER
SEFTON DR
SOUTHWICK, MA 01077

WESTFIELD FOOD CO-OP
JOANNE MEYER
OLD FEEDING HILLS ROAD
WESTFIELD, MA 01085

S. BERKSHIRE COMM ACTION
JANET VOLCKHAUSEN
144 MAIN ST
GREAT BARRINGTON, MA 01230

MONTEREY CO-OP
ELLEN BLOUNT
BOX 104
MONTEREY, MA 01245

OCTOBER UNION CO-OP
ROBIN ASHLEY
BOARDMAN ST.
SHEFFIELD, MA 01257

BUCKLAND FOOD CO-OP
NICKI WOLENTIS
COLRAIN, MA 01340

MONTAGUE FOOD CO-OP
MICHAEL NAUGHTON
BOX 207 BARTLETT FARM
MONTAGUE, MA 01351

OUR DAILY BREAD
BOX 377
ORANGE, MA 01364

GOOD FOOD UNION
RICK STONE
34 WILLIAM ST
SHELBURNE FALLS, MA 01370

GREENFIELD FOOD CO-OP
JULIE LEIGHTON
28 S. HIGH ST.
TURNERS FALLS, MA 01376

UNITED COOPERATIVE SOCIETY OF
FITCHBURG
815 MAIN ST.
FITCHBURG, MA 01420

COMMON CO-OP
LINDA FALSTEIN
AYER RD
HARVARD, MA 01451

NORTHBOROUGH FOOD CO-OP
MARIANN GORSUCH
1 LELAND DR
NORTHBOROUGH, MA 01532

WORCESTER NATURAL GARDENERS FD CLB
MS K G ANDERSON
OLD CRAWFORD RD.
NORTHBORO, MA 01532

COMMUNITY STOMACH
205 MILLBURY ST.
WORCESTER, MA 01604

NEW SPITIT FOOD CO-OP
BOB SHURTLEFF
1127 WORCESTER RD
FRAMINGHAM, MA 01701

1ST PARISH FRAMINGHAM CO-OP
HEATHER TAYLOR
633 CENTRAL ST
FRAMINGHAM, MA 01701

ACTON FOOD CO-OP
JERRY MAGUIRE
14 REVOLUTIONARY RD
ACTON, MA 01720

BEDFORD CONSUMERS CO-OP
PETEY PALAZA
30 BURLINGTON RD
BEDFORD, MA 01730

CARLISLE FOOD CO-OP
ALYN & NANCY ROBIN
TOPHET RD.
CARLISLE, MA 01741

WEST CONCORD FOOD & FRIENDSHP CO-OP
BOX 32
CONCORD, MA 01742

LINCOLN CONSUMER CO-OP
MS. ROSS
TODD POND RD.
LINCOLN, MA 01773

WESTON ORGANIC FOOD CO-OP
PAUL & JULIE REDSTONE
45 RICE SPRING LN
WAYLAND, MA 01778

ANDOVER CONSUMERS CO-OP
68 MAIN ST.
ANDOVER, MA 01810

ANDOVER FOOD CO-OP
62 OSGOOD ST.
ANDOVER, MA 01810

CONSUMER CO-OP ALLIANCE
HARRY BEDELL
123 CHESTNUT ST.
ANDOVER, MA 01810

CHELMSFORD CO-OP
PAT TYO
1 SANTE FE RD.
CHELMSFORD, MA 01824

THE OTHER SIDE FOOD CO-OP
2 LINDEN ST REAR
READING, MA 01867

FAMILY FOOD CLUB
DEE KASTANOTIS
24 STORY AVE.
LYNN, MA 01902

SWAMPSCOTT CO-OP
10 ROCKLAND ST
SWAMPSCOTT, MA 01907

CAPE ANN FOOD CO-OP
DERRY HEASLEY
1248 WASHINGTON
GLOUCESTER, MA 01930

MOUTH OF THE RIVER
MIKE PENDERGAST
10 MARKET ST
NEWBURYPORT, MA 01950

FRANKLIN CO-OP
RICK BOURNE
900 ELM ST
FRANKLIN, MA 02038

SCITUATE CO-OP II
VIKKI LIA
61 KINGS WAY
SCITUATE, MA 02066

WEST END CO-OP
RICHELLE SAUNDERS
90 SUMMER ST.
SCITUATE, MA 02066

STOUGHTON FOOD CO-OP
JUDY STOLOW
11 HORAN WAY
STOUGHTON, MA 02072

NORWEST CO-OP
HELI TOMFORD
127 THATCHER ST
WESTWOOD, MA 02090

PINTO BEAN CO-OP
JERRY RINGER
22 WILLOW FARM RD
WESTWOOD, MA 02090

TRINITY FOOD CO-OP
43 EAST ST.
WRENTHAM, MA 02093

RAINBOW GROCERIES
72 KILARNOCK
BOSTON, MA 02115

LRI FOOD CO-OP
BOOKSMITH
1075 COMM. AVE
BOSTON, MA 02117

JAMAICA PLAIN FOOD CO-OP
107 ARMORY ST
ROXBURY, MA 02117

MISSION HILL FOOD CO-OP
55 BEACH GLEN ST
ROXBURY, MA 02119

DORCHESTER/ROXBURY FOOD CO-
389 BOWDOIN ST.
DORCHESTER, MA 02122

ALLSTON-BRIGHTON FOOD CO-OP
11 MYRICK
ALLSTON, MA 02134

NEFCO DIRECTORY ASSISTANCE
DON LUBIN
8 ASHFORD ST.
ALLSTON, MA 02134

NEFCO BULK PURCHASING
DIANE HALPERIN
14 A ASHFORD ST
ALLSTON, MA 02134

CAMBRIDGE SOUTH FOOD CO-OP
BILLIE MILLER
39 FENNO ST.
CAMBRIDGE, MA 02138

FRESH POND CO-OP
BARBARA FAY
503 HURON
CAMBRIDGE, MA 02138

HARVARD S.U. FOOD CO-OP
3 SACRAMENTO ST.
CAMBRIDGE, MA 02138

JORDON FOOD CO-OP
RADCLIFFE COLLEGE
91 WALKER ST
CAMBRIDGE, MA 02138

PINTO BEAN CO-OP
LISA BRADLEY
33 LINE ST
CAMBRIDGE, MA 02138

SHAILER LANE FOOD CO-OP
CONNIE KIRWAY
2 KENWAY ST.
CAMBRIDGE, MA 02138

BEANSPROUT
JOYCE THOMOSON
12 DOUGLAS ST.
CAMBRIDGE, MA 02139

CAMBRIDGE CENTRAL FOOD CO-OP
PETER SALVERSTONE
253 1/2 BROADWAY
CAMBRIDGE, MA 02139

CAMBRIDGE FOOD CO-OP
580 MASS. AVE
CAMBRIDGE, MA 02139

CAMBRIDGE HEADSTART CO-OP
639 MASS AVE
CAMBRIDGE, MA 02139

CAMBRIDGE PRESBYTERIAN FOOD CO-OP
FIRST UNITED PRESBYTERIAN
1418 CAMBRIDGE ST
CAMBRIDGE, MA 02139

CAMBRIGEPORT CO-OP
BILL CAVALINI
269 PEARL ST.
CAMBRIDGE, MA 02139

HANCOCK ST. CO-OP
JUDY BIBBINS
314 HARVARD ST.
CAMBRIDGE, MA 02139

RISING EARTH CO-OP
271 BROOKLINE ST.
CAMBRIGE, MA 02139

NORTH CAMBRIDGE FOOD CO-OP
NANCY HAMMETT
31 BUENA VISTA PARK
CAMBRIDGE, MA 02140

DUCK VILLAGE FOOD CO-OP
LARRY ROSENBURG
64 DANE ST
SOMERVILLE, MA 02143

WEST SOMERVILLE FOOD CO-OP
GEORGE ALLEN
26 GRANITE ST. #2
SOMERVILLE, MA 02143

BROADWAY FOOD CO-OP
KAREN FALER
99 PUTIYAN RD
SOMERVILLE, MA 02145

NEW UNION CO-OP
16A UNION SQUARE
SOMERVILLE, MA 02145

MYSTIC CO-OP
ELIZABETH PEABODY HOUSE
6 RIVER ROAD
SOMERVILLE, MA 02145

MALDEN SHOESTRING CO-OP
LARRY O HEARN
24 CLINTON
MALDEN, MA 02148

HGS CO-OP
RICHARD SPOOL
164 CHARLES RIVER RD #E3
WALTHAM, MA 02154

TUFTS FOOD CO-OP
JOHN WEINROT
30 ADAMS ST
MEDFORD, MA 02155

EKOS CO-OP
CATHY LANTIGUA
34 PARK ST.
NEWTON, MA 02158

NEWTON CORNER CO-OP
SALLY LOCKE
12 WILLARD ST.
NEWTON, MA 02158

PEACE & BEANS FOOD CO-OP
ELLIOT CHURCH
NEWTON CORNER, MA 02158

BEST FOOD CO-OP
HELEN OSHIMA
52 BERWICK RD
NEWTON CENTRE, MA 02159

NEWTON CENTRE CO-OP
RITA RICHMOND
833 COMMONWEALTH AVE.
NEWTON CENTRE, MA 02159

WEST NEWTON FOOD CO-OP
RUTH HEESPLINK
45 PLEASANT ST.
NEWTON CENTRE, MA 02159

NEWMAN HOUSE CO-OP
442 WALNUT ST
NEWTONVILLE, MA 02160

UNITARIAN CHURCH CO-OP
FIRST UNITIARIAN CHURCH
1326 WASHINGTON ST
W. NEWTON, MA 02165

AUBURNDALE CHURCH CO-OP
46 HANCOCK ST
AUBURNDALE, MA 02166

BOSTON COLLEGE FOOD CO-OP
BOSTON COLLEGE
NEWTON, MA 02167

NEWTON HIGHLANDS FOOD CO-OP
BARBARA FELSTAD
14 ROSLYN RD
WABAN, MA 02168

WABAN CO-OP
CLAUDIA ROSEN
GLASTONBURY OVAL
WABAN, MA 02168

QUINCY COMMUNITY FOOD CO-OP
SOUTHWEST COMMUNITY CENTER
372 GRANITE ST.
QUINCY, MA 02169

WOLLASTON COMMUNITY CO-OP
SUZANNE WAGNER
465 NEWPORT AVE
WOLLASTON, MA 02170

LEXINGTON FOOD CO-OP
KAREN DOOKS
5 MOHAWK DR
LEXINGTON, MA 02173

LEXINGTON FREE CO-OP
ST. BRIDGET
RENE FINE
52 ELDRED ST.
LEXINGTON, MA 02173

FIVE FIELDS CO-OP
JOANNA ROTBERG
14 BARBERRY RD
LEXINGTON, MA 02173

ARLINGTON CHEESE CO-OP
JUNE ROWE
1 KENSINGTON RD.
ARLINGTON, MA 02174

ARLINGTON FOOD CO-OP
LORETTA WHITNEY
65 WOLLASTON AV
ARLINGTON, MA 02174

ARLINGTON FOWLER CO-OP
LURLINE FOWLER
19 WINTER ST.
ARLINGTON, MA 02174

ARLINGTON MEAT CO-OP
DAN LINDBERG
8 CANDIA ST.
ARLINGTON, MA 02174

JASON FOOD CO-OP
MARTHA HERBERT
22 LAKEVIEW ST.
ARLINGTON, MA 02174

KENDALL AREA FOOD CO-OP
C.O.D.E., INC
396 CONCORD AVE
BELMONT , MA 02178

U.U.M. FOOD CO-OP
MARGARET GOOD
6 MONTVALE RD
WELLESLEY, MA 02181

NEEDHAM FOOD CO-OP
SUSAN ABBOTT
254 FOREST ST.
NEEDHAM, MA 02192

BOSTON FOOD CO-OP
12 BABBIT ST.
BOSTON, MA 02215

DUXBURY FOOD CO-OP
JOAN WITHAM
78 SURREY LANE
DUXBURY, MA 02332

CHURCH HILL CO-OP
KAY GRANT
79 MYRTLE ST.
HANOVER, MA 02339

BOURNE FOOD CO-OP
ROSE FEMIA
9 BLUEBERRY RD
BOURNE, MA 02531

FALLMOUTH FOOD CO-OP
LAURA JACKSON
22 HERITAGE CREEK
FALLMOUTH, MA 02540

WOODS HOLE FOOD CO-OP
BOB GOLDSBOROUGH
5GARDENER ROAD
WOODS HOLE, MA 02543

CANAL CONSUMERS ASSN
SHIRLYANN WASKIEWICZ
10 BAKSIS RD
SANDWICH, MA 02563

LOWER CAPE FOOD CO-OP
JOHN KRAUSE
87 BRADFORD
PROVINCETOWN, MA 02657

ORLEANS FOOD CO-OP
METHODIST CHURCH
BOX 356
S. ORLEANS, MA 02662

WELLFLEET FOOD CO-OP
JUDY STETSON
CHEQUESSETT NECK RD.
WELLFLEET, MA 02667

FALL RIVER FOOD CO-OP
637 S. MAIN ST.
FALL RIVER, MA 02721

NEW BEDFORD FOOD CO-OP
1426 ACUSHNET AVE
NEW BEDFORD, MA 02743

RHODE ISLAND

R.I. WORKERS ASSN CO-OP
WALTER DIONNE
716 DEXTER ST
CENTRAL FALLS, RI 02863

ALTERNATIVE FOOD CO-OP
ELEANOR ROOSEVELT HALL BSMT
UNIVERSITY OF RHODE ISLAND
KINGSTON, RI 02881

FAMILY FOOD CO-OP
DAVID EVANS
16 PROSPECT AVE.
NARRAGANSETT, RI 02882

WESTERLY FOOD CO-OP
JOE LIGHT
12 NARRAGANSETT AVE
WESTERLY, RI 02891

GET BACK FOODS
CATHY BALDWIN
39 SECOND ST
PROVIDENCE, RI 02906

STAFF OF LIFE CO-OP
LYNN BLAKE
258 WATERMAN ST
PROVIDENCE, RI 02906

FOOD FOR FRIENDS
P.A.C.E.
557 PUBLIC ST.
PROVIDENCE, RI 02907

PREMIE CO-OP
VINNY AZZARONE
191 ONTARIO ST.
PROVIDENCE, RI 02907

R. I. COMMUNITY COLLEGE
FOOD CO-OP
NANCY WHIT
141 OAKLAND AVE
PROVIDENCE, RI 02908

NEW HAMPSHIRE

DEERFIELD CO-OP
TERRY & THAYER MCCAIN
RFD 1
DEERFIELD, NH 03037

MILFORD CO-OP MARKET
CAROL LASELLE
PEASELEE RD
MERRIMACK, NH 03054

V.O.I.C.E. CO-OP
2 SHATTUCK ST.
NASHUA, NH 03060

WEST CO-OP
MANCHESTER CAP
227 S. MAIN ST. BSMT
MANCHESTER, NH 03102

NEW HAMPSHIRE CO-OPS
LUCILLE HOLT & TERRY BECKER
260 ORANGE ST.
MANCHESTER, NH 03103

MANCHESTER COMMUNITY FOOD CO-OP
MIKE & TERRY BECKER
355 LAKE AVE.
MANCHESTER, NH 03104

BRADFORD CO-OP
HARRY PAGE
RFD
BRADFORD, NH 03221

LAKES REGION CO-OP
PAT NAYES
RFD 1
LACONIA, NH 03246

SURRY ALLIED CONSUMERS, INC
KEN SMITH
CRAIN RD
SURRY, NH 03431

MONADNOCK FOOD CO-OP
DOLLY WIPPIE
105 GROVE ST.
PETERBOROUGH, NH 03458

FRANCONIA FOOD CO-OP
TATWANASI NATURAL FOODS
FRANCONIA, NH 03580

HANOVER CONSUMER COOPERATIVE SOCTY
45 S. PARK ST.
HANOVER, NH 03755

LISTEN FOOD BUYING CLUB
LISTEN CENTER
92 HANOVER ST.
LEBANON, NH 03766

DO IT STORE
52 MAIN ST.
W. LEBANON, NH 03784

VALLEY FOOD CO-OP
MARK REIS
EATON CENTER, NH 03832

EXETER FOOD CO-OP
REBECCA DAMSELL
NEWMARKET RD.
EXETER, NH 03857

NEWTON FOOD CO-OP
BRUCE GALLANT
BOX 244 RT 2
PLAISTOW, NH 03865

MAINE

ULIB FOOD BUYING GROUP OF YORK CY
JAN PERKINS
CAPE NEDDICK, ME 03902

YORK COUNTY FOOD CLUB
LORRAINE MOULTON
BOX 520
YORK HARBOR, ME 03911

BATH/BRUNSWICK CONSUMER ASSN
BOX F
BRUNSWICK, ME 04011

GORHAM FOOD CO-OP
ROBERT CARTER, JR.
59 SOUTH ST.
GORHAM, ME 04038

KENNEBUNKPORT-ARUNDEL FOOD CO-OP
ELLIE DOW
BOX 347
KENNEBUNKPORT, ME 04046

LONG ISLAND CO-OP
PETER ELLIOT
LONG ISLAND, ME 04050

SACO RIVER CO-OP
GREGORYS MARKET
45 SCAMMON ST.
SACO, ME 04072

RURAL CUMBERLAND CY PURCHASING CO-O
836 GRAY RD.
S. WINDHAM, ME 04082

SANFORD-SPRINGVALE CO-OP
10 OAK ST.
SPRINGVALE, ME 04083

COMMITTEE FR COORDN OF MAINE CO-OPS
JAY ROBBINS
14 PERKINS ST.
TOPSHAM, ME 04086

KENNEBUNK-WELLS CO-OP
PAT STEINER
PORT RD
WELLS, ME 04090

GOOD DAY CO-OP
59 CENTER ST.
PORTLAND, ME 04111

PORTLAND FOOD CO-OP
BENNETT PUDLIN
GOOD DAY MARKET
59 CENTER ST
PORTLAND, ME 04111

ANDROSCOGGIN FOOD CO-OP
28 BATES ST.
LEWISTON, ME 04240

GREATER LIVERMORE FOOD & WHATEVER
LAYNE & PAT VINJE
RFD 2
LIVERMORE FALLS, ME 04254

OXFORD HILLS BUYING CLUB
PRISCILLA COOK
RFD 2
NORWAY, ME 04268

PROMISED LAND FOOD BUYING CO-OP
ABBIE PAGE
FRESH ONION ORGANIC FARM
POLAND SPING, ME 04274

RUMFORD BUYING CLUB
PRISCILLA JASUT
RUMFORD CENTER, ME 04278

MEXICO NEIGHBORLY BUYING CLUB
OXFORD CO. E.O.C.
35 MARKET SQUARE
S. PARIS, ME 04281

GOAT CO-OP
NORRIS PERLMAN
RFD 1 BOX 54
W. PARIS, ME 04289

COMMUNITY BUYING CLUB
GENERAL DELIVERY
WEST PERU, ME 04290

AUGUSTA CO-OP
MATT KORAL
12 WYMAN ST
AUGUSTA, ME 04330

PITTSTON FOOD CO-OP
CHARIL SDELINGER
RT 2
GARDINER, ME 04345

KENNEBEC COUNTY CO-OP
SUSAN EMMERLING
183 1/2 WATER ST.
HALLOWELL, ME 04347

FEDERATION OF CO-OPS
BOX 107
132 WATER ST.
HALLOWELL, ME 04347

VERNON VALLEY CO-OP
BERNARD GRAY
RFD
MT. VERNON, ME 04352

WHITEFIELD CO-OP
DIANE CUREWITZ
RFD
WHITEFIELD, ME 04362

BANGOR FOOD BUYING CLUB
UNITARIAN CHURCH
23 FRANKLIN
BANGOR, ME 04401

COBBS FOOD CO-OP
PO BOX 562
BANGOR, ME 04401

U.M.V.E.T.S. CO-OP
FRED JUDKINS
37 WILEY ST
BANGOR, ME 04401

SUMMIT CO-OP
RFD SUMMIT
BURLINGTON, ME 04417

RISING SUN FOOD CO-OP
MARGUERITE SHEEHAN
GIVEN FARM
HUDSON, ME 04449

COASTAL BUYING CLUB
DAVE DAVIS
ORLAND, ME 04472

OFF CAMPUS BUYERS CO-OP
MEG HANSON
OFF-CAMPUS BOARD OFFICE
MEMORIAL UNION, U OF MAINE
ORONO, ME 04473

ORONO-OLD TOWN FOOD CO-OP
ROBERT CATES
BOX 294
ORONO, ME 04474

BOOTHBAY REGION FOOD CO-OP
CHRIS HOUSE
RIVER ROAD
BOOTHBAY HARBOR, ME 04538

BRISTOL FOOD CO-OP
JOE STEINBERGER
BRISTOL, ME 04539

EDGECOMB AREA CO-OP
LYNN ARNOLD
MARY ISLAND RD
EDGECOMB, ME 04545

SALT BAY CO-OP
SARAH MACK
RFD
NEWCASTLE, ME 04553

THE COOPERATIVE MARKET
MCKINNE STIRES
RT 2 BOX 320
WISCASSET, ME 04578

COASTAL CO-OP
ELLEN BJERRUM
RFD 3
WALDOBORO, ME 04572

ALLIED STOMACH
COLLEGE OF THE ATLANTIC
105 EDEN
BAR HARBOR, ME 04609

DOWNEAST CO-OP
WILLIAM CROLL, JR
SPRAGUS FALLS RD
CHERRYFIELD, ME 04622

SUNSPOT, INC
KAREN GOOD
RFD 1 EDMUNDS
DENNYSVILLE, ME 04628

PEMBROKE-TOOTHPICK CO-OP
BARBARA TOOTHPICK/ALAN HORSERADISH
PEMBROKE, ME 04666

CHRISTY HILL CO-OP
RON SALMON
SEDGEWICK, ME 04676

CARIBOU ECONOMISERS
MARY BRUNER
R2 BOX 154
CARIBOU, ME 04736

HOULTON BUYING CLUB
NORMA HARPER
MONTICELLO, ME 04760

MADAWASKA THRIFTERS
BEA CAMBERLAIN
ST. AGATHA, ME 04772

ROCKLAND FOOD CO-OP
CHARLANE CONRAD
59 BEECH ST.
ROCKLAND, ME 04841

WARREN FOOD CO-OP
NANCY ZISSE
MID-COAST CLINIC
414 MAIN ST
ROCKLAND, ME 04841

PITCHER POND CO-OP
PEG MILLER
RFD 2
LINCOLNVILLE, ME 04849

LINCOLNVILLE FOOD CO-OP
RFD #1
LINCOLNVILLE, ME 04849
JEANETTE SILVERIO

CAMDEN FOOD CO-OP
19 KNOWLTON ST.
CAMDEN, ME 04853
(207)236-2161
MARCIA KEIDEL

FOG HORN CO-OP
GEORGE & JOSIE BAGGETT
BOX 140
TENANTS HARBOR, ME 04860

YANKEE PEOPLES BUYING CLUB
KAREN LOGODMOS
BOX 25
THOMASTON, ME 04861

NOT NOW CO-OP
BUMP HILL ROAD
UNION, ME 04862
SUE NERSESSIAN

COMMUNITY CO-OP
RUTH DENNETT
76 WEST RIVER RD
WATERVILLE, ME 04901

HUNGRY CHUCKS INEVITABLE FOOD CO-OP
KIT PENNEY
9 WINTER
WATERVILLE, ME 04901

CHICKEN CO-OP
KAREN KIEVITT
36 NORTHPORT
BELFAST, ME 04915

MONROE FOOD CO-OP
BITSA WOOD
RFD 1
BROOKS, ME 04921

CENTRAL MAINE NATURAL FOOD CO-OP
BRIAN DELANEY
RFD #3 BOX 97
DEXTER, ME 04930

PEAK MOUNTAIN CO-OP
ARIEL WILCOX
RFD #1
DIXMONT, ME 04932

FRIENDS FOOD CO-OP
KATHY HRUSKA
BOX 161
LIBERTY, ME 04949
(207)589-2521

MOOSE POND CO-OP
LARRY MCCRAIG
52 HAMILTON
PITTSFIELD, ME 04967

HARD TIMES CO-OP
AL POWELL
MADISON AVE
SKOWHEGAN, ME 04976

SANDY RIVER CO-OP
LEON BRESSLOFF
TEMPLE, ME 04984

TROY CO-OP
JUDY ROCK
WHITAKER RD
TROY, ME 04987

VERMONT

WEST LEBANON WAREHOUSE
RFD 1
EAST THETFORD, VT 05043

GOOD FOOD RESTAURANT
COMMON GROUND
25 ELLIOT ST.
BRATTLEBORO, VT 05301

PUTNEY CONSUMERS CO-OP
BOX 55
PUTNEY, VT 05346

ONION RIVER FOOD CO-OP
77 ARCHIBALD ST.
BURLINGTON, VT 05401

ADDISON COUNTY BUYERS CLUB
15 MAIN ST.
BRISTOL, VT 05443

FOOD FOR THOUGHT
LAURA BENIS
BOX 32
E. FAIRFIELD, VT 05448

FRANKLIN/GRAND ISLE BUYING CLUB
165 LAKE ST
ST. ALBANS, VT 05478

FOOD FOR THOUGHT
TAIL OF THE TIGER
BARNET, VT 05821

ADAMANT FOOD CO-OP
CINDY MARTIN
ADAMANT, VT 05640

MORRISVILLE CO-OP
JOHN ROGERS
RFD 1
MORRISSVILLE, VT 05661

NEPCOOP
BOX 247
PLAINFIELD, VT 05667

PLAINFIELD CO-OP
BOX 157
PLAINFIELD, VT 05667

RUTLAND NATURAL FOODS CO-OP
117 WEST ST.
RUTLAND, VT 05701

MIDDLEBURY CO-OP
ANN FOX
19 WAYBRIDGE ST.
MIDDLEBURY, VT 05753

GOOD EARTH
BOX 417
LYNDONVILLE, VT 05851

NORTHEAST KINGDOM CO-OP
BOX 272
BARTON, VT 05822

CONNECTICUT

MANCHESTER CO-OP
WOMEN'S CENTER
MANCHESTER COMMUNITY COLLEGE
MANCHESTER, CT 06040

SIMSBURY FOOD CO-OP
ANGELE MOKHIBER
32 COUNTRY LANE
SIMSBURY, CT 06070

WORKER COOPERATIVE UNION
STAFFORD SPRINGS, CT 06076
37 SISSON AVE
HARTFORD, CT 06105

WILD FLOUR CO-OP
JILL CHARRON
38 MERRIMAN ST
UNIONVILLE, CT 06085

CONSUMERS CO-OP ASSN.
461 FLATBUSH AVE
HARTFORD, CT 06106

BLUE HILLS FOOD CO-OP
CLIFF ROSENTHAL
95 CANTERBURY ST.
HARTFORD, CT 06112

DOWN TO EARTH FOOD CO-OP
16 MAPLEWOOD AVE
WEST HARTFORD, CT 06119

CHRISTIAN CO-OP
LARRY BERNIER
RT 2 BOX 532
DAYVILLE, CT 06241

VALLEY CO-OP
94 MAIN ST.
ANSONIA, CT 06401

NORTH END CAC CO-OP
183 N. MAIN ST.
ANSONIA, CT 06401

GOOD HARVEST
686 MAIN
MIDDLETOWN, CT 06457

CHESTER CO-OP
CAROLYN LINTELMANN
35 DYERS PT. RD
OLD SAYBROOK, CT 06475

NEW HAVEN FOOD CO-OP
490 GREENWICH AVE
NEW HAVEN, CT 06519

RAINBOW CO-OP
1720 WHITNEY AVE
NEW HAVEN, CT 065XX

N.O.W. BUYING CLUB
NEW OPPORTUNITIES FOR WATERBURY
769 MAIN ST.
WATERBURY, CT 06704

NEW JERSEY

MID EASTERN COOPERATIVES
FRANK ANASTASIO
75 AMOR AVE.
CARLSTADT, NJ 07072

NEW JERSEY NATURAL FOODS
216 BELMONT AVE
OCEAN, NJ 07712

GOOD FOOD DISTRIBUTORS
249 MT. KEMBLE AVE
MORRISTOWN, NJ 07960
CAROL MCCABE/267-3735

MORRISTOWN FOOD CO-OP
50 WESTERN
MORRISTOWN, NJ 07960
DONNA GOODWIN/235-5616/MORRISTOWN FRIEND

STOCKTON COLLEGE CO-OP
STOCKTON COLLEGE
STOCKTON, NJ 08559

COUNTRY NATURAL BAKERY
BOX 5193
CLINTON, NJ 08809

HUNTERDON CITY CO-OP
ANNANDALE RD
CLINTON, NJ 08809

NEW YORK

PEOPLES WAREHOUSE
21 2ND AVE
NEW YORK, NY 10003

GOOD FOOD CO-OP
58 E.4 ST.
MANHATTAN, NY 10003
PATRICIA 260-4712

PEOPLES CO-OP
508 E. 6TH ST.
MANHATTAN, NY 10009
GINO GARCIA/677-2787
MICHAEL/228-7840

CORNUCOPIA
201 E 4TH ST.
NEW YORK, NY 10009
(212)475-9894
DENISE/673-6319

15TH ST. MEETING HOUSE CO-OP
EILEEN LAWCOR
82 WASHINGTON PL #4D
NEW YORK, NY 10011

SABRINA FOOD CONSPIRACY
243 W. 20 ST.
MANHATTAN, NY 10011

INTEGRAL YOGA
227 W. 13 ST.
MANHATTAN, NY 10011
(212)929-0585/0586 M-S/930-930
TRIMOORTI LEVY/929-1918

WEST VILLAGE CO-OP
135 W. 4 ST.
MANHATTAN, NY 10012
BARBARA 242-2309
ALEX/741-1873

ALTERNATIVE 491
491 HUDSON
NEW YORK, NY 10014
GARY/(212)243-0364

NATURAL LIFE CO-OP
1111 E. 34TH
MANHATTAN, NY 10016

COMMUNITY ACTION CO-OP
436 AMSTERDAM AVE (81ST)
NEW YORK, NY 10024
BEAULAH/799-1290

GREENHOUSE ASSOC.
466 AMSTERDAM AVE.
NEW YORK, NY 10024
GUS 787-3042, MIKE (9-5) 732-8551

BROADWAY LOCAL FOOD CO-OP
95 AND COLUMBUS
MANHATTAN, NY 10025
TONY/663-2266
NATALIE/865-8928

HOUSE OF KUUMBA
FREDERICK DOUGLAS COMMUNITY CENTER
104TH ST AND COLUMBUS AVE
NEW YORK, NY 10025
CHUMMIE READING/865-4615

97TH ST CO-OP
50 W. 97TH ST
NEW YORK, NY 10025
HOLIMA TORE/666-8648

WEST SIDE FOOD BUYING CLUB
1050 AMSTERDAM AVE.
NEW YORK, NY 10026

HARLEM RIVER CONSUMERS CO-OP
270 LENNOX
NEW YORK, NY 10027
(212)427-7252

KUDIN KOWAP
526 W. 123RD ST
NEW YORK, NY 10027
JIMMY/865-7715
DON/864-0241

NATURAL FOODS CENTER
ROOM 105, EARL HALL
COLUMBIA UNIVERSITY
NEW YORK, NY 10027

BIRD
875 W 181ST ST
NEW YORK, NY 10033

PRIME & PUMP
415 W 126TH ST
NEW YORK, NY 10027
GARY/850-7866

PROJECT ABLE
15 ST. JAMES PL
MANHATTAN, NY 10038

SHANTI FOOD CONSPIRACY OF ST.GEORGE
104 WESTERVELT AVE.
STATEN ISLAND, NY 10301
(212)447-9227
GEORGE ZARILLO/447-9232

OSSINING COMMUNITY COOPERATIVE, INC
47 SPRING ST.
OSSINING, NY 10562
(914)762-9731
RICHARD CROSS

RAINBOW FOODS
166 SPENCER ST.
BROOKLYN, NY 11205
(212)522-4033
ARLENE DREXLER

CONSUMER ACT PROG OF BEDFORD-STUYV
ADOLF ALAYSON
501 MARCY AVE
BROOKLYN, NY 11206
(212)388-1601
ADOLFO ALAYON

MONGOOSE
782 UNION ST.
BROOKLYN, NY 11211
DON 499-6643
JACK 768-3959

BROWNSVILLE COOPERATIVE BUYING CLUB
388 ROCKAWAY AVE.
BROOKLYN, NY 11212
(212)385-4697/385-6282
WILLIAM LAING

FAMILY BUYING CLUB
202 ROCKY HILL RD
BAYSIDE, QUEENS, NY 11361

ORGANIC ENERGY
68-06 FRESH MEADOW LANE
FLUSHING, NY 11365
( )762-8517
PAHOO 463-9497
REST. 359-2391

SOUTH OZONE PARK COMM BUYING CLUB
14205 ROCKAWAY BLVD
S. OZONE PARK, NY 11436
(212)529-3427
BETHENIA ROUSE

BAY CO-OP
11 LINDER COURT
BROOKHAVEN, NY 11719

HUNTINGTON COLLECTIVE
BOX 81
HUNTINGTON, NY 11743

PEOPLE'S TOWN HALL FOOD CO-OP
488 NEW YORK AVE.
HUNTINGTON, NY 11743
JOHN BRUSH

SOUND FOOD CO-OP
541 LAKE AVE.
ST. JAMES, NY 11780

STONY BROOK FREEDOM FOODS CO-OP
JACK SOGRO
STAGE XII CAFETARIA
SUNY
STONYBROOK, NY 11790

COHOES COOPERATIVE BUYING CLUB
C/O COHOES COMM ACTION PROGRAM, INC
98 MOHAWK ST.
COHOES, NY 12047
(518)237-9201
MILLIE MARCELLE

DOVE FOOD CO-OP
JUDY BRAUN
RT 2, BOX 79
SELKIRK, NY 12158

SOUTH END FOOD COOPERATIVE
142 S. PEARL ST.
ALBANY, NY 12202
(518)472-9107
HELEN HERBERT

PENNY PINCHERS FOOD CO-OP
RANDY GREENE
MILLBROOK RD STAR RTE
MARGARETVILLE, NY 12455

BEGGARS BANQUET
FAMILY
16 ROCK CITY RD
WOODSTOCK, NY 12498
(914)679-2485/338-2370
NATURES PANTRY
NATE

COLUMBIA CITY FOOD CO-OP
MARGARIE WALKER
RT 1
HUDSON, NY 12534

GOOD FOOD RESTAURANT
18 CHURCH ST.
NEW PALTZ, NY 12561

REAL FOOD STORE
53 MAIN ST.
NEW PALTZ, NY 12561

SARATOGA CO-OP
62 DEEKMAN
SARATOGA SPRINGS, NY 12866

NORTH COUNTRY HEALTH FOODS CO-OP
30 SMITH
PLATTSBURGH, NY 12901

GROCERY CO-OP
LOIS PROIETTE
7 WHITAKER RD.
FULTON, NY 13069

OSWEGO COUNTY CO-OP STORE
W. 3RD AND VORHEES ST
FULTON, NY 13069

NATURES STOREHOUSE
2 WARREN ST.
AUBURN, NY 13201

COMMUNITY FOOD CO-OP
120 DELL ST.
SYRACUSE, NY 13210

SYRACUSE REAL FOOD CO-OP
550 WESTCOTT
SYRACUSE, NY 13210
(315)479-6456
DENNIS & HARRIET LERNER/503 ALLEN

GOOD FOOD STORE
315 WAVERLY
SYRACUSE, NY 13210

CHEAP FOOD LTD.
CHAPEL HOUSE, OFFICE R.
711 COMSTOCK AVE.
SYRACUSE, NY 13210

OSWEGO COUNTY CO-OP STORE
104 W. BRIDGE ST.
OSWEGO, NY 13216

GLENFIELD FOOD COOPERATIVE
RURAL ROUTE
GLENFIELD, NY 13343
(315)376-7468
MS. ARITY MITCHELL

MEADOW CO-OP
BOX 1052
HAMILTON, NY 13346

MOLINE CO-OP
21 W. KENDRICK
HAMILTON, NY 13346

LOWVILLE FOOD BUYING CLUB
RURAL ROUTE
LOWVILLE, NY 13367
(315)376-3671
MS. RICHARD HILL

SOUTH LYONS FOOD BUYING CLUB
RURAL ROUTE
LYON FALLS, NY 13368
(315)348-8292
JOAN DARLING

BEAVER FALLS FOOD BUYING CLUB
RURAL ROUTE
CASTORLAND, NY 13620
(315)346-6082
CONNIE LOUSEY/SHADY AVE CROGHAN 13327
MILFORD REGGIE/BEAVER FALLS 13305

NORTH FAMILY FAIR
ANDREW SHELTON
R.D. #1
GOUVERNEUR, NY 13642

POTSDAM COMMUNITY CO-OP
34 MAPLE
POTSDAM, NY 13676

NORTH VALLEY BUYERS CLUB
RURAL DELIVERY 2 PO BOX 200
NEWARK VALLEY, NY 13811
(607)642-8958
FLORENCE FRANKS

RICHFORD PENNYPINCHERS
RURAL DELIVERY
RICHFORD, NY 13835
(607)657-4495
MARTHA DAMON

OFF CENTER
MANAGER
73 STATE ST.
BINGHAMTON, NY 13905

EAST SIDE COMMUNITY COOPERATIVE
300 WILLIAMS ST.
BUFFALO, NY 14204
(716)852-0182
GERALDINE WEST

GREENFIELD ST. RESTAURANT
25 GREENFIELD
BUFFALO, NY 14214

N. BUFFALO COMMUNITY AND FOOD CO-OP
3225 MAIN ST
BUFFALO, NY 14214

DIVINE FOOD CO-OP
681 LINWOOD
BUFFALO, NY 14215
(716)883-0436
PETER WALSH

LEXINGTON REAL FOODS CO-OP
224 LEXINGTON AVE.
BUFFALO, NY 14222

BROCKPORT FOOD CO-OP
37 MAIN ST. SOUTH
BROCKPORT, NY 14420
KEN/352-0246,637-5103

GENESEO FOOD BUYING CLUB
20 ELM ST
GENESEO, NY 14454
(716)926-3586
LYNN ISRAEL

GENEVA CO-OP
190 LEWIS
GENEVA, NY 14456

CLEAR EYE WAREHOUSE
367 ORCHARD
ROCHESTER, NY 14606

FEDERATION OF ROCHESTER KOOPERATIVS
713 MONROE AVE
ROCHESTER, NY 14607

GENESEE CO-OP
713 MONROE AVE
ROCHESTER, NY 14607
(716)244-3900 <271-3770>

BLESSED THISTLE BAKERY
942 MONROE AVE.
ROCHESTER, NY 14607

REGULAR RESTAURANT
715 MONROE
ROCHESTER, NY 14607

JAMESTOWN FOOD CO-OP
273 FAIRMONT
JAMESTOWN, NY 14701
(716)488-0971

CATTARAUGUS BUYERS COOPERATIVE, INC
22 W. WASHINGTON ST.
ELLICOTTVILLE, NY 14731
(716)699-4551
RODNEY CROCKER

ITHACA REAL FOOD CO-OP
140 W. STATE
ITHACA, NY 14850
(607)273-9012/1782 TWTH/730PM-9 SA/11-6
FRANKIE WHITMAN/273-1782/4415 ELM
MONTANA/277-0904/308 BRYANT

SOMADHARA BAKERY
215 N. CAYUGA
ITHACA, NY 14850

PENN YAN AREA CO-OP
SUNRISE FARM
RD 1
PRATTSBURG, NY 14873
(607)522-4302
SALLY LARRICK

KOSMOS RESTAURANT
17 W. MAIN
TRUMANSBERG, NY 14886

TRUMANSBERG CO-OP
15 CONGRESS
TRUMANSBERG, NY 14886

SPENCER BUYERS CLUB
RURAL DELIVERY 2
SPENCER, NY 14883
(607)589-6267
JERRY CATLIN

PENNSYLVANIA

MIREILLE
REVOLUTIONARY EUROPE
P.O. BOX 4288
PITTSBURGH, PA 15203

SEMPLE STREET FOOD COOPERATIVE
3459 WARD ST.
PITTSBURGH, PA 15213
(412)687-1227
SARA DE JOSEPHINE

DIVINE FOOD CO-OP
1364 DENNISTON AVE
PITTSBURGH, PA 15217
(412)421-5970
SANDY OLCHEK

MEAT BUYERS CLUB
WESTMORELAND CNTY CONF FOR
ECONOMIC OPPORTUNITY
128 E. PITTSBURGH ST.
GREENSBURG, PA 15601
(412)837-6050
JEANETTE LEWIS

ERIE EDINBORO FOOD CO-OP
522 SHENLEY AVE
ERIE, PA 16505
JERRY HERTZ/454-0084

RAINBOW FOODS
513 W 67TH ST
ERIE, PA 16507
DOUG & BARB DAILEY/455-3872

KINGSLEY CO-OP
FRED PREUSS
526 E. 10TH
ERIE, PA 165XX

OUR STORE
MOLLY VERENE
336 RIDGE AVE
STATE COLLEGE, PA 16801
(814)238-7789 TU/4-7, TH/3-7
BOBBY HARRISON

ADAMS COUNTY BUYING CLUB
PO BOX 205
GETTYSBURG, PA 17325
(717)334-8322
DEBBIE SPAIN

CROCUS
RT 2 BOX 116
NEW RINGOLD, PA 17960

BETHLEHEM CO-OP
353 BROADWAY
BETHLEHEM, PA 18015

MOUNTAIN FOOD CO-OP
126 RIDGEWAY
STROUDSBURG, PA 18360

GOOD EARTH
ST. ASAPHS CHURCH
57 E. LEVENING MILL
BALA CYNWOOD, PA 19004

FOOD CO-OP H
HAVERFORD COLLEGE
C/O ERIC STERLING
HAVERFORD, PA 19041

LANSDOWNE CO-OP
25 S. LANSDOWNE
LANSDOWNE, PA 19050
CHUCK NELSON/623-9987

SWARTHMORE CO-OP
317 N. CHESTER
SWARTHMORE, PA 19081
JANE PACKARD/KI4-5886

SWARTHMORE CO-OP
401 DARTMOUTH AVE
SWARTHMORE, PA 19081
WILLIAM SHIRLEY/543-9805

PRINCETON FOOD CO-OP
WAYNE MOSS
217 PINE TREE RD.
RADNOR, PA 19087

SPRING ST. CO-OP
2122 SPRING ST.
PHILADELPHIA, PA 19103
MS. PETER LISTER/569-2167

COMMUNITY FOOD CO-OP OF WEST PHIL.
C/O CRADY ABNEY
3907 SPRUCE ST.
PHILADELPHIA, PA 19104
( )349-7770
MICHAEL ABNEY HARRY AUGUST

DIVINE FOOD CO-OP
3519 LANCASTER
PHILADELPHIA, PA 19104
(215)387-6288
PAUL WILLIAMS

ECOLOGY FOOD CO-OP
301 N. 36TH ST
PHILADELPHIA, PA 19104
(215)222-5142 M-F/10-7 SA/10-6 SU/10-2
787-6782,222-6103/3416 RACE ST
NINA OLSON/BA2-6103

PHILADELPHIA FDERATN OF FOOD CO-OPS
POWELLTOWN WAREHOUSE
ED PLACE
3300 RACE ST.
PHILADELPHIA, PA 19104

POWELTON BAKING CO-OP
33RD AND RACE ST
PHILADELPHIA, PA 19104

POWELTON CO-OP
33RD AND RACE ST
PHILADELPHIA, PA 19104
ED PLACE/222-7185

PEOPLES CO-OP OF MT. AIRY
C/O SUMMIT PRESBYTERIAN CHURCH
WESTVIEW AND GREENE ST.
PHILADELPHIA, PA 19119
CAROL LISI/849-0240

THE WEAVERS WAY CO-OP
555-559 W. CARPENTER LN
PHILADELPHIA, PA 19119
(215)843-6945 T-S/9-7
JULES TIMMERMAN/848-4459/513 W. CARPENTE
LARRY BELLIKOFF/438-3375/541 W. CARPENTE

CHURCH OF THE ADVOCATE
18TH AND DIAMOND ST
PHILADELPHIA, PA 19121
GLADYS UNDERWOOD/236-0568

ST. ELIZABETH
1845 N. 23RD ST
PHILADELPHIA, PA 19121
ERNIE COMEGYS/987-9932/236-8073

WHARTON CENTER
1708 N. 22ND ST.
PHILADELPHIA, PA 19121

TEMPLE COMMUNITY FOOD CO-OP
1439 NORRIS ST. W
PHILADELPHIA, PA 19122
NORMAL WEISS/849-1485

FRANKFORD
YMCA
ARROTT AT UZIPER
PHILADELPHIA, PA 19124
PEG BROMLEY/744-3639
CLAIRE MEYER/8725-3249

OAK LANE FOOD
11TH AND OAK LANE
PHILADELPHIA, PA 19126
MARYLN LAPIDAS/549-2591
LISA WALLACE/424-9193 TH

WEST OAK LANE CO-OP
LAMONT AME CHURCH
1500 CHELTENHAM AVE.
PHILADELPHIA, PA 19126
HARRIET FLEISCHMAN/6738 OLD YORK RD

MANAYUNK FOOD CO-OP
ST. DAVIDS EPISCOPAL CHURCH
DUPONT & KRANSAU OR DUPONT & SMICK
PHILADEOPHIA, PA 19127
BETTY JONES/483-5069/117 DUPONT OR 482-
JEAN TURVEY/483-9022/4546 RITCHIEST

EAST FALLS BUYING CLUB
EAST FALLS HOMES
4513 MERRICK RD
PHILADELPHIA, PA 19129
LOVEY BLAND/438-0280
MS. OVERTON/

CROSS ROADS COMM. CENTER
2916 N 6TH ST. OR 2016
PHILADELPHIA, PA 19133
MARK MILLER/223-7897

OPEN, INC
2431 N. 6TH ST.
PHILADELPHIA, PA 19133

ST. EDWARDS
2417 N. 8TH ST
PHILADELPHIA, PA 19133
SR. MARY AGNES/684-1700

SPRING GARDEN COMM CENTER
1812 GREEN ST.
PHILADELPHIA, PA 19136

MARIPOSA
4726 BALTIMORE AVE.
PHILADELPHIA, PA 19143
( )SA9-9462
PAM SH2-4783, ANN EV4-8282
ARLENE RENGERT/726-4514

STONEHOUSE LIFE CENTER FOOD CO-OP
1006 S. 46
PHILADELPHIA, PA 19143
KEITH MILLER/386-1371
BOB MORRIS/476-6796

GERMANTOWN PEOPLES FOOD CO-OP
GERMANTOWN COMM PRES CHURCH
GREEN & TULPEHEN
PHILADELPHIA, PA 19144
TERRY STERN 843-7284

PEOPLES CO-OP
CALVERY CHURCH
MANNHEIM AND PULASKI
PHILADELPHIA, PA 19144
BILL TIRRILL/848-4244

TOGETHERNESS HOUSE
32 E. ARMATT
EAST GERMANTOWN, PA 19144
LOUISA ODONNELL/844-3387

ETHNIC HERITAGE AFFAIRS INSTITUTE
2635 WHARTON ST
PHILADELPHIA, PA 19146
RICH APPEL/463-0888

SOUTH ST. COMMUNITY CO-OP
624 S. 4TH
PHILADELPHIA, PA 19147
SUE COLELLA/9220631

HOLMES CIRCLE
8109 FARNSWORTH ST
PHILADELPHIA, PA 19152
MS. URBANSKI/332-4212

GREENWICH NEIGHBORS FOOD CO-OP
2029 S. 8TH ST.
PHILADELPHIA, PA 19148

HORN OF PLENTY
FOOTLIGHTER THEATRE
MAIN AND 1ST AVE
BERWYN, PA 19312
ARDIS RYDER/644-8499

MARCHWOOD CO-OP
430 CONCORD AVE
EXTON, PA 19341
P DEHAVEN

KIMBERTON CO-OP
40 GALACIA DR.
PHOENIXVILLE, PA 19460

PERIWINKLE VALLEY CO-OP
26 BUCHWALTER
PHOENIXVILLE, PA 19460

DELAWARE

COMMUNITY FOOD CO-OP
282 W. MAIN
NEWARK, DL 19711
JOY SCHWEIZER/731-1288
JOHN HICHEY/932-4805/4 BRIAR LANE

DISTRICT OF COLUMBIA

COMMUNITY WAREHOUSE
2010 KENDALL ST NE
WASHINGTON, DC 20002

FREEDOM TRUCKING COLLECTIVE
010 KENDALL ST NE
WASHINGTON, DC 20002
SKI CLARK/232-3608
ARTHUR/265-4609

FINDERS ASSOCIATE II
MARGARET WARD
3918 W. ST NW
WASHINGTON DC 20007

FIELDS OF PLENTY
2447 18TH ST. NW
WASHINGTON, DC 20009
(202)483-3884/MTTHF/10-8 W/10-7 SA/9-7
JULIE RAICA/232-3895/1751 KILBOURNE
JIM BENN/232-7345/1731 NEW HAMPSHIRE #62

STONE SOUP COMMUNITY MARKET
1801 18TH ST. NW
WASHINGTON, DC 20009
(202)234-7665 M/10-7 TF/10-8 SA/9-7
STEVE CLARK/234-7665/1802 BELMONT

DIVINE FOOD CO-OP
3235 MCKINLEY ST NW
WASHINGTON, DC 20015
(202)362-0545
MATT REILLY

MARYLAND

GLUT FOOD CO-OP
4005 34TH ST.
MOUNT RANIER, MD 20822
(301)779-1978 M-SU/10-7
A LIGHT/(202)387-2872/1879 S ST NW/DC 20
TOM FLECKNOE/234-9286

RAINBOW BRIDGE
5604 KENILWORTH
RIVERDALE, MD 20840
(301)864-1460 M-SA/10-8 SU 12-6
DOUG/464-2085/11705 ANNAPOLIS/GLENDALE 2

GREENBELT CONSUMER SERVICES
8547 PINEY BRANCH RD
SILVER SPRING, MD 20901
JOHN BROWN

MORRIS CO-OP 2
LOIS FISH
6815 GREENSPRING
BALTIMORE, MD 21209
JUDY BLANK/3404 DEEP WILLOW/21208

THE CO-OP
JANE DANIELS
210 RIDGEWOOD
BALTIMORE, MD 21210

SPRING BOTTOM NATURAL FOODS
RT. 1
BELAIR, MD 21213

BROTHERS NATURAL FOODS
3123 BELVIDERE
BALTIMORE, MD 21215
NONI

RESEVOIR HILL FOOD CO-OP
NANCY LAWLER
3035 PARK
BALTIMORE, MD 21217

GURUKU NATURAL FOODS
322 N. CHARLES
BALTIMORE, MD 21218

WAVERLY PEOPLES FOOD CO-OP
3207 INDEPENDENCE
BALTIMORE, MD 21218
CAROL CUBLEY

GOOD FOOD CO-OP
1617 SHAKESPEARE
BALTIMORE, MD 21231
TERRY MOORE/(301)732-4371

ANNAPOLIS FOOD CO-OP
1991 VALLEY RD RT 11
ANNAPOLIS, MD 21401

VIRGINIA

SHARE
5220 LIGHTHORNE
BURKE, VA 22015
MILDRED SNYDER

LAKE JACKSON FOOD CO-OP
11426 DUMFRIES
MANASSUS, VA 22110

COBELIA CO-OP
BOX 259
HILLSBORO, VA 22132

DALE CITY FOOD BUYERS CO-OP
HARRY LEICHTER
14308 N. BELLEVILLE
DALE CITY, VA 22193

STOREHOUSE CO-OP
752 N. VAN DORN
ALEXANDRIA, VA 22304
MS. KENT HUFF

NIMRODEL
727A LITTLE BACK RIVER RD.
HAMPTON, VA 22369
ELLEN MITCHELL

CARROT SEED CO-OP
BOX 224
FLINT HILL, VA 22627

CHARLOTTESVILLE CO-OP
THE PRISON
RUGBY RD
CHARLOTTESVILLE, VA 22903

KRISHNAS KITCHEN
11 ELLIEWOOD
CHARLOTTESVILLE, VA 22903

CHARRLETTSVILLE FOOD CO-OP
C/O WESLEY HUBBARD
RT1, BOX 45A
ROSELAND, VA 22967

SUNSHINE
1001 LAFAYETTE ST.
WILLIAMSBURG, VA 23184
PETER TYREE

EXODUS FOOD CO-OP
1101 FLOYD ST.
RICHMOND, VA 23220

FORTE FOUNDATION
PO BOX 403
VIRGINIA BEACH, VA 23458
(804)428-7747
601 10TH ST

NEW AGE FOOD CO-OP
4706 HAMPTON RD
NORFOLK, VA 23509
(804)497-8115
ISABEL CHENG/441-3508/620 GRESHAM 106/23
SANDI DUNAVENT/497-8115,857-4768/537 BEL

ROANOKE COOPERATIVE ASSN. LTD
813 5TH ST SW
ROANOKE, VA 24016
(703)982-9664 M-S/11-7
FRED $APLANTE/342-5423
EVA JO WU/774-8729

EATS NATURAL FOODS CO-OP
217 W. COLLEGE
BLACKSBURG, VA 24060
STAN DAVIS/703-382-0390
STEVE DUNCAN/951-2636

PITTSYLVANIA CNTY COMM ACTION INC
BUYING CLUB
PO BOX 936
CHATHAM, VA 24531
(703)432-8250
ANNE SOLENSKI

WEST VIRGINIA

FREEMAN, WOLF, & ASSOC COMMUNITIES
BUYING CLUB
FREEMAN, WV 24724
(304)248-4361
EVELYN WILSON

GROWING TREE COUNTRY STORE
128 1/2 COURT ST.
SPENCER, WV 25276
CAROLEE/(304)927-4324

EVERYBODYS CO-OP/HARRISVILLE
S.J. LANAHAN
RR1
OXFORD, WV 26414

BIG NICKEL
FAIRMONT STATE COLLEGE
FAIRMONT, WV 26554

NORTH CAROLINA

COUNTRY CO-OP
BOX 111
PITTSBORO,NC 27312

CHAPEL HILL FOOD CO-OP
COMMUNITY BOOKSTORE
409 W ROSEMARY ST
CHAPEL HILL, NC 27514

COMMUNITARIAN EARTH STORE
122 HARRISON
RALEIGH, NC 27603

PEOPLES INTERGALACTIC FOOD CO-OP
1413 JAMES
DURHAM, NC 27707
JONATHON CARMEL/427-8731

CHOWAN COOPERATIVE PRODUCE EXCHANGE
PO BOX 398
EDENTON, NC 27932
(919)482-2786
SHERWOOD LAYTON

CHARLOTTE FOOD CO-OP
2505 E5TH ST.
CHARLOTTE, NC 28204
JERRY MILES/332-1854
STEVE NELSON/333-0874

MOUNTAIN FOOD CONSPIRACY
BOX 176
VILAS, NC 28692
STEPHEN GELLER/297-3662
HENRY HALL/963-5458

SOUTH CAROLINA

COLUMBIA CO-OP
221 PICKENS
COLUMBIA, SC 29205

WOODLAND COMMUNITY PROGRESS GROUP
RTE 1 PO BOX 353
GEORGETOWN, SC 29440
RUBEN DAVIS

PEOPLES COMMUNITY COOPERATIVE
RIVERS STREET EXTENSION
WALTERBORO, SC 29488
(803)549-1624
WILLIE MAE WILLIAMS

LIFE CO-OP
BARBARA CLAY
BOX 2279
N. MYRTLE BEACH, SC 29577

HAMPTON COUNTY BUYING CLUB
PO BOX 706
HAMPTON, SC 29924
(803)943-4812
JAMES MCCARTHY

GEORGIA

NEW MORNING FOOD CO-OP
QUAKER HOUSE
1384 FAIRVIEW RD NE
ATLANTA, GA 30306
(404)373-7986/0914

ELIZABETH ST. FOOD CO-OP
VIC BUBBETT
206 ELIZABETH ST. NE #6
ATLANTA, GA 30307
(404)577-6889

MORNING STAR INN
1451 OXFORD RD NE
EMORY, GA 30307

SEVANANDA
431 MORELAND AVE NE
ATLANTA, GA 30307
DIINGA DANSHI/MIKE/404-681-2831

ATLANTA FOOD CO-OP
731 LAWTON ST SW
ATLANTA, GA 30310
(404)755-1641

GEORGE WASHINGTON CO-OP
428 FLAT SHOALS RD SE
ATLANTA, GA 30316
(404)483-0959/522-2892
WILLIAM & MADELINE WORDES

SUN-MEC BUYING CLUB
C/O SUN-MEC NEIGHBORHOOD SERVCE CTR
71 GEORGIA AVENUE S.W.
ATLANTA, GA 30315
(404)577-1351
HARRIET DARNELL

FOOD CO-OP
2030 CLIFF VALLEY NE
ATLANTA, GA 30329
(404)634-6138
STAN METCALF

GEORGIA INSTITUTE OF TECHNOLOGY
TOGETHER FOOD CO-OP
STUDENT GOVERNMENT
ATLANTA, GA 30332
(404)894-2814

FLORIDA

EAST SIDE SPRINGFIELD FOOD CO-OP
JACKSONVILLE, FL 32005
(904)353-8701
BEVERLY SHIELDS

DAYTONA BEACH FOOD CO-OP
STAN BARBER
RT1 BOX 33
ORLANDO BEACH, FL 32074
(904)677-1589

LEON COUNTY FOOD CO-OP
702 S. MACOMB
TALLAHASSEE, FL 32304
(904)222-9916
JOHN, CLAIRE, PAT, JOE

PEOPLES SOUTHEASTERN WHSE
702 S MACOMB
TALLAHASSEE, FL 32304

HOGTOWN GRANARY
114 S. MAIN
GAINESVILLE, FL 32601
(904)377-5186
MARCO, STEVE, JIM

BAY COUNTY FOOD CO-OP
800 AIRPORT ROAD
PANAMA CITY, FL 32401
(904)785-5506
HARRIETT, GAIL, LENNY

YELLOW SUN FOOD CO-OP
2911 1/2 E. JACKSON
PENSACOLA, FL 32503

EVERYMAN NATURAL FOODS CO-OP
2902 12TH AVE
PENSACOLA, FL 32503
ALLEN REACH/904-438-0402

DIVINE FOOD CO-OP
518 NE 4TH AVE
GAINESVILLE, FL 32601
(904)378-8184
PAUL KITTAS

DE LAND BUYING CLUB
259 WEST VOORHIS ST.
DE LAND, FL 32720
(904)734-2513
MS. LEGERTHA HENRY

SUNSEED CO-OP
6290 ATLANTIC AVE
CAPE CANAVERAL, FL 32920
SANDY

CHELA CENTER
614 E. ATLANTIC BLVD
POMPANO VEACH, FL 33060

SUNSHINE COOPERATIVE ASSN
4306 NW SECOND AVE
MIAMI, FL 33127

ALTERNATIVE VITTLES
STAN ALTLAND
1478 GULF TO BAY
CLEARWATER, FL 33515

SKYBIRD
HUDSON PLAZA
RT 19
HUDSON, FL 33568

SUNFLOWER
THE SARASOTA FOOD STORE
1549 MAIN ST. OR 1817
SARASOTA, FL 33577

THE CO-OP STORE
1230 N. NEBRASKA OR 120303
TAMPA, FL 33612
TERRI, DAVE

BO TREE
2255 34TH ST.
ST. PETERSBURG, FL 33713

ALABAMA

TENNESSEE

NEIGHBORHOOD SERVICE CENTER BC
1116 8TH AVE S
NASHVILLE, TN 37203
(615)747-4671
GWENDOLYN MCLEAN

THE PAPER BAG CO-OP
EAST SEVIER AVE
KINGSPORT, TN 37660
BILL JENNINGS

MISSISSIPPI

OXFORD CONSUMER COOPERATIVE
512 JACKSON AVE
OXFORD, MS 38655
(601)252-2579
MS. BERNIE FREEMAN

KENTUCKY

SUNSHINE SHOPPE
1802 BARDSTOWN RD
LOUISVILLE, KY 40204
(502)452-1152

WHOLESOME HORIZONS CO-OP
ANANDA MARGA
2013 LONGEST AVE
LOUISVILLE, KY 40204
(502)452-6795

HAPPY HOLLOW
ELLIOTTVILLE, KY 40317

GOOD FOODS CO-OP
314 1/2 S. ASHLAND AVE
LEXINGTON, KY 40502

HARLAN BUYING CLUB
C/O HARLAN CNTY COMM ACTION AGENCY
314 S. MAIN ST.
HARLAN, KY 40831
(606)537-5331
DANNY DAVIS

OHIO

RACOON VALLEY FOOD FRIENDS CO-OP
ANN HAGEDORN
17 SAMSON PLACE
GRANVILLE, OH 43023

COLUMBUS CONSUMERS CO-OP
PHYLLIS BYARD
87 ORCHARD LN.
WORTHINGTON, OH 43085
(614)846-2747

COMMON MARKET WAREHOUSE
BOX 8253
COLUMBUS, OH 43201
(614)294-0145,4343
MIKE GATES, BOB LUCE LARRY CROY

OSU FOOD CO-OP
HARVEY FORSTAG
2377 N. 4TH ST.
COLUMBUS, OH 43201

NEW DAWN BAKERY
82 E 16TH
COLUMBUS, OH 43204
DICK MOORE/614-299-6490/294-3088

SOUTHSIDE FOOD CO-OP
1156 PARSONS
COLUMBUS, OH 43207
ANNIE/614-443-3782
WALLIE CASH/443-4619

BUCKEYE VILLAGE FOOD CO-OP
2661 DEFIANCE
COLUMBUS, OH 43210
JEANENE BECKER/614-267-4275/651 TRUMBULL

COLUMBUS COMMUNITY FOOD CO-OP
82 E 16TH AVE
COLUMBUS, OH 43210
(614)294-3088 M-F 1-8/S 10-5
WILLIAM FINZEL/261-7819/2166 SUMMIT #3
BARRY CHERN/421-1679/348 W 8TH

DIVINE FOOD CO-OP
1074 E BROAD OR 851 NEIL
COLUMBUS, OH 43215
(614)294-4520
GREG ZIEGLER/258-8491

FOUNTAIN CITY MERCHANTS
131 N MAIN
BRYAN, OH 43506

EARTH FOOD CO-OP
CHERYL BROWN
1952 FREEMAN
TOLEDO, OH 43606

CHESTER FOOD CO-OP
L. JEFFREY
7484 CEDAR RD
CHESTERLAND, OH 44026

OBERLIN COMM FOOD CO-OP
JACQUES RUTZLEY
OBERLIN COLLEGE
BOX 2296
OBERLIN, OH 44074

OBERLIN GOOD FOOD CO-OP
C/O CO-OP BOOKSTORE
37 W. COLLEGE SC.
OBERLIN, OH 44074

PAINESVILLE FOOD CO-OP
JOHN UPDIKE & JERRY KING
ST. JAMES EPISCOPAL CHURCH
PAINESVILLE, OH 44077

FRUIT AND VEGATABLE CO-OP
NORTH PRESBYTERIAN CHURCH
4001 SUPERIOR
CLEVELAND, OH 44103

INNER CITY CO-OP
HOUGH AVE. UNITED CHURCH OF CHRIST
65 AND HOUGH
CLEVELAND, OH 44103
ROBERT EVANS 361-5984
FRED CRAIG 391-2150

FOOD C.O.O.P.
12408 EUCLID
CLEVELAND, OH 44106
(216)421-7654

COVENANT FOOD CO-OP
11205 EUCLID
CLEVELAND, OH 44106

GENESIS RESTAURANT
12-200 EUCLID
CLEVELAND, OH 44106

GLENVILLE AFRO-AMERICAN CO-OP
C/O AUDREY JETER
GLENVILLE OPPORTUNITY CENTER
1073 E. 105
CLEVELAND, OH 44108
(216)268-1600

NORTHWEST SIDE-FREMONT FOOD CO-OP
808 LITERARY
CLEVELAND, OH 44113
(216)771-1202/696-4407
DOT GRICE

METROPOLITAN CO-OP SERVICES, INC
METRO MEATS, INC.
2624 DETROIT AVE
CLEVELAND, OH 44113
(216)241-0864
MICHAEL BIBLER 781-5745

NEAR WEST SIDE-FREMONT FOOD CO-OP
3004 CLINTON
CLEVELAND, OH 44113
( )241-6523
JOANNE WASCO

GARDEN VALLEY FOOD CO-OP
7100 KINSMAN
CLEVELAND, OH 44120

BROADWAY FOOD CO-OP
4825 BROADWAY
CLEVELAND, OH 44127
SHARON WILLIAMS/781-2944-295

SCHADEN BUYING CLUB
10309 PARK HEIGHTS
GARFIELD HEIGHTS, OH 44130

CLARK-REDEEMER CO-OP
2970 W. 30TH ST
CLEVELAND, OH 44131

EUCLID FOOD CO-OP
101 E. 272ND
EUCLID, OH 44132

KENT FOOD CO-OP
228 GOUGLER
KENT, OH 44240

COMM ACTION COUNCIL FOOD CO-OP
230 WEST CENTER ST.
AKRON, OH 44302
(216)375-2118
LUCILLE DAVID

ROSY CHEEKS COMMUNITY STORE
JACKIE JOHNSTON
459 E. EXCHANGE
AKRON, OH 44304
(216)376-2750

WHOLE WHEAT & HONEY COOP
87 W. STATE STREET
AKRON, OH 44308
(216)376-8181

WISC FOOD CO-OP
224 S MARKET ST.
WOOSTER, OH 44691

HOLLYWOOD COMMUNITY CENTER
FOOD BUYING CLUB
101 WALNUT ST.
FRANKLIN, OH 45005
(513)746-2311
BOB VONDRELL

EAST END FOOD CO-OP (BC)
C/O CARTERS
2624 EASTERN
CINCINNATI, OH 45202

CINCINNATI FOOD CO-OP
245 W. MCMILLAN
CINCINNATI, OH 45219
(513)621-8569 M3-7,W3-9,SA10-5
J LUGENBILL/721-1753/1805 LANG 45210
W BROOMFIELD/651-3179/2338 STRATFORD

DIVINE LIGHT
520 HOWELL
CINCINNATI, OH 45220
(513)281-1160

COLUMBUS CO-OP
437 DELTA
CINCINNATI, OH 45226
MIKE/877-2217

GREENE COUNTY BUYING CLUB
132 N. DETROIT ST.
XENIA, OH 45385
(513)376-1351
LAVADA THORPE

REAL GOOD FOOD CO-OP
ANTIOCH COLLEGE UNION
RR #1
YELLOW SPRINGS, OH 45387

MIDDLE EARTH CO-OP
2101 RAVENSWOOD
DAYTON, OH 45406

THE ARC RESTAURANT
20 E. STATE
ATHENS, OH 45701
JIM CAMPBELL/614-593-7592
JO ANDRES

ATHENS ORGANIC FOOD COP
BOX 1094
ATHENS, OH 45701

COMMUNITY FOOD CO-OP STORE
C/O LIMA-ALLEN CY COMMUNITY A.C.
MEMORIAL HALL
ELM AND ELIZABETH ST.
LIMA, OH 45801
(419)222-5371
JOSEPH CLARK

INDIANA

NORTHSIDE FOOD CO-OP
46 TH AND WINTHROP
INDIANAPOLIS, IN 46205

DIVINE FOOD CO-OP
115 S. AUDUBON RD
INDIANAPOLIS, IN 46219
(317)352-1641
MARCIA CARROLL

PEACE AND FREEDOM FOOD CO-OP
TIM CURTAIN
471 STATE ST. #2
INDIANAPOLIS, IN 46229

INDIANAPOLIS CO-OP
1555 MAXINE
INDIANAPOLIS, IN 46240

RAINBOW GROCERY
ROB FRIEND
1011 E. WASHINGTON
SOUTH BEND, IN 46617
(219)282-1511

NO BALONEY
1125 W. THOMAS
S. BEND, IN 46625
(219)287-8406

PEOPLES BUYING CLUB
2502 WINTER ST.
FORT WAYNE, IN 46803
(219)456-7620 OR 672-3777

YE OLDE FOOD CO-OP
1232 CRESCENT
FT. WAYNE, IN 46805

PEOPLES PANTRY
BOB BUCHER
104 MAPLE STREET
N. MANCHESTER, IN 46962
JON BLICKENSTAFF
MARK SHIRKEY

PEOPLES FOOD CO-OP
2509 S. MAIN
NEW CASTLE, IN 47362

EARLAM EAT
REID BAILEY
BOX 31
RICHMOND, IN 47374

BLOOMINGTON FOOD CO-OP
RUSH ROBINSON
1407 S. LINCOLN
BLOOMINGTON, IN 47401
MERRY CUNNINGHAM/RT5 BOX 274

CLARK FIELD CO-OP
ST. JOHNS CHURCH
4617 MELLEMEADE
EVANSVILLE, IN 47713
(812)424-9261

TERRE HAUTE FOOD CO-OP
11 S. NINTH
TERRE HAUTE, IN 47803

SOUTH SIDE FOOD CO-OP
210 GREEN ST
LAFAYETTE, IN 47901

WEST SIDE FOOD CO-OP
335 N. WESTERN
WEST LAFAYETTE, IN 47906

MICHIGAN

GOOD EARTH CO-OP/BIRMINGHAM
COMMON GROUND CRISIS CENTER
1090 S. ADAMS
BIRMINGHAM, MI 48011
TED RICE/313-645-9676

HARVESTERS CO-OP
CARLYN CHATTERTON
24520 GLEN ORCHARD DR.
FARMINGTON, MI 48024
(313)477-5963

LAKE ORION FOOD CO-OP
C/O KAREN MOORE
1230 ORION RD.
LAKE ORION, MI 48035

MILFORD CO-OP/GREEN BAGGERS
MARION SCHOENING
312 CANAL
MILFORD, MI 48042

MT. CLEMENS FOOD CO-OP
JIM OKRAGKESKI
12 MURDOCK PL
MT. CLEMENS, MI 48043

OXFORD-ORION CO-OP
40 DENNISON
OXFORD, MI 48051

CARROT PATCH CO-OP
DORIS CHAPMAN
5786 CRESCENT DR.
PONTIAC, MI 48054
(313)682-6585

HOMINID SERVICES,INC
C/O PAT LYONS OR DOUG BROWN
1114 DORIS ROAD
PONTIAC, MI 48057
(313)373-9022 7A-9P
ROCHESTER

NEW AGE BAKERY AND BUYING CLUB
OKRA GLESKI'S
5309 LINDA
WARREN, MI 48092

YPSILANTI COMMUNITY INITIATIVE
707 1/2 W. CROSS #2
YPSILANTI, MI 48092

GREEN VALLEY CO-OP
JENNY HENRY
4169 LA FOREST
WATERFORD, MI 48095
(313)623-6113

SHADY ACRES
LIZ MORAY
2206 FOSS
ANN ARBOR, MI 48103

ANN ARBOR BAKERY
208 N. 4TH
ANN ARBOR, MI 48104

MICHIGAN FEDERATION OF FOOD CO-OPS
PEOPLES WHEREHOUSE
4111 JACKSON RD
ANN ARBOR, MI 48104

ANN ARBOR ITEMIZED PRODUCE CO-OP
BILL DONNER
1409 WELLS
ANN ARBOR, MI 48104

NEIGHBORHOOD FOOD CO-OP
GWEN JOHNSON
543 N. MAIN
ANN ARBOR, MI 48104
(313)769-3771/761-3142

PEOPLES FOOD CO-OP OF ANN ARBOR
212 N. 4TH AVE
ANN ARBOR, MI 48104
DAVID, CAROL, SHEILA, RUTH, ROB

ANN ARBOR PEOPLE'S PRODUCE
PEGGY TAUBE
JULIE CARROLL
1006 LINCOLN
ANN ARBOR, MI 48104

ARROWHEAD HILLS CO-OP
BOB BENEDICT
2675 ARROWHEAD TRAIL
ANN ARBOR, MI 48105

PONTIAC HEIGHTS
ELLEN PSEKE
2733 ARROWOOD TRAIL
ANN ARBOR, MI 48105

FAMILY GROUP
BERT COPPOCK
2329 STONE DR
ANN ARBOR, MI 48105

NOAHS PANTRY
1418 DIX-TOLEDO RD
LINCOLN PARK, MI 48146

EL CHEAPO FOOD CO-OP
32044 MAINE
LIVONIA, MI 48150

CASS CORRIDOR
4200 CASS
DETROIT, MI 48203
(313)831-5036

THREE FOR THREE FOOD CO-OP
150 BELMONT
DETROIT, MI 48203
(313)867-5855, DONNA 821-7611

MASJIC
ABU HANIF
6412 VAN BUREN
DETROIT, MI 48204

BIG RAPIDS TRUCKING CO.
6100 VERNOR
DETRIOT, MI 48209

EARTH CENTER RESTAURANT
11464 MITCHELL
HAMTRAMCK, MI 48212
(313)891-9746

RAINBOW GROCERY
20534 W. 7-MILE RD
DETROIT, MI 48219
(313)535-1490
PHIL BOMARITO

GRAND BLANC
ARMAND HOAVE
1159 HANNAH
GRAND BLANC, MI 48439

BEEHIVE CO-OP
WILLIAM RENDEL
15566 FALK RD
HOLLY, MI 48442

KARMA CO-OP
COURTNEY KING
503 JEFFERSON
SAGINAW, MI 48601

YELLOW STALK CO-OP
RT 1, BOX 18
LAKE, MI 48632

ANSAR CO-OP
14592 SUSSEX
DETROIT, MI 482XX

FEMINIST FOOD CO-OP
RESOURCE CENTER
2445 8-MILE RD
DETROIT, MI 482XX

KARMA MIDLAND
LANCE & LYNN SIMPSON
3612 LAWNDALE DR
MIDLAND, MI 48640
(517)835-1139

MIDLAND CO-OP
KATHY & L. BOERKE
306 N. MEADOW BROOK
MIDLAND, MI 48640
(517)835-1139

KARMA CO-OP OF BAY CITY
PAY HAYNER
1184 W. HAMPTON RD
ESSEXVILLE, MI 48732
DAVE ROUSSE ( )893-6529
KAREN 893-6529 DAYS,894-2087 NITES

BELDING FOOD CO-OP
STEVE JOHNSON
5346 BELDING
BELDING, MI 48809

INDEPENDENT PURCHASING ASSN
320 STUDENT SERVICES BLDG
MICHIGAN STATE UNIVERSITY
EAST LANSING, MI 48824

LANSING AREA FOOD CO-OP
606 S. WALNUT
LANSING, MI 48910

RAINBOW GROCERY
231 S. HOSMER
LANSING, MI 48912

WOLF MOON FOOD CO-OP
2011 E. MICHIGAN
LANSING, MI 48912
(517)482-0038
ALEX,TOREY, JOEL, CHRIS

DIVINE FOOD CO-OP
305 STUART ST
KALAMAZOO, MI 49007
BILL PATTERSON

PEOPLE'S FOOD CO-OP OF KALAMAZOO
141 BURR OAK
KALAMAZOO, MI 49001
(616)342-5686 M-SAT 11-7
MARIE GREENING/323-2762/7943 S 25 49002
JO ANN MARTIN

WILD BILLS WALK ON WATER BAKERY
143 BURR OAK
KALAMAZOO, MI 49001
(616)342-5686 7-SA/8-5
GENE JANIK/342-4488

BATTLE CREEK PEOPLES FOOD CO-OP
455 W. DICKMAN
BATTLE CREEK, MI 49015

BATTLE CREEK CO-OP
MICHIGAN SELF HELP ACTION
21 GREENWOOD
BATTLE CREEK, MI 49017

BENTOTN HARBOR, FOOD CO-OP
JIM KING
3925 US 33 N
BENTON HARBOR, MI 49022

ADRIAN FOOD CO-OP
848 HOCH AVE
ADRIAN, MI 49221

ALBION FOOD CO-OP
JACK HICKS
927 N. EATON
ALBION, MI 49225

ALBION VARIETY FOOD CO-OP
209 W. CENTER
ALBION, M 49224

HILLSDALE FAMILY FOOD CO-OP
388 W. BACON RT 4
HILLSDALE, MI 49242
HELENE/439-1300

MOUNTAIN PEOPLE
BARB HUNTER
SANDY ACRES
RT 2
REMUS, MI 49340

HOLLAND FOOD CO-OP
RICH WILLIAMS
HOLLAND, MI 49423

HOLLAND FOOD CO-OP
COLIN BRAAT
2374 MAKSHBA TRAIL
MACAATAWA, MI 49434

GOOD EARTH CO-OP/ALLENDALE
JAYMI LEE
12317 LINDEN
MARNE, MI 49435
(616)677-3273

SAUGATUCK FOOD CO-OP
SANDY WENK
GENERAL DELIVERY
SAUGATUCK, MI 49453
KAY PEHLDPHS/857-4129

HAPPY FARMER CO-OP
141 MICHIGAN
SHELBY, MI 49455

WESTOWN FOOD CO-OP
149 BUTTERWORTH
GRAND RAPIDS, MI 49504

GRAND RAPIDS FOOD CO-OP
EPWORTH MEHTODIST
600 LAFAYETTE NE
GRAND RAPIDS, MI 49505

EASTOWN FOOD CO-OP
1440 WEALTHY SE
GRAND RAPIDS, MI 49506
JIM PONGONES/(616)454-8838

MESICK CORNUCOPIA CO-OP
HARRY LAWRENCE
RT 1 BOX 22
MESICK, MI 49668

GRAYLING CO-OP GROUP
JIM SIGVET
RT 1, BOX 1388
GRAYLING, MI 49738

GRAIN TRAIN NATURAL FOODS CO-OP
311 1/2 E. MITCHELL #8
PETOSKEY, MI 49770
(616)347-2381 BILL, TIM

COUNTRY HEARTH CO-OP
416 N. STATE
ST. IGNACE, MI 49781

MARQUETTE ORGANIC FOOD CO-OP
GINNY THOMPSON
230 W. OHIO ST.
MARQUETTE, MI 49855
(906)249-3567,228-8232 5-11

MUNISING CO-OP
JIM MCMAHAN
BOX 431
MUNISING, MI 49862

ORYANA FOOD CO-OP
123 1/2 W FRONT
TRAVERSE CITY, MI 49684
R. ROTANCKER/113 STATE

KEWWWNAW CO-OP
1029 ETHEL ST.
HANCOCK, MI 49930

KEEWENAW CO-OP
409 SHELDON
HOUGHTON, MI 49931

KARMA CAFE
409 SHELDON
HOUGHTON, MI 49931

HARVESTORS CO-OP
DALE & MARIE LAPOINTE
19353 SEMINOLE
REDFORD TOWNSHIP, MI

IOWA

MUTUAL AID FOOD ASSN
114 DES MOINES
AMES, IA 50010

GRINNELL CONSUMER CO-OP
QUIET HOUSE
1127 PARK ST
GRINNELL, IA 50112
DAN STEIN

DES MOINES FOOD CO-OP
RUFUS JONES HOUSE
1535 11TH STREET
DES MOINES, IA 50314
(515)243-5761 MARY DISNEY
LYNN PRICE,DAN MELBOURN/262-6846/1310 7T
MARILYN SNYDER/277-7463/518 28TH

ALGONA BUYING CLUB
MEL MERTZ
RR2
ALGONA, IA 50511

COTTON-TOP CO-OP
VANCE JENISON
202 E MAIN ST
CEDAR FALLS, IA 50613

GREEN ISLAND CO-OP
JOHN HONNEYWELL
RR1
GREEN ISLAND, IA 52010

ONEOTA COMMUNITY CO-OP
1007 PAINE ST.
DECORAH, IA 52101
LEE VANDERLAAN/(319)382-2047/RR #3
SUSAN WARREN PALM/RR3

BLOOMING PRAIRIE WAREHOUSE
529 S GILBERT
IOWA CITY, IA 52240

NEW PIONEER CO-OP SOCIETY
529 S GILBERT
IOWA CITY, IA 52240
(319)337-4471

GOOD NEWS GENERAL STORE
100 16TH AVE SW
CEDAR RAPIDS, IA 52404

EDEN NATURAL FOODS
1605 HARRISON
DAVENPORT, IA 52803
(319)323-0731

WISCONSIN

HARTFORD FOOD CO-OP
29 S MAIN
HARTFORD, WI 53027

C.S.C. CO-OP FOOD CLUB
STUDENT LIFE
U. OF WISCONSIN-PARKSIDE
KENOSHA, WI 53140

KENOSHA FOOD CO-OP
5411 23RD AVE
KENOSHA, WI 53140

BITS & PIECES CORNER CO-OP
487 W. MAIN
WAUKESHA, WI 53186
(414)544-9130

FULL CIRCLE
GEORGE JOHNSON
645 E. GENEVA
WILLIAMS BAY, WI 53191

MILWAUKEE CO-OP FOODS
3145 W LISBON AVE
MILWAUKEE, WI 53208
(414)344-2332
DAVID KORESSEL

GORDON PARK CO-OP FOODS
821 E. LOCUST
MILWAUKEE, WI 53212
(414)263-9126

ONF CO-OP
833 E. LOCUST
MILWAUKEE, WI 53212

HEAD START FOOD CO-OP
1315 N. WISCONSIN AVE.
RACINE, WI 53402
(414)632-5193 CARL HUBBARD

RACINE ALTERNATIVE HIGH SCHOOL
620 LAKE AVENUE
RACINE, WI 53403
(414)632-3158 RIC GLINES

BELOIT COLLEGE FOOD CO-OP
BELOIT COLLEGE
BOX 219, B-708 CLANY ST.
BELOIT, WI 53511

QUERCUS ALBA BAKERY
121 S. MAIN
OREGON, WI 53575
(608)835-5816

RICHLAND BUYERS CO-OP
CAP
COURTHOUSE 2ND FLOOR
RICHLAND CENTER, WI 53581

GOOD KARMA
311 STATE ST. UNDERGROUND
MADISON, WI 53703
(608)251-0555

MAIN COURSE LTD
306 N BROOKS ST.
MADISON, WI 53703

MIFLIN STREET CO-OP
32 N. BASSETT
MADISON, WI 53715
(608)251-9800
MICHAEL LILLIE 8-10 M-SA/10-10 SU

NATURES BAKERY
1101 WILLIAMSON ST.
MADISON, WI 53715

WHOLE EARTH LEARNING COMMUNITY
817 E. JOHNSON ST
MADISON, WI 53715
(608)256-8828 F-M/10-7 T,TH/10-830
DICK MCLEESTER/255-5843/844 WILLIAMSON
BRYAN BUCKER/241-2987/1026 TROY

WILLIAMSON ST. GROCERY
1014 WILLIAMSON ST.
MADISON, WI 53715

EAGLE HEIGHTS CO-OP
611 EAGLE HEIGHTS
MADISON, WI 53715
(608)238-2166

COMMON MARKET
1335 GILSON ST.
MADISON, WI 53715

GREEN LANTERN EATING CO-OP
604 UNIVERSITY AVE
MADISON, WI 53715

INTRA-COMMUNITY COOPERATIVE
1335 GILSON ST.
MADISON, WI 53715

WHOLE EARTH
101 E. ELM
RIVER FALLS, WI 54022
M-TH/1-5 F/1-7 SA/10-5
DEBBIE BROADFOOT/(715)425-2898/311 N LEW
ROGER BROWNE/425-5874/RT 1

MENOMINEE COUNTY CO-OP
KESHENA, WI 54135
(715)799-3500
WAYNE PECORE

N.E.W. WHOLE FOODS CO-OP
1264 E. MASON
GREENBAY, WI 54301

STEVENS POINT AREA FOOD CO-OP
2501 WELSLEY
STEVENS POINT, WI 54481
(715)341-1555 F12-7/SA10-4
RHONDA FORD/344-8942/1917 WATDRST
KAREN CARLESON/341-5880/220 W R DR

LACROSSE PEOPLES CO-OP
212 N 14TH ST
LACROSSE, WI 54601

ETTRICK CO-OP
RT 2 BOX 3
ETTRICK, WI 54627

CONSUMERS COOPERATIVE OF EAU CLAIRE
2221 HIGHLAND AVE
EAU CLAIRE, WI 54701

EAU CLAIRE CO-OP
MIKE MCKENLEY
1028 CUMMINGS
EAU CLAIRE, WI 54701

CONNERVILLE FOOD CO-OP
WINDING ROAD FARM
BOYCEVILLE, WI 54725
PAUL, RICE, TONY THOM, HELEN

MENOMONIE BUYING CLUB
JIM MCELHATTON
1209 8TH ST
MENOMONIE, WI 54751

SHANGRA-LA BUYING CLUB
KATY PLUNKETT
RT 1 BOX 143
STOCKHOLM, WI 54769

CCC
BOX 485
ASHLAND, WI 54806

CHEQUAMEGON BAY AREA BUYING SERVICE
BOX 472
ASHLAND, WI 54806

RICE LAKE BUYING CLUB
JERRY GOBLER
119 S. WISCONSIN OR 35 S. MAIN
RICE LAKE,WI 54868
LYNN S KRUSKY

SUPERIOR FOOD BUYING CLUB
904 TOWER AVE
SUPERIOR, WI 54880
(715)394-9758
FERN BRUNNER

GOOD LIFE NATURAL FOODS
600 N. MAIN
OSHKOSH, WI 54901

FOX RIVER VALLEY CO-OP
217 E. COLLEGE
APPLETON, WI 54911

MINNESOTA

UNITED CO-OP
MARY HUBBS
7380 HEYDRUM
COTTAGE GROVE, MN 55016

NATURES NOOK
7 NW 3RD ST
FARIBAULT, MN 55021

FOREST LAKE BUYING CLUB
RALPH & FERN DOEBBLING
8360 202 DN ST N
FOREST LAKE, MN 55023

STEELE COUNTY BUYING CLUB
C/O DODGE-STEELE-WASECA CTZ ACT CNL
OWATONNA, MN 55060
(507)451-9100
SIDNEY GLOCK

COMMONPLACE RESTAURANT
374 SELBY
ST. PAUL MN 55102

SELBY FOOD CO-OP
516 SELBY
ST. PAUL, MN 55102
(612)227-1453

MERRI-GROVE CO-OP
1675 SELBY
ST. PAUL, MN 55104
(612)644-7033

SAINT ANTHONY PARK FOODS
1435 N. CLEVELAND
ST. PAUL, MN 55108

GREEN GRASS GROCERY
928 RAYMOND
ST. PAUL, MN 55113
(612)646-6667

LAKE REGION ENTERPRISES
ANNANDALE, MN 55302
(612)274-5632
MS. LOUIS HILL

GLENCOE SAVERS BUYING CLUB
GLENCOE, MN 55336
(612)864-3827

PRIOR LAKE BUYING CLUB
MS DEAN FINKY
RR3
PRIOR LAKE, MN 55372

CLEAR LAKE FOOD BUYING CLUB
WATKINS, MN 55389
(612)764-2185/764-2795
DELORES FABER

GOOD GRITS
1343 LASALLE
MINNEAPOLIS, MN 55403
(612)333-9984

MILL CITY CO-OP
2552 BLOOMINGTON AVE S.
MINNEAPOLIS, MN 55404
(612)721-2072

NEW RIVERSIDE CAFE
CEDAR & RIVERSIDE
MINNEAPOLIS, MN 55404

NORTH COUNTRY CO-OP
2129 RIVERSIDE
MINNEAPOLIS, MN 55404

PEOPLE'S WAREHOUSE
123 E 26TH ST
MINNEAPOLIS, MN 55405

POWDERHORN CO-OP
3440 BLOOMINGTON AVE S.
MINNEAPOLIS, MN 55404
(612)724-9681

PRODUCE COLLECTIVE
EMMA EVECHILD
1205 E 21ST
MINNEAPOLIS, MN 55404

RED STAR APOTHECARY
123 E. 26TH ST
MINNEAPOLIS, MN 55404

RED STAR MILL
2601 STEVENS AVE S
MINNEAPOLIS, MN 554XX

SCOOP
PEOPLES WAREHOUSE
123 E. 26TH ST.
MINNEAPOLIS, MN 55404

SEWARD CO-OP
2201 FRANKLIN AVE.E
MINNEAPOLIS, MN 55404
(612)724-9681

WHOLE FOODS
2500 1ST AVE OR 2502 S. 1ST AVE
MINNEAPOLIS, MN 55404

DIVINE FOOD CO-OP
734 E. LAKE ST. #200
MINNEAPOLIS, MN 55407

PEOPLE'S COMPANY
1534 E. LAKE
MINNEAPOLIS, MN 55407

THE BEANERY
3008 LYNDALE AVE. S.
MINNEAPOLIS, MN 55409

GARDEN BAKERY
820 W. 36TH ST
MINNEAPOLIS, MN 55409

NORTHSIDE FOOD COMMUNITY
1111 W. BROADWAY
MINNEAPOLIS, MN 55411
(612)522-2236

SOUTHEAST CO-OP
1023 EIGHTH ST. SE
MINNEAPOLIS, MN 55414

YORK CO-OP
10409 YORK AVE, SO
BLOOMINGTON, MN 55431

BREAD OF LIFE COMMUNITY
2549 NW 103RD AVE
COON RAPIDS, MN 55433

NUTRITION STUDY GROUP
EMILE COLLINS
8816 MORRIS RD
BLOOMINGTON, MN 55437

COOK COUNTY BUYING CLUB
BOX 15
GRAND MARAIS, MN 55604

COOK BUYERS CLUB
RT 1 BOX 163
ANGORA, MN 55703

HURDS HEALTH HAVEN
RT1 BOX 86A
CHISHOLM, MN 55719

NORTH WOODS WHOLE FOODS
6 W. SHERIDAN
ELY, MN 55731

HIBBING BUYING CLUB
STAR RT 4,BOX 114A
HIBBING, MN 55746
JIM CARTIER

J.I.B. WHOLE FOODS CO-OP
BOX 156
NASHWAUK, MN 55769

VIRGINIA BUYING CLUB
PAT WEIR
5 MORE DR.
VIRGINIA, MN 55792

COMMUNITY FOOD STORE
307 S. BROAD
MANKATO, MN ?????

MIDLAND COOPERATIVES
FOOD AND CLOTHING DEPT
AXEL LAINE
217 LAKE AVE. S.
DULUTH, MN 55802

WHOLE FOODS COMMUNITY CO-OP
LORENA GOTHARD
631 E 8TH ST
DULUTH, MN 55805
(218)727-9855
MURIEL ENGSTROM/722-5036/231 W 5TH

LA CRESCENT BUYING CLUB
RTE 2 PO BOX 152
LA CRESCENT, MN 55947
(507)895-4785
MS. FRANK HARRIS

SPRING VALLEY BUYING CLUB
SPRING VALLEY, MN 55975

FAMINE FOODS
120 E. 2ND
WINONA, MN 55987
LIZ & DAVE STERLING/RR2/BOX 82/MABEL
SUE SATLEL/1402 W 6TH/452-9672

RIVERBEND CAFE
3RD & MAIN
WINONA, MN 55987

WINONA BUYING CLUB
723 E. 4TH ST.
WINONA, MN 55987
MS. JEROME ROBERTS

WINTER GREEN COMMUNITY CO-OP
103 N. BROADWAY
ALBERT LEA, MN 56007
(507)373-0386
SARA AIKENS

NATURAL FOODS CO-OP
EDGAR & ELLEN MOREY
RT 1 BOX 25 A
MAPLETON, MN 56065

WASECA COUNTY BUYING CLUB
WASECA COMMUNITY CENTER
WASECA, MN 56093
(207)835-4119
RALPH SUTLIEF

FAMILY FOOD CO-OP
CHARLES HYRD
413 MASON
MARSHALL, MN 56258

PENNY PINCHERS BUYING CLUB
OLIVIA, MN 56277
(612)523-2125
MS. RAY MINKLE

ST. CLOUD ORGANIC FOOD CO-OP
4396 1ST AVE S
ST. CLOUD, MN 56301
(612)253-2131 MTTHF/12-530 W/12-8 SA/4-6
JIM BOLTON/685-8350/RR2 COLD SPRING 5632
ROGER DAHLIN/252-8076/RR1 KIMBALL

RISING MOON CO-OP
RT 1
AITKIN, MN 56431

SWAN VALLEY CO-OP
BOX 9
LEADER, MN 56462

STAPLES PEOPLES PANTRY
RR2
STAPLES, MN 56479

GOOD FOODS STORE
LENGBY, MN 56651
(218)668-3351/3655

JOHN SALMI MEMORIAL CO-OP
LAKE CABETOBAMA
RAY, MN 56669

SOUTH DAKOTA

HARVEST MOON FOODS
13 MARKET ST
VERMILLION, SD 57069

COOPERATIVE BUYING CLUB INC.
1024 QUINCY ST.
RAPID CITY, SD 57701
(605)342-9531
HOLLEY LAMB

STURGIS BUYING CLUB
MEADE COUNTY COMMUNITY CENTER
1130 MAIN ST.
STURGIS, SD 57785
(605)347-2646
DAN PETERSON/BOULDER CANYON RT
TERRY HABERLIN/1937 AMES/SPEARFISH

E. DAKOTA CO-OP
PETER DYE
GARRETSON, SD 57030

NORTH DAKOTA

FOOD REALIZATION CO-OP
BRUCE BELL
RR 1
FARGO, ND 58102

FOOD CO-OP OF GRAND FORKS
1202 2ND AVE N
GRAND FORKS, ND 58201

CARRINGTON BUYING CLUB
CHRIS LEECE
RR 1
CARRINGTON, ND 58421

PURE PRAIRIE GENERAL STORE
110 8TH ST. SE
MINOT, ND 58701

MONTANA

BILLINGS CO-OP
SAT NAM SHOP
2615 MONTANA
BILLINGS, MT 59101

FRIENDSHIP CENTER MEAT BUYING CLUB
1503 GALLATIN ST.
HELENA, MT 59601
(406)442-6800

BOZEMAN CO-OP
BILL NELL
321 N. TRACY
BOZEMAN, MT 59715
PATTY/25S. WALLACE

FREDDYS FEED & READ
1221 HELEN
MISSOULA, MT 59801

THE GOOD FOOD STORE
118 W. MAIN
MISSOULA, MT 59801
(406)728-5823 M-S 11-6
JEFF NORTHFIELD/527 RIVER ST.
MARCIA & CAROL HERRIN/504 N. 2ND ST.

MISSOULA CONSUMERS CO-OP
716 DICKENS
MISSOULA, MT 59801
AL WATSON/728-9755

THE NEW LITTLE FOOD CO-OP
BOX 854
LIBBY, MT 59923
MARSHA ALEXANDER, MARCI MOLES

LIBBY CO-OP
RT3, BOX 1636
LIBBY, MT 59923

FLATHEAD FOOD CO-OP
345 PARK
WHIETFISH, MT 59937
(406-862-3958

ILLINOIS

HOFFMAN ESTATES CO-OP
JOAN MARIE WERMES
THE TRIB
400 LAKE COOK RD
DEERFIELD, IL 60015

GOOD PEOPLES
TANYA KEATON
1242 WHITE ST.
DES PLAINES, IL 60018

MACLANE FOGG CO-OP
1000 ALLASON RD
MUNDELEIN, IL 60060

ECCLESIA FELLOWSHIP
3305 EVERGREEN
WAUKEGAN, IL 60085

NEW LIFE
PETER KNOBEL
1510 CENTRAL
WILMETTE, IL 60091

DUCK SOUP COUP
LOIS TUCKER
134 1/2 LINCOLN HWY
DEKALB, IL 60115

ELGIN CO-OP
MAIGNON BAITY
1933-C PEACHTREE LN
ELGIN, IL 60120

FAR OUT WEST CO-OP
JOYCE BODEEN
200 E. ROOSEVELT, BOX 203
LOMBARD, IL 60148

MAYWOOD BUYING CLUB
JOE RATLEY
151 MADISON
BELLEWOOD, IL 60104
(   )343-4100

NEAR WEST SUBURBAN CO-OP
2151 W. MADISON
BELLEWOOD, IL 60104
MAGGIE KINGSDAD

SCHAUMBURG CO-OP
BILL ROSENTHAL
700 HUNTINGTON LN
SCHAUMBURG, IL 60172

NORTH CHICAGO
VERLAINE RIEK
2712 HARRISON
EVANSTON, IL 60201
(312)491-0039

POOR RICHARDS
BERT SCHOMER
1019 SEWARD
EVANSTON, IL 60202
DOROTHY NAGELBACH/475-7063
STEVEN & DIANE DUBEY0677-5204

MIXED NUTS
PEGGY DALEIDEN
1235 HINMAN
EVANSTON, IL 60202

REBA PLACE FELLOWSHIP
727 REBA PLACE
EVANSTON, IL 60202

FOREST PARK CO-OP IN OAK PARK
SUE & JOHN FERGUSON
105 WASHINGTON BLVD
OAK PARK, IL 60302

SOUTH OAK PARK CO-OP
C. MILLER
1009 S. ELMWOOD AVE
OAK PARK, IL 60304

CHICAGO HEIGHTS
EUNICE JONES
145 E. 14TH ST
CHICAGO HEIGHTS, IL 60411

HARVEY CO-OP
NELDA CHILDRESS, HELEN JERZ
HARVEY NEIGHBORHOOD SERVICE ORGNZN
14726 S. OAKLEY
HARVEY, IL 60426

METRO BUYING CLUB
JOHN TOMASKO
709 WILCOX
JOLIET, IL 60435

PARK FOREST
DOROTHY COLSON
21 KROTIAK
PARK FOREST, IL 60466
(312)481-7970

AURORA FEED THE HUNGRY
MARIE WILKINSON
648 NORTH VIEW
AURORA. IL 60506

SMALL PLANET
807 B OGDEN AVE
DOWNERS GROVE, IL 60515

RECOOP
ANN BIECHLER
701 HITCHCOCK
LISLE, IL 60532

RIVERSIDE CO-OP
JUDY MARQUANDT
369 OLMSTEAD
RIVERSIDE, IL 60546

FOOD CO-OP PROJECT
LOOP COLLEGE
64 E. LAKE ST.
CHICAGO, IL 60601

GREATER ILLINOIS PEOPLES
COOPERATIVE WAREHOUSE
FOOD CO-OP PROJECT
64 E. LAKE ST
CHICAGO, IL 60601
(312)269-8101
DAVID, TOM, JULIO, DEBBIE

DIVINE LIGHT MISSION
220 S. STATE #726
CHICAGO, IL 60604
(312)939-9194
CARL

BEACON HOUSE
IDELLA TYLER
1440 S. ASHLAND
CHICAGO, IL 60608
(312)243-8100-7

FEED THE HUNGRY
CURTIS MILLER
108 S. WATER MARKET
CHICAGO, IL 60608

WENTWORTH GARDENS COMMUNITY STORE
3750 S. WELLS
CHICAGO, IL 60609
(312)791-8738
HALLEI AMY/WA4-0416
MARY WILLIAMS/624-0764

CHURCH OF THE ASCENSION
1133 N. LASALLE
CHICAGO, IL 60610

ST. MALACHY CHURCH
RICHARD EHRENS
2248 W. WASHINGTON
CHICAGO, IL 60612
(312)733-1068

NEAR NORTH FOOD CO-OP
ST. THERESA CHURCH HALL
1950 N. KENMORE
CHICAGO, IL 60614

HYDE PARK COOPERATIVE SOCIETY
GLADYS SCOTT
1526 E. 55TH ST
CHICAGO, IL 60615

HYDE PARK DISTIRBUTION CENTER
57TH AND UNIVERSTIY
CHICAGO, IL 60615

ST. BONIFACE FOOD CO-OP
921 NOBLE
CHICAGO, IL 60622

LITTLE BROTHERS OF THE POOR
BELLE WHALEY
3745 W. OGDEN
CHICAGO, IL 60623
(312)522-2644

PARENT-CHILD CENTER
KAREN IVEY
3121 W. JACKSON
CHICAGO, IL 60624
(312)533-3350

LAWNDALE FOOD CO-OP
3324 W. ROOSEVELT
CHICAGO, IL 60624
(312)722-0240,826-8180

HARVEST CO-OP
ROBERTA FISHMAN
7421 N. WOLCOTT
CHICAGO, IL 60626
(312)262-3691

SELF HELP ACTION CENTER
DOROTHY SHAVERS
11013 INDIANA
CHICAGO, IL 60628
(312)C04-4557

SUNRISE CO-OP
SUE ADAMOWSKI
6053 NEWBURG
CHICAGO, IL 60631

KOSHER CO-OP
HILLEL HOUSE, UNIV OF CHIC
5715 S. WOODLAWN
CHICAGO, IL 60637

SOUTH CO-OP
4840 S. DORCHESTER
CHICAGO, IL 60637

MEDILL AVE LUTHERAN CHURCH
4917 W. MEDILL
CHICAGO, IL 60639
CARL

UPTOWN FOOD CO-OP
4524 N. BROADWAY
CHICAGO, IL 60640

UPTOWN HULL HOUSE
4520 N. BEACON
CHICAGO, IL 60640
WARREN KMIEC/561-8033,334-0914,1293
STEVE GAG/334-8185,769-4432

LUTHERAN CHURCH OF REDEEMER
4900 W. BERENICE
CHICAGO, IL 60641
DELL

OUR SAVIOR
5155 W. BERTEAU
CHICAGO, IL 60641
DENNIS

BEVERLY CO-OP
EVE DUDEK
10338 S. BELL
CHICAGO, IL 60643

JCC CO-OP
3003 W. TOUHY
CHICAGO, IL 60645

HOLY ORDER OF MANS
GEN TEITELBAUM
2328 N. OAKLEY
CHICAGO, IL 60647
(312)278-0006

NORTHSIDE YMCA
DEBORAH GONZALES
2750 W. NORTH AVE
CHICAGO, IL 60647
(312)227-0111

SOUTH SHORE COMMUNITY CO-OP
SOUTH SHORE COMMUNITY CHURCH
7401 YATES
CHICAGO, IL 60649

LUTHERAN REDEEMER BUYING CLUB
1406 N. LARAMIE
CHICAGO, IL 60651
PHIL JOHNSON/637-1735
CARL JENSON/622-0443

BELMONT NATION
SECOND UNITARIAN CHURCH
656 W. BARRY
CHICAGO, IL 60657
BARBARA WARREN/248-0874
JUDY BURNBAUM/935-0234

BREAD SHOP
3400 N. HALSTED
CHICAGO, IL 60657

CENTRO LATINO
ALFREDO & LYDIA VALDEZ
3225 N. SHEFFIELD AVE
CHICAGO, IL 60657
(312)549-7550

RAINBOW GROCERY
946 W. WELLINGTON
CHICAGO, IL 60657

SHREE GANASHAS NUTRITIOUS
AND DELICIOUS F.C.
3002 N. SHEFFIELD
CHICAGO, IL 60657

CORNUCOPIA
BOX 2559
CHICAGO, IL 60690

FRIENDLY FOOD CO-OP
DORIS PETER
1217 MICHIGAN
ROCKFORD, IL 61102
(815)964-0716

WAY OF LIFE
1722 4TH
PERU, IL 61354
PAUL EBENER

TOMPKINS STREET CO-OP
488 W. TOMPKINS ST
GALESBURG, IL 61401
ARTIE WARD/342-3555
LOUANNA MARTINEZ/343-9772

MACOMB COMMUNITY CO-OP
C/O JOANN CARTWRIGHY
803 BOBBY AVE
MACOMB, IL 61455
SHERRY DAVIS/837-4147/627 E. CALHOUN

NORTHSIDE BUYERS CLUB
410 WAYNE
PEORIA, IL 61603
(309)676-5322 MARY K & SAM CONVER
JULIA PETERSON/676-5803

PEOPLE'S FOOD CO-OP
36 WHITES PL.
BLOOMINGTON, IL 61701

DICK-FREEMAN TRUCKING COLLECTIVE
204 S. ROOSEVELT
BLOOMINGTON, IL 61701

WHITEWOOD CO-OP
LAY-Z-J
COOKSVILLE, IL 61730
(309)725-3503
DAVE, DENNY CRAIG

THE FOOD CO-OP
202 S. LINCOLN
CHAMPAIGN, IL 61801
CYNDY FELTY/384-7114
GEORGE FINCH/367-6326

STRAWBERRY FIELDS
1310 W. MAIN
URBANA, IL 61801

HOMESTEAD COMMUNITY BAKERY
ST. JOSEPH, IL 61873

PEOPLES COOPERATIVE BUYING CLUB
1015 LIBERTY
E. ST.LOUIS, IL 62201
(618)271-4794
LEOLA HOLMES

GOOD EARTH
960 N. JORDAN
DECATUR, IL 62521

CARLINVILLE FOOD CO-OP
LARRY BUXBAUM
718 E. MAIN
CARLINVILLE, IL 62626
(217)854-4381

SPOON RIVER CO-OP
122 S. 4TH ST.
SPRINGFIELD, IL 62701
(217)523-3523

KING HARVEST FOOD CO-OP
LYNN KIENZLER
1441 N. 5TH STREET
SPRINGFIELD, IL 62702
(217)522-3541

SPRINGFIELD AND SANGAMON CNTY B.C.
1310 E. ADAMS ST.
SPRINGFIELD, IL 62703
(217)525-1117
EDNA GARNER

CARBONDALE CO-OP
GAIL
305 W. MAIN
CARBONDALE, IL 62901

MISSOURI

LACLEDE CO-OP
PEACOCK COMMUNITY CENTER
LACLEDE & EWING STREETS
ST. LOUIS, MO 63103
SUE PETERSON/535-8839

DEMUN COMMUNITY CENTER FOOD CO-OP
700 DEMUN
ST. LOUIS, MO 63105
JAN KEPCHAR, GORGEA

MIDWEST CO-OP ASSN
925 S. BEMISTON
ST. LOUIS, MO 63105

FOREST PARK CO-OP
4140 W. PINE
ST. LOUIS, MO 63108
NANCY BECK/535-9101
4389 LACLEDE

WEST PINE NEIGHBORS
4530 OAKLAND
ST. LOUIS, MO 63110
MARY GALLAGHER/652-0826

PEOPLES PRODUCE
5899 DELMAR
ST. LOUIS, MO 63112
HELEN GRIGSBY/862-5010
DENNY GOOCH 727-7096

SPRINGDALE CO-OP
LINCOLN FUQUA
7738 SPRINGDALE #7
ST. LOUIS, MO 63121
(314)383-8089

K-W CO-OP
346 LEE
KIRKWOOD, MO 63122
BERNICE WEHRMEYER/966-8515/201 COUCH

OLIVETTE CO-OP
DELCREST BUILDING
8350 DELCREST
ST. LOUIS, MO 63124
MARSHA BREGAN/997-0726

LIMIT AVENUE FOOD CO-OP
554 LIMIT
ST. LOUIS, MO. 63130
(314)721-1146WTH,9-5 F9-12 <725-7295 B4
CAROL SNYDER/725-7295/6255 CLEMENS
MIKE REYNOLDS/726-6284/ EASTGATE

SOUTHSIDE FOOD SERVICE
1301 S. 12TH
ST. LOUIS, MO
BRUCE/862-2832

WELLS-GOODFELLOS CO-OP
5625 WELLS AVE
ST. LOUIS, MO
MS. WHITE/385-8925

LOGAN FARM CO-OP
100 OLD FARMHOUSE RD
ST. CHARLES COUNTY, MO

WATER TOWER FOOD CO-OP
4522 N. 9TH STREET
ST. LOUIS, MO 63147
DICK HASS 534-5656

CAPE CO-OP
CAROL QUICK
126 A S. LOUISIANA
CAPE GIRARDEAU, MO 63701

HACE CO-OP SUPERMARKET
BOX 49
HOWARDVILLE, MO 63869
HENRIETTA GRANT/(314)688-5080

LIVE CENTER FOOD CO-OP
BRIAN MCINERNEY
915 W. 17TH ST.
KANSAS CITY, MO 64108

DIVINE FOOD CO-OP
15 E. 30TH ST
KANSAS CITY, MO 64109

REDSTAR FOOD CO-OP
3130 OLIVE
KANSAS CITY, MO 64109

CITY-WIDE GRAIN STORE
BOB WIRTH
4306 FOREST
KANSAS CITY, MO 64110
(816)561-0288

KANSAS CITY WAREHOUSE
3917 TROOST
KANSAS CITY MO 64110

WESTPORT CO-OP
ESTHER MARKUS
4830 CAMPBELL
KANSAS CITY, MO 64110
(816)931-8130
ELLEN BENJAMIN/4330 WALNUT 64111
3666 BELLVIEW

COLUMBIA COMMUNITY GROCERY
100 ORR
COLUMBIA, MO 65201
(314)442-2116 M,T,TH,F/10-6
BOB ROMAN/387-4571
RICH MCKEEVER/4422360

PAQUIN STREET CAFE
1100 PAQUIN ST.
COLUMBIA, MO 65201

SPRINGFIELD NATURAL FOODS CO-OP
BOX 1642
SPRINGFIELD, MO 65805
(417)866-2300/M-F/6-8 SA/12-4
DOUG TAYLOR/866-2300/1118 E BROWER #2
BOB SHAW/866-7841/800 S. CAMPBELL #6

KANSAS

WESTERN WYANDOTTE MINI MARKET
121 ALLCUTT ST.
BONNER SPRINGS, KS 66012
(913)HA2-5477
MIKE MCNEILY

FOOD CO-OP
1220 OHIO
LAWRENCE, KS 66044
JIM/843-6119

LAWRENCE FOOD CO-OP
1309 OHIO
LAWRENCE, KS 66044
VIC,TOM/843-7815

LAWRENCE MILK RUN
PAUL JOHNSON
788 LOCUST
LAWRENCE, KS 66044
( )841-5597
ROBIN, 1224 OHIO

PENN HOUSE
1035 PENNSYLVANIA
LAWRENCE, KS 66044

BETHEL-RIVERVIEW ACTN GRP B.C.
73 S. 7TH ST.
KANSAS CITY, KS 66101
(913)321-2508
MS. FRANCES COTTON

NORTHEAST ACTION GROUP BUYING CLUB
950 QUINDERO BLVD
KANSAS CITY, KS 66101
(913)DR1-0840

TOTAL ACTION GROUP BUYING CLUB
1620 S. 37TH ST.
KANSAS CITY, KS 66101
(913)HE2-7555
MS HELEN HARPER

RAINBOW FOODS
3950 RAINBOW
KANSAS CITY, KS 66103

MANHATTAN FOOD CO-OP
4 FM HOUSE
615 FAIRCHILD
MANHATTAN, KS 66502

TOPEKA FOOD CO-OP
834 WASHBURN
TOPEKA, KS 66606
(913)357-7650 M-F/10-9 S/12-6
CHARLES GARDINER/853-0873/2324 W 25
CARL SEAL/2525 SUNSET RD/66614

COMMUNITY FOOD PROGRAMS
573 S. WEST
WICHITA, KS 67213
FRED JOHNSON

PARSONS BUYERS CLUB
2530 1/2 MAIN ST.
PARSONS, KS 67357
(316)421-2060
NAOMI LONG

NEBRASKA

CORNHUSKERS CO-OP
1319 R. ST.
LINCOLN, NB 68501

STARSEED FOOD CONSPIRACY
PRUDENCE GADLER
2928 SOUTH ST.
LINCOLN, NB 68503

LOUISIANA

OCTUPUS
CENTRAL CITY E.O.C.
2020 JACKSON
NEW ORLEANS, LA 70113

COMMUNITY CO-OP
1038 RAMPART
NEW ORLEANS, LA 701XX

CAJUN CO-OP
PELLUCIDAR
117 E. UNIVERSITY AVE
LAFAYETTE, LA 70501

ARKANSAS

UPSTAIRS FOOD
BOX 5009
LITTLE ROCK, AR 72205
CYNTHIA EVANS

EUREKA SPRINGS FOOD CO-OP
4 N. MAIN
EUREKA SPRINGS, AR 72632

OZARK FOOD CONSPIRACY
347 N. WEST
FAYETTEVILLE, AR 72701

ARKANSAS FOOD CO-OP
306N VANCOUVER
RUSSELLVILLE, AR 72801
DUNCAN CAMPBELL

OKLAHOMA

LONE WOLF CO-OP
MARK CHALOM
214 W. SYMMES
NORMAN, OK 73069
RITA MAUPIN/2808 S. RYAN B-13

LOVELIGHT
755 JENKINS
NORMAN, OK 73069

BETHLEHEM COMMUNITY CENTER
937 NE 6TH
OKLAHOMA CITY, OK 73105
(405)236-5939

WESLEY COMMUNITY CENTER
431 SW 11TH
OKLAHOMA CITY, OK 73125
(405)236-0521

TULSA FOOD CO-OP
BOX 1072
TULSA, OK 74101

TEXAS

DALLAS FOOD CO-OP
ELLIE RICHARDSON
4502 RIDGE
DALLAS, TX 75203

COOPERATION
5423 DRUID LN
DALLAS, TX 75209

HOUSTON FOOD CO-OP
915 WELCH
HOUSTON, TX 77006
(713)529-6444
WAYNE VOGEL

WOODY HILLS FOOD STORE
1015 W. LYNN
AUSTIN, TX 78703

AUSTIN COMMUNITY PROJECT
1602 W 12TH
AUSTIN, TX 78703

CLARKSVILLE BAKERY
1013 WEST LYNN
AUSTIN, TX 78703

DELLWOOD FOOD CO-OP
PAT TERENTEAU
1408A ASHWOOD
AUSTIN, TX ?????

SATTVA
2434 GUADALUPE
AUSTIN, TX 78705

THE FOOD CO-OP
KATHY & TERRY DUBOISE
807 W 28 1/2
AUSTIN, TX 78707
(512)477-5849

THE FOOD CO-OP
DENNIS FORTASSIN
THE ARK
2000 PEARL ST.
AUSTIN, TX 78705
DEBBIE MONAS/2115 W. 10TH/78703

THE AVENUES
4115 GUADALUPE
AUSTIN, TX 78751

NATURAL FOOD CO-OP
6282 DONIPHAN
EL PASO, TX 79932

COLORADO

DIVINE LIGHT MISSION
DIVINE FOOD COORDINATOR
MARK RETZLOFF
BOX 532
DENVER, CO 80201

COMMON MARKET FOOD CO-OP
1100 CHAMPA
DENVER, CO 80204

RAINBOW GROCERY
2260 E. COLFAX
DENVER, CO 80206
(303)320-1664
DAVE RICHARD

CLARE GARDENS BUYING CLUB
2626 OSCEOLA
DENVER, CO 80212
AL JOHNSON

CARNIVAL CAFE
1843 BROADWAY
BOULDER, CO 80302

PEOPLES FOOD CO-OP
862 1/2 CHEYENNE
GOLDEN, CO 80401

IDAHO SPRINGS FOOD CO-OP
BOX 1574
IDAHO SPRINGS, CO 80452
CHER EPPINGA/567-4258

LEADVILLE CO-OP
411 W. 8TH
LEADVILLE, CO 80461

FT. COLLINS FOOD CO-OP
700 W. MOUNTAIN ST
FT. COLLINS, CO 80521
STEVE JOHNSON/303-493-9506

GREELY FOOD CO-OP
4028 DENVER
EVANS, CO 80620

US TOO, INC
COOPERATIVE EXTENSION SERVICE
27 E. VERMIJO
COLORADO SPRINGS, CO 80903
(303)471-5764
LARRY DUNN

JUST US FOOD CO-OP
611 E. ESPRALA
COLORADO SPRINGS, CO 80907

ROCINANTE GROCERY STORE
GARDNER, CO 81040
(303)746-2981
MS. JOSEPHINE SANDERS

DURANGO FOOD CO-OP
78 FOLSOM PL.
DURANGO, CO 81301

DOVE CREEK FOOD CO-OP
DOVE CREEK, CO 81324

MOUNTAIN CO-OP
BOX 515
TELLURIDE, CO 81435

WYOMING

LARAMIE PEOPLES MARKET
111 IVINSON ST.
LARAMIE, WY 82070
(307)745-9753

IDAHO

JOLLY GOOD FELLOWS
1123 IDAHO
LEWISTON, ID 83201
(208)746-2384

MAGIC VALLYE CONSUMERS CO-OP
139 FIFTH
TWIN FALLS, IS 83301
(208)734-7826
MICHELLE MARKIEWICZ

FOOD CO-OP
COMMUNITY ACTION AGENCY
BOX 268
LEWISTON, ID 83501

BOISE CONSUMER CO-OP
1743 BROADWAY OR 1515 N 13TH
BOISE, ID 83706
(208)342-6652

EARTH FOODS INN
801 PARK BLVD
BOISE, ID 83706

COUNTRY GARDEN
BOX 694
BONNERS FERRY, ID 83805

CO-OP
C/O GOOD FOOD STORE
112 E. 2ND ST.
MOSCOW, ID 83843
DAVE NESBITT

UTAH

H STREET CO-OP
135 H ST.
SALT LAKE CITY, UT 84103

TODAHAIDEKANI NALYEHE BAHOOGHAN
BEEAHOOTA INC.
PO BOX 402
BLUFF, UT 84512
DAVID JONES

HALCHIITA NALYEHE BAHOOGAN INC.
PO BOX 45
MEXICAN HAT, UT 84531
(602)674-3219
JANET SLOAN

CAP CO-OP
MOAB, UT 84532

ARIZONA

DIVINE FOOD CO-OP
91 W. LYNWOOD
PHOENIZ, AZ 85003
(602)253-5155
ANDY HARRIS

SUNBOW
1401 E. SHERIDAN
PHOENIX, AZ 85006
(602)253-9800
MAX, JEFF

GENTLE STRENGTH CO-OP
38 E. 5TH
TEMPE, AZ 85281
(602)968-4831 M-SA/9-6

PEOPLES FOOD CO-OP
2219 E. APACHE
TEMPE, AZ 85281
(602)968-7526
ROBERT TASH

BISBEE GENERAL STORE CO-OP
BOX D-F
BISBEE, AZ 85603
M-SA 10-6
MAXINE, CHRIS

TAO FOOD CONSPIRACY
BOX 739
MT. LEMMON, AZ 85619
STEVEN GOLD, DONDELION, LOVE 22
SLEEPY HOLLOW RD #19

SANTA CRUZ VALLEY CO-OP
BOX 387
TUMACACORI, AZ 85640

GANJA GROCERS
FAYE DETLASS
6860 LACHNAD
TUCSON, AZ 85704
(602)297-4175

ALTERNATIVE WAYS
JOANNE PETERS
1037 E. BLACKLIDGE
TUCSON, AZ 85705
(602)624-8998

FLOWING WELLS CO-OP
BETTY PERKINS
4035 N. FLOWING WELLS
TUCSON, AZ 85705
(602)887-9489

FOOD CONSPIRACY
412 N. 4TH AVE.
TUCSON, AZ 85705
(602)624-4821 M-SU/9-8
VERONICA ANGEL/792-9301

LOOSE AZZA GOOSE
411 N 7TH
TUCSON, AZ 85705

PEOPLES WAREHOUSE
411 N 7TH
TUCSON, AZ 85705

OBLIVION CO-OP
1015 E 6TH ST.
TUCSON, AZ 85719
FRANK MILAN, MICHAEL, WENDY,
KATHLEEN, ERIC
(602)622-9873

NA-AH-TEE CO-OP INC.
INDIAN WELLS RURAL BRANCH
INDIAN WELLS, AZ 86031
(602)738-2356
MILLER NEZ

TOOD-DINE BENALYEBAHOWAN
PO BOX 410 STAR ROUTE
WINSLOW, AZ 86047
(602)686-6224
MARY ALICE RIGGS

NEW PROSPECT NATURAL FOODS CO-OP
236 MONTEZUMA ST
PRESCOTT, AZ 86301
LINDA/602-445-7740

ROUGH ROCK BLACK MESA ENTERPRISE
ROUGH ROCK DEMONSTRATION SCHOOL
BOX 97
CHINLE, AZ 86503
(602)728-3311-233
PETER BELCETTO

GANADO FEED AND CONSUMER CO-OP
PO BOX 767
GANADO, AZ 86505
(602)755-9500
CAROLYN BLUEHOUSE

DINEH-BI-NAA-YEI COOPERATIVE
PO BOX 566
PINON, AZ 86510
(602)674-5323
LOIS TSO

BLUE GAP FOOD COOPERATIVE
PINON, AZ 86515
KATIE CHEE

NEW MEXICO

ACOMA FOOD COOPERATIVE
PO BOX 67
SAN FIDEL, NM 87038
CONNIE GRUBE

BLESSED LIGHT JUICE CO
612 BROADWAY NE
ALBUQUERQUE, NM 87102
ERNISTO/505-873-2493

TORREON FOOD STAMP CO-OP ASSN
PO BOX 193
CUBA, NM 87103

BABAS FAMILY STORE
107 MESA SE
ALBUQUERQUE, NM 87106
RUDRA & DEVA/505-247-0991

SUNDANCE CO-OP RESTAURANT
127 HARVARD SE
ALBUQUERQUE, NM 87106

OSHA CO-OP
8812 4TH ST. NW
ALAMEDA, NM 87114
(505)898-7018
MARSHA,BARBARA W-SA/9-6

EASTERN NAVAHO FEED STORE CO-OP ASN
PO BOX 104
CROWNPOINT, NM 87313
(505)786-5697
WAYNE FREELAND

NEW LIFE COOPERATIVE
S. REILLY
207 JEFFERSON
SANTA FE, NM 87501
JANE, ERNIE/827-3141
LOLOMA NURSERY/RODEO RD

AMIGOS DE SALUD COOPERATIVA
BOX 453
EL PRADO, NM 87529
RUTH ANN/758-9972 MWF/10-4 SA/10-1230

OLD TOWN NATURAL FOODS
174 BRIDGE
LAS VEGAS, NV 87701

LITTLE CREEK CO-OP
20 E FEIGELSON BOX 143
ALTO, NM 88312
(505)336-4464

NEVADA

MIDWAY BUYERS CLUB
OLD JUNIOR HIGH SCHOOL
LEAD ST.
HENDERSON, NV 89015
(702)648-3280
MARVIN MITCHELL

COMMUNITY ACTION SELF-HELP
ECONOMIC OPPORTUNITY BOARD
OF CLARK COUNTY
960 W. OWENS
LAS VEGAS, NV 89106
(702)648-3280
MARVIN MITCHELL

ACTION OVER 55 COOPERATIVE
1632 YALE ST.
LAS VEGAS, NV 89107
(702)648-3280
MARVIN MITCHELL

CALIFORNIA

DIVINE FOOD SERVICE
316 N. LARCHMONT BLVD
LOS ANGELES, CA 90004
MICHAEL SHADWICK

WATTS CO-OP
MARIA SMALL WOOD
3925 S. RIDGELY DR.
LOS ANGELES, CA 90008

JEFFERSON BUYING CLUB
9TH AVE & JEFFERSON
LOS ANGELES, CA 90016
(   )734-2668
FLO KUSHNER/732-4051

CHICANO AMERICANOR SERVICIOS ASSN
BERT N. CORONA
214 ECHANDIA 11
LOS ANGELES, CA 90023

COMMUNITY SERVICE ORGANIZATION
TONY RIOS
2820 E. WHITTIER BLVD.
LOS ANGELES, CA 90023

WESTWOOD BAYIT
619 LANDFAIR
LOS ANGELES, CA 90024
VICKIE/213-478-9326
MOSHE HALFON/479-2578

BAHAI
MONA GRIESER
11548 ROCHESTER #4
LOS ANGELES, CA 90025

GOOD HERB & COOPORTUNITY
556 SANTA MONICA BLVD
LOS ANGELES, CA 90025
(213)479-7122
GEORGE TUCKER, EYTAN

SAFER WAY
TONY & DONNA ZERO
1545 BROCKTON
LOS ANGELES, CA 90025

CHINATOWN CO-OP
CLYDE LOO
1431 ALLISON AVE
LOS ANGELES, CA 90026
(213)628-9704

ECHO PARK/SILVERLAKE
1336 ECHO PARK AVE
LOS ANGELES, CA 90026
(213)661-6292
ART GOLDBERG (213)665-7625
VICTOR ROY/665-3898

SUNRISE NATURAL FOODS
3817 SUNSET BLVD.
LOS ANGELES, CA 90026

EAST HOLLYWOOD CO-OP
HERB ELSKY
4161 RUSSELL AVE
LOS ANGELES, CA 90027

IMMACULATE HEART CO-OP
C/O MARIE GAMBOA
IMMACULATE HEART COLLEGE
2021 N. WESTERN AV.
LOS ANGELES, CA 90027
MIKE KAHOE, 1844 N. KINGSLEY #11

SOUTHERN CALIF COOPERATING COMMUNTY
WAREHOUSE & DIRECTORY ASS'T
5300 SANTA MONICA
LOS ANGELES, CA 90029

SAFER WAY
UCLA MARRIED STUDENT HOUSING
GILIA & GERRY GARDNER
3167 SEPUL VEDA BLVD
LOS ANGELES, CA 90034

GOOD TIMES CO-OP
1840 S. BEDFORD
LOS ANGELES, CA 90035
DENNY/839-8451
STAN/836-4950

ORIENTAL FOOD CO-OP
JEFF TA
C/O ORIENTAL COLLEGE
BOX 0
LOS ANGELES, CA 90041

HIGHLAND PARK FOOD CO-OP
JACKIE DAVIS
6243 STRICKLAND OR 1181 GLEN ARBOR
LOS ANGELES, CA 90042
(213)257-5386
FRED (213)222-6816
K LEECH/257-1163/J FAUVRE/795-2402

CORNUCOPIA
MITCH EISENBERG/JOYCE JAYRO
927 N. MARTEL
LOS ANGELES, CA 90046
(213)874-8744

THE GATHERING
JOHN DUGAS
4506 S. WESTERN AVE.
LOS ANGELES, CA 90062

LOS ANGELES NATURAL FOODS CO-OP
CAROLE ROBERTS
6665 1/2 FRANKLIN AVE.
HOLLYWOOD, CA 90068
(213)874-9351

UCLA-VILLAGE CO-OP
BARBARA BROIDE
228 ALMONT #1
BEBERLU MILLS, 90211

FREE VENICE CO-OP
C/O MARVENA KENNEDY
440 VENICE WAY
FREE VENICE, CA 90291
(213)821-1774
PAUL DONN 399-4841

VEGETARIAN CO-OP
RALPH MEYER
218 ENTRADA DR
SANTA MONICA, CA 90402

VENICE CO-OP
525 GEORGINA
SANTA MONICA, CA 90402

ANANDA MARGA
1508 17TH ST
SANTA MONICA, CA 90404

ONE LIFE
202 PIER
OCEAN PARK, CA 90405

SAN PEDRO FOOD CO-OP
LOUIS WRIGHT
715 N. MEYLER
SAN PEDRO, CA 90731
(213)831-3257

SAN PEDRO FOOD CO-OP
JOHN & KAREN
1807 ELREY RD
SAN PEDRO, CA 90732

LONG BEACH FOOD CONSPIRACY
DONDA &DON HUGHES
1105 CHERRY ST
LONG BEACH, CA 90802
(213)599-6158
MIKE SWEENEY/1810 E. ANAHEIM/599-7718
PHINIUS 591-9150

POOR & SIMPLE FOOD CO-OP
3322 E. ANAHEIM
LONG BEACH, CA 90815

ALTADENA FOOD CO-OP
BILL & SUI YEE FENWICK
3737 CANYON CREST ROAD
ALTADENA, CA 91001
(213)798-3542 792-7541

THROOP MEMORIAL CHURCH CO-OP ASSN
300 S. ROBLES
PASADENA, CA 91106
BILL WATTER/213-795-7437

CHATSWORTH CO-OP
10465 1/2 SANTA SUSANA RD
CHATSWORTH, CA 91311
BRUCE GUSTIN/882-1039

CREATIVE PARENTHOOD CO-OP
PAM LEVIN
4314 PETIT
ENCINO, CA 91316

ORGANIC CELLAR
3450 OLD CONETO RD
NEWBURY PARK, CA 91320
(805)498-1824

CAL ARTS
25252 FOURL
NEWHALL, CA 91321
RAY WEISLING/805-259-1822

VALLEY STATE FOOD CO-OP
LES SPITZA
8445 AMIGO #12
NORTHRIDGE, CA 91324
(213)885-0419
JO ANN 344-6566

HARVEST FOODS CO-OP
ANN & VIN GOLIA
17949 HATTON
RESEDA, CA 91335

THE ONION
DICK
10606 DANUBE
MISSION HILLS, CA 91340

SEPULVEDA CO-OP
SHEILA & MIKE BERNARD
8935 LANGDON
SEPULVEDA, CA 91343

VAN NUYS FOOD CO-OP
CAROL STEVENS
16611 PARK LANCE CIRCLE
VAN NUYS, CA 91401
CAROL/476-6065

CLAREMONT FOOD CO-OP
BOX 813
CLAREMONT, CA 91711
(714)626-0578/TERRY GIVENS/442 GUILFORD

ALHAMBRA-MT WASHINGTON
MARGARET SANSTED
2300 COMMONWEALTH
ALHAMBRA, CA 91803
(213)281-8442

SOLANA BEACH PEOPLES FOOD
503 N. HIGHWAY 101
SOLANA BEACH, CA 92075

GOLDEN HILLS CO-OP
RANDY LUNOMARIC
3354 LINCOLN
SAN DIEGO, CA 92104
(714)282-4547

GOLDEN HILLS CO-OP
2963 BEECH ST
SAN DIEGO, CA 92105

HARMONY
NATURAL VEGETARIAN CO-OP REST.
1877 CABLE ST. (O.B.)
SAN DIEGO, CA 92107
(714)223-1144

DESERT COLLECTIVE
BOX 114
COACHELLA, CA 92236
(714)347-1778

OCEAN BEACH PEOPLES STORE
TOM KOZDEN
4859 VOLTAIRE
SAN DIEGO, CA 92107
(714)224-0110

PRANA
O.O.B. 7306
SAN DIEGO, CA 92107
(714)280-6390

MEDICINE WHEEL
BOX 1121
IDYLLWILD, CA 92349

ECOLOGY CLUB OF LAGUNA BEACH
2141 LAGUNA CANYON RD OR 2137
LAGUNA BEACH, CA 92651
(714)494-4677 TWTH/8-12,3-8 F-SA/9-1
DORINDA GORSILINE/494-0091/620 THALIA
TRISHA GAMEZ/494-4677

ISLA VISTA FUD CO-OP
6583 PARDALL
ISLA VISTA, CA 93017

GREEN DOT CO-OP
DAVE DAVENPORT
2897 E. OJAI AVE
OJAI, CA 93023

POONEAL
8183 SULFUR MOUNTAIN RD
OJAI, CA 93023
TED COSSAIRT

DESERT SUNRISE
44759 N. SIERRA HWY
LANCASTER, CA 93534

OUR STORE
FRESNO FOOD COLLECTIVE
1940 ECHO
FRESNO, CA 93784

CARMEL CO-OP
ROOM 29 BERNADELLI SQUARE
CARMEL, CA 93921

CARMEL VALLEY CO-OP BUYING ASSN
BERNADELLI SQUARE
CARMEL VALLEY, CA 93924
BOB INTERSIMONE

CONS CO-OP SOC OF MONTERAY PEN, INC
BOX 1427
MONTERAY, CA 93940
MARY BEARD/17 CIELO VISTA TERR.

THE GRANARY
1124 FOREST
PACIFIC GROVE, CA 93950

EVERGREEN CO-OP
MS. BROENKOW
2935 SLOAT RD
PEBBLE BEACH, CA 93953

BRIARPATCH CO-OP MARKET
687 BAY RD
MENLO PARK, CA 94025
(408)321-1215

COMMUNITY BUYERS CLUB
MORSE SCHOOL
707 MORSE
SUNNYDALE, CA 94086

NORTHSIDE BUYERS CLUB
FAIRWOOD SCHOOL
SUNNYVALE, CA 94086

SUNNYVALE BUYING CLUB
ROBIN CLUTE
667 TOYON AVE.
SUNNYVALE, CA 94086

ZEN CO-OP
319 PAGE ST.
SAN FRANCISCO, CA 94102

NATURALLY GOOD BUYING CLUB NO 2
787 22ND AVE.
SAN FRANCISCO, CA 94107
(415)386-4423

PFP FOOD CO-OP
3245 MISSISSIPPI AVE
SAN FRANCISCO, CA 94107
(415)552-2366

WHITE PANTHER FOOD
151 KING ST
SAN FRANCISCO, CA 94107
(415)543-0335

DIVINE FOOD CO-OP
2380 VAN NESS AVE
SAN FRANCISCO, CA 94109
(415)885-1171
RICH ISRAEL

BERNAL HEIGHTS COMMUNITY CO-OP
320 WINFIELD
SAN FRANCISCO, CA 94110
(415)826-4388

FREE FOOD CO-OP
41 NEVADA ST.
SAN FRANCISCO, CA 94110
(415)285-4960

INNER MISSION CO-OP
837 SOUTH VAN NESS
SAN FRANCISCO, CA 94110

RED STAR CHEESE CO
3030 20TH ST
SAN FRANCISCO, CA 94110

ST. PETER'S FOOD BUYING CLUB
1200 FLORIDA ST.
FLORIDA AND 24TH ST.
SAN FRANCISCO, CA 94110

SEEDS OF LIFE
3021 24TH ST.
SAN FRANCISCO, CA 94110
(415)826-6814
MARGIE (415)647-3125

HEALTHY HUNZA BUYING CLUB
233 BRUNSWICK ST.
SAN FRANCISCO, CA 94112
(415)333-0140

S.F. FOOD BUYING PROGRAM
239 VIENNA ST.
SAN FRANCISCO, CA 94112
(415)585-6737

EUREKA VALLEY FOOD CHAIN
4529 18TH ST.
SAN FRANCISCO, CA 94114
(415)431-0245

ROSE HIPS BUYING CLUB
107 NOE ST.
SAN FRANCISCO, CA 94114
(415)863-5287

COMMUNITY FOOD CLUB
2590 SACRAMENTO ST.
SAN FRANCISCO, CA 94115
(415)648-7295

ONGOING PICNIC CO-OP
2234 20TH AVE.
SAN FRANCISCO, CA 94116
(415)665-1610

WESTERN ADDITION FOOD BUYING CLUB
457 HAIGHT ST.
SAN FRANCISCO, CA 94117
(415)861-6840

COMMON MARKET BUYING CLUB
HAIGHT ASHBURY FOOD CONSPIRACY
1446 COLE ST.
SAN FRANCISCO, CA 94117
(415)647-4302

EAT GOOD BUYING CLUB
1310 HAIGHT ST.
SAN FRANCISCO, CA 94117
(415)668-3580

GROUPHEAD BUYING CLUB
977 CLAYTON ST.
SAN FRANCISCO, CA 94117
(415)665-7737

HAIGHT COMMON MARKET
COMMUNICATIONS COLLECTIVE
1919 PAGE ST.
SAN FRANCISCO, CA 94117
(415)661-9142

NATURALLY GOOD BUYING CLUB NO 1
200 CHERRY ST.
SAN FRANCISCO, CA 94118
(415)752-2897

COMMON GOOD BUYING CLUB
1259 46TH AVE.
SAN FRANCISCO, CA 94122
(415)681-2204

INNER SUNSET FOOD CO-OP
24 IRVING ST.
SAN FRANCISCO, CA 94122
(415)558-2164

SEASIDE ONE BUYING CLUB
1370 40TH AVE.
SAN FRANCISCO, CA 94122
(415)566-8834
N & L O'SULLIVAN/165 BELVEDERE

SAN FRANCISCO COOPERATING WAREHOUSE
1559 BANCROFT
SAN FARNCISCO, CA 94124

PALO ALTO TENANT UNION FOOD CONSP.
424 LYTTON AVE
PALO ALTO, CA 94301
ED WILLIGER & ROBERTA KANS/321-7387

CONSUMER CO-OP SOCIETY
JUD REEVES
164 S. CALIFORNIA AVE.
PALO ALTO, CA 94306

ECOLOGY ACTION/COMMON GROUND
2225 EL CAMINO REAL
PALO ALTO, CA 94306

THE FOURTH ESTATE
PO BOX 11176
PALO ALTO, CA 94306

SANGHA
1611 COLLEGE
PALO ALTO, CA 94306
MICHAEL GOLDSTEIN/415-321-5059

BERKELEY FOOD CO-OP
RANDY ELLIOT
2027 HEARST
BERKELEY, CA 94504

MA REVOLUTION'S NATURAL FOODS
2566 TELEGRAPH AVE.
BERKELEY, CA 94604

ALTERNATIVE DISTRIBUTING CO.
6448 BAY ST.
EMERYVILLE, CA 94608 OR 94126

EDIBLE DRY GOODS CONSPIRACY
363 62ND ST.
OAKLAND, CA 94618

OAKLAND FOOD CO-OP
C/O PEOPLES FOOD MARKET
5520 COLLEGE AVE.
NORTH OAKLAND, CA 94618
(415) 8-9298
JULIE CARSON 655-6745
LAURIE S ER 655-4887

THE PEOPLES ALTERNATIVE FOOD STORE
5520 COLLEGE AVE
OAKLAND, CA 94618

BERKELEY FOOD CONSPIRACY
DARYL MCLEOD
1317 CORNELL
BERKELEY, CA 94702

LOAVES AND DISHES
2314 BANCROFT WAY
BERKELEY, CA 94704

ONE WORLD FAMILY RESTAURANT
2455 TELEGRAPH
BERKELEY, CA 94704

WHITE PANTHER FOOD CO-OP
2307 HASTE
BERKELEY, CA 94704

ASSOCIATED COOPERATIVES
ROBERT NEPTUNE
4801 CENTRAL AVE.
RICHMOND, CA 94804

CONSUMERS CO-OP OF BERKELEY
DON ROTHENBERG
4805 CENTRAL AVE.
RICHMOND, CA 94804

MR. NATURALS
PO BOX 148
BROOKDALE, CA 95007

VILLA ROMA BUYING CLUB
ANN MANDEL
840 QUINCE AVE.
SANTA CLARA, CA 95051

KRESGE FOOD CO-OP
LEONARD ARMSTRONG
KRESGE COLLEGE UNIV OF CA
SANTA CRUZ, CA 95060

SANTA CRUZ NEIGHBORHOOD FOOD CO-OP
105 HARVEY WEST BLVD
SANTA CRUZ, CA 95060
( )426-6820/1299
PRISILLA LOWENSTEIN

SANTA CRUZ CONSUMERS CO-OP
1725 COMMERCIAL WAY
SANTA CRUZ, CA 95065

INTEGRAL YOGA INSITIUTE
817 PACIFIC
SANTA CRUZ, CA 95068
(408)427-1845
BRO JIVAKAW CHRITANYA/423-8366/20 GRANIT

CHAZ LORD
3355 CAZADERO HWY
CAZADERO, CA 95421

COMMUNITY FOOD STORE
R.R.M.S.C. BOX 818
MONTE RIO, CA 95421

RUSSIAN RIVER MULTI SERVICE CO-OP
COMMUNITY FOOD STORE
BOX 61
VILLA GRANDE, CA 95486

ARCATA CO-OP
957 H ST.
ARCATA, CA 95521
(707)822-4150
CINDY STAPENHORST/443-6881/RT1 BOX 786

PEOPLES FOOD CONSPIRACY
437 F ST.
DAVIS, CA 95616
(916)756-4892 M-F/5-7PM
ANN EVANS/752-2878/212 WALKER UCD/M-F 9-
DWIGHT PATTERSON/756-1305/627 E ST.

DIVIDE COMMUNITY ACTION COUNCIL
PO BOX 11
KELSEY, CA 95643
(916)622-0952
RAMONA ALLEMAN

SACRAMENTO CONSUMER CO-OP
BOX 335
FAIR OAKS, CA 95628
ANN HOYT/41302 VIENTO LN/WOODLAND, CA 9

WE THE PEOPLE NATURAL FOOD CO-OP
BOX 348
TAHOE VISTA, CA 95732
(916)546-9954 10-6
BOB CANTISANO, JAN TODD

SACRAMENTO NATURAL FOODS CO-OP
1525A 16TH ST
SACRAMENTO, CA 95814
(916)442-0380
SUSIE CREAMCHEES/2008 N ST. #C

CHICO NATURAL FOODS CO-OP
1146 NORMAL
CHICAO, CA 959

HURDS GULCH CO-OP
TOM CLINGMAN
FORT JONES, CA 96032

MT. SHASTA CO-OP
BOX 618
MT. SHASTA, CA 96067

HAWAII

NORTH SHORE FOOD CO-OP
59-450 A ALAPIO RD
HALEIWA, HONOLULU, HI 96712
JOAN, DUNCAN/638-8190

THE HILO COMMUNITY FOOD CO-OP
P.O. BOX 651
HILO, HI 96720

FRIENDLY NEIGHBORHOOD STORE
BOX 822
KALAHEO, KAUAI, HI 96741

MANNA TRADING CO.
P.O. BOX 527
KEALAKEKUA, HI 96750

PRASADAM
BOX 1021
WAILUKU, MAUI,HI 96793

MAUI COMMUNITY CO-OP
GARDEN OF ETEN
1910 VINEYARD
WAILUKU, MAUI, HI 96793
RUSS PETRUSHA

PEOPLE NON-PROFIT NUUANU
2017 COIN
HONOLULU, HI 96814
(808)941-0448

KOKUA COUNTRY FOODS, INC
DOLLY FOSTER
2357 S. BERETANIA ST.
HONOLULU, HI 96814

OAIHO
29 KOWANANAKOA PL
NUUANU, HONOLULU, HI 96817
SUSY/(808)538-7790

PEOPLE NON-PROFIT WAIKIKI
2480 KIA AVE K-38
HONOLULU, HI 96819
RON STANGLER/923-7794

ECO FOODS CO-OP
404 PIIKOI
HONOLULU, HI 96822

OREGON

THE DALLES NATURAL FOODS
314 COURT ST.
THE DALLES, OR 97058

PEOPLES FOOD STORE
RT 1, BOX 818
WILSONVILLE, OR 97070
(503)638-8377

ESTACADA CO-OP
RT1 BOX 47
ESTACADA OR 97023

ASTORIA CO-OP
1120 MARINE DR
ASTORIA, OR 97103

HOPE CO-OP
BOX A
BUXTON, OR 97109

GOOD FOOD CO-OP
12540 WILSON RIVER HWY
TILAMOOK, OR 97141

PURE EARTH FOODS
BOX 41
CANNON BEACH, OR 97110

PEOPLES WAREHOUSE
3029 SE 21ST
PORTLAND, OR 92202

DIVINE GIFT
1233 S.W. MORRISON
PORTLAND, OR

THE WAYFARER
435 N.W. GLISAN
PORTLAND, OR 97209
(503)228-9063

NATURES FOODS
2733 S.W. FIRST
PORTLAND, OR 972XX

SUNSHINE NATURAL FOODS
714 S.W. MADISON
PORTLAND, OR

FOOD FRONT CO-OP
1618 NW 23RD #5
PORTLAND, OR 97210
(503)222-5658
STEVE BYERS/227-2151/2222 NW IRVING

MAIN ST. GATHERING
5124 N.E. CLEVELAND
PORTLAND, OR 97211

FRIENDS 'N FOOD
301 S.E. 16TH
PORTLAND, OR 97214
(503)232-6551

PEOPLES FOOD - PORTLAND
3029 SE 21ST ST.
PORTLAND, OR 97214
GORDON WHITEHEAD

SUNSHINE NATURAL FOODS
WHOLESALE WAREHOUSE
229 S.E.ALDER ST.
PORTLAND, OR 97214

DIVINE FOOD CO-OP
RT 1 BOX 92
PORTLAND, OR 97231
(504)286-8412
BRUCE BARTLETT

HELIOTROP NATURAL FOODS
2060 MARKET ST.
SALEM, OR 97301
(503)362-5487

SALEM COMMUNITY CO-OP
1635 FAIR GROUNDS
SALEM, OR 97303

1ST ALTERNATIVE
1007 SE 3RD
CORVALLIS, OR 97330
DON,DENNIS 753-3115

LINCOLN CRACKER BARREL CO-OP
1640 N.E. HWY 101
LINCOLN CITY, OR 97367
GEORGEUS

SWEET HOME AND NEIGHBORS FOOD CO-OP
1325 N. 18TH ST.
SWEET HOME, OR 97386
(503)367-3046
JIM BIGELOW

GROWERS MARKET
454 WILLAMETTE
EUGENE, OR 97401
(503)687-1145

EUGENE COMMUNITY PRODUCE
SANDY BISHOP
410 CLARK
EUGENE, OR 97401
(503)345-3277

HOME FRIED TRUCK STOP
1414 ADLER
EUGENE, OR 97401

STARFLOWER
385 LAWRENCE
EUGENE, OR 97401

AMRIT FAMILY BAKERY
136 E. 11TH
EUGENE, OR 97402

WEST END GENERAL STORE
1525 W. 6TH
EUGENE, OR 97402
(503)485-0680
STEPHEN JAFFE/936 ADAMS/345-0743

WILLAMETTE PEOPLES CO-OP
1391 E. 22ND
EUGENE, OR 97403
(503)343-6694

PEOPLES CAFE
787 OLIVE
EUGENE, OR 974XX

ARC
BILL SLATTERY
835 ASH AVE
COTTAGE GROVE, OR 97424

MUSTARD SEED
BOX 729
DRAIN, OR 97435

HUE
BILL WHITE MEMORIAL COUNTY CO-OP
MILO, OR 97455

HEALTH FOOD & POOL STORE
145 N. "A" ST.
SPRINGFIELD, OR 97477
(503)747-9142

ASH VALLEY CO-OP
TILLER, OR 97484

EMILY FOOD CO-OP
4930 COYOTE CREEK
WOLF CREEK, OR 97497

GINGER HUBBARD
13520 LOWER GRAVE CR. RD
WOLF CREEK, OR 97497

FOREST ACRES CO-OP
3362 TABLE ROCK RD.
CENTRAL POINT, OR 97501

ASHLAND PEOPLES FOOD CO-OP
3RD ST
ASHLAND, OR 97520

TAKILMA FOOD CO-OP
10008 TAKILMA RD.
CAVE JUNCTION, OR 97523

FIELDS OF MERIT
1615 NE 6TH ST.
GRANTS PASS, OR 97526

WONDER NATURAL FOODS
11711 REDWOOD HIGHWAY
WONDER, OR 97543

OREGON CO-OP COALTION
VSI
18930 SW BOONES FERRY RD
TUALITIN, OR 97602

MT. EMILY CO-OP
1005 W. AVE
LA GRANDE, OR 97850

WASHINGTON

CLOVERGREEN CO-OP
W. STEVEN TACHERA
23017 45TH AVE. SE
BETHELL, WA 98011

WHOLESOME FOODS CO-OP
110 RAILROAD AVE S
KENT, WA 98031

ABUNDANT LIFE CO-OP
1703 202 PLACE S.W.
ALDERWOOD MANOR, WA 98036

FERTILE EARTH FOODS
13840 N.E. 175TH
WOODINVILLE, WA 98072

CASCADE COMMUNITY CO-OP
224 MINOR AVE.N.
SEATTLE, WA 98101

COMMUNITY PRODUCE
1510 PIKE PLACE OR 1426 ALASKA WAY
SEATTLE, WA 98101
(206)624-1681 M-SA/9-6

CORNER PRODUCE
90 PIKE ST.
SEATTLE, WA 98101

ALMOST EDEN
1510 PIKE PLACE
SEATTLE, WA 98101
(206)622-4856

SOUP & SALAD RESTAURANT
LOWER PIKE PL
SEATTLE, WA 98101

FAMILY PROVIDER
6508 N.E. 175TH
WOODINVILLE, WA 98072

GROWING FAMILY
6239 WOODLAWN AVE N
SEATTLE, WA 98103
(206)523-3259

PHINNEY ST. CO-OP
400 N. 43RD ST
SEATTLE, WA 98103
(206)633-2354

TINA EASTERLING
5218 16TH N.E.
SEATTLE, WA 98105

MOTHER MORGANS GUMBO/LIVE-IN HONEY
431-15TH AVE EAST
SEATTLE, WA 98112

SUNSHINE CO-OP
146 NE 64TH
SEATTLE, WA 98115

UPFRONT CAFE
LITTLE BREAD CO
8050 15TH AVE NE
SEATTLE, WA 98115

PUGET CONSUMERS CO-OP
2261 65TH AVE. NE
SEATTLE, WA 98115

CAPITOL HILL CO-OP
1835 12TH AV
SEATTLE, WA 98122
(206)325-1524 OR 3638 MWFSA/11-6 TTH/11-
BILL CORR/EA4-8918
DANIEL HOOK

MADRONA FOOD CO-OP
1135 34TH AVE
SEATTLE, WA 98122

RAINBOW GROCERY
1607 SUMMIT
SEATTLE, WA 98122
(206)325-4778
PETER LEIGHTON

SEATTLE WORKERS BRIGADE
402 15TH AVE E
SEATTLE, WA 98122
(206)284-0371

MT. BAKER CO-OP
3716 39TH AVE S
SEATTLE, WA 98144

BURION CO-OP
1507 24TH S.W.
SEATTLE, WA 98166
(206)243-7226

COOPERATING COMMUNITY GRAINS
4030 22 AVE W.
SEATTLE, WA 98199

LYNN ST. CO-OP
511 MALDEN AVE E #4
SEATTLE, WA 98199

LAKESIDE CO-OP
7321 4TH AVE NE
SEATTLE, WA 98205

COMMUNITY FOOD CO-OP
1000 HARRIS ST,
BELLINGHAM, WA 98225
(206)734-0083

FAIRHAVEN CO-OP MILL
1000 HARRIS AVE
BELLINGHAM, WA 98225

LOW-INCOME MEAT & PRODUCE CO-OP
2512 ELDRIDGE AVE
BELLINGHAM, WA 98225
(206)734-9940
BEA JIMENEZ

BAKER RIVER CO-OP
BOX 86
CONCRETE, WA 98237

SARAH HART CONSPIRACY
BOX 236
FRIDAY HARBOR, WA 98250

SUNSET CO-OP
BOX 306
LANGLEY, WA 98260

SOUTH WHISBEY CO-OP
BOX 306
LANGLEY, WA 98260

CASCADE CO-OP
BOX 32
MARBLEMOUNT, WA 98267

SKAGIT VALLEY FOOD CO-OP
619 2ND ST.
MOUNT VERNON, WA 98273

SNOHOMISH FOOD CO-OP
BOX 510 606 MAPLE
SNOHOMISH, WA 98290J
(206)355-4595

KITSAP COMMUNITY ACTION
1200 ELIZABETH AVE
BROMERTON, WA 98310

FORKS CO-OP
BOX 152
FORKS, WA 98331

HOMESTEADERS CO-OP
GENERAL DELIVERY
KINGSTON, WA 98346

AMBROSIA NATURAL FOODS
RT S, BOX 60
MORTON, WA 98356
(206)496-5885
LONGVIEW, WA 98362 OR 632

GRAINERY
527 NEVADA DR.
LONGVIEW, WA 98362 OR 632

THE FOOD CO-OP
617 TYLER ST.
PORT TOWNSEND, WA 98368

KITSAP GROCERY
RT1, BOX 375
POULSBO, WA 98370

FOOD BAG
914 BROADWAY #11
TACOMA, WA 98402
(206)NA7-9456

ARTICHOKE MEDE
203 W. 4TH ST
OLYMPIA, WA 98501

FOOTE ST. CO-OP
1103 W. 6TH AVE
OLYMPIA, WA 98502

MCPHEE FOOD CO-OP
RT 11, BOX 251A
OLYMPIA, WA 98502

OLYMPIA GENERAL FOOD
RT 14, BOX 37
OLYMPIA, WA 98502

THE FOOD CO-OP
904 E. 4TH
OLYMPIA, WA 98506
(206)943-9440

COOPERATIVE FEDERATION
BOX 1621
OLYMPIA, WA 98507
(206)357-8323

RIVERFRONT CO-OP
BOX 128
RAYMOND, WA 98577

TROUTLAKE TRADING POST
BOX 62
TROUTLAKE, WA 98650

GOLDEN FLORINS
BOX 1463
CHELAN, WA 98816

CONJUNCTION GENERAL STORE
RT 1, BOX 226
TONASKET, WA 98855

METHEW VALLEY CO-OP
RT1, BOX 61
WINTHROP, WA 98862

HOSANA CO-OP
203 E. CHESTNUT
YAKIMA, WA 98903

YELLOW BUTTERFLY
607 N. SPRAGUE
ELLENSBURG, WA 98926

PULLMAN FOOD CO-OP
NE 850 A ST.
PULLMAN, WA 99163

GILL MCGEE
1608 E. 39TH
SPOKANE, WA 99203
(509)624-1608

THE STORE
2630 SUNSET BLVD
SPOKANE, WA 99204

NORTHWEST FOOD CO-OP
1130 FARI ST
CLARKSTON, WA 99403

ALASKA

S.E.C. CO-OP
RT 1, BOX 463
KETCHIKAN, AK 99901

CANADA

KARMA FOOD CO-OP
DUPONT STREET
TORONTO, ONTARIO

NATURES WAY
ETHEREA NATURAL FOOD
341 BLOOR
TORONTO, ONTARIO

NEILL WYCK FOOD CO-OP
BOB LUKER
REGISTRAR NW COLLEGE 22 FLOOR
96 GERRARD ST E
TORONTO, ONTARIO M5B1G7 CANADA

COOPERATIVE D'AILMENTS
NATURALES ET MACROBIOTIQUES
4616 PANIEAU
MONTREAL, QUEBEC

MONTREAL CO-OP
4800 ST. DOMONIQUE
MONTREAL, QUEBEC

BANYAN TREE
C/O KEITH
474 JESSE ST.
WINNEPEG, MANITOBA

FED-UP CO-OP
304 E. 1ST AVE
VANCOUVER, B.C. CANADA
872-0712

COOPERATIVES RESOURCE SERVICE
2141 PANDORA
VANCOUVER, BC
254-1158

AMOR DE COSMOS
58 PANDORA AVE
VICTORIA, B.C., CANADA
386-1532

COOPERATIVE COLLEGE OF CANADA
141-105TH ST W
SASKATOON, SASK. S7N 1NS

Index